1

The Original
WOLFHOUND

Guide to Evening Classes
Adult & Leisure Learning
2006/2007

in Dublin City & County

WOLFHOUND PRESS

Contents

Introduction page 5

Alphabetical Subject Listing
pages 8 - 225

Index of email addresses & websites
pages 227 - 240

ACKNOWLEDGEMENTS:
Our thanks to all who have assisted and facilitated our research on this year's edition, including schools' authorities and the organisers of adult education courses at the various centres.

Details are correct at time of going to press. Our listings are based on information provided by the course providers. Every effort has been made to ensure accurate and comprehensive listings, but the editor and publisher accept no responsibility for inaccuracies that may appear herein, for the quality of the courses provided, nor for any changes in prices, days, or times of the courses we have listed.

© 2006 Research, compilation, editing & advertising: Seamus Cashman, 68 Mountjoy Square, Dublin 1 (email: cprojectsltd@eircom.net).

Design and layout © 2006 Merlin Publishing

Published by
Wolfhound Press
An Imprint of Merlin Publishing
16 Upper Pembroke Street, Dublin 2
Tel: (01) 6764373
Fax: (01) 6764368
publishing@merlin.ie
www.merlinwolfhound.com

Trade Edition   10-Digit ISBN 0-86327-939-2
                       13-Digit ISBN 978-0-86327-939-3

Non-Trade Edition   10-Digit ISBN 0-86327-940-6
                       13-Digit ISBN 978-0-86327-940-9

Cover design by M & J Graphics
Printed and bound in Cox and Wyman Ltd., Britain

Introduction

Welcome to the 32nd edition of this original, bestselling guide to adult day and evening learning courses and leisure activities for the greater Dublin region.

Long known as *The Wolfhound Guide to Evening Classes*, it is many years since the 'evening' of its title became 'day and night'! Our new edition contains a wide-ranging offering of choices and information to help you select the perfect evening or daytime learning course. *The Wolfhound Guide* has been market leader for three decades and contains a most comprehensive range of evening and part-time day courses and leisure activities throughout Dublin and surrounding areas. Select a course, workshop or programme from the some 4,000 entries here – whether classroom or home-study based – and you will be participating in the knowledge revolution.

There really are exciting opportunities on offer, from Yoga to Acting or Aerobics; from a myriad Computer based involvements to the more simple Keep-Fit; from Art, Philosophy and History to the practical and useful trade and DIY type activities; or perhaps you might try the newer age alternatives, be it the art of stillness or the energetic Salsa beat! All of these and more can be found in a radius from the Spire to the sea and the inland to the mountains and hills surrounding the capital. Also included are distance learning options for home study by correspondence, online and email. Everything is arranged in an easy to search alphabetical subject listing: from **A** (accordion) to **Z** (Zoology).

Confidence

Creativity

THE GAIETY SCHOOL OF ACTING

PART TIME ADULT DRAMA COURSES:

- One Year Performance Course
- One Year Advanced Performance Course
- One Year Performance Theatre Company
- Introduction to Drama
- Page to Stage
- Introduction to Improvisation
- Acting for Camera
- Stagecraft
- Audition Technique
- Creative Writing
- Voice Weekend Workshops
- Make a 'Short' Short W/end Wkshops
- Stage Combat

YOUNG GAIETY AND YOUTH THEATRE COURSES
(4-19 Year Olds)

- Young Gaiety Saturday School
- Youth Theatre Workshop
- Youth Theatre Company

Summer and Easter Courses for all ages.
Plus our acclaimed 2 year full-time course.

Courses in Temple Bar, Bray, Sutton, Cork and Kerry.

For bookings, a brochure, or more information:
Tel: 01 679 9277 / 1890-25 83 58
Email: info@gaietyschool.com   or visit our website www.gaietyschool.com

The subject cross-references provided are not comprehensive. They are intended to assist in searching for courses relating to your area of interest. There is a directory of email and website addresses at the end of the book.

We include prices where possible, but be forewarned: not all centres had finalised prices or times as we went to press. Dates, times and prices will be available from the relevant centre by late August or before. Most evening courses begin at 7 or 7.30 (and are generally of 1-2 hours duration). But again, 6.30pm is not an infrequent start time and I've noticed 5pm starts and 10pm ends this year. Early registration is advisable: places are often limited, and much sought after. For more expensive courses, it is vital to make a clear decision before paying in full because fees are usually non-refundable. Some course prices are reduced for Senior Citizens and the unwaged. Almost all adult learning and leisure courses remain inexpensive – probably the best value options in Ireland today.

Next to calling in to enroll in person, the telephone remains your most effective means of contact. Enrolment days/evenings generally take place from the second week of September, and most courses begin in mid- to late September. Academic terms vary from 8-12 weeks, and some courses will either continue, or restart again, in January – so keep *The Wolfhound Guide* close to hand throughout the year. We hope that you enjoy your course choices.

And remember
that you found it in
The Wolfhound Guide

ACCORDION Music

Comhaltas Ceoltóirí Éireann 32 Belgrave Sq Monkstown (2800295) - button

Donahies Community School Streamville Rd 13 (8482217) - button accordion, Mon 8.30-10pm 10 wks €85 (BC tuning)

Dún Laoghaire Music Centre 130A Lr George's St Dún Laoghaire (2844178)

Nolan School of Music 3 Dean St 8 (4933730) - also day

Scoil Shéamuis Ennis, Naul, Co Dublin (8020898 087 7870138) - button accordion

Waltons New School of Music 69 Sth Gt George's St 2 (4781884) - also day, see ad page 155

ACCOUNTANCY / ACCOUNTS Book-keeping / Business / Computerised Accounts / Management

ACCA (Assoc of Chartered Certified Accountants) 9 Leeson Pk 6 (4988900) - chartered certified accountancy; also day / dip in financial management - nationwide

CTA Computer Training Academy, St James's Tce Malahide (8454070) - manual

DIT Faculty: Business Aungier St 2 (4023000) - ACCA exam, €761 per stage

Dorset College 64 Lr Dorset St/ 8 Belvedere Pl 1 (8309677) - accounting & finance cert/dip, Mon & Wed, 6.30-9.30, 1-2 yrs

Dublin Business School 13/14 Aungier St 2 (4177500) - ACCA, Mon to Thurs, 6.15pm-9.45, 3-4 years / BA (Hons) Acc & Finance, 4 yrs / Dip, Acc & Finance, 1 yr / CIMA, 3-4 yrs, Certified Dip in Financial Management, ACCA, 1 eve per wk, 1 yr: all 6.15-9.30pm / Dip in International Reporting Standards, ACCA Dip IFRS, 6mths/1yr, wkends

Eden Computer Training Rathfarnham 16 & 1 Green St 7 (4953155) - tas, sage, take 5

FAS Training Centre Tallaght Cookstown Indl Est 24 (4045200)

Griffith College Dublin Sth Circular Rd 8 (4150400) - ACCA & CPA, p/t revision, both 3 stages over 3 yrs, 2 eves per wk; also w/ends/ IATI & ACA revision, both 2 stages over 2 yrs, 2 eves per wk/ BA in accounting & finance, 3yrs HETAC f/time

Hartstown Community School Clonsilla 15 (8209863) - & accounts beginners/ intermediate 10wks, €85 each/ computerised accounts 10 wks €95, attendance cert

Inst of Certified Public Accountants in Ireland 9 Ely Pl 2 (6314649) - CPA centres of ed at: Griffith College; Plunket College; BPP Professional Education; Business Management Institute; Senior College Dún Laoghaire Col of Further Ed. Full time, p/time, wkend & eve courses

Institute of Technology Tallaght ITT Dublin, Tallaght 24 (4042101) - Higher Cert, Business (Accounting), NFQ level 6 2 Yrs/ Bachelor of Business Accounting NFQ Level 7 1 yr (add on)/ Bachelor of Business (Hons) Accounting NFQ Level 8 1 yr (add on)

Kilroy's College Wentworth House Grand Canal Street Lr 2 (6620538 1850-700700) - tutor supported home study: book-keeping & accounts, self-employed/ farm

Marino College 14-20 Marino Mart 3 (8332100) - for your new business, 8pm Thurs 10 wks €65

Newpark Adult Education Centre, Newtownpark Ave Blackrock (2884376 / 2883725) - manual accounts, Thurs 7.30-9.45 10 wks €120/ accounts & taxation introduction, Wed, 7.30-9.45pm 10 wks €120

Palmerstown CS - Pobailscoil Iosolde, Kennelsfort Rd 20 (6260116) - manual/ computerised: Thurs 8.15-9.45 10 wks €90

Pitman Training Centre 6-8 Wicklow St 2 (6768008) - foundation in finance, full/pt-time, day eve sats, dip

Dorset College

Tel: 01) 8309677 E-mail: info@dorset-college.ie   www.dorset-college.ie
66 Lower Dorset Street, Dublin 1 (Head Office)

Excellence Through Life-Long Learning

SCHOOL OF COMPUTING
Computer Applications
  Complete Beginner – Equalskills
  ECDL-European Computer Driving Licence
  e-Citizen • Microsoft Office Specialist
Web Design
  CIW v5 Foundations / Site Designer / e-Commerce
Network Systems Professional
  CompTIA A+ / CompTIA Network+ / Security+ / Server+
  Red Hat Linux • CISCO – Certified Computer Network Associate
Microsoft Certified Professional
  MCSA-Microsoft Certified System Administrator
  MCSE-Microsoft Certified System Engineer
  MCAD-Microsoft Application Developer
Programming
  Sun Certified Programmer for JAVA
School of Business
  Certificate & Diploma Business Studies ICM
  Diploma Marketing, Advertising and PR ICM
  Diploma Project Management
  CIPD – Certificate in Personnel Practice
  Travel & Tourism - FETAC Level 5
Short-Term Business Courses – 60% FAS Funded
  Introductory Diploma in Management - ILM
  First Line Management Certificate - ILM
  Supervisory Management & Leadership - ILM
  Team Leading Certificate – ILM • Project Management ILM
  Risk Management/ Crisis Management ILM
School of Legal Studies
  Legal Studies Certificate & Diploma ICM
School of Training & Development
  JEB Teachers' Diploma Information Communication Technology - Skills
  TEFL-Teaching English as Foreign Language
  CIPD-Certificate in Training Practice
School of Accounting
  ACCA Certified Accounting Technician
  ACCA Professional Scheme
  Certificate/Diploma Accounting & Finance
  Manual & Computerised Accounts - FETAC Level 5
  Manual & Computerised Payroll - FETAC Level 5
School of Design
  Diploma in Interior Design
  Higher Diploma in Interior Design & Architecture
  AutoCAD 2D / 3D City & Guilds
  Desk Top Publishing
School of Health, Nursing and Childcare
  Childcare Studies - FETAC Level 5
  Working with Children with Special Needs
Psychology
  Diploma in Psychology
  Certificate in Child Psychology
  Certificate in Forensic Psychology

Plunket College Swords Rd, Whitehall 9 (8371689) - IATI cert in business management/ law/ accounting/ taxation: 27wks morns, Mon,Wed, Fri/ Certified Public Accountant- 1 & 2: 25 wks/ also leaving cert(H,O), Tues, 27 wks €283

Pobalscoil Rosmini Adult Ed Grace Pk Rd 9 (8371015) - finance & accounting for small business, Tue 7-8.20 €90

Westmoreland College for Management Studies 11 Westmoreland St 2 (6795324/7266) - ACCA dip in Financial Management

ACCOUNTING TECHNICIAN

ACCA 9 Leeson Pk 6 (4988900) - certified - nationwide, also day

Ashfield College Main St Templeogue 6W (4900866) - certified, 2 yr p/time, from Sept

Ballyfermot CFE, Ballyfermot Rd 10 (6269421) - IATI foundation yr 1/ admission yr 2: 20 wksMon/Wed 7-10pm + some Sats; tasbooks

Bray Institute of FE, Novara Ave (2866111 / 2829668) - IATI cert, yrs 1 & 2, Mon & Wed 7-10pm €450 pa; +€180 for Tasbooks for yr2

Colaiste Ide Cardiffsbridge Rd Finglas W 8443233 11 (8342333) - admission/foundation, Tues & Thurs, 7-10pm, each 25 wks, €470, IATI

Crumlin College of FE, Crumlin Rd 12 (4540662) - IATI Yr 1 foundation: business management & IT, accounting 1, business law, taxation 1/ yr 2 admission: IT in business, computerised accounts (Tas books), company law, accounting 2, taxation 2 : Mon, Tue, Wed eves

DIT Faculty: Business Aungier St 2 (4023000) - IATI exams, 2 yrs, €777 per stage

Dorset College 64 Lr Dorset St/ 8 Belvedere Pl 1 (8309677) - ACCA cert CAT, Mon & Wed 6.30-9pm 2yr

Dublin Business School 13/14 Aungier St 2 (4177500) - IATI, 2 eves per wk, 6.15-9.30pm, 2yrs

I.T. Blanchardstown Rd North 15 (8851000) - IATI cert, 2 yrs, €800 pa p/time

Inchicore CFE, Emmet Rd 8 (4535358)

Institute of Accounting Technicians in Ireland 87/89 Pembroke Rd 4 (6377363) - information on accredited courses

Institute of Technology Tallaght ITT Dublin, Tallaght 24 (4042101) - accounting technician 2 yrs IATI cert

McKeon Murray Business Training, Elm House Leopardstown Office Pk 18 (2959087)

Plunket College Swords Rd, Whitehall 9 (8371689) - IATI Foundation: Accounts- [1] Taxation/ Business Management & Law/IATI Admission Accounts- [2] IT/ Company Law/ Taxation 2; Computerised Accounts/ Costing & Budgeting - 28 wks

Senior College Dún Laoghaire, CFE Eblana Ave Dún Laoghaire (2800385) - IATI foundation/admission, €480

Stillorgan CFE, Old Road Stillorgan (2880704) - Tue & Thurs 7-10pm 24 wks

Westmoreland College for Management Studies 11 Westmoreland St 2 (6795324/7266) - IATI/foundation & admission

ACRYLIC PAINTING

Ballsbridge CFE, Shelbourne Rd 4 (6684806) - intro to, Mon 7.45/ Thurs 6 & 7.45: each 10 wks €60

Brian Byrnes Art Studio 3 Upr Baggot St 4 (6671520 / 6711599) - 8wk, €15, also day

Cabinteely Community School Johnstown Rd 18 (2857455) - improvers, 10wk, €95

Firhouse Community College Firhouse Rd 24 (4525807) - accrilic & oils, Tue 7.30-9.30pm 8 wks €104

Jean Strong (2892323) - ongoing, beginners-improvers, 10wks, €170/also day:- Blackrock & Dundrum

Kilternan Adult Education Centre Ballybetagh Rd Kilternan 18 (2952050) - Mon, Tue 9.30am/ 7.30pm 10 wks €130

Kylemore College Kylemore Rd 10 (6265901) - Mon 10 wks 7-9pm

Meridian Art Group c/o St Paul's College Raheny 5 (8310688)

St Tiernan's Community School Parkvale Balally 16 (2953224) - intro, Mon 7.30 10 wks €95

ACTING Drama / Speech & Drama / Theatre

Ballsbridge CFE, Shelbourne Rd 4 (6684806) - 'art of physical action on stage' Tue 6-9pm 10 wks €150

Ballyfermot CFE, Ballyfermot Rd 10 (6269421) - skills & techniques, Fetac 5, 22 wks Mon 7-10pm

Betty Ann Norton Theatre School 11 Harcourt St 2 (4751913) - acting dip / adult foundation course

Corporate Club 24 Elmcastle Green Tallaght 24 (4610935)

Donahies Community School Streamville Rd 13 (8482217) - beginners, Tue 7.30 10 wks €85

Gaiety School of Acting Sycamore St Temple Bar 2 (6799277) - 2 yr full time acting course/ 1 yr courses: Performance, Adv. Performance, Performance Theatre Company/ 10 wk courses: Intro to Drama / Page to Stage / Acting for Camera / Comedy Improv / Stage Combat / Stagecraft / Audition Technique / Dramatic Writing/ Wkend Workshops: Voice / Stage Combat / Make a 'Short' Short/ Young Gaiety & Youth Theatre Workshops/ Easter & Summer Courses. venues: Temple Bar, Bray, Sutton, Cork & Kerry

Hartstown Community School Clonsilla 15 (8209863) - stage combat, 10 wks €85

Leinster School of Music & Drama Griffith College Campus South Circular Rd 8 (4150467)

Network Club 24 Elmcastle Green Tallaght 24 (4524415)

New Media Technology College 13 Harcourt St 2 (4780905) - intro, speech & drama, 8 wks 6.30-9.30 or Sat 10-1 or 2-5pm

Newpark Adult Education Centre, Newtownpark Ave Blackrock (2884376 / 2883725) - drama workshop, Tue 7.30-9.45 10 wks €120

Plunket College Swords Rd, Whitehall 9 (8371689) - intro: Wed, 10 wks 7.30 €90

Rathmines CFE - Senior College, Town Hall 6 (4975334) - intro to drama & acting, 7-9pm 10 wks €90

ACUPUNCTURE Medicine

Acupuncture Foundation Training School Milltown Pk College 6 (1850 577405) - professional practitioner training, wkend modules

Irish College of Traditional Chinese Medicine ICTCM House Merchants Road 3 (8559000) - PT licentiate in acupuncture and traditional chinese medicine, 3 yrs 12 wkends pa, Lic. TCM recognised by Guangzhou Uni of TCM; VHI, BUPA approved.

Our Lady's Hospice Harold's Cross 6 (4068806 4068810) - intro for health care professionals, 5 Dec06 10-4pm €100 incl lunch

ADDICTION STUDIES see Drugs & Alcohol Abuse

Ballyfermot CFE, Ballyfermot Rd 10 (6269421) - NUI Maynooth cert, 23 wks/100hrs, Mon 7-10, some Sats

Liberties College Bull Alley St 8 (4540044) - foundation in addiction studies, Wed 7-9pm 10 wks €90

Maynooth NUI Adult & Community Ed Dept (7084500) - Maynooth NUI campus, evenings; also at: Ballymermot CFE 6269421) Mon 7-10pm; St Kilian's Bray (2864646); Drogheda (041 9836084); Clonliffe D3 (8360911); Carmen's Court Dublin 8 (4549772) Wed 10am-4pm; DAP Cross Care Dublin 3 (8360911) - NUI cert

ADMINISTRATION Chartered Secretaries / Hospital & Health Services / Leisure / Teachers

Ballyfermot CFE, Ballyfermot Rd 10 (6269421) - arts admin, 15 wks Wed 7-9.30

Westmoreland College for Management Studies 11 Westmoreland St 2 (6795324/7266) - ICM dip in business studies/ ICM dip corporate management/ ICM dip health services management

ADULT EDUCATION
Ballyfermot CFE, Ballyfermot Rd 10 (6269421) - adult & community ed, NUI Maynooth cert, 23 wks/100 hrs, Mon 7-10pm

FETAC East Point Plaza East Point Business Park 3 (8659500) - national certification body

Holistic Healing Centre 38 Dame St 2 (6710813)

Maynooth NUI Adult & Community Ed Dept (7084500) - Ballyfermot CFE (6269421) Mon 7-10pm; Tallaght Partnership D24 (4664280)

UCD Adult Education Centre Belfield (7167123) - adults and learning; contemporary issues in adult education: mon/ course delivery; designing learning experience; facilitation skills; planning skills: adult education: each Sat morn/ facilitation skills and group learning, Thurs; new ideas in adult teaching, Mon; philosophy of adult education (Tue, 10 wks); supporting the adult learner, Tue

ADULT EDUCATOR'S TRAINING COURSE Teachers
Ballymun Trinity CS, Adult Ed Centre 9 (8420654) - literacy tutor training, €free

Crumlin College of FE, Crumlin Rd 12 (4540662) - for adult literacy tutors, Mon (4547054)/ ESOL tutor course, Wed, Thurs 6.45

Finglas Adult Reading & Writing Scheme Colaiste Eoin Cappagh Rd 11 (8340893) - literacy tutor training, 12 wks Tues 7-9pm

ADULT LITERACY see English Literacy / Basic Education
Crumlin College of FE, Crumlin Rd 12 (4540662) - various day + eve adult reading & writing courses: one-to-one, spelling groups, numeracy, FETAC foundation in communications, spelling through computers; junior cert maths, English; Tues & Thurs 7.45-9.45/ adult educ guidance service 4540662 ext119

DATE Centre CFE, Dundrum 14 (2964322 (9.30am-12pm)) - Southside Adult Literacy Centre, wide range of classes, group, 1-1, call 2964321

Dublin Adult Learning Centre 3 Mountjoy Sq 1 (8787266) - Read, Write, Spell - various courses; also tutor training

Irish Deaf Society 30 Blessington St 7 (sms 8828001/Minicom:8601910/fax 8601960) - literacy classes for deaf adults, €free

Kilroy's College Wentworth House Grand Canal Street Lr 2 (6620538 1850-700700) - tutor supported home study: English, spelling & arithmetic; dip courses

KLEAR Grange Park View Kilbarrack 5 (8671845) - self-esteem/ computer literacy/ storysacks/ spelling group/ basic maths/ sums/ learn through cookery/ reading & writing/ reading with children: day courses

Malahide Community School Malahide (8460949) - Tue, Thurs 7.30 20 wks no fee

Rathmines CFE - Senior College, Town Hall 6 (4975334) - adult literacy service Tue eves - reading, writing, spelling, numeracy

ADVENTURE SKILLS
Clondalkin Sports & Leisure Centre Nangor Rd Clondalkin 22 (4574858) - day

St Kevin's College, Clogher Rd Crumlin 12 (4536397) - ISA, ICU, NCVA, 1yr, day

ADVENTURE SPORTS & HOLIDAYS
An Oige 61 Mountjoy Street 7 (8304555) - walking, hiking, photography, cycling, hostelling, voluntary work, conservation

Corporate Club 24 Elmcastle Green Tallaght 24 (4610935) - snow skiing abroad

Network Club 24 Elmcastle Green Tallaght 24 (4524415) - hillwalking, walking,

sailing, windsurfing, canoeing, orienteering, snow skiing (abroad)

Portmarnock Sub-Aqua Club Colin Murray Diving Instructor (087 2428575) - scuba diving

ADVERTISING Graphics / Marketing

Communications & Management Institute Regus Hse, Harcourt Rd 2 (4927070) - marketing, PR, advertising & sales dip, Tue+Thurs, 1 yr €1550/ advertising cert, Thurs 10 wks €750

DIT Faculty: Business Aungier St 2 (4023000) - professional dip: executive/ creative, 1 yr €744 each

Dorset College 64 Lr Dorset St/ 8 Belvedere Pl 1 (8309677) - marketing, advertising, PR dip ICM, Mon & Wed, 6.30-9pm 1 yr

Dublin Business School 13/14 Aungier St 2 (4177500) - Dip in Marketing, Advertising, Sales & PR, 2 eves wkly 1 yr, 6.15-9.30pm

Fitzwilliam Institute Ltd Temple Court Temple Rd Blackrock (2834579) - dip in advertising (with e-commerce, marketing & PR modules) 14 wk - 2 eves wkly Mon&Wed: 6.30-9.30, €1395 incl exam fee; city centre: accredited by Assoc Advert Ireland

Irish Academy of Public Relations (2780802) - courses at UCD, Belfield: dip in pr, advertising & marketing, 1 yr 2 evs, €1850; cert in advertising and marketing, 12 wks 1 ev, €730

Westmoreland College for Management & Business 11 Westmoreland St 2 (6795324/7266) - ICM dip, marketing, advertising & PR

AEROBICS see also Keep Fit

Cabinteely Community School Johnstown Rd 18 (2857455) - intermediate, €45 step, €50 10wks each

Clondalkin Sports & Leisure Centre Nangor Rd Clondalkin 22 (4574858) - & step aerobics, also day

Coolmine Community School Clonsilla 15 (8214583) - tae bo style, 1 & 2: Mon. Tue, 7 & 8.10pm, 10 wks €60

Corporate Club 24 Elmcastle Green Tallaght 24 (4610935) - aqua

Danzon (087 9172939) - cardiosalsa, all levels €9.50 per class, Mon 5.45pm ongoing: Wynn's Hotel Lr Abbey St 1

Dundrum Family Recreation Centre Meadowbrook 16 (2984654)

Firhouse Community College Firhouse Rd 24 (4525807) - Mon 7.30-9pm 8 wks €78

Foxrock Institute Kill o' the Grange, Kill Lane Blackrock (4939506) - Tue eve 8 wks €105

Greendale Community School Kilbarrack 5 (8322735) - Thurs 8.30 10 wks €60

Hartstown Community School Clonsilla 15 (8209863) - 10wk, €55

Holy Family Community School Rathcoole (4580766)

Jackie Skelly's Fitness 42 Clarendon St, 2; Park West, Nangor Rd, 12 & Applewood Village, Swords, & Ashbourne (6770040) - step, pump, spin, toning, taebo, pilates, body sculpt - membership includes classes

Lucan Community College Esker Drive (6282077) - to music, Mon 7.30 & 8.30 10 wks €65 ea

Marino College 14-20 Marino Mart 3 (8332100) - Tues, 6pm 10wks, €45

Motions Health & Fitness Training (087 2808866) - Fitness Instructor training diploma course (ITEC), part-time, 9 hours per week. Venue Citywest Hotel & Leisure Centre, Naas Rd

National Aquatic Centre Snugborough Rd Blanchardstown 15 (6464300) - aerobics in water, aquafit

National Training Centre 16a St Joseph's Parade Dorset St 7 (8827777)

Network Club 24 Elmcastle Green Tallaght 24 (4524415) - aqua

Palmerstown CS - Pobailscoil Iosolde, Kennelsfort Rd 20 (6260116) - Mon, 10 wks, 8-8.45p m €60

Phibsboro Gym 1st Floor, Phibsboro SC 7 (8301849) - step/boxercise

Portmarnock Sports & Leisure Club Blackwood Lane Carrickhill Portmarnock (8462122) - also aqua fit

Ringsend Technical Institute Cambridge Rd 4 (6684498) - Tue 6.30 10 wks €50

St MacDara's CC, Wellington Lane Templeogue 6W (4566216) - Mon beginners/ tummy & thigh, 7 & 8.15 8 wks, €52 ea

AERONAUTICAL ENGINEERING & RELATED COURSES see also Aviation

DIT Faculty: Engineering Bolton St 1 (4023000) - jet engine overhaul 1 yr €950/ aeronautical knowledge; also catagory A: €650 1 eve wk modules; €950 2 eve wk modules

Kilroy's College Wentworth House Grand Canal Street Lr 2 (6620538 1850-700700) - tutor supported home study: avionics - basic aircraft electronics, dip course

AIKIDO see also Karate / Martial Arts

Aikido Federation of Ireland 1, Park Lane East Pearse St 2 (6718454) - beginners: Mon/ Wed; improvers: Tue/Thurs - 7.45; Sat 1pm/ regular Mon/Wed/Fri 6pm. Fees from €4-€10 per class; also student rates

Irish Aikido Association Scoil Caitriona Baggot St Upr 2 (087 2940735) - intro, Thurs eve, advanced, Sun (day): ea 10 wks €50; ongoing / College of Surgeons, York St 2, Wed 3-5pm, 10 wks €50

Natural Health Training Centre 1 Park Lane E Pearse St 2 (6718454) - beginners: Mon/ Wed; improvers: Tue/Thurs - 7.45; Sat 1pm/ regular Mon/Wed/Fri 6pm. Fees from €4-€10 per class; also student rates

Phibsboro Gym 1st Floor, Phibsboro SC 7 (8301849)

Public Service Aikido Club St Andrew's Resource Cntr Pearse St 2 (4923551 Mary) - all yr except bank hols, Mon & Thurs, classes 7.30-9.30, €5 per class (consesions)

ALARM INSTALLATIONS

Hi-Tech Training 4 Nth Gt George's St 1 (1850-759759) - 50% practical, hands-on, 7-10pm, 10 wks, cert/ digital communicators text & voice, cert 1 day 10am-5pm/ fire alarm foundation, 3 day 10-5pm cert: 50% practical hands-on

ALCOHOL ABUSE see Drugs

St Anthony's House St Lawrence Rd Clontarf 3 (8335300) - AA, also Sat

ALEXANDER TECHNIQUE

Alexander Technique Postural Re-education Frank Kennedy 35 Callary Rd Mt Merrion (2882446) - also day/ stress management

ALTERNATIVE & COMPLEMENTARY THERAPIES & LIFESTYLES

Ballyfermot CFE, Ballyfermot Rd 10 (6269421) - Mon 7-9pm 15 wks

Greenhills College Limekiln Ave Walkinstown 12 (4507779/4507863) - angel therapy, Mon, 8wks, €104

Harmony Healing 41 Beneavin Pk Glasnevin 11 (8641768)

Hartstown Community School Clonsilla 15 (8209863) - holistic life skills/just for me - 10wks, €85 each

Healing House 24 O'Connell Ave Berkeley Rd 7 (8306413) - wide range of courses & therapies

Irish Yoga Association PO Box 9969 7 (4929213/ 087 2054489) - qualified teachers available all over Ireland/ 4 yr Teacher Training courses

Margaret Macken Yoga Stephen's Gr/Adelaide Rd/Clontarf (8332954) - Iyengar Yoga, 6 wk course; also relaxation, stress management and meditation

Newpark Adult Education Centre, Newtownpark Ave Blackrock (2884376 / 2883725)

Obus School of Healing Therapies, 53 Beech Grove Lucan (6282121) - accupressure 6 day course, €475 / Hopi ear candling, 1 day wkend €150, cert

Our Lady's Hospice Harold's Cross 6 (4068806 4068810) - complementary therapies & creative arts 18 May 07/ Dream Tending, 14 & 20 July 07: each 1 day, 10am-4pm €100 incl lunch/ holistic approach to cancer care, 1 day workshop 26 Nov06;3 March07; 20 Oct07: 10-4pm €100 incl lunch

Rathmines CFE - Senior College, Town Hall 6 (4975334) - holistic lifestyle, Tue & Wed 10 wks €90

Shiatsu Ireland classes at 44 Adelaide Rd 2 (2962839) - shiatsu & massage - beginners & advanced

Walmer College & Holistic Centre First Floor, River Hse Raheny Shopping C 5 (8329645) - auragraphics, wkend workshops/ body spirit/ various massage courses/ relaxation - meditation, etc

ANATOMY

Aspen's College of Beauty Therapy 83 Lr Camden St 2 (4751079/ 4751940) - ITEC anatomy & physiology

Bronwyn Conroy Beauty School Temple Hall, Temple Rd Blackrock (2107848) - anatomy, physiology & massage

Colaiste Ide Cardiffsbridge Rd Finglas W 8443233 11 (8342333) - ITEC dip in anatomy, physiology & body massage, 20 wks Tue & Thurs 7-10 €500

Crumlin College of FE, Crumlin Rd 12 (4540662) - ITEC dip in anatomy & physiology & body massage, for registered nurses only

Dún Laoghaire CFE, 17 Cumberland St Dún Laoghaire (2809676) - anatomy & physiology, 20 wks Tue 6.45-8.45 €300

Galligan Beauty Group 109 Grafton St 2 (6703933) - and phjysiology dip, ITEC/CIB-TAC, €800

Healing House 24 O'Connell Ave Berkeley Rd 7 (8306413) - anatomy & physiology diploma course, ITEC, Tues, Wed, Thurs or 1 w/end mthly, €750

Irish Academy of Massage & Complementary Therapies 33 Monkstown Lawns, Clondalkin 22 (4640126) - anatomy and physiology, €600, ITEC dip

Motions Health & Fitness Training (087 2808866) - Diploma in Holistic Massage (ITEC), part-time course, 3 hours per week. Castleknock, Citywest & Naas

Portobello School 43 Lr Dominick St 1 (8721277) - anatomy, physiology & body massage, ITEC dip

Senior College Dún Laoghaire, CFE Eblana Ave Dún Laoghaire (2800385) - dip in anatomy, physiology and body massage, CIBTAC, 25 wks, €720

Walmer College & Holistic Centre First Floor, River Hse Raheny Shopping C 5 (8329645) - & physiology, ITEC dip

ANGELS see Meditation, etc

Balbriggan Community College Pine Ridge Chapel St (8412388/9) - angel threapy, Wed 8 wks 7.30-9.30 €104

Ballyfermot CFE, Ballyfermot Rd 10 (6269421) - Mon 7-9, 12 wks

Ballymun Trinity CS, Adult Ed Centre 9 (8420654) - Tue 7.30 6 wks €75

Firhouse Community College Firhouse Rd 24 (4525807) - Tue 7.30-9pm 8 wks €78

Grange Community College Grange Abbey Rd Donaghmede 13 (8471422) - 7-9pm Mon 10 wks Angel therapy

Hartstown Community School Clonsilla 15 (8209863) - spiritual development, 8 wks €85

Killester CFE, Collins Ave 5 (8337686) meditation & healing, 10 wks Tue 7.30, €60

Marino College 14-20 Marino Mart 3 (8332100) - healing with angels, 8pm Tues €65

St Finian's Community College Swords (8402623) - Angel therapy, 8 wks

TACT St Dominic's School St Dominic's Rd Tallaght 24 (4596757)

Walmer College & Holistic Centre First Floor, River Hse Raheny Shopping C 5 (8329645)

ANGLING

Irish Federation of Sea Anglers c/o H O'Rourke 67 Windsor Drive Monkstown (2806873)

ANIMALS / ANIMAL CARE

Brian Byrnes Art Studio 3 Upr Baggot St 4 (6671520 / 6711599) - painting/drawing, 8wk, €140, also day

Coláiste Dhúlaigh CFE,Barryscourt Rd Coolock 17 (8481337) - animal welfare program, Mon 7-9.30, 10 wks

Killester CFE, Collins Ave 5 (8337686) - per care & animal grooming beginners Mon/ improvers Tue: 7-9.30 10wks €110

Tagnrye Dog Services various locations (4513324) - how to train your dog, in your home, eve & day, 6 wks €100

ANIMATION

Ballyfermot CFE, Ballyfermot Rd 10 (6269421) - computer animation 15 wks Mon/Wed, 7-10pm

New Media Technology College, 13 Harcourt St 2 (4780905) - macromedia flash/ 3D character animatioin; 3D studio max: each 8 wks 6.30-9.30/ sat 10-1pm or 2-5pm

ANTHROPOLOGY

All Hallows College Gracepark Rd Drumcondra 9 (8373745) - logic: philosophical anthropology & intro to psychology, Mon 7.45-10pm, 24 wks €590

International Foundation for Adult Education PO Box 93 Eglinton St Cork (022-29358 / 0818 365305) - dip, distance learning, IFAE-Netherlands

ANTIQUES Furniture Restoration

Irish Auctioneers & Valuers Institute 38 Merrion Sq E 2 (6611794) - fine art appreciation

Newpark Adult Education Centre Newtownpark Ave Blackrock (2884376 / 2883725) - furniture: restoration & repair, Mon, Thurs, 7.30-9.45, 10wks, €125

UCD Adult Education Centre Belfield (7167123) - Antiques Today: An Expert Overview, Mon 8 wks

APIARY see Bee-Keeping

ARABIC see also Languages

Sandford Language Institute Milltown Pk Sandford Rd 6 (2601296) - all levels, 15wks €285

ARCHAEOLOGY

Hartstown Community School Clonsilla 15 (8209863) - in a global society, 10 wks €85

UCD Adult Education Centre Belfield (7167123) - What is Archaeology? Tue / Prehistoric landscapes, South Dublin & North Wicklow; also in S Wicklow, Carlow Kildare: both 1 day trips Sat/ Cert in Archaeology - Out of the Distant Past, Thurs/ Celtic societies: Europe & Ireland 750BC-950AD/ Expanding Horizons: Ireland, Europe and Atlantic Worlds, Thurs spring

ARCHERY

Clondalkin Sports & Leisure Centre Nangor Rd Clondalkin 22 (4574858)

Greendale Community School Kilbarrack 5 (8322735) - Tue, 7.30pm, 10wks, €95

ARCHITECTURE Art History / Draughtsmanship

Irish Georgian Society 74 Merrion Sq 2 (6767053) - lectures, tours, visits to historic houses etc, for members

Pearse College Clogher Rd Crumlin 12 (4536661/4541544) - draughting 1 €150 / 2: €170, day

Trinity College 2 (8961000) - (8968589), extra mural, intro to European, €255, 22 wks day/ renaissance & baroque architecture Italy; Romanesque art & architecture: day 22 wks €130 each

UCD Adult Education Centre Belfield (7167123) - Understanding and Appreciating Georgian Dublin, Tue 8 wks/ Understanding Irish Historic Buildings, Mon 10 wks/ The Great House in Britain & Ireland, Wed 10 wks spring

AROMATHERAPY

Aspen's Beauty Clinic & College 83 Lr Camden St 2 (4751079/ 4751940) - ITEC

Berni Grainger 21 Grangemore Ave 13 (8472943/ 086 2694214) - massage & use of oils, intro, w/end, €180

19

Bray Institute of FE, Novara Ave Bray (2866111 / 2829668) - 10wks, €85 beginners Wed 7.30-9.30pm

Coláiste Dhúlaigh CFE, Barryscourt Rd Coolock 17 (8481337) - & body massage, Mon, 10 wks, 7.30-9.30/ for home use, Fri 10-12pm 10 wks

Colaiste Ide Cardiffsbridge Rd Finglas W 8443233 11 (8342333) - ITEC dip, 20 wks Tue 7-10 €300

Coolmine Community School Clonsilla 15 (8214583) - Wed 7.30 10 wks €70

Galligan College of Beauty 109 Grafton St 2 (6703933) - ITEC & CIBTAC, Sept - June p/time, €1200

Grange Community College Grange Abbey Rd Donaghmede 13 (8471422) - 7-9pm Mon 10 wks

Harmony Healing 41 Beneavin Pk Glasnevin 11 (8641768) - essential oils & massage

Hartstown Community School Clonsilla 15 (8209863) - 10wks, €85

Healing House 24 O'Connell Ave Berkeley Rd 7 (8306413) - international ITEC dip - Feb-Dec07, weekly or 1wkend mthly €1250 / essential oils, basic massage, 1 or 2 day workshops, €100/€175, cert

Holistic Healing Centre 38 Dame St 2 (6710813) - ITEC dip

Lucan Community College Esker Drive (6282077) - Tue 7.30-8.30 10 wks €130

Malahide Community School Malahide (8460949) - Thurs 7.30 10 wks €90

Melt, Temple Bar Natural Healing Centre 2 Temple Ln 2 (6798786) - face-packs, essential oils: day/wk/end, €200 cert

Obus School of Healing Therapies, 53 Beech Grove Lucan (6282121) - professional, 1yr, dip, Leixlip

Our Lady's Hospice Harold's Cross 6 (4068806 4068810) - advanced clinical, Pt 1: 2 day workshop (Sat/Sun) 9-4.30pm €195 incl lunch

Pearse College Clogher Rd Crumlin 12 (4536661/4541544) - ITEC dip, day

Portobello School 43 Lr Dominick St 1 (8721277) - ITEC dip

Ringsend Technical Institute Cambridge Rd 4 (6684498) - massage, 6.30-8pm/ 8-9.30: each 10 wks €70

Senior College Dún Laoghaire, CFE Eblana Ave Dún Laoghaire (2800385) - CIBTAC dip, €660/ intro to aromatherapy & massage, €120

Tallaght Community School Balrothery 24 (4515566) - intro to massage & aromatherapy, 7.30-9.30 8 wks €60

Walmer College & Holistic Centre First Floor, River Hse Raheny Shopping C 5 (8329645) - aromatherapy ITEC dip

ART Acrylics / Animation / Architecture / Design / Drawing / Glass / Graphics / Oils / Painting / Picture Framing / Portrait / Sketching / Watercolours

Balbriggan Community College Pine Ridge Chapel St (8412388/9) - watercolours, 8 wks, Wed 7.30-9.30pm €104

Ballymun Trinity CS, Adult Ed Centre 9 (8420654) - oils, watercolours, painting, beginners/improvers, Mon Wed 7.30 10wk, €100

Ballymun Men's Centre Lift Shaft 4 Shangan Rd Ballymun 9 (8623117) - painting, watercolours, acrylics, etc, Tues afternoon

BASE Ballyboden Adult Social Education Whitechurch Library Taylor's Lane 16 (4935953) - beginners / improvers / FETAC art foundation: 10 wks

Brian Byrnes Art Studio 3 Upr Baggot St 4 (6671520 / 6711599) - 8wk, €150 also day, landscapes, animals, portraits, flowers & gardens

Coláiste Dhúlaigh CFE,Barryscourt Rd Coolock 17 (8481337) - art foundation, Fetac 3 Mon 20 wks 10-11am

Coláiste Eanna, Kilkieran Rd Cabra 7 (8389577) - sketching/painting, 10wk, Tues, 7-9pm

College of Further Education Main St Dundrum 14 (2951376) - oils, sketching, watercolours: Tue 7-9pm 8 wks €104

Coolmine Community School Clonsilla 15 (8214583) - drawing & painting, beginners, Mon, Wed improvers 7.30; oils & acrylics Tue, Wed, 7.30: 10wks, €80 ea/workshops, Sat 7 Oct 10-1pm €25

DATE Centre CFE, Dundrum 14 (2964322 (9.30am-12pm)) - beginners, watercolour 9.30am acryllic 11am/ flower painting: each 10 wks, €97, day

Dundrum Family Recreation Centre Meadowbrook 16 (2984654)

Finglas Adult Reading & Writing Scheme Colaiste Eoin Cappagh Rd 11 (8340893) - art & design, FETAC level 3 & 4: 30 wks Weds 1-4pm

Firhouse Community College Firhouse Rd 24 (4525807) - Mon 7.30-9.30pm 8 wks €104

Gallery Art Centre The Mill, Celbridge Co Kildare (6276206) - painting made simple, day/ eve, 9 wks €110/ also for children

Greenhills College Limekiln Ave Walkinstown 12 (4507779/4507863) - beginners/ intermediate 10 wks, €130

Hartstown Community School Clonsilla 15 (8209863) - 10 wks/watercolour 10 wks €85

Holy Family Community School Rathcoole (4580766)

Inchicore CFE, Emmet Rd 8 (4535358) - art & design

Institute of Art Design & Technology Dún Laoghaire (2414631) - various courses

Jean Strong (2892323) - ongoing, beginners-improvers, 10wks, €170/also day:- Blackrock & Dundrum / unlock latent creativity with 'The Artist's Way' - paint, write, compose music, Mon, Tue 14 wks €250

Kilternan Adult Education Group Ballybetagh Rd Kilternan 18 (2952050) - all mediums, each 10 wks €113.75

Knocklyon Youth & Community Centre, 16 (4931213) - Wed, Fri, 10am/12pm, 8 wks €90/ intermediate Mon 8pm 8 wks €90

Kylemore College Kylemore Rd 10 (6265901)

Marysha, Old National School Dunboyne Co Meath (8222929 087 6853452) - drawing & painting for adults, watercolours & acrylics, Thur 7.15-9.15 8 wks, all thru' year

Maynooth NUI Adult & Community Ed Dept (7084500) - community art for community development, Old Bawn CS D24 (4526137)

Meridian Art Group c/o St Paul's College Raheny 5 (8310688)

Newpark Adult Education Centre, Newtownpark Ave Blackrock (2884376 / 2883725) - painting/drawing/watercolours, sketching/ oil: Mon, Tue, Thurs, 10 wks 7.30-9.45pm €120

Old Bawn Community School Tallaght 24 (4526137) - intro to drawing, design, watercolours & oils (materials not incl); beginners, Thurs, improvers Tues: 7.30-9.30, 10wks €95 each

Plunket College Swords Rd, Whitehall 9 (8371689) - beginnerscolour, form, paints: Tues 7.30, €90/ painting & sketching for active retired, 2-4pm Wed €55

Pobalscoil Rosmini Adult Ed Grace Pk Rd 9 (8371015) - beginners techniques of drawing, painting, composition, Mon/Tue 8.20pm €95

Portmarnock Community School Carrickhill Rd (8038056) - basic elements, beginners/ improvers, Tue 7.30 10 wks €100

St MacDara's CC, Wellington Lane Templeogue 6W (4566216) - Tue beginners, Mon: 7.30-9.30pm, 8 wks, €104

Stillorgan Senior College Old Road Stillorgan (2880704) - beginners, Mon 7.30 8 wks €104

Pobalscoil Rosmini
Adult Education Programme 2006 / 2007
Enrolment: Mon 4th September – Fri 15th September 9.30am - 12.30pm
Evening Enrolment: Mon 18th & Tues 19th September 7.30 - 9.30pm
Classes begin from Mon 25th September – late enrolling if places available
Tel/Fax: 8371015 Email: adulted@pobalscoilrosmini.ie

TACT St Dominic's School St Dominic's Rd Tallaght 24 (4596757)

Taney Parish Centre Taney Rd Dundrum 14 (2985491) - Mon/Tue 2981853/ art zone, Thur 0868159073, day

TARGET St Kevin's School Newbrook Rd, Donaghmede 13 (8671967) - beginners/ improvers/ advanced: day only 10 wks

UCD Adult Education Centre Belfield (7167123) - Art for All, Wed: 10 wks/ bookmaking, Sat 1 day

ART & DESIGN

Coláiste Dhúlaigh CFE,Barryscourt Rd Coolock 17 (8481337) - art, design, craft level 3, Wed 2-5pm 20 wks

ART APPRECIATION Art History

Cabinteely Community School Johnstown Rd 18 (2857455) - history of art, Tue 10 wks €95

Gallery Art Centre The Mill, Celbridge Co Kildare (6276206) - modern art, am/pm 6 wks €70

Institute of Professional Auctioneers & Valuers 129 Lr Baggot St 2 (6785685) - fine & decorative arts, cert, 15 wks €750

National Gallery of Ireland Merrion Sq W 2 (6615133) - 1 term 12 wks 6.30: season ticket €85; €8 per class/ public lectures Sun 3pm & Tues 10.30am: free/ guided tours incl for visually/hearing impaired - book in writing 3 wks in advance/ Saturday family prog adults with children, 3-4pm, Sept-Nov, free

People's College for Continuing Education & Training 32 Parnell Sq 1 (8735879) - exploring modern Irish art, €60

Plunket College Swords Rd, Whitehall 9 (8371689) - Mon 7.30-9.30 10 wks €90

Portmarnock Community School Carrickhill Rd (8038056) - visual awareness (Mr D Higgins), Mon 7.30-9.20, 10 wks €100

Trinity College 2 (8961000) - (8968589) - extra mural, intro to Euro painting, 22 wks €255, day / the Arts of Japan, 22 wks, €130 eve

UCD Adult Education Centre Belfield (7167123) - an introduction to, Fri pm 10 wks/ mapping the city, Mon: ea 10 wks

ART HISTORY see also Art Appreciation

DATE Centre CFE, Dundrum 14 (2964322 (9.30am-12pm)) - history & appreciation, 10 wks, €97, day

National Gallery of Ireland Merrion Sq W 2 (6615133) - 1 term 12 wks 6.30: season ticket €85 or €8 per class

Newpark Adult Education Centre, Newtownpark Ave Blackrock (2884376 / 2883725) - European paintings, Thurs 10 wks 7.30-9.45 €120

Rathmines CFE - Senior College, Town Hall 6 (4975334) - artistic creative development, art history & life drawing, Mon 7-9pm 10 wks €90

Trinity College 2 (8961000) - (8968589) - history of European painting, 22wks €255 day / (8963151) Irish art & its contexts, eve 17wks, €120/ 18th century painting Britain & Ireland, day, 22 wks €130; / painting & sculpture in 17th century Europe, day 22 wks €130/ arts of Japan, eve 22 wks €130

UCD Adult Education Centre Belfield (7167123) - dip in history of european art, 24 wks Tue & Wed/ intro to the Renaissance in Florence, Rome and Venice, Sat morn 10 wks

ART METAL WORK see Jewellery

ARTS/CRAFTS see also Crafts; Jewellery

Ballymun Trinity CS, Adult Ed Centre 9 (8420654) - mosaics & stained glass, Tue 7.30 10 wks €130

Ceramic Forms Michelle Maher 9 Fernleigh Cl Castleknock 15 (6405614 087-2047695)

Coláiste Dhúlaigh CFE,Barryscourt Rd Coolock 17 (8481337) - Tue 10.20-12.20pm/ 7.15-9.15pm, 10 wks ea

College of Progressive Education 27-29 Carysfort Ave Blackrock (4884300) - creative activities for children

Coolmine Community School Clonsilla 15 (8214583) - mosaic magic, Mon 7.30-9.30, 10 wks €80

Hartstown Community School Clonsilla 15 (8209863) - creative card making, 10 wks €85

Killester CFE, Collins Ave 5 (8337686) - art of paper making, card making & gift wrapping, Tue 7.30 10 wks €80

KLEAR Grange Park View Kilbarrack 5 (8671845) - creative arts, day

Kylemore College Kylemore Rd 10 (6265901) - for childcare 0-6 yrs, 13 wks Wed 7-9pm

Malahide Community School Malahide (8460949) - glass mosaics, Thurs 10 wks €100

Marysha, Old National School Dunboyne Co Meath (8222929 087 6853452) - for children, throughout year, Thurs 4.30-6.30

Newpark Adult Education Centre Newtownpark Ave Blackrock (2884376 / 2883725) - intro to mosaics, 10wks, Mon €120/ jewellery & bead design €120/ stained glass 10 wks Tues

Palmerstown CS - Pobailscoil Iosolde, Kennelsfort Rd 20 (6260116) - mosaic, Tues 7.30, 10 wks €70

Portobello School 43 Lr Dominick St 1 (8721277) - visual display, dip

Tracy Miley Cabinteely venue 18 (086 8485394) - mosaic, all levels, 7.30-9.39pm, 8 wks/ hand built ceramics beginners, improvers: 8 wks, day: €140 each, materials supplied

UCD Adult Education Centre Belfield (7167123) - papercrafting - making cards, Sat 10am 1 day

ASSERTIVENESS / EMPOWERMENT see also Enneagram / Personal Development

Ballsbridge CFE,, Shelbourne Rd 4 (6684806) - Thurs, 6.30 10 wks, €90

Bray Institute of FE, Novara Ave Bray (2866111 / 2829668) - 10 wks, €85 Wed 7.30-9.30

Cabinteely Community School Johnstown Rd 18 (2857455) - 10wk, €95

Centre for Professional & Personal Development 44 Westland Row 2 (6612291) - wkend, €500

Coláiste Dhúlaigh CFE,Barryscourt Rd Coolock 17 (8481337) - and communication skills, Mon 7.15 10 wks

Communication & Personal Development 30/31 Wicklow St 2 (6713636/ 6613225)

Eden Computer Training Rathfarnham 16 & 1 Green St 7 (4953155)

Enriching Careers 38 Clonliffe Rd 3 (6589091)

Harmony Healing 41 Beneavin Pk Glasnevin 11 (8641768)

Marino College 14-20 Marino Mart 3 (8332100) - Tue 6pm €85 / 8pm €90 10wks/ Wed 1.30-3.30 €85

Old Bawn Community School Tallaght 24 (4526137) - self discovery, Tue, 7.30-9.30, 10wks €90

Our Lady's Hospice Harold's Cross 6 (4068806 4068810) - assertiveness & listening skills, 1 day workshop €100 incl lunch

Quantum Communications Ken McCready 39 Emerald Sq, Dolphin's Barn 8 (086 1502604) - empowerment training, at Teachers Centre, 36 Parnell Sq 1, 6 wks €239

The Professional Training and Coaching Consultancy (087 6379765/ 045 865783) -
 6 wks, Terenure / Lucan / Dundrum

Training Options Plus 6-8 Wicklow St 2 (6717787) - 1 day, cert

ASTROLOGY

Astroleg 10 Griffith Close 11 (085 1561697) - beginners / intermediate/ advanced

Cabinteely Community School Johnstown Rd 18 (2857455) - illustrated with music
 & film, Mon 10 wks €95

ASTRONOMY

Astronomy Ireland PO Box 2888 5 (8470777) -beginners classes, from 5 Oct & 8 Feb:
 10 wks 7.30-9.30 €120 incl membership & mag

Dunsink Observatory Dunsink Lane Castleknock 15 (838 7911/7959) - Public open
 nights 1st/3rd Wed of each month, Oct-Mar, 8pm. Must send SAE for free tickets

Foxrock Institute Kill o' the Grange, Kill Lane Blackrock (4939506) - Mon eve 8 wks €105

Irish Astronomical Society PO Box 2547 Brian Keene (President) 14 (086 2389252)
 - 1meeting a mth, 1st mondays, Ely Hse

Lucan Community College Esker Drive (6282077) - Mon 7.30-9.30 10 wks €65

UCD Adult Education Centre Belfield (7167123) - introduction, Wed 10 wks spring

ATHLETICS

Athletics Association of Ireland 18 Joyce Way Parkwest 12 (6251101) - the national
 body, 320 clubs

Clondalkin Sports & Leisure Centre Nangor Rd Clondalkin 22 (4574858)

AUCTIONEERING

DIT Faculty: Built Environment Bolton St 1 (4023000) - BSc in Property Studies, 4
 yrs ptime IAVI (661794)

Institute of Professional Auctioneers & Valuers 129 Lr Baggot St 2 (6785685) - estate
 agent practical, cert

Institute of Technology Tallaght ITT Dublin, Tallaght 24 (4042101) - auctioneering &
 estate agency, eve 2yrs IPAV cert

AUTOMOBILE ENGINEERING see Engineering

AVIATION see also Paragliding

DIT Faculty: Engineering Bolton St 1 (4023000) - flight ops officer dispatcher, 2yr
 €1150; €850 yr2/ private aircraft pilot licence theory, 1 yr €950

Eircopter Helicopters Weston Aerodrome Celbridge (6280088) - helicopter private
 pilot licence, ground school, 12 wks €600/ also, introductory flying lessons, 30 min
 €250, 60min €450

Kilroy's College Wentworth House Grand Canal Street Lr 2 (6620538 1850-700700)
 - tutor supported home study: avionics - basic aircraft electronics, dip course

National Flight Centre Flight School Weston Airport Leixlip Co Kildare (6282930) -
 private pilot / commercial pilot: licence; multi-engine / night / intrument / instructor:
 rating; introductory filghts €95 & €180

AYURVEDA

Coolmine Community School Clonsilla 15 (8214583) - 10 wks, Tue 7.30-9.30 €80

BADMINTON

Badminton Centre Whitehall Rd Terenure 12 (4505966) - 7 days a week: adults/
 beginners/ improvers

Baldoyle Badminton Centre Unit 4 Baldoyle Ind Est Grange Rd 13 (8393355)

Corporate Club 24 Elmcastle Green Tallaght 24 (4610935)

Network Club 24 Elmcastle Green Tallaght 24 (4524415)

Pobalscoil Rosmini Adult Ed Grace Pk Rd 9 (8371015) - beginners / improvers Tue 8.20 / 8.30pm €90 each

Portmarnock Community School Carrickhill Rd (8038056) - Mon 16 wks 7-9.30pm

Portmarnock Sports & Leisure Club Blackwood Lane Carrickhill Portmarnock (8462122)

Ringsend Technical Institute Cambridge Rd 4 (6684498) - beginners/ improvers, Mon 7&8.30 10wks, €70

Taney Parish Centre Taney Rd Dundrum 14 (2985491) - Tues, Thurs (2981853) day

BAKERY STUDIES

DIT Faculty: Tourism & Food Cathal Brugha St 1 (4023000) - professional baking German breads & German cake, each 3 classes, cert €300/ pastries & snacks 1, €400; also 2; each 36hrs; sweetbreads 1 36 hrs, €400 hrs, also 2, 10 classes

BALLET see also Classical & Jazz /Dance

Coiscéim Dance 14 Sackville Pl 1 (8780558) - for adults: city centre studio, intermediate: Thurs, 6.15 8 wks €100

Dance Theatre of Ireland Bloomfields Centre, Lr George St Dún Laoghaire (2803455) - Mon, 6.45-8pm, 10 wks €80

Dublin School of Dance 13 Stamer St Portobello 8 (4755451) - ballet & jazz dance, adult beginners, eve 15 wks €134

Dundrum Family Recreation Centre Meadowbrook 16 (2984654)

Inchicore CFE, Emmet Rd 8 (4535358)

Ingrid Nachstern (2600663) - classical ballet, beginners, 10 wk, Tues, Sandymount, €80 per term; also, for adults Tues eve 10 wks €80

BALLROOM DANCING see also Dancing / Old Time

Bray Institute of FE, Novara Ave Bray (2866111 / 2829668) - 10 wks €85 beginners Wed 7.30

Cabinteely Community School Johnstown Rd 18 (2857455) - quickstep, foxtrot, waltz, tango 10wk, €50

Dance Classes & Ballroom of Romance Presentation Primary Sch Terenure 6 (6211514/ 087 2484890) - waltz, quickstep, tango, slow foxtrot all levels & teacher training, Fri 8pm €10 per class

Dance Club Rathmines & Rathgar (2893797) - beginners

Dundrum Family Recreation Centre Meadowbrook 16 (2984654)

Hartstown Community School Clonsilla 15 (8209863) - beginners/intermediate, 10 wks, €60

Just Dance (8273040 087 8473518) - Blackrock, Drumcondra, Castleknock, Blanchardstown, for fitness & fun

Morosini-Whelan School of Dancing 46 Parnell Sq W 1 (8303613) - incl waltz, rock- 'n'roll, quickstep, swing, Mon & Wed 8-9pm €8

Pobalscoil Rosmini Adult Ed Grace Pk Rd 9 (8371015) - beginners 1 & 2: Wed 7pm & 8.30 €90 each

BANJO

Comhaltas Ceoltóirí Éireann 32 Belgrave Sq Monkstown (2800295)

Waltons New School of Music 69 Sth Gt George's St 2 (4781884) - also day, see ad page 155

BANKING AND FINANCE see also Financial Services

Dublin Business School 13/14 Aungier St 2 (4177500) - Institute of Bankers joint finanacial services dip, 2 eves, 2 yrs, 6.15-9.30pm / dip in stockbroking investment/ advanced dip in stockbroking, i eve , 14 weeks, 6.15-9.30; certs in mortgage practice / banking operations / credit & lending / customer relationships & services (Inst of Bankers), 1 eve a wk, 6.15-9.30pm, 1 yr

Westmoreland College for Management Studies 11 Westmoreland St 2 (6795324/7266) - ACCA Dip in financial management

BASIC EDUCATION may include English / Irish / Maths / Writing / Computers - day and evening courses see also Adult Literacy

Ballymun Trinity CS, Adult Ed Centre 9 (8420654) - spellwell - 10wk/ read write numeracy computers, education guidance: free (8622402)

Crumlin College of FE, Crumlin Rd 12 (4540662) - adult reading & writing courses, one-to-one tuition, spelling groups, ESOL; numeracy, intro to computers; FETAC foundation in communications; also day

Dublin Adult Learning Centre 3 Mountjoy Sq 1 (8787266) - basic English/ jnr cert English/ leaving cert English

Finglas Adult Reading & Writing Scheme Colaiste Eoin Cappagh Rd 11 (8340893) - one-to-one read/write tuition, Mon & tue eve, 30 wks; also daytime; / spelling groups 10 wks thurs am, Mon 7-9/ basic English 10 wks tues 7-9pm/ creative writing for basic skills 10 wks Mon 11-12.30/ basic maths 10 wks Wed 9.30-11; 30 wks FETAC lev el 3, wed 11-12.30; Mon 7-9pm/

KLEAR Grange Park View Kilbarrack 5 (8671845) - general knowledge./ basic English/Maths group/ spelling - phonics & pronounciation; day only

Pearse College Clogher Rd Crumlin 12 (4536661/4541544) - literacy drop-in centre 4547054

People's College for Continuing Education & Training 32 Parnell Sq 1 (8735879) - English, Irish basic €15

Southside Adult Literacy Scheme 4 Glenville Tce Dundrum 14 (2964321) - basic English, maths, FETAC

BASKET-MAKING see Crafts

BASKETBALL

Basketball Ireland National Basketball Arena Tallaght 24 (4590211)

Clondalkin Sports & Leisure Centre Nangor Rd Clondalkin 22 (4574858)

Network Club 24 Elmcastle Green Tallaght 24 (4524415)

Portmarnock Sports & Leisure Club Blackwood Lane Carrickhill Portmarnock (8462122)

BASSOON

Dún Laoghaire Music Centre 130A Lr George's St Dún Laoghaire (2844178)

BATIK/TIE-DYE

Plunket College Swords Rd, Whitehall 9 (8371689) - intro to: for wall hangings, shirts, etc: Wed 7.30 10 wks €90

BEAUTICIAN see also Beauty Therapy / Manicure

Aspen's Beauty Clinic & College of Beauty Therapy 83 Lr Camden St 2 (4751079/ 4751940) - professional make-up, ITEC/ also short courses spray-tan/ threading/ Brazillian & Hollywood/ ear-piercing/ false eyelashes

Bronwyn Conroy Beauty School Temple Hall, Temple Rd Blackrock (2107848) - beautician / also f/time CIDESCO/ CIBTAC / p/time CIBTAC

Coogan-Bergin Clinic & College of Beauty Therapy Glendenning Hse 6-8 Wicklow St 2 (6794387) - CIBTAC Mon & Wed 6-9pm, €2495/ also 1 day wkly/ beautician, body therapy & electrolysis CIBTAC, day €5790, also, CIDESCO CIBTAC €5995

Galligan College of Beauty 109 Grafton St 2 (6703933) - ITEC & CIBTAC, Sept - June p/time, Beauth Specialist €2600

Irish Academy of Training 33 Monkstown Lawns, Clondalkin 22 (4640126) - beauty specialist, ITEC dip, €2150 p-time/ ITEC dip f-time 4-day wk €4400/ make-up ITEC cert tue eve €850 from Oct06

BEAUTY CARE (GROOMING, MAKE-UP, etc.) see also Grooming / Manicure & Pedicure / Skin Care

Ballymun Trinity CS, Adult Ed Centre 9 (8420654) - Mon 6 wks, €75

Cabinteely Community School Johnstown Rd 18 (2857455) - simply beautiful course, 8wk, €80

Coláiste Eanna, Kilkieran Rd Cabra 7 (8389577) - beauty & make-up, Thurs 7pm 10 wks

Coolmine Community School Clonsilla 15 (8214583) - style coaching, Tue 7.30-9.30 10 wks €70

Crumlin College of FE, Crumlin Rd 12 (4540662) - CIBTAC course, skin treatments dip 20 wk, Mon & Wed 6.45; also Tue 9.15-4.15pm/ nail treatments dip 13 wks; waxing dip 13 wks, Tues & Thurs 6.45 each/ star-nail dip: acrillic/jell 8 wks Thurs 6.45pm

Foxrock Institute Kill o' the Grange, Kill Lane Blackrock (4939506) - for tutors in ladies colour analysis, Wed eve

Geraldine Brand Style Image Consultant City Centre (8327332) - courses for all ages, men, women; grooming individual 2 hr day €250

Grange Community College Grange Abbey Rd Donaghmede 13 (8471422) - 7-9pm Mon 10 wks

Greenhills College Limekiln Ave Walkinstown 12 (4507779/4507863) - skin care, 10wks Mon, €130

Hartstown Community School Clonsilla 15 (8209863) - 5wks, €65

Killester CFE, Collins Ave 5 (8337686) - Tue 7.30-9, 10 wks 70

Marino College 14-20 Marino Mart 3 (8332100) - make-up & beauty therapy, Tue & Thurs 6.30 10 wks €75 ea/ gel nail technician cert Thurs 10 wks 7.30 €90

Newpark Adult Education Centre, Newtownpark Ave Blackrock (2884376 / 2883725) - intro Thurs, 10 wks €120

Old Bawn Community School Tallaght 24 (4526137) - classic style, Tues, 7.30-9.30pm, 10 wks €90

Palmerstown CS - Pobailscoil Iosolde, Kennelsfort Rd 20 (6260116) - Thurs 7.30-9.30 8wks €90

Pobalscoil Rosmini Adult Ed Grace Pk Rd 9 (8371015) - techniques of, Wed 7.30-9.30 €120/ introductory tips & essentials for ladies, Tue 8.30 €90

Senior College Dún Laoghaire, CFE Eblana Ave Dún Laoghaire (2800385) - make-up & skin care, €120

BEAUTY THERAPY & THERAPIST see also Manicure & Pedicure

Aspen's Beauty Clinic & College of Beauty Therapy 83 Lr Camden St 2 (4751079/ 4751940) - ITEC

Bronwyn Conroy Beauty School Temple Hall, Temple Rd Blackrock (2107848) - beautician/ also f/time CIDESCO / CIBTAC / p/time CIBTAC

Coogan-Bergin Clinic & College of Beauty Therapy Glendenning Hse 6-8 Wicklow St 2 (6794387)

Galligan College of Beauty 109 Grafton St 2 (6703933) - CIDESCO beautician, body massage, electrolysis Sept - June f/time/ spa therapy €1200/ stone therapy €900/ body therapy 2000

Grange Community College Grange Abbey Rd Donaghmede 13 (8471422) - 7.30-9.30 8 wks

Newpark Adult Education Centre, Newtownpark Ave Blackrock (2884376 / 2883725) - introduction, €120 Thurs 7.30-9.45pm

Portobello School 43 Lr Dominick St 1 (8721277) - beauty therapy, 6.30pm 32 wks/ waxing; manicure & pedicure; nail technology; facial make-up: all ITEC cert, 16 wks

BEE-KEEPING

Fingal-Nth Dublin Beekeepers Assoc Sec. John McMullan 34 Ard Na Mara Cr Malahide (8450193) - beginners bee-keeping course, February/March 2007, 6wk, 2hrs pw + outdoor demonstration

BELLY DANCING

Ballymun Trinity CS, Adult Ed Centre 9 (8420654) - Mon, 7pm 10 wks €100

Belly Dance Ireland with Valerie Larkin, Hollywood Academy Sackville Place 1 (2963856) - Egyptian & original, eve; workshops/ private lessons by appt/ beginners welcome. Venues also at Tallaght, and O'Fiach College, Dundalk

Bray Institute of FE, Novara Ave Bray (2866111 / 2829668) - beginners Mon Tue 7.30 €55 8 wks/ improvers Wed €85 10 wks

Coolmine Community School Clonsilla 15 (8214583) - beginners/ improvers, Tue 10 wks 7 & 8pm €60

Foxrock Institute Kill o' the Grange, Kill Lane Blackrock (4939506) - 8 wks €105

Hartstown Community School Clonsilla 15 (8209863) - 10wks, €60

Malahide Community School Malahide (8460949) - for beginners, 10 wks €75

Marino College 14-20 Marino Mart 3 (8332100) - Thurs 6.30, 10 wks €65

Palmerstown CS - Pobailscoil Iosolde, Kennelsfort Rd 20 (6260116) - Mon, beginners 7.30/ intermediate 8.15: 10 wks €75 ea

Pobalscoil Rosmini Adult Ed Grace Pk Rd 9 (8371015) - Tue 7pm & 8.30pm €90

Rakassah School for Egyptian Belly Dance, Temple Lane Studios Cecelia St 2 (087 6841492) - beginners to advanced: with professional Egyptian-trained performer/ teacher Veronica Coughlan (087 7785127) - various venues

BEREAVEMENT (Aspects of dealing with loss)

Foxrock Institute Kill o' the Grange, Kill Lane Blackrock (4939506) - bereavement counselling, Wed eve 8 wks €105

Our Lady's Hospice Harold's Cross 6 (4068806 4068810) - why do bad things happen to good people, 1 day workshops 29 Nov; 14 Feb07; 13 June07/ grieving: understanding the process, 1 day workshops, 15 Feb07; 14 June07: each 10-4pm €100 incl lunch/ creative writing skills for use in bereavement or loss, 1 day workshop 22 Jan07 9-4.30pm €100 incl lunch/ anticipatory grief for medical social workers, 2 day workshop 5-6 Oct06 €200 incl lunch/ rites of passage: understanding Islam, 1 day workshop 7 Dec06/ 15 June07 9-4pm €100 incl lunch/ loss & bereavement up-to-date, lectures for social workers from 7 Sept06 Thurs 7-9pm

BIBLE STUDIES see Scripture / Theology / Religion

BIOLOGY

Coláiste Dhúlaigh CFE,Barryscourt Rd Coolock 17 (8481337) - microbiology level 2, Mon 7-9.30 16 wks

Kilroy's College Wentworth House Grand Canal Street Lr 2 (6620538 1850-700700) - tutor supported home study: leaving cert course

Plunket College Swords Rd, Whitehall 9 (8371689) - leaving cert(h,o), 27 wks, €425

BIRDS & BIRDWATCHING see Ornithology

BODHRAN see also Irish Traditional/ Music

Comhaltas Ceoltóirí Éireann 32 Belgrave Sq Monkstown (2800295)

Donahies Community School Streamville Rd 13 (8482217) - beginners Mon 7.30-9pm 8 wks €85 (own bodhran)

Old Bawn Community School Tallaght 24 (4526137) - beginners/ improvers: Tues, 10 wks, 7.15 or 8.30 €65

Waltons New School of Music 69 Sth Gt George's St 2 (4781884) - also day, see ad page 155

BODY BUILDING see also Keep Fit, PE etc.

Tony Quinn Centre 66/67 Eccles St 7 (8304211) - annual membership (8304998)

BODY CONDITIONING

Bray Institute of FE, Novara Ave Bray (2866111 / 2829668) - toning, Mon or Tue 7.50-8.50 8 wks €45

Greendale Community School Kilbarrack 5 (8322735) - Tue, 7-8pm, 10wks, €60

Hegarty Fitness Centre 53 Middle Abbey St 1 (8723080) - cellulite removal/ slimming/figure therapy, 4-10wks, €28 ea, also day

Hegarty Fitness Centre 53 Middle Abbey St 1 (8723080) - body treatments - cellulite removal/ slimming/ figure therapy, 4-10 wks, €28 each, also day

Kilroy's College Wentworth House Grand Canal Street Lr 2 (6620538 1850-700700) - tutor supported home study: fitness, health, nutrition dip

Palmerstown CS - Pobailscoil Iosolde, Kennelsfort Rd 20 (6260116) - Mon 7pm 10 wks €60

Irish Payroll Association
IPASS House, H4, Centrepoint Business Park,
Oak Road, Dublin 12.
Phone: 4089100   Fax: 4089102
Email: ask@ipass.ie   Website: www.ipass.ie

Certified Payroll Technician
Diploma in Payroll Management

The only nationally recognised payroll qualification
Classes in more than 40 centres nationwide – distance learning also available.

Venues: Rathmines, Bray, Mount Street, Dun Laoghaire, Sandyford, Tallaght, Ballyfermot, Lucan, Blanchardstown, Swords, Griffith Avenue and South Circular Road (Sat mornings).

Certified VAT Technician

The only nationally recognised VAT qualification – essential for accounts and bookkeeping staff – distance learning also available.

Venues: Mount Street, Dun Laoghaire, Tallaght, Blanchardstown, Griffith Avenue and South Circular Road (Sat mornings).

Pobalscoil Rosmini Adult Ed Grace Pk Rd 9 (8371015) - Mon, ladies 7pm/ men 8.30 €90

Ringsend Technical Institute Cambridge Rd 4 (6684498) - Mon 6.30 10 wks €50

BODY THERAPY

Coogan-Bergin Clinic & College of Beauty Therapy Glendenning Hse 6-8 Wicklow St 2 (6794387) - beautician electrolysis CIBTAC €3795

Motions Health & Fitness Training (087 2808866) - Diploma in Holistic Massage (ITEC), part-time course, 3 hours per week. Castleknock, Citywest & Naas

Roebuck Counselling Centre 59 Rathgar Rd 6 (4971929) - bodywork course for counselling & healthcare practitioners, 1 day wkend monthly 12 mths

BOOK CLUB/ READING GROUPS see also Literature, Libraries, etc

DATE Centre CFE, Dundrum 14 (2964322 (9.30am-12pm)) - reading circle, Mon 11am, 10 wks €97

Kilternan Adult Education Centre Ballybetagh Rd Kilternan 18 (2952050) - monthly 2nd Fri 215-3pm

SPI Society of Publishers in Ireland - for people in book publishing and related activities

TACT St Dominic's School St Dominic's Rd Tallaght 24 (4596757) - book club

BOOK-KEEPING see also Accounts / Computerised Accounts / PAYE

Cabinteely Community School Johnstown Rd 18 (2857455) - European Institute of Technology, calculator required, 10wks, €95

Coláiste Dhúlaigh CFE,Barryscourt Rd Coolock 17 (8481337) - manual, Mon 7.30 10 wks

CTA Computer Training Academy, St James's Tce Malahide (8454070) - manual

Dorset College 64 Lr Dorset St/ 8 Belvedere Pl 1 (8309677) - manual & computerised, Mon & Wed, 6.30-9.30pm, 12 wks

Dún Laoghaire CFE, 17 Cumberland St Dún Laoghaire (2809676) - manual & computerised Tue 20 wks 7-9pm €300

FAS Training Centres - manual & payroll: Baldoyle 13 (8167400) / Cabra Bannow Rd 7 (8821400) 20 wks / Finglas Jamestown Rd 11 (8140200) / Loughlinstown Wyattville Rd, DL (2043600) 10 wks

Greenhills College Limekiln Ave Walkinstown 12 (4507779/4507863) - VAT, PAYE, purchases, sales, etc made easy, 10ks, €130

Hartstown Community School Clonsilla 15 (8209863) - & accounts, beginners/ intermediate 10wks, €85 each

Irish Payroll Association (IPASS) IPASS Hse, Centerpoint Business Pk Oak Rd 12 (4089100) - nationally recognisedl VAT qualification: Certified VAT Technician, 1 night per week, 10 weeks for both Parts 1 and 2. Venues: City Centre, Griffith Ave, Blanchardstown, Tallaght, Dún Laoghaire, Sth Circular Rd (Sat morns)

Kylemore College Kylemore Rd 10 (6265901) - basic manual & computerised accounts, 12 wks Thurs 7-9pm

Lucan Community College Esker Drive (6282077) - Mon 7.30-8.30 10 wks €130

Old Bawn Community School Tallaght 24 (4526137) - PAYE, PRSI & VAT, ea 10 wks: Tues, 7.15-9.45 €120/ computerised accounting with Tas, intro Thurs, 7.30-9.30 10 wks €145

Pitman Training Centre 6-8 Wicklow St 2 (6768008) - basic skills, cert, 10 hrs, day, eve, sats

BOOK-PRODUCTION see see also Printing / Publishing

Trinity College 2 (8961000) - (8968589) history of the book: writing, reading and printed word 3000BC-2000AD, eve 9 wks €60

BOTANY see Gardening, Horticulture

BOWLING (LAWN)

Saint Anthony's House St Lawrence Rd Clontarf 3 (8335300) - indoor, annual membership, also day

BOWLING (TEN-PIN)

Leisureplex Malahide Rd, Coolock (8485722); Stillorgan (2881656); Blanchardstown (8223030); Tallaght (4599411)

Network Club 24 Elmcastle Green Tallaght 24 (4524415)

BOXING see Sport

BRAILLE

Pobalscoil Rosmini Adult Ed Grace Pk Rd 9 (8371015) - beginners reading & writing, Mon 7.30-9.50 €90

BREATHING EXERCISES

Holistic Healing Centre 38 Dame St 2 (6710813)

Irish Yoga Association PO Box 9969 7 (4929213/ 087 2054489) - qualified teachers available all over Ireland/ 4 yr Teacher Training courses

BRIDGE (BASIC - ADVANCED)

Ballsbridge CFE, Shelbourne Rd 4 (6684806) - beginners 6pm/ continuation 7.45: Thurs 10 wks €80

Ballymun Trinity CS, Adult Ed Centre 9 (8420654) - Mon, Tue: 7pm 10wk, €100 ea

Bray Institute of FE, Novara Ave Bray (2866111 / 2829668) - beginners, Mon/improvers, Wed: 7.30 10wks, €85 ea

Brian's Bridge School Brian or Elizabeth at (4501541) - home tuition & absolute beginners a speciality, expert tutor (25+yrs exp), also day, wkend, 6wks

Cabinteely Community School Johnstown Rd 18 (2857455) - 10wk, €95

Civil Service Bridge Club 72 Heytesbury St 8 (4750083 eve; 6282729 day) - beginners 10wk, €75

Contract Bridge Assoc of Ireland Paul Porteous Templeogue House Templeogue Rd 6W (4929666)

Coolmine Community School Clonsilla 15 (8214583) - beginners, Mon, Tue/improvers Tue: 7.30pm 10wk, €80

Corporate Club 24 Elmcastle Green Tallaght 24 (4610935)

DATE Centre CFE, Dundrum 14 (2964322 (9.30am-12pm)) - bridge club Wed 10.15am

Donahies Community School Streamville Rd 13 (8482217) - beginners Wed/improvers Mon/ Advanced Tue: 10am 10 wks €110

Dundrum Family Recreation Centre Meadowbrook 16 (2984654)

Greendale Community School Kilbarrack 5 (8322735) - beginners/ cont. Tue 7.30 €95

Greenhills College Limekiln Ave Walkinstown 12 (4507779/4507863) - Tue 10 wks €130

Killester CFE, Collins Ave 5 (8337686) - beginners, 10 wks Mon 7.30 €60

Kilternan Adult Education Centre Ballybetagh Rd Kilternan 18 (2952050) - beginners, Mon 7.30-9.30pm 10 wks €130

KLEAR Grange Park View Kilbarrack 5 (8671845) - for beginners, day / club 10 wks supervised play, day

Malahide Community School Malahide (8460949) - for novice/ improvers, 10 wks €90

Marino College 14-20 Marino Mart 3 (8332100) - Thurs 7.30 10 wks €90/ Wed 1.30 €85

Network Club 24 Elmcastle Green Tallaght 24 (4524415)

Newpark Adult Education Centre Newtownpark Ave Blackrock (2884376 / 2883725) - basic, 10wks, €120 Mon, Tue 7.30-9.45pm

Palmerstown CS - Pobailscoil Iosolde, Kennelsfort Rd 20 (6260116) - absolute beginners/ improved, 7 & 8.30, 10 wks, €70 each

Pobalscoil Neasáin Baldoyle 13 (8063092) - Tue, 10 wks

Pobalscoil Rosmini Adult Ed Grace Pk Rd 9 (8371015) - Tue 7-9.30 €100

Ringsend Technical Institute Cambridge Rd 4 (6684498) - beginners, 7.30-10pm Thurs 10 wks €115

Saint Tiernan's Community School Parkvale Balally 16 (2953224) - beginners Mon 7.30-9.30pm, 10 wks (086 3859953)

St Anthony's House St Lawrence Rd Clontarf 3 (8335300) - club, 7-11pm

TACT St Dominic's School St Dominic's Rd Tallaght 24 (4596757)

Taney Centre Taney Rd Dundrum 14 (2985491) - Mon, Wed & Fri (2788340) day/ capricorn Wed eve, 2884020

Templeogue Castle Community Bridge Club Templeogue House 6W (4931204 / 4934889) - beginners classes commence Sept at Templeogue Bridge Centre

BROADCASTING see Communications / Media / Writing
BRONZE CASTING
NCAD Centre for Continuing Educ 100 Thomas Street 8 (6364214) - intro & intermediate mouldmaking & waxwork, 21-22wk
BUDDHISM - Meditation / Philosophy
Buddhist Centre Kilmainham Well House 56 Inchicore Rd Kilmainham 8 (4537427)
Dublin Buddhist Centre 42 Lr leeson St (Basement) 2 (6615934) - 5wk, €150 waged, €95 unwaged
Melt, Temple Bar Natural Healing Centre 2 Temple Ln 2 (6798786) - Tibetan meditation, Sun 10am €50.00
Tara Buddhist Centre 18 Long Lane 8 (7078809) - ongoing: €8 per class, Tues, Thurs 7.30; also at Melt, Temple Lane Mon 6.45-8, €6, and Adult Ed Centre, Sion Hill Tues 8pm €8
BUILDING CONSTRUCTION see also Construction / House Maintenance / Surveying
DIT Faculty: Built Environment Bolton St 1 (4023000) - construction technology higher cert, 3yr p/time €2900; also, BTech, 1 yr ptime, each €1000/ building technology, 1yr, €1250, cert/ site management higher cert, 3 yr, 1 day & eve wkly, €900/€1300 pa/
BUILDING TRADES see also Construction
St Kevin's College, Clogher Rd Crumlin 12 (4536397) - pre-apprenticeship, 1yr, day
BUSINESS ADMINISTRATION / STUDIES Banking / Finance / Management / Office Procedure / Secretarial
The Asian Institute, Nova UCD, Belfield 4 (2899608) - doing business with the Koreans / with the Chinese / with the Japanese: all on-site
Cabinteely Community School Johnstown Rd 18 (2857455) - future studies (computer, office, busniess skills) NCVA cert, 9.15-12.30, Sept-May, €100
Communications & Management Inst Regus Hse, Harcourt Rd 2 (4927070) - business studies dip/ graduate dip: each 20 wks €1450
CTA Computer Training Academy, St James's Tce Malahide (8454070) - business skills & computer appreciation, p/time day 10 wks
DIT Faculty: Business Aungier St 2 (4023000) - MBA - in international marketing, entrepreneurship; accounting & finance; facilitiles management; construction project managemnt, 2yr p/time €9000 pa/ BBS (Hon) in Business studies, 4 stages/yrs ptime €1525 pa/ BSc in business & legal studies, modular €1525pa
Dorset College 64 Lr Dorset St/ 8 Belvedere Pl 1 (8309677) - business studies admin FETAC 5/ secretarial Mon-Fri 9.20-2pm 1 yr/ HETAC 6 higher cert in business, Mon-Fri 9.30-2.30, 2 yrs/ cert & dip in business studies, ICM Tue & Thurs 6.30-9.30 1-2 yrs
Dublin Business School 13/14 Aungier St 2 (4177500) MBA Executive Masters in Business Admin; MBS Master of Business Studies: each 2 eves 6.15-9.30pm 2 yrs / BA (Hons) Business Studies 6.15-9.30pm 4 yrs / Higher Dip Business Studies 2 eves 6.15-9.30pm 16 mths / Dip Business Studies 2 eves 6.15-9.30pm 1 yr Dip International Business Studies 2 eves 6.15-9.30pm 1 yr / BA (Hons) Business & Psychology 6.15-9.30pm 4 yrs / Higher Dip Business Studies in Information Technology / Human Resource Management / e-Business: each 2 eves 6.15-9.30pm 16 mths / BA (Hons) Business Management; Business Management - HRM; Law;

Accounting; Marketing: 6.15-9.30pm, 4 yrs each

Eden Computer Training Rathfarnham 16 & 1 Green St 7 (4953155) - ecommerce/ project panagement

FAS Net College (2043732 ecollegeinfo@fas.ie) - business courses, online

Greenhills College Limekiln Ave Walkinstown 12 (4507779/4507863) - intro to business management, Mon / Tue 10 wks €130

Griffith College Dublin Sth Circular Rd 8 (4150400) - higher cert, 2 yrs, HETAC, f/t/ BA in Business Studies, 3 yrs, HETAC, p/t, 3 eves per wk, also f/t

I.T. Blanchardstown Rd North 15 (8851000) - Higher Cert in Business Studies, 2 yrs €1575 pa p/time

Inchicore CFE, Emmet Rd 8 (4535358) - business admin with legal studies, day 2 yr HND

Institute of Public Administration 57-61 Lansdowne Rd 4 (2403600) - public management & business studies degree & dip courses/ one yr part-time cert

Irish Management Institute Sandyford Rd 16 (2078400) - Henley Masters in Busines Admin, 3 yr prog

Kilroy's College Wentworth House Grand Canal Street Lr 2 (6620538 1850-700700) - tutor supported home study: leaving cert/ business management, dip

National College of Ireland Mayor St IFSC 1 (4060500/ 1850 221721) - BA (Hons) in Business, 4 years, Mon, Wed, Thurs eve, €3,285; Higher Certificate in Business, 2 years, €2,500; NCI Diploma in Business, 2 years, Mon eve, €1,420/ BSc (Hons) in Business Information Systems, 4 years, €3,600

Old Bawn Community School Tallaght 24 (4526137) - NCI Higher Cert in Business, Tue & Thurs 6.30-9.30+6 Sats €2500

Palmerstown CS - Pobailscoil Iosolde, Kennelsfort Rd 20 (6260116) - FETAC 5, Thurs 7pm 16 wks €299/ higher cert in business HETAC, 2 yrs 2 eve wkly €1800

Pearse College Clogher Rd Crumlin 12 (4536661/4541544) - & international trade/& retail management, day

Pitman Training Centre 6-8 Wicklow St 2 (6768008) - effective business communication, 18 hrs, cert/ business skills dip, full/pt-time: day eve sats

School of Business & Humanities IADT Dún Laoghaire (2144764) - Bachelor of Business Studies (H), one yr add-on, 2 eve wkly + Sat workshops - finance, taxation, marketing, HRM, policy, information systems, entrepeneurship

Senior College Dún Laoghaire, CFE Eblana Ave Dún Laoghaire (2800385) - ICM cert, €450/ dip, €250

The Open University Enquiry / Advice Centre Holbrook House, Holles St 2 (6785399)

Transactional Analysis in Ireland (4511125) - in everyday situations, mthly workshop, donation

Trinity College 2 (8961000) - (8961039) - business & IT BSc hons, 4yr, 24wks per yr

UCD Adult Education Centre Belfield (7167123) - access to commerce, 16 wks/ export marketing, 10 wks/ international trade 10 wks

Westmoreland College for Management Studies 11 Westmoreland St 2 (6795324/7266) - ICM cert, dip, business studies/ ICM dip corporate management/ ICM dip, health services management/ ICM grad dip management

BUSINESS, SMALL see also Book-keeping

St Tiernan's Community School Parkvale Balally 16 (2953224) - small business finance, tax, accounts, law, Mon, 7.30pm, 10 wks, €95

BUSINESS, START YOUR OWN

Ashfield College Main St Templeogue 6W (4900866) - 7.30-9.30, 8 wks

Bray Institute of FE, Novara Ave Bray (2866111 / 2829668) - Mon 7.30, 10wks, €85

Dún Laoghaire CFE, 17 Cumberland St Dún Laoghaire (2809676) - running your own business, Mon 20 wks 7.30-9.30pm €230

Eden Computer Training Rathfarnham 16 & 1 Green St 7 (4953155)

Enriching Careers 38 Clonliffe Rd 3 (6589091)

FAS Training Centres Ballyfermot 10 (6055900); Cabra Bannow Rd 7 (8821400) - 10 wks; Finglas Jamestown Rd 11 (8140200) - 10 wks; Jervis St 1 (8044600) - 6-9pm 10 wks; Tallaght Cookstown Indl Est 24 (4045200); Wyattville Rd, DL (2043600) - 10 wks

Hartstown Community School Clonsilla 15 (8209863) - 10wks, €85

Holy Family Community School Rathcoole (4580766)

Marino College 14-20 Marino Mart 3 (8332100) - Thurs, 6pm 10 wks €85

Newpark Adult Education Centre Newtownpark Ave Blackrock (2884376 / 2883725) - 10wks, €150. Tue 7.30-9.45pm

Old Bawn Community School Tallaght 24 (4526137) - developing the idea, Tue, 10 wks €95

Positive Success Group, Applewood Med Centre Swords (8956820)

CABINETMAKING / CHAIRMAKING see Furniture

CALLANETICS

Taney Centre Taney Rd Dundrum 14 (2985491) - Wed (087 2445425)

CALLIGRAPHY

Ballymun Trinity CS, Adult Ed Centre 9 (8420654) - Wed, 7.30, €100

Bray Institute of FE, Novara Ave Bray (2866111 / 2829668) - Wed 7.30 10 wks €85

Coolmine Community School Clonsilla 15 (8214583) - calligraphy brushwork & graphics: Mon, 10wk, €70/ workshop sat 7 Oct 10am-1 €25

DATE Centre CFE, Dundrum 14 (2964322 (9.30am-12pm)) - beginners/ advanced: each 9.30am, 10 wks, €97

Foxrock Institute Kill o' the Grange, Kill Lane Blackrock (4939506) - 8wks, €105

Hartstown Community School Clonsilla 15 (8209863) - 10 wks €85

Holy Family Community School Rathcoole (4580766)

Old Bawn Community School Tallaght 24 (4526137) - italic handwriting, scroll making, ribbons & seasonal cards, 10 wks €95

Palmerstown CS - Pobailscoil Iosolde, Kennelsfort Rd 20 (6260116) - Thurs, 7.30 10 wks €70

Peannairí, Irish Scribes St Mary's Sec School Haddington Rd 4 (8337621 2980470) - Wed: beginners, 10 wks €97 (start 28/09/06); advanced 10 wks €97 (start 20/09/06); eve 7.30-9.30pm, 10 wks (starts 20/09/06)/ Thurs morns 9.30-11am (starts 28/09/06)

CAMOGIE

Cumann Camogaiochta na nGael Pairc an Chrocaigh St Joseph's Ave 3 (8364619)

Portmarnock Community School Carrickhill Rd (8038056) - GAA junior/ intermediate camogie, 16 wks 7-9pm

CAMPANOLOGY(Art & Science of Bell/Change-Ringing)

Society of Change Ringers Christchurch Cathedral 8 (6778099) - lectures, demos & participation, Fri 7-9 practice night/ Sun 10-11, 3-3.30 ringing

CANOEING see also Adventure Sports

Clondalkin Sports & Leisure Centre Nangor Rd Clondalkin 22 (4574858) - also day

Corporate Club 24 Elmcastle Green Tallaght 24 (4610935)

Fingal Sailing School Malahide (8451979) - kayaking, canoeing

Irish Canoe Union Sport HQ Park West 12 (6251105) - introductory courses summer and spring, 7-9.30pm, 6 wks; assessment for Kayak proficiency cert, €175, all technical equipment supplied, at Strawberry Beds, Chapelizod/ introductory courses, wkend 10am-4pm 2-day €130, level 1 kayak proficiency

Network Club 24 Elmcastle Green Tallaght 24 (4524415)

CANTONESE see also Languages

Aisling Ireland 137 Lr Rathmines Rd 6 (4971902) - begin & post-begin, 7.30 10 wks €200

The Asian Institute, Nova UCD, Belfield 4 (2899608) - beginners, post-beginners, conversational, native-speaking teacher 10 wks €200+book

CARD PLAYING see also Bridge

Ballyfermot CFE, Ballyfermot Rd 10 (6269421) - intro to poker, Wed 7-9.30 10 wks

Network Club 24 Elmcastle Green Tallaght 24 (4524415)

Palmerstown CS - Pobailscoil Iosolde, Kennelsfort Rd 20 (6260116) - poker, whist, etc: Mon 8.15 10 wks €70

Saint Anthony's House St Lawrence Rd Clontarf 3 (8335300) - Tues

CAREERS/CAREER GUIDANCE see also Job Seeking Skills / Parents Courses

Centre for Professional & Personal Development 44 Westland Row 2 (6612291) - eve/ w/end, €420, cert

CTA Computer Training Academy, St James's Tce Malahide (8454070) - CV skills, 3 hrs

Enriching Careers 38 Clonliffe Rd 3 (6589091)

ETC Consult 17 Leeson Pk 6 (4972067) - comprehensive career guidance report & discussion

Hartstown Community School Clonsilla 15 (8209863) - Life coaching 10 wks €85

Irish Payroll Association (IPASS) IPASS Hse, Centerpoint Business Pk Oak Rd 12 (4089100) - Certified Payroll Technician and Certified VAT Technician, both by classroom courses and distance learning. Venues: City Centre, Griffith Avenue, Swords, Blanchardstown, Ballyfermot, Lucan, Tallaght, Dún Laoghaire, Sandyford, Bray, Rathmines, Mount St, Sth Circular Rd (Sat morns)

Pearse College Clogher Rd Crumlin 12 (4536661/4541544) -soccer career development, day, 1 yr FETAC/FAI certs / FUTSAL coaching awards

UCD Adult Education Centre Belfield (7167123) - career planning & personal development, Sat 2-day

CARERS, COURSES FOR - incl Caring for the Elderly / Nursing Studies

College of Progressive Education 27-29 Carysfort Ave Blackrock (4884300) - FETAC level 5 full time health care support DHSXX, part time modules care of the older person, care support, safety and health at work, care skills, communications, work experience, nutrition, introduction to nursing, intellectual and physical disability studies and caring for people with disabilities

Inchicore CFE, Emmet Rd 8 (4535358) - caring services (social care); cert in social studies; caring for people with disabilities

Our Lady's Hospice Harold's Cross 6 (4068806 4068810) - holistic approach to cancer care / workshops for care assistants: 1 day €100: palliative care, 23 Nov 06; 8 Feb 07; 14 June 07 / hospice approach for care of the older person: 3 day €250, 11-13 Oct 06; 27-29 June 07; 24-26 Oct 07: all, 9am-4pm incl lunch/ Bowen technique & reflexology in cancer care support, 1 day Sat: 23 Sept 06; 22 Sept 07 10-4pm 100 incl lunch

CARING FOR THE ELDERLY

College of Progressive Education 27-29 Carysfort Ave Blackrock (4884300) - FETAC level 5 care of the older person, care support, caring for people with disabilities, care skills for health care assistants, communications, nutrition

41

St Tiernan's Community School
Pobalscoil Tiarnain, Parkvale, Balally, Dublin 16
Tel: 2953224; 087 2235741; Fax: 2953225
www.tiernans.ie   johndillane@eircom.net
Adult Education Programme September 2006
Enrol by post or by telephone after 3rd July 2006.
Enrolment nights: Mon. 11th and Tue. 12th September 2006 from 7.30 - 9.00 pm
All classes commence on the week beginning Monday 25th September 2006.

CARPENTRY see also Trade Courses / Woodwork

St Tiernan's Community School Parkvale Balally 16 (2953224) - Tue 7.30 €110

CARTOONING see also Animation

Ballyfermot CFE, Ballyfermot Rd 10 (6269421) - cartoon & illustration, Mon 7-10pm 12 wks

CATECHETICS see Religion

CATERING see also Cookery

DIT Faculty: Tourism & Food Cathal Brugha St 1 (4023000) - professional restaurant service 1 & 2, cert, 16 wks €275 each/ cert in: advanced kitchen, 16 wks €615 per module (advanced; pastry; international cuisine 1&2; ethnic; kitchen management)/ culinary arts, higher cert 3 yrs €780 pa/ meat management 2 yrs €520 pa

CCTV INSTALLATION

Hi-Tech Training 4 Nth Gt George's St 1 (1850-759759) - priliminary 1 day, cert/ cctv foundation, 3-day practical course, 10am-5pm, cert/ digital & remote access, 3 day 10-5pm, cert

CEARD-TEASTAS GAEILGE see Teaching

CEILI DANCING see also Irish Dancing

Cáirde Rince Ceili na hÉireann St Louis High School Charleville Rd Rathmines 6 (4982422) - Thursdays 8-9.30pm €5 (Eilis Ni Mhearrai)

Palmerstown CS - Pobailscoil Iosolde, Kennelsfort Rd 20 (6260116) - Mon 8.30 10 wks €70

CELLO

Bray Music Centre Florence Rd Bray (2866768)

Dún Laoghaire Music Centre 130A Lr George's St Dún Laoghaire (2844178)

Newpark Music Centre Newtownpark Ave Blackrock (2883740) - also day

Waltons New School of Music 69 Sth Gt George's St 2 (4781884) - also day, see ad page 155

CELTIC STUDIES

Saor-Ollscoil na hÉireann 55 Prussia St 7 (8683368) - early Irish History

CERAMICS see also Pottery

Ceramic Forms Michelle Maher 9 Fernleigh Cl Castleknock 15 (6405614 087-2047695) - pottery/ ceramic hand building, 6 wk (all mats) €150; Mon, Tue, Wed 7.30/ also Tues 10.30-12.30am; ongoing; also wkend workshops & parties

Donahies Community School Streamville Rd 13 (8482217) - hand built ceramics & pottery, Mon 7.30-9.30pm 10 wks €100

NCAD Centre for Continuing Educ 100 Thomas Street 8 (6364214) - intermediate c.22wk; also, introduction to pottery & ceramics

St Finian's Community College Swords (8402623) - 8 wks

Tracy Miley Cabinteely venue 18 (086 8485394) - hand built, beginners, improvers, 7.30-9.39pm 8 wks, €140, materials supplied

CERTIFICATION

FETAC East Point Plaza East Point Business Park 3 (8659500) - national certification body

Irish Academy of Public Relations (2780802) - Academy House, 1 Newtown Park, Blackrock Co Dublin: certification for Introduction to Public Relations course nationwide

Public Relations Institute of Ireland 78 Merrion Sq 2 (6618004) - certification body

CHEMISTRY

DIT Faculty: Science Kevin St 8 (4023000) - BSc chemical sciences, 2 yr €910pa

Kilroy's College Wentworth House Grand Canal Street Lr 2 (6620538 1850-700700) - tutor supported home study: leaving cert

CHESS

Bray Institute of FE, Novara Ave Bray (2866111 / 2829668) - intro to, Tue 7.30-9.30 10 wks €85

Corporate Club 24 Elmcastle Green Tallaght 24 (4610935)

Network Club 24 Elmcastle Green Tallaght 24 (4524415)

CHILD CARE & DISTANCE LEARNING

College of Progressive Education 27-29 Carysfort Ave Blackrock (4884300) - foundation & advanced studies in childcare / dip. in crêche management ILM/ cert in childcare & crêche work / foundation in montessori method / cert in classroom assistants training / child psychology / business skills of running a crêche/ FETAC level 5 after school care, caring for children 0-6, early childhood education, child development, special needs assistant training and caring for people with disabilities/ FETAC level 6 dip. in special needs assistants, classroom assistant conversion to special needs dip

CHILD CARE AND DEVELOPMENT see also Classroom Assistant/ Distance Learning / Montessori / Parents / Pre-School

Ballyfermot CFE, Ballyfermot Rd 10 (6269421) - Fetac 6, 2 yrs x 22 wks , Mon & Wed 7-10pm/ supervisor, Fetac 6 2 yrs x 22 wks

BASE Ballyboden Adult Social Education Whitechurch Library Taylor's Lane 16 (4935953) - FETAC level 2, all yr

Bray Institute of FE, Novara Ave Bray (2866111 / 2829668) - play - the developing child, Tue 7.30-9.30 10 wks €95

Childminding Ireland Wicklow Enterprise Pk The Murrough Wicklow Town (0404 64007) - distance learning courses: registered childminding cert, €250/ professional practice €75 cert

Coláiste Dhúlaigh CFE,Barryscourt Rd Coolock 17 (8481337) - play & the developing child, Mon 7-9.30pm 8 wks

Coláiste Eanna, Kilkieran Rd Cabra 7 (8389577) - Fetac level 4 & 5, tue/ thurs 10 wks 7-9pm

College of Further Education Main St Dundrum 14 (2951376) - pre-school playgroup IPPA cert, Tue & Thurs 7-9pm 10 wks €130

College of Progressive Education 27-29 Carysfort Ave Blackrock (4884300) - working with young children, crêche management UCD, childcare & early education course for childcare workers & carers of special needs, f-time/ therapeutic play/ working in childcare/ child development/ early childhood programme/ montessori method/ creative activities & arts and crafts for children/ FETAC level 5 special needs assistant training, play and the developing child, caring for the child from 0-6, working in childcare, child development, caring for people with disabilities and after school care./ FETAC level 6 supervision in childcare, early childhood programmes, therapeutic play skills and montessori practical life exercises

Coolmine Community School Clonsilla 15 (8214583) - caring for the child 0-6yr FETAC 5, Tue 7-9.45pm €600 (College of Prog Ed course)

Donahies Community School Streamville Rd 13 (8482217) - working with young children, College of Prog Ed cert, Tue 10 wks €400/ play & the developing child, Tue 7.30 10 wks €85

Dorset College 64 Lr Dorset St/ 8 Belvedere Pl 1 (8309677) - Childcare Studies: caring for children (0-6)/ working in childcare/ child development/ early childhood education/ art & craft for childcare or English level 2/ communications/ work experience/ safety & health at work/ working with special needs children: each 6.30-9pm FETAC / childcare studies, - FETAC level 5, Mon-thurs 9.30-2.30pm 1 yr

Dún Laoghaire CFE, 17 Cumberland St Dún Laoghaire (2809676) - play & the developing child, IPPA cert, Wed, 10 wks 7-9, €125/ cert in child care, yr 1 & yr 2: 20 wks Mon + Wed 7-9.30pm €490 ea/ art & craft for children, Wed, 10 wks 7-9.30pm €200

Greenhills College Limekiln Ave Walkinstown 12 (4507779/4507863) - play & developing child, Tue, 10wks €130

Inchicore CFE, Emmet Rd 8 (4535358) - child-care, pre-nursing/ nursery studies: day/ BTEI p-time FETAC 4-6

IPPA - the Early Childhood Org, Unit 4 Broomhill Business Complex, 24 (4630010) - various short courses, IPPA, FETAC, C&G certs

KLEAR Grange Park View Kilbarrack 5 (8671845) - child development

Kylemore College Kylemore Rd 10 (6265901) - caring for children & child development and play , 13 wks Mon 9.30-12, FETAC1 L4; also Level 3 16 wks tue 7-9pm/ early childhood ed & working in childcare, 14 wks tue 9.30-12 FETAC2 L5/ child development, 13 wks Tue 7-9pm/ individual modules Mon, W ed, Thurs 7-9pm: development; disabilities; early education; care provision, practice; art+craft

Liberties Vocational School Bull Alley St 8 (4540044) - early childhood education, Mon / art & craft for childcare, Wed / social studies, Wed: / child development, Mon/ caring for children, Mon / working in childcare: Mon / work experience, Wed: all FETAC level 5: 10 wks, 7-9pm, €105 ea

Lucan Community College Esker Drive (6282077) - play & the developing child, Tue 7.30-8.30 10 wks €130

Malahide Community School Malahide (8460949) - play & the developing child,

Tues, 10 wks €90 - IPPA course / FETAC level 1, Tue 7.30pm 20 wks €200

Marino College 14-20 Marino Mart 3 (8332100) - childcare supervision FETAC 6, 2 yr Tue 6.30, €465/ childcare FETAC 5 cert, Thurs 6.30 24 wks €380

Montessori Education Centre 41-43 Nth Gt George's St 1 (8780071) - Montessori teacher training dip: course (1 nursery) 0-6 yrs, eve 9 mths Mon & Tue 6.30-8.30 €2100; also by distance learning; (2 junior) 6-9 yrs, (3 primary) 9-12 yrs: by distance learning, 10 mths, €1500, dip

Plunket College Swords Rd, Whitehall 9 (8371689) - working in childcare FETAC 5 30 wks Tue+ 1 Sat mthly, 7-10pm €900

Pobalscoil Rosmini Adult Ed Grace Pk Rd 9 (8371015) - working in childcare/ after school care: each FETAC 5, 20 wks Mon 7.30-9.30 + 2 Sats €90 each

Portobello School 43 Lr Dominick St 1 (8721277) - caring for children, FETAC 16 wks / facilities management, dip/ childcare c&g cert, 6.30pm 32 wks/ FETAC level 2, 6.30-9.30, 2 yrs 2 eve per wk/ early childhood education; Child development: each FETAC, 16 wks

South Dublin Learning Centre 4 Glenville Tce Dundrum 14 (2964321) - child development, FETAC cert

St MacDara's CC, Wellington Lane Templeogue 6W (4566216) - play & the developing child, Tue 7.30-9.30 8 wks €104

Transactional Analysis in Ireland (4511125) - in everyday situations, mthly wkshop, donation

CHILD CARE MANAGEMENT

College of Progressive Education 27-29 Carysfort Ave Blackrock (4884300) - business skills for the c_che ILM/ cert in crèche management UCD / cert in childcare & crèche work (NCFE) / FETAC Level 5 caring for children 0-6 / FETAC level 6 supervision in childcare

IPPA - the Early Childhood Org, Unit 4 Broomhill Business Complex, 24 (4630010) - various short courses, IPPA, FETAC, C&G certs

CHILD PROTECTION STUDIES

Tennis Ireland Dublin City University Glasnevin 9 (8844010) - workshops (contact: Ursula Martin)

CHILDREN'S LITERATURE see Literature for Children

CHINESE CULTURE/LANGUAGE see also Languages

Aisling Language Services 137 Lr Rathmines Rd 6 (4971902) - mandarin chinese, all levels, 7.30-9.30 10 wks €20

The Asian Institute, Nova UCD, Belfield 4 (2899608) - mandarin chinese, all levels, conversational, native-speaking teacher 10 wks €200+book; also, for practical business use, on-site

Bray Institute of FE, Novara Ave Bray (2866111 / 2829668) - Tues 7.30-9.30 10 wks €85

Dún Laoghaire CFE, 17 Cumberland St Dún Laoghaire (2809676) - Tue 10 wks 7-8.30pm €95

Irish Chinese Cultural Society 67 Cowper Rd Rathmines 6 (4971505) - monthly meetings on Chinese culture, fourth Wed, September to May at United Arts Club, 3 Upper Fitzwilliam St 2

Language Centre NUI Maynooth Co Kildare (7083737) - language, beginners, 18wk, €350 cert

Marino College 14-20 Marino Mart 3 (8332100) - mandarin, Thurs 8pm 10 wks €65
Newpark Adult Education Centre, Newtownpark Ave Blackrock (2884376 / 2883725) - language Thurs 7.30-9.30pm 10 wks €120
Ringsend Technical Institute Cambridge Rd 4 (6684498) - beginners, Wed 7-9pm 10 wks €90
Sandford Language Institute Milltown Pk Sandford Rd 6 (2601296) - all levels, 15 wks €350
Trinity College 2 (8961000) - (8961560) - extra mural, intro to language & culture, 24wk, €365/ post-beginners/intermediate language, 24wks, €365
CHOIR/CHORAL SINGING see also Music
Cor Duibhlinne Foras Na Gaeilge 7 Merrion Sq 2 (086 3948492) - womens, in Irish, Mon eves ongoing €5 per night
Dún Laoghaire Music Centre 130A Lr George's St Dún Laoghaire (2844178)
CHRISTIANITY see Bible / Meditation / Ministry / Pastoral / Religion
CINEMA see also Film Appreciation / Media / Video / Writing, Creative
Corporate Club 24 Elmcastle Green Tallaght 24 (4610935)
Film Institute of Ireland Irish Film Centre 6 Eustace St Temple Bar 2 (6795744)
CIRCUS SKILLS see Juggling
CITIZENSHIP see also Policital Studies, Current Affairs
Pamphlet, '*Step Together - From Pillar to Spire: A Proposal for Citizens Day* available €3.00 post free from The OtherWorld Press, BookConsulT 68 Mountjoy Square 1
CIVIL SERVICE (confined and open)
Kilroy's College Wentworth House Grand Canal Street Lr 2 (6620538) home study
CLARINET see also Music
Abbey School of Music 9b Lr Abbey St 1 (8747908) - Ronan O'Sullivan
Bray Music Centre Florence Rd Bray (2866768)
Dún Laoghaire Music Centre 130A Lr George's St Dún Laoghaire (2844178)
Leinster School of Music Griffith College Campus South Circular Rd 8 (4150467)
Newpark Music Centre Newtownpark Ave Blackrock (2883740) - also day

Nolan School of Music 3 Dean St 8 (4933730) - also day

Waltons New School of Music 69 Sth Gt George's St 2 (4781884) - also day, see ad page 155

CLASSICAL STUDIES see also Cultural Studies

College of Further Education Main St Dundrum 14 (2951376)

DATE Centre CFE, Dundrum 14 (2964322 (9.30am-12pm)) - Thurs 10 wks, €97, day

KLEAR Grange Park View Kilbarrack 5 (8671845) - intro to classical studies, Fri 11.30am

Old Bawn Community School Tallaght 24 (4526137) - heros & heroines of ancient Greece, Thurs 7.30-9.30 €90

Saor-Ollscoil na hÉireann 55 Prussia St 7 (8683368) - Tues

CLASSROOM ASSISTANT / SPECIAL NEEDS

College of Progressive Education 27-29 Carysfort Ave Blackrock (4884300) - classroom assistants training / FETAC level 5 & 6 in special needs assistant training / also distance learning classroom conversion to special needs assistant

Old Bawn Community School Tallaght 24 (4526137) - thurs 7-9.45 18wks, 2 Sats €850 Froebel & FETAC 5 module (College of Progressive Ed course)

Pobalscoil Neasáin Baldoyle 13 (8063092) - Tue eve: contact 4884300 (College of Progressive Ed course)

CLAY MODELLING see also Arts/Crafts

CLAY PIGEON SHOOTING

East Coast Shooting Club (087 2243829)

CLIMBING see Adventure Sports

COACHING see also Life Skills, Personal Development / Sport Coaching

Athletics Association of Ireland 18 Joyce Way Parkwest 12 (6251101) - courses in coaching, introductory & levels 1-3, NCTC approved

Basketball Ireland National Basketball Arena Tallaght 24 (4590211)

Centre for Professional & Personal Development 44 Westland Row 2 (6612291) - accredited dip in life & business coaching, 6 mths €2550

Coláiste Dhúlaigh CFE, Barryscourt Rd Coolock 17 (8481337) - for success Mon 7.15-9.30 9 wks/ coaching detox, thurs 11am-1pm 12 wks

Communications & Management Inst Regus Hse, Harcourt Rd 2 (4927070) - coaching dip, eve & wkends 11 mths €9450/ post-grad dip, Mon & Weds 11 mths €9450/ mentoring & executive coaching dip, Mon, Wed, Wkends, 6mths €3450

Enriching Careers 38 Clonliffe Rd 3 (6589091)

Firhouse Community College Firhouse Rd 24 (4525807) - be your own life coach, Mon 7.30-9pm 8 wks €104

Football Assoc of Ireland 80 Merrion Sq Sth 2 (6766864)

Hartstown Community School Clonsilla 15 (8209863) - life coaching, 10 wks €85

Marino College 14-20 Marino Mart 3 (8332100) - life coaching, thurs 8pm 10 wks €65

Plunket College Swords Rd, Whitehall 9 (8371689) - business coaching for self-employued, tue 7.30-9.30 1-10 wks €90

Pobalscoil Rosmini Adult Ed Grace Pk Rd 9 (8371015) - life coaching, Wed 7pm & 8.30 €90 each

Positive Success Group Applewood Med Centre Swords (8956820)

Senior College Dún Laoghaire, CFE Eblana Ave Dún Laoghaire (2800385) - intro to lifestyle coaching, €120

Success Partners Compass Hill Kinsale Co Cork (021 4772564 087 6142980) - 1:1 full day coaching: life; business; executive; personal

The Professional Training and Coaching Consultancy (087 6379765/ 045 865783) - fulfil goals & ambitions: Grainne Carrickford-Kingston, Accredited Life Coach

COLOUR THERAPY

School of Reiki Ivy House Sth Main St Naas (045 898243 086 3084657) introductory

TACT St Dominic's School St Dominic's Rd Tallaght 24 (4596757)

COMMERCIAL STUDIES see Business / Book-keeping

COMMUNICATION SKILLS see also Drama / Media / Personal Development / Public Speaking / Women, Courses for / Facilitation

Ballymun Men's Centre Lift Shaft 4 Shangan Rd Ballymun 9 (8623117) - personal effectiveness, self development, improved literacy and computer literacy

Centre for Professional and Personal Development 44 Westland Row 2 (6612291) - 6 wks, €400, cert

Corporate Club 24 Elmcastle Green Tallaght 24 (4610935)

Eden Computer Training Rathfarnham 16 & 1 Green St 7 (4953155)

Finglas Adult Reading & Writing Scheme Colaiste Eoin Cappagh Rd 11 (8340893) - FETAC, each 30 wks, level 3 Tues 9.30-11.30am & Mon 7-9pm/ level 4 Mon 7-9pm

Gael Linn 35 Dame St 2 (6751200) - classes held @35 Dame St 2

Junior Chamber Ireland - email pro@jci-ireland.org for info

Leinster School of Music Griffith College Campus South Circular Rd 8 (4150467)

Liberties College Bull Alley St 8 (4540044) - Mon 7-9pm FETAC 5 10 wks €105

Maynooth NUI Adult & Community Ed Dept (7084500) - communication & group skills for managers: NUI Maynooth campus; also Ballyfermot CFE (6269421)

Network Club 24 Elmcastle Green Tallaght 24 (4524415)

Newpark Adult Education Centre Newtownpark Ave Blackrock (2884376 / 2883725) - public speaking, 10wks, €120, Mon 7.30-9.45

UCD Adult Education Centre Belfield (7167123) - communication across the life-span; dramatic communication; history of communication; intercultural communication & mass communication (summer); psychology of interpersonal comm, Tue; public communication; reading skills, Wed: each 8-10 wks/ speak with confidence workshop 1 Fri / Sat am/pm Blackrock/ writing skills Wed 10 wks spring

COMMUNICATION SKILLS IN BUSINESS

Communication & Personal Development 30/31 Wicklow St 2 (6713636/ 6613225)

Kilroy's College Wentworth House Grand Canal Street Lr 2 (6620538 1850-700700)
- tutor supported home-study dip course
Portobello School 43 Lr Dominick St 1 (8721277) - business communications, - ICM
subject cert, 6.30-9.30, 3 wkends
Training Options Plus 6-8 Wicklow St 2 (6717787) - customer care/ telephone
receptioin/ presentation skills (2 day)/ executive PA/ time management/ meetings
& minutes: each 1 day, cert

COMMUNICATION STUDIES

Ballyfermot CFE, Ballyfermot Rd 10 (6269421) - group skills for managers, NUI
Maynooth cert, 100 hrs x 2 yrs, Wed 7-10pm
Coláiste Dhúlaigh CFE,Barryscourt Rd Coolock 17 (8481337) - Fetac level 2, Tue
7-9.15 17 wks
Communication & Personal Development 30/31 Wicklow St 2 (6713636/ 6613225)
KLEAR Grange Park View Kilbarrack 5 (8671845) - Thurs eve; also day

National College of Ireland Mayor St IFSC 1 (4060500/ 1850 221721) - NCI Diploma in Effective Communication, 1 year, 1 wk day,2wkends, €2,650

COMMUNITY DEVELOPMENT

FAS Training Centre Ballyfermot 10 (6055900) - various local community training activities, citywide

Maynooth NUI Adult & Community Ed Dept (7084500) - community development & leadership: Ballymun Axis Arts Centre (8832132); Adult Ed Centre, 7-9.30pm (065 6824819); St Helena's Family Resource Centre, Finglas South 11 (8640285) Dunshaughlin Community College, Meath (8259137); Slane (0469280790) / community arts development, Old Bawn CS D24 (4526137)

Old Bawn Community School Tallaght 24 (4526137) - NUI cert, community arts for community development, 10am-5pm, one Tue & Wed monthly for 9 mth

COMMUNITY INFORMATION CENTRES

Community & Youth Info Centres 1 - Ashbourne 8351806/ Balbriggan 8414600/ Ballyfermot 6264313/Ballymun 8421890/Blanchardstown 8220449/ Bray 2869590/ Clondalkin 4579045/ Crumlin 4546070/ Dún Laoghaire 2844544/ Dundrum 2960713/ Finglas 8641970/Killester 8511438/Lucan 6241975/ Malahide 8450627/ Palmerstown 6263050/ Rialto 4539965/ St Vincents 8305744/ Liberties 4536098/ Skerries 8494443/ Stillorgan 2885629/ Swords 8406877/ Tallaght 4515911/ Nat Assn for Deaf People 8723800

COMMUNITY STUDIES

Ballyfermot CFE, Ballyfermot Rd 10 (6269421) - adult & community ed, NUI maynooth cert, 23 wks/100 hrs, Mon 7-10pm/ youth & community work, NUI dip (UCC), Mon 7-10pm/ cert in community development, 100hrs, NUI (UCC), Wed 7-10pm

Inchicore CFE, Emmet Rd 8 (4535358) - community care & education; business studies, 2 yr morns

COMMUNITY WORK, Voluntary see Voluntary Work

COMPUTER (INTRODUCTION TO THE) Computer Training / ECDL / Keyboard / Word Processing

Balbriggan Community College Pine Ridge Chapel St (8412388/9) - computer literacy & pc skills Mon/ Tue: 8 wks €140 each

Ballinteer Community School Ballinteer 16 (2988195)

Ballsbridge CFE, Shelbourne Rd 4 (6684806) - computers for beginners, Mon 6pm & 7.45; Thur 6pm: 10wks €90 ea

Ballymun Trinity CS,s Adult Ed Centre 9 (8420654) - beginners, Mon, Tue: 10wk, €120

Ballymun Men's Centre Lift Shaft 4 Shangan Rd Ballymun 9 (8623117) - FETAC Level 3 Thurs morning & Fri afternoon & Level 4 Wed Morning & Wed Afternoon

Bray Institute of FE, Novara Ave Bray (2866111 / 2829668) - beginners Mon, Tue 7pm €85; Wed 7.30 €90: 10 wks each; Stage 2 Mon, Tue 8.30 10 wks €85

Cabinteely Community School Johnstown Rd 18 (2857455) - intro to ms office 97, windows, 10wk, €110/ improvers, word, email, powerpoint, file management, 7 & 8.30, 10 wks €110

Coláiste Dhúlaigh CFE, Barryscourt Rd Coolock 17 (8481337) - for beginners step 1, Tue 7.50-9.40 10 wks/ intro for retired people, 10 wk Mon.6-9pm

Colaiste Ide Cardiffsbridge Rd Finglas W 8443233 11 (8342333) - pre-ECDL, Thurs, 7pm, 15 wks, €200 (IIPMM)

College of Further Education Main St Dundrum 14 (2951376) - Tue & Thurs 7-9pm 8 wks €140

Coolmine Community School Clonsilla 15 (8214583) - begin. wkshp Sat 7 Oct 10am-1, €25

Crumlin College of FE, Crumlin Rd 12 (4540662) - beginners, general introduction, Mon 6.45/8.15 10 wks / self-tuition daytime, open learning centre (4531202)/ intro to computers Mon 10.15am; Thurs 6.45

CTA Computer Training Academy, St James's Tce Malahide (8454070) - appreciation; basic applications, word, email, internet, day/eve/Sat

DIT Faculty: Tourism & Food Cathal Brugha St 1 (4023000) - applications for the hospitality & services industry - data summary, 12 wks eve €130

Donahies Community School Streamville Rd 13 (8482217) - beginners Mon/ intro to Wed/ improvers Tue €110/ general intro; keyboard skills; for home use; internet: each 7.30 Mon €110/ for older adults level 1 & 2: Tue, Wed, Thurs morns €110

Dorset College 64 Lr Dorset St/ 8 Belvedere Pl 1 (8309677) - complete beginners - equalskills course, Mon&Wed 6.30-9.30pm, 10 wks

Dún Laoghaire CFE, 17 Cumberland St Dún Laoghaire (2809676) - beginners/ improvers, Mon, Tue & Wed, 5pm, 6.45 & 8.45, €120 ea

Eden Computer Training Rathfarnham 16 & 1 Green St 7 (4953155)

FAS Training Centre Baldoyle 13 (8167400) - 10 wks; Ballyfermot 10 (6055900); Cabra Bannow Rd 7 (8821400) - 10 wks; Finglas Jamestown Rd 11 (8140200) -

10 wks; Jervis St 1 (8044600) - pre-ecdl; Tallaght Cookstown Indl Est 24 (4045200); Wyattville Rd, DL (2043600) - 10 wks

Finglas Adult Reading & Writing Scheme Colaiste Eoin Cappagh Rd 11 (8340893) - basic FETAC 3 10 wks tue 9.30-11.30; Mon & Tue 7-9pm/ intermediate FETAC 4 Mon 9.30-12pm

Firhouse Community College Firhouse Rd 24 (4525807) - beginners, Mon / Tue equal skills cert: 7.30-9.30pm 8 wks €140 ea

Grange Community College Grange Abbey Rd Donaghmede 13 (8471422) - intro to basics, word internet & email; also improvers courses

Greendale Community School Kilbarrack 5 (8322735) - for absolute beginners, Tue+Thur, 10 wks 7pm €125

Greenhills College Limekiln Ave Walkinstown 12 (4507779/4507863) - 10 wks, €166

Hartstown Community School Clonsilla 15 (8209863) - beginners/intermediate, 10wks, €95 each

Holy Family Community School Rathcoole (4580766)

Inchicore CFE, Emmet Rd 8 (4535358)

Irish Academy of Computer Training 98 St Stephen's Green 2 (4347662) - IACT webmaster dip, 12 wks/ intro to programming; C; visual basic: ea 8 wks/ access, 8 wks cert/ word; excel; powerpoint: ea 4 wks cert/ C++, 10 wks; VC++; java 12 wks: cert / ECDL bootcamp, 10 wks: day/eve

Killester CFE, Collins Ave 5 (8337686) - intro to & improv: each 10 wk Mon 7.30-9.30 €110

Kilternan Adult Education Centre Ballybetagh Rd Kilternan 18 (2952050) - for fun Mon, Thur, Fri: 10 wks €166/ beginners Mon 7.30 €133/ improvers Tue Wed 7.30 €133/ 9.30am €166: each 10 wks

KLEAR Grange Park View Kilbarrack 5 (8671845) - computer literacy, Thurs eve/ also day

Kylemore College Kylemore Rd 10 (6265901) - beginners/ easy pace/ further skills: each 10 wks 7-9pm/ also Mon & Sat 10.30-12.30pm; Wed 2-4pm

Lucan Community College Esker Drive (6282077) - beginners, Tue 7.30-8.30 10 wks €166

Malahide Community School (8460949) - Wed, day, 10 wks €100; Tues, 10 wks €130

Marino College 14-20 Marino Mart 3 (8332100) - basic, equal skills 6pm Thurs, ecdl course book & cert €130/ pre-ECDL Wed 10 wks, 10.30 €140/ 2pm €100

Newpark Adult Education Centre Newtownpark Ave Blackrock (2884376 / 2883725) - intro to, 10wks, €170/ ECDL, 20wks, €550

Old Bawn Community School Tallaght 24 (4526137) - basic introductory & intermediate courses - word, excel, internet: 10 wks each/ also, introduction for over 50s, Wed 10 wks

Open Learning Centre at Crumlin CFE 12 (4531202/ 4540662) - self-tuition basic to advanced: Mon-thurs 9.15am-12.15/ 2.15-4.15pm/ Fri 9.15-12.15pm

Palmerstown CS - Pobailscoil Iosolde, Kennelsfort Rd 20 (6260116) - for beginners, Mon 6.45 & 8.45, Wed 2-3pm/ level 2 Mon 7.45pm Wed 3-4pm: each 10 wks €70

Pearse College Clogher Rd Crumlin 12 (4536661/4541544) - work skills, day/ also advanced skills, day, FETAC 2 cert business studies/ ebusiness: €233; advanced €220

People's College for Continuing Education & Training 32 Parnell Sq 1 (8735879) - €60

Pitman Training Centre 6-8 Wicklow St 2 (6768008) - intro to, day, eve sats, 45 hrs, cert

Plunket College Swords Rd, Whitehall 9 (8371689) - beginners, Tues, €100/ intermediate, Wed, €100: 10 wks/ for active retired, Wed 2-4pm €55

Pobalscoil Neasáin Baldoyle 13 (8063092) - beginners, Tue 7.30 10 wks €120/ everyday use of, 10 wks €120

Pobalscoil Rosmini Adult Ed Grace Pk Rd 9 (8371015) - equal skills, Wed 7pm & 8.30pm €160 each ICS cert/ for mature learners 1 Wed 7-8.20; 2 8.30-9.50 €150 ea/ special 'stand alone' class for absolute beginners, Wed 1.30-2.50pm €150

Portmarnock Community School Carrickhill Rd (8038056) - beginners, Tue/ improvers, Mon: 7.30-9.20 10 wks €140

Rathmines CFE - Senior College, Town Hall 6 (4975334) - applications, beginners & improvers, 10 wks, €95 ea, Mon, Tue 6 & 7.30pm

Saint Finian's Community College Swords (8402623) - 8 wks

School of Computer Technology 21 Rosmeen Gdns Dún Laoghaire (2844045) - intro to - unix; linux; java; C++; perl; PHP; visual basic; website design: each €35 per hr, C&G

Senior College Dún Laoghaire, CFE Eblana Ave Dún Laoghaire (2800385) - intro to computers & the internet, Ecdl, €150

St Kevin's College, Clogher Rd Crumlin 12 (4536397) - 10wks

St MacDara's CC, Wellington Lane Templeogue 6W (4566216) - beginners, Mon, Tue, 7.30 8 wks, €140 each

St Tiernan's Community School Parkvale Balally 16 (2953224) - level 1 Mon €130/ level 2 +excel, internet & email, Tue €120: all 7.30, 10 wks

Sth Dublin Co Libraries (4597834-admin only) - introduction to computers, free: Ballyroan (4941900), Castletymon (4524888)

Clondalkin (4593315), Lucan (6216422), Tallaght (4620073).

Stillorgan Senior College Old Road Stillorgan (2880704) - Mon 7.30 8 wks €166

TACT St Dominic's School St Dominic's Rd Tallaght 24 (4596757)

Tallaght Community School Balrothery 24 (4515566) - intro to ms applications, 7.30-9.30 10 wks €150

COMPUTER AIDED DESIGN see also Design, Graphic

Ashfield Computer Training Main St Templeogue 6W (4926708) - autoCAD2000

Ballsbridge CFE, Shelbourne Rd 4 (6684806) - photoshop CS2, Thurs 7.45-9.15 10 wks €90

Ballyfermot CFE, Ballyfermot Rd 10 (6269421) - games analysis, Fetac 5 22 wks Wed 7-10pm

Bray Institute of FE, Novara Ave Bray (2866111 / 2829668) - cad 2, C&G cert, 7.30-10pm 25wks, €430/ photoshop for beginners, Wed 7.30 10 wks €170

Coláiste Dhúlaigh CFE, Barryscourt Rd Coolock 17 (8481337) - 2D CAD, C&G cert, Mon/Tues, 9 wks. 7 - 9.30

Colaiste Ide Cardiffsbridge Rd Finglas W 8443233 11 (8342333) - C&G computer aided draughting & design, AutoCad, Tue 7-10pm, 25 wks, €300 CILT

DIT Faculty: Engineering Bolton St 1 (4023000) - intro to com aid draughting, 10 wks €370/ solid modelling CAD/CAM 1 yr €500

Dorset College 64 Lr Dorset St/ 8 Belvedere Pl 1 (8309677) - autoCAD, C&G, 2D; 3D

Dublin Institute of Design 25 Suffolk St 2 (6790286) - AutoCad 2D/ AutoCad 3, each c&g cert, 1 eve 12 wks

Dún Laoghaire CFE, 17 Cumberland St Dún Laoghaire (2809676) - 2D AutoCAD 2005 (ECDL Tue)/ Autodesk Viz4 foundation, Mon): each 20wks 7-10pm, €430

Eden Computer Training Rathfarnham 16 & 1 Green St 7 (4953155)

FAS Training Centre Ballyfermot 10 (6055900); Finglas Jamestown Rd 11 (8140200) - photoshop digital imaging, 10 wks/ autocad 10 wks; Loughlinstown Wyattville Rd, DL (2043600) - AutoCAD intro, 10 wks/ advanced photoshop 10 wks; Tallaght Cookstown Indl Est 24 (4045200)

Griffith College Dublin Sth Circular Rd 8 (4150400) - AutoCAD - 2D C&G/ AutoCAD - 3D, C&G, both p/t, end user, 1 eve per wk

Irish Academy of Computer Training 98 St Stephen's Green 2 (4347662) - quarkXpress; corel draw; ms publisher; adobe photoshop; framemaker; intro to CAD design for engineers: all 8 wks, cert/ powerpoint, 4 wks, cert/ desktop publishing master course 12 wks, dip: day/eve

Moresoft IT Institute 44 Lr Lesson St 2 (2160902) - autocad, 1 & 2/ 3D drawing & modelling: ea 6-9pm 12 wks

New Media Technology College, 13 Harcourt St 2 (4780905) - 3D studio Max/ dreamweaver; animation; flash, director / also p/time day

Plunket College Swords Rd, Whitehall 9 (8371689) - CAD FETAC 5 30 wks Mon 7-10pm €431

Ringsend Technical Institute Cambridge Rd 4 (6684498) - autoCAD beginners Thurs 6.30, 10wks, €105/ - CAD Ecdl cert, Thurs 8-10pm 20 wks €400

Senior College Dún Laoghaire, CFE Eblana Ave Dún Laoghaire (2800385) - CAD computer aided design, ECDL, €310

St Kevin's College, Clogher Rd Crumlin 12 (4536397) - autoCAD, 20wks

COMPUTER APPRECIATION

Irish Academy of Computer Training 98 St Stephen's Green 2 (4347662) - becoming computer literate 4wk; PC survival 2wk; word, excel, powerpoint: 4 wk each; office,

smartsuite, 4-8 wks each/ internet & email, 3wk; desktop pub, 6 wk; ms publisher, ms frontpage; access: 8 wk each: all cert, day/eve

Ringsend Technical Institute Cambridge Rd 4 (6684498) - home computers things to do, Wed 7pm 10 wks €140

COMPUTER MAINTENANCE / Technical Support

Adelaide Computers 14 Pembroke Lane Ballsbridge 4 (2696213)

Ashfield Computer Training Main St Templeogue 6W (4926708) - PC Maintenance / Microsoft- MCP, MCSA, MCSE/ CompTia's A+, Network+, Security+, Linux+, Server+; Cisco-CNNA, CCNP/ Citrix - CCA / CIW- master Designer Track: all courses offered morns, eves and accelerated

Ballsbridge CFE, Shelbourne Rd 4 (6684806) - troubleshoot your own, Thur 6 30 10 wks €120

BCT Institute, 30 Fitzwilliam St 2 (6616838 /891) - A+ PC hardware technician: A+ Core, Mon, 6.45-9pm 10 wks; A+ OS technologies, Tue 6.45-9pm 11 wks/ server hardware engineer, Server+, Wed 6.45-9pm 14 wks

Coláiste Dhúlaigh CFE,Barryscourt Rd Coolock 17 (8481337) - maintenance & networks, Fetac Tue 6.45 20 wks

Crumlin College of FE, Crumlin Rd 12 (4540662) - build & maintain your PC, Wed 10 wks 7-9pm/ computer & network support technicians, f/time day/ comp TIA A+ 25 wks; comp NET+; CISCO CCNA 20 wks ea

Dorset College 64 Lr Dorset St/ 8 Belvedere Pl 1 (8309677) - compTIA certification: A+, 20 wks Mon & Wed 6.30; network+, security+; linux+; server+ Sat 10-1pm/

MCSA administrator Tue & Thurs: windows XP 3 wks; server 2003 7 wks; network hosts 3 wks; network services 7 wks; exchange server 7 wks / MCSE/ MCAD

Eden Computer Training Rathfarnham 16 & 1 Green St 7 (4953155)

FAS Net College (2043732 ecollegeinfo@fas.ie) - online courses

FAS Training Centre Ballyfermot 10 (6055900)

Hartstown Community School Clonsilla 15 (8209863) pc upgrade & repair, - 8wks €95

Hi-Tech Training 4 Nth Gt George's St 1 (1850-759759) - pc set-up and maintenance, levels 1&2, 50% practical hands-on, 7-10pm, 10wks 1 eve each; cert

Irish Academy of Computer Training 98 St Stephen's Green 2 (4347662) - pc troubleshooting & repair, 8 wks cert/ A+ , network+ : certs 20 wks each/ windows 2000 server, 12 wks MCP; MCSA cert 26 wks; CCNA 20 wks; Linux admin 12 wks: all cert, day/eve

Moresoft IT Institute 44 Lr Lesson St 2 (2160902) - fast-track MCSA cert, eve, Sat 17 wks

Pitman Training Centre 6-8 Wicklow St 2 (6768008) - A+ computer technician, cert, 120hrs, day, eve, sats

Pobalscoil Rosmini Adult Ed Grace Pk Rd 9 (8371015) -PC maintenance, Tue 7.30-9.30 €150

Rathmines CFE - Senior College, Town Hall 6 (4975334) - troubleshooting your PC Wed 6.30-9 10 wks €140

Ringsend Technical Institute Cambridge Rd 4 (6684498) - Tue/ Thurs: 7-9pm 10 wks €140 each

COMPUTER NETWORKS see also Computer Training, etc

BCT Institute, Institute 30 Fitzwilliam St 2 (6616838 /891) - cisco certified network associate, CCNA, Mon + Wed 6.45-9pm 7 wks; CCNA, Wed 6.45-9pm 14 wks; Thurs 6.45-9pm 14 wks/ CCNA remote access, Tue 6.45-9pm 15wks; CCNA routing, Thurs 6.45-9pm 15wks; certified network wireless administrator, Fri 6.45-9pm 12; network engineer foundations, network+, Thurs 6.45-9pm 11 wks; networking fundamentals, Mon, 6.45-9pm 11 wks; network security specialist, security+, Thurs, 6.45-9pm 12 wks; network eng.foundations, network+, Thurs 6.45-9pm 11wks

Crumlin College of FE, Crumlin Rd 12 (4540662) - CISCO CCNA prep course, Tue 6.45-9.45, 25 wks/ A+ prep course 20 wks Wed 6.45/ comp NET+; CISCO CCNA 20 wks ea

Dorset College 64 Lr Dorset St/ 8 Belvedere Pl 1 (8309677) - CompTIA network+, Tue & Thurs 6.30-9pm 15 wks/ MCSA administrator Tue & Thurs: windows XP 3 wks; server 2003 7 wks; network hosts 3 wks; network services 7 wks; exchange server 7 wks/ MCSE infrastructure 7 wks; active directory 7 wks; exchang e server 3.5 wks

Eden Computer Training Rathfarnham 16 & 1 Green St 7 (4953155)

FAS eCollege (2043732 ecollegeinfo@fas.ie) - online courses

FAS Training Centre Jervis St 1 (8044600) - intro to pc networks, 6-9pm 10 wks

I.T. Blanchardstown Rd North 15 (8851000) - cisco network academy prog: CCNA, 1 yr €3900/ IT Essentials 1 & 2 €750 each: p/time

Institute of Technology Tallaght ITT Dublin, Tallaght 24 (4042101) - Cisco cert network associate prog, 1 yr CNNA

Kilroy's College Wentworth House Grand Canal Street Lr 2 (6620538 1850-700700)

- tutor supported home study, network+

New Media Technology College 13 Harcourt St 2 (4780905) network professional cert, 1 yr C&G

COMPUTER PROGRAMMING see also Systems Analysis

Ashfield Computer Training Main St Templeogue 6W (4926708) - VBA, Java, Javascript, SQL, Crystal Reports

BCT Institute, 30 Fitzwilliam St 2 (6616838 /891) - mastering java programming, Mon 6.45-9pm 14 wks; mastering javascript prog, Fri 6.45-9pm 12 wks

CITAS Computer & IT Training 54 Middle Abbey St 1 (8782212) - C++, MCSE, etc

Crumlin College of FE, Crumlin Rd 12 (4540662) - f/time day/ MS visual basic 10 wks Tue 8.15-9.45pm

DIT Faculty: Engineering Bolton St 1 (4023000) - programmable logic controllers, 10wks €350 per stage; C&G cert 20 wks €500

Dorset College 64 Lr Dorset St/ 8 Belvedere Pl 1 (8309677) - MCAD applications developer courses - visual basic; visual studio; ADO.net; XML web services;

COM+ applications; programming with XML: 4 to 7 wk courses / Sun cert programmer for Java 2, Tue & Thurs 6-9pm 12 wks

Dún Laoghaire CFE, 17 Cumberland St Dún Laoghaire (2809676) - 10 wks 7-10pm €200

Eden Computer Training Rathfarnham 16 & 1 Green St 7 (4953155)

FAS Training Centres: Cabra Bannow Rd 7 (8821400) & Finglas Jamestown Rd 11 (8140200) - java, intro 10 wks / Loughlinstown Wyattville Rd, DL (2043600) - java, intro 10 wks/ programmable logic controllers 10 wks

Fitzwilliam Institute Ltd Temple Court Temple Rd Blackrock (2834579) - dip in oracle database programming, ICM, 10 wk - 2 eve wkly, Tue & Thurs, 6.30-9.30pm, €1265 incl exam fees; city centre; accredited by ICM

Irish Academy of Computer Training 98 St Stephen's Green 2 (4347662) - intro to programming; 8wk cert; IACT webmaster in web design 12 wk dip/ C, 8wk, C++, Visual C++ 10wk ea; visual basic premier; visual basic for programmers, adv VB; Visual Basic MCP prep; Visual Basic .NET prog: all 8 wk cert/ ms access 8 wk; java for programmers, 10wk; VBScript & ASP programming 10wk: all cert, day/eve

Kilroy's College Wentworth House Grand Canal Street Lr 2 (6620538 1850-700700) - home study visual basic 6.0

New Media Technology College 13 Harcourt St 2 (4780905) - advanced tech cert, C&G 1 yr f/time / web programming, active server pages/ digital media

School of Computer Technology 21 Rosmeen Gdns Dún Laoghaire (2844045) - unix/linux LPI cert, €825/ java; C++; visual basic: C&G certs/ SQL; perl; PHP: all 36 hrs, €750 ea/ also day

COMPUTER SCIENCE / ELECTRONICS see also Digital / Information Technology

Cabinteely Community School Johnstown Rd 18 (2857455) - ECDL, 20 wks, €575

DIT Faculty: Engineering Bolton St 1 (4023000) - MSc applied computing for technologists; MSc engineering computation: each 2yr p/t 6 modules, €400pa & Thesis €700/ BTech in computing, modular €1800

Griffith College Dublin Sth Circular Rd 8 (4150400) - BSC in computing science, 3-5 yrs, HETAC, p/t, 3 eves per wk; also f/t 4 yrs/ MSc in computing 18 mths p/t, 3 eves per wk; also 1 yr f/time / higher dip, 18 mths, p/t, 3 eve wkly, also 1 yr f/time/ higher cert in computing, 2 yrs, HETAC, mon to fri, also 3 eve per wk/ BSc in computing f/t 3yrs

I.T. Blanchardstown Rd North 15 (8851000) - higher dip in science in computing, 18 mths €3200/ - higher cert in computing, 2 yr €1700 / MSC in computing €4400 p/time

Institute of Technology Tallaght ITT Dublin, Tallaght 24 (4042101) - MSc in Distributed and Mobile Computing NFQ Level 9 1 yr/ BSc in Information Technology NFQ Level 7 3 yrs

Irish Academy of Computer Training 98 St Stephen's Green 2 (4347662) - IATC webmaster, 12 wks dip/ programming; PC troubleshooting & repair: each 8 wks, cert/ A+; network+: each 20 wks, cert day/eve

National College of Ireland Mayor St IFSC 1 (4060500/ 1850 221721) - H.Dip in Science in Computing in eLearning, 1 year, €3,000; Higher Certificate in Science in Computing in Applications & Support, 2 years, Tues, Thurs eve, €3,600/ BSc (Hons) in Software Systems, 4 years, Tues, Thurs eve, €3,600

The Open University Enquiry/Advice Centre Holbrook House, Holles St 2 (6785399)

Trinity College 2 (8961000) - (8962732) - BSc hons, 4yr, 24wks per yr/ (8962414) management of info systems, MSc degree, eve, 2 yr course

COMPUTER TRAINING & Applications

Adelaide Computers 14 Pembroke Lane Ballsbridge 4 (2696213) - for beginners, six 1hr lessons/ intro to/ word/ accerss/ excel/ powerpoint/ windows/ms office beginners/ publisher

Ashfield Computer Training Main St Templeogue 6W (4926708) - MS Office all levels, all versions/ ECDL, MOS, ECDL advanced / Microsoft MCSA, MSCE / CompTIA -A+, Network+, Security+, Linux+,Server+/ Cisco - CCNA, CCNP/ Citrix - CCA/ CIW - Master Designer Track/ JEB - Teaching training dip in ICT/ DTP - Quark, Photoshop, Illustrator, Publsiher, Acrobat; Digital Photog; all courses offered morns, eves and accelerated

Ballinteer Community School Ballinteer 16 (2988195) - ECDL

Bray Institute of FE, Novara Ave Bray (2866111 / 2829668) - ECDL €480, Tue, Wed 7.30 25 wks

BCT Institute, 30 Fitzwilliam St 2 (6616838 /891) - ECDL Fri 6.45-9pm 11 wks

CITAS Computer & I.T. Training 54 Middle Abbey St 1 (8782212) - ECDL/ MOS

College of Further Education Main St Dundrum 14 (2951376)

CTA Computer Training Academy, St James's Tce Malahide (8454070) - basic/ ecdl / mos: day/eve/Sat

DIT Faculty: Engineering Bolton St 1 (4023000) - computer applications, 3 yr higher cert, €1000

Dorset College 64 Lr Dorset St/ 8 Belvedere Pl 1 (8309677) - ECDL, all modules, 6.30-9pm 15 wks; Sats 9.30-2pm 15 wks/ MOS excel, word: core & expert; access core; project; outlook

Eden Computer Training Rathfarnham 16 & 1 Green St 7 (4953155) - word, excel, access, powerpoint, ecdl, MOS, web-design, MCP, A+, network+, MCSE, MCSA, Server+

FAS Net College (2043732 ecollegeinfo@fas.ie) - online courses

FAS Training Centre Jervis St 1 (8044600) - intro to pc networks/ ecdl/ pre-ecdl: all 10 wks, 6-9pm; Wyattville Rd, DL (2043600) - MOS core modules: access, excel, word: each 10 wks

Fingal Co Libraries County Hall Main St Swords (8905520) - books, audio, CDs, DVDs, language course, self-learning language & computer courses, adultliteracy, internet access, Balbriggan: 8411128; Baldoyle: 8906793; Blanchardstown: 8905563; Howth: 8322130; Malahide: 8452026; Mobile Library HQ: 8221564; Schools Library:8225056; Skerries: 8491900; Housebound Service: 8604290

Foxrock Institute Kill o' the Grange, Kill Lane Blackrock (4939506) - beginners/ intermediate/advanced certs 6-8wks, from €130 also Sat

Grange Community College Grange Abbey Rd Donaghmede 13 (8471422) - ms word/ internet / powerpoint, improvers 10wks

Greendale Community School Kilbarrack 5 (8322735) - spreadsheets, graphics, internet, 10 wks €125

Greenhills College Limekiln Ave Walkinstown 12 (4507779/4507863) - ECDL, 20wks, €365

Holy Family Community School Rathcoole (4580766)

Inchicore CFE, Emmet Rd 8 (4535358)

Irish Academy of Computer Training 98 St Stephen's Green 2 (4347662) - IACT webmaster, 12 wks dip/ word processing; spreadsheets: 4 wks ea/ databases, 8wk; graphics (freelance, powerpoint); programming / windows 200, XP, Linux; networking; desktop publishing; presentation tools; new technologies; ms; lotus; IBM; corel; Sun: all cert, day/eve

Keytrainer Ireland Ltd 6W (4922223) - tailored courses

Kilroy's College Wentworth House Grand Canal Street Lr 2 (6620538 1850-700700) - tutor supported home study: beginners, ECDL, MOS, PC repair/assembly, networking, data processing, visual basic 6.0, A+, i.Net+

Kylemore College Kylemore Rd 10 (6265901) - excel & access 10 wks Tues 7-9pm

Malahide Community School Malahide (8460949) - ECDL qualification, 3 modules 10 wks Thurs €220

Moresoft Computers Ltd 44 Lr Lesson St 2 (2160902) - word, excel, access, powerpoint, outlook, project: all levels, 6-9pm/ MOS 2000; xp; 2003: eve, Sats/ visio

Newpark Adult Education Centre, Newtownpark Ave Blackrock (2884376 / 2883725) - ms word, internet, excel, powerpoint, file management

Old Bawn Community School Tallaght 24 (4526137) - ECDL, all 7 modules, Tues or Thurs, 28 wks, 7.30-9.40

Pitman Training Centre 6-8 Wicklow St 2 (6768008) - Windows, 12 hrs./ Ms Office specialist dip, 6 wks /ECDL, various courses/ MS Skills dip, full/pt-time/ Ms office applications, 16-20 hrs, cert/ day, eve, sats

Portobello School 43 Lr Dominick St 1 (8721277) - Galileo travel reserv / Autocad c&g cert/ British Airways level 1; Virgin Air fares & ticketing level 1&2, eve 16 wks each

Ringsend Technical Institute Cambridge Rd 4 (6684498) - ecdl

School of Computer Technology 21 Rosmeen Gdns Dún Laoghaire (2844045) - unix/linux LPI cert, €825/ java; C++; visual basic: C&G certs/ SQL; perl; PHP; website design: all 36 hrs, €750 ea/ also day

Senior College Dún Laoghaire, CFE Eblana Ave Dún Laoghaire (2800385) - computer applications beginners, Ecdl €320

Tallaght Community School Balrothery 24 (4515566) - ECDL, 25wk, €500 5 terms (payable by term €200, €200, €100)

TARGET St Kevin's School Newbrook Rd, Donaghmede 13 (8671967) - day only, intro to; Pre-ECDL / ECDL

COMPUTERISED ACCOUNTS see also Accounts/ Book-keeping

Ashfield Computer Training Main St Templeogue 6W (4926708) - Tas Books / Sage

Bray Institute of FE, Novara Ave Bray (2866111 / 2829668) - Take 5, 22 wks, €400

CITAS Computer & I.T. Training 54 Middle Abbey St 1 (8782212) - sage & tasbooks, payroll, Thurs 6-8pm €600

Coláiste Dhúlaigh CFE,Barryscourt Rd Coolock 17 (8481337) - tasbooks, Tue 7.15-9.30 10 wks

CTA Computer Training Academy, St James's Tce Malahide (8454070) - Take5 / Sage: day/eve/Sat

Dorset College 64 Lr Dorset St/ 8 Belvedere Pl 1 (8309677) - manual & computerised - FETAC, Mon & Wed, 6.30-9pm, 12 wks

Eden Computer Training Rathfarnham 16 & 1 Green St 7 (4953155)

FAS Training Centres: Baldoyle 13 (8167400) - 10 wks; Ballyfermot 10 (6055900); Cabra Bannow Rd 7 (8821400) - 10 wks; Finglas Jamestown Rd 11 (8140200) - 10 wks; Jervis St 1 (8044600) - 6-9pm 10 wks; Loughlinstown Wyattville Rd, DL (2043600) - 10 wks; Tallaght Cookstown Indl Est 24 (4045200)

Hartstown Community School Clonsilla 15 (8209863) - 10 wks €95 cert of attendance

Irish Academy of Computer Training 98 St Stephen's Green 2 (4347662) - excel; lotus 1-2-3; ea 4 wks, cert; day/eve

Plunket College Swords Rd, Whitehall 9 (8371689) - tasbooks Tue 7-10 10 wks €273

Pobalscoil Rosmini Adult Ed Grace Pk Rd 9 (8371015) - for small business, Tue 7pm & 8.30 €160 incl materials

Senior College Dún Laoghaire, CFE Eblana Ave Dún Laoghaire (2800385) - Tas Books, IATI, €150

COMPUTERS, for ELECTRICIANS, ENGINEERS see also Computer Maintenance

BCT Institute, 30 Fitzwilliam St 2 (6616838 /891) - Red Hat linux computing essentials, RH030, Tue, 6.45-9pm 15; linux core system admin, RH130, Thurs, 6.45-9pm 15 wks; network engineer foundations, network+, Thurs 6.45-9pm 11 wks

Dorset College 64 Lr Dorset St/ 8 Belvedere Pl 1 (8309677)

Eden Computer Training Rathfarnham 16 & 1 Green St 7 (4953155)

Kilroy's College Wentworth House Grand Canal Street Lr 2 (6620538 1850-700700) - home study PC repair & upgrading, Assembly & A+

Moresoft IT Institute 44 Lr Lesson St 2 (2160902) - updating systems engineer skills, 6-9pm 3 wks/ fast-track MCSE cert, eve/Sat 32 wks

CONCERTINA see also Music

Comhaltas Ceoltóirí Éireann 32 Belgrave Sq Monkstown (2800295)

Na Piobairi Uileann 15 Henrietta St 1 (8730093) - weds

CONFECTIONERY / CAKE MAKING / DECORATION

DIT Faculty: Tourism & Food Cathal Brugha St 1 (4023000) - professional baking: bread 1 €400; break 2 €300; cake 1 €400; cake 2; each 36 hrs, cert/ sweetbreads 1 36 hrs, 2 10 classes/ pastries & snacks 1 & 2 36 hrs €400 ea

Foxrock Institute Kill o' the Grange, Kill Lane Blackrock (4939506) - sugar craft & cake icing, Wed 6 wks €95

Hartstown Community School Clonsilla 15 (8209863) - sugar craft & cake decoration, 10wk, €85

Newpark Adult Education Centre Newtownpark Ave Blackrock (2884376 / 2883725) - cake icing, beginners / improvers, Mon/Tue: 7.30-9.45 10wks, €125

Old Bawn Community School Tallaght 24 (4526137) - cake icing/ sugar art, beginners/ advanced/ 10 wks, Tues/thurs, 7.30 €95

St MacDara's CC, Wellington Lane Templeogue 6W (4566216) - sugar craft, cake art, Mon, 7.30-9.30pm, 8 wks, €104

CONFLICT RESOLUTION see also Social Justice / Personnel / Peace

Trinity College 2 (8961000) - conflict & dispute resolution studies, 1yr postgrad dip, 24 wks (2601144)

UCD Adult Education Centre Belfield (7167123) - Conflict Resolution & Mediation Skills: Module 1 & 2: Thurs 7 wks

CONSERVATION see also Environment / Forestry

Irish Peatland Conservation Council Bog of Allen Nature Centre Lullymore, Rathangan Co Kildare (045 860133) - wet, wild & wonderful bogs & fens, 6 wks; lectures, workshops & full day field trips from 6 Feb, Tues eves

CONSTRUCTION see also Building

DIT Faculty: Built Environment Bolton St 1 (4023000) - construction economics & management (BSc Surveying), 6 yrs p/time, €2400 pa

FAS Training Centre Tallaght Cookstown Indl Est 24 (4045200) - construction skills cert scheme: operators/ technicians/ etc (6070500)

Trinity College 2 (8961000) (8961007) applied building: repair & conservation, 24 wks, Fri eve + Sat morn postgrad dip/fire safety in practice, eve + Sat morn 24 wks 1 yr postgrad dip/ highway & geothechnical eng, postgrad dip 1 yr / construction law & contract admin, 1yr postgrad dip, 24wks, Fri pm & Sat am

CONSTRUCTION TECHNICIANS see Surveying

CONSUMER EDUCATION see also Law / Know Your Rights

Consumer's Assoc of Ireland 43-44 Chelmsford Rd Ranelagh 6 (4978600) - independent non-profitmaking org working for the Irish consumer, publish *Consumer Choice* monthly

KLEAR Grange Park View Kilbarrack 5 (8671845) - consumer awareness, day

CONTEMPORARY DANCE see also Dance / Modern Dance

Coiscéim Dance 14 Sackville Pl 1 (8780558) - for adults: city centre studio, beginners welcome: Mon & Tues, 6.15 & 7.45, 8 wks €100

Dance Theatre of Ireland Bloomfields Centre, Lr George St Dún Laoghaire (2803455) - beginners Thurs 6.54-8pm/ intermediate Tue, Wed 6.45-8pm; body conditioning throughdance Sats 12-1.15pm: 10 wks €80

COOKERY / FAMILY COOKING see also Catering / Confectionery / Health Food / Hostess / Hotel / Vegetarian

Alix Gardner Catering 71 Waterloo Road 4 (6681553) - cookery / intermediate 1 / around the world cuisine: each 10wks, 6.30-9.30, €700, cert/ healthy eating/ vegetarian/ gluten free

Ashfield College Main St Templeogue 6W (4900866) - gourmet cookery & wine selection / entertaining at home, new recipes / 7.30-9.30, 8 wks each

Ballymun Trinity CS,s Adult Ed Centre 9 (8420654) - for all, family meals, Tues 8wk, €90/ oriental: Mon 7pm 10 wks €120

Bray Institute of FE, Novara Ave Bray (2866111 / 2829668) - basic everyday, Mon; imaginative everyday: Tue 7.30 10 wks €95 each/ European vegetarian cooking, Wed 7.30 10 wks €90

Cabinteely Community School Johnstown Rd 18 (2857455) - for special occasions, 8wk, €90 /oriental, 8wk, €100/ simple cooking, Tue 8 wks €110

Coláiste Dhúlaigh CFE, Barryscourt Rd Coolock 17 (8481337) - Tue 7-9.15pm 10 wks/ Chinese, Mon, 8 wks, 7.30-9pm

Coláiste Eanna, Kilkieran Rd Cabra 7 (8389577) - Italian, simple recipes & pasta, Tue 7pm 10 wks

Coolmine Community School Clonsilla 15 (8214583) - healthy home fare: Mon 10 wks €90 / workshop Sat 7 Oct 10am-1, €25

Crumlin College of FE, Crumlin Rd 12 (4540662) - beginners / healthy eating: Tue 7.30 international, Mon: all 10 wks/ gourmet cookery special occasions, Wed 10 wks 7.30-9.30 ea

DIT Faculty: Tourism & Food Cathal Brugha St 1 (4023000) - various professional short courses

Donahies Community School Streamville Rd 13 (8482217) - demonstration class, Mon 7.30 10 wks €95

Firhouse Community College Firhouse Rd 24 (4525807) - Asian (demo) Mon 7.30-9.30pm 8 wks €119

Hartstown Community School Clonsilla 15 (8209863) - joy of cooking/ holistic nutrition: each 10wks, €85/ Indian eve 10wks €85

Hartstown Community School Clonsilla 15 (8209863) - Asian, 10 wks €85

Kylemore College Kylemore Rd 10 (6265901) - Italian, Tue/ Thai & Indian, Thurs: each 6 wks 7-9pm/ food, cookery & nutrition foundation FETAC, 12 wks Wed 1.30-4pm

Lucan Community College Esker Drive (6282077) - made simple, Mon, Tue: 7.30-8.30 10 wks €120

Malahide Community School Malahide (8460949) - for special occasions, Mon 7.30 8 wks €100

Marino College 14-20 Marino Mart 3 (8332100) - for all, for special occasions: Tues €75/ Chinese €105/ Indian €85/ Italian €105: Spanish €85: Thurs: 10wks

Newpark Adult Education Centre Newtownpark Ave Blackrock (2884376 / 2883725) - basic, for all/ Asian - Thai, Malaysian, Vietnamese/ Indian/ Italian, €135: each 10 wks €135

Old Bawn Community School Tallaght 24 (4526137) - meals in minutes, Thurs/ across the globe, Tues 10 wks €120

Palmerstown CS - Pobailscoil Iosolde, Kennelsfort Rd 20 (6260116) - beginners home baking: Mon / Italian, Tue: ea 7.30pm 10 wks €90

Pobalscoil Neasáin Baldoyle 13 (8063092) - Indian, Tue, 10 wks

Ringsend Technical Institute Cambridge Rd 4 (6684498) - dinner party ideas Wed 7pm10 wks €120

St Tiernan's Community School Parkvale Balally 16 (2953224) - world cuisine, hands-on, Thurs, 7.30pm, 10 wks €140

Tallaght Community School Balrothery 24 (4515566) - 10wk, 7.30-9.30 €100

TARGET St Kevin's School Newbrook Rd, Donaghmede 13 (8671967) - colourful creative cooking, 10 wks, day only

Vegetarian Society of Ireland PO Box 3010 Dublin 4

CORRESPONDENCE SCHOOLS & HOME STUDY see also Distance Learning

College of Progressive Education 27-29 Carysfort Ave Blackrock (4884300) - see distance learning for child and health care related courses

Esperanto Assoc of Ireland 9 Templeogue Wood 6W (4945020) - Esperanto, €free

International Foundation of Adult Education PO Box 93 Eglinton St Cork (022-29358 / 0818 365305) - social studies/psychology/anthropology/sociology: IFAE-Netherlands

Irish Academy of Public Relations (2780802) - intro to PR, cert/ practical journalism, cert, 1 yr, €390/€440 each by email or correspondence

Irish Payroll Association (IPASS) IPASS Hse, Centerpoint Business Pk Oak Rd 12 (4089100) - nationally recognised payroll or VAT qualification. Certified Payroll Technician or Certified VAT Technician

Kilroy's College Wentworth House Grand Canal Street Lr 2 (6620538 1850-700700)

McKeon Murray Business Training, Elm House Leopardstown Office Pk 18 (2959087)

National Training Authority ITEC Hse Cornelscourt 18 (2070597)

The Garden School (094 9649943) - RHS cert, horticulture/ gardening courses

The Open University Enquiry/Advice Centre Holbrook House, Holles St 2 (6785399) - BA/BSc / dips/ postgrad degrees/ progs in management, education, health & welfare

COUNSELLING SKILLS see also Bereavement, Psychology, etc

Ballsbridge CFE, Shelbourne Rd 4 (6684806) - NUI Maynooth course, Tue 6pm 20 wks +some Sats, €1230/ intro to, Tue 6pm, 10 wks €90

Ballymun Trinity CS, Adult Ed Centre 9 (8420654) - NUI cert, wed 7-10pm, 25 wks €1300

Bray Institute of FE, Novara Ave Bray (2866111 / 2829668) - NUI cert, 25 wks €1230

Clanwilliam Institute 18 Clanwilliam Tce 2 (6761363) - marital & family therapy: foundation, 1yr/ professional, 3yrs

Coláiste Dhúlaigh CFE, Barryscourt Rd Coolock 17 (8481337) - counselling, Mon 7-9.30: 20 wks, cert/ skills, Tue 7.15-9.15, 8 wks

Coolmine Community School Clonsilla 15 (8214583) - NUI cert, Mon 7- 10pm, €1230

Donahies Community School Streamville Rd 13 (8482217) - NUI Maynooth cert, €1230

Dublin Business School 13/14 Aungier St 2 (4177500) - BA(Hons) in Counselling & Psychotherapy, 4 yrs / Higher Dip in Counselling & Psychotherapy , 1 yr/ MSc Counselling & Psychotherapy 2 yrs

Dún Laoghaire CFE, 17 Cumberland St Dún Laoghaire (2809676) - NUI, foundation in counselling skills, 25wks, Mon 7-10pm +4 Sats, €1350

Foxrock Institute Kill o' the Grange, Kill Lane Blackrock (4939506) - intro to, Wed eve 8 wks €110

Greendale Community School Kilbarrack 5 (8322735) - inrto to counselling & psychology, Wed morn 10am 10 wks €100

Greenhills College Limekiln Ave Walkinstown 12 (4507779/4507863) - Mon, 10 wks €130

Hanly Centre Eblana Ave Dún Laoghaire (2807269) - pre-intervention counselling/ one-to-one

IICH Education 118 Stillorgan Road 4 (2017422) - workshops; certs; diplomas

Institute of Creative Counselling & Psychotherapy 82 Upr George's St Dún Laoghaire (2802523) - intro to counselling & psychotherapy, 10th October 10 wks, 6.30-9pm €350

Roebuck Counselling Centre

59 Rathgar Road, Dublin 6. Phone: 4971929

email: roebuckcounsellingcentre@eircom.net

- **One year Certificate Course in Communication Skills and Group Dynamics** Starts November 2006

- **Accredited Diploma in Counselling and Psychotherapy (3 years)** Starts November 2006 ends May 2007
  Fridays: 4.00pm - 10.00pm
  Saturdays: 8.00am - 2.00pm

For more information on these and other courses Phone 4971929

Irish Association of Holistic Medicine 66 Eccles St 7 (8500493) - diploma in holistic psychotherapy & counselling, 2 yr over 6 wkends + 6day module per yr, €2850pa

Knocklyon Youth & Community Centre, 16 (4931213) - NUI Maynooth cert, tue 9.30am/12.30pm 30 wks €1230

Kylemore College Kylemore Rd 10 (6265901) - intro to, Tue/ intro to counelling & reality therapy, Thurs: each 10 wks 7-9pm

Marino College 14-20 Marino Mart 3 (8332100) - intro to, Tue 10 wks €90

Maynooth NUI Adult & Community Ed Dept (7084500) - NUI cert: at Ballsbridge CFE (6684806); Ballyfermot CFE (6269421); Ballymun CS (8420654); Bray, St Thomas CS (2866111); Coolmine (8214583); Donaghies CS (8473522); Dunlaoghaire CFE (2809676); Drogheda (041 9836084); Knocklyon (4943991); NUI Maynooth campus (7083784) Thurs 7-10pm; Naas (045 898923); Old Bawn Tallaght (4526137); Trim (046 9438000)

Newpark Adult Education Centre, Newtownpark Ave Blackrock (2884376 / 2883725) - intro to, Tue 7.30 10 wks €120

Old Bawn Community School Tallaght 24 (4526137) - foundation, NUI Maynooth cert, 1yr, Tue, 100 hours

Palmerstown CS - Pobailscoil Iosolde, Kennelsfort Rd 20 (6260116) - intro, Tue 7.30 10 wks

People's College for Continuing Education & Training 32 Parnell Sq 1 (8735879) - €60

Roebuck Counselling Centre 59 Rathgar Rd 6 (4971929) - one yr introductory course in counselling skills & group dynamics/ also dip in counselling & psychotherapy (3 yr), Fri 4-10pm, Sat 8am-2pm/ ongoing training for trained counsellors, wkends/ start-up for qualified counsellors to set up practice & pre-accreditation, Thurs eve ongoing

CRAFTS GENERAL see also Applique / Arts & Crafts / Basket-making / Batik / Crochet / Jewellery/ Lace / Patchwork / Quilting / Tapestry

Ballymun Trinity CS, Adult Ed Centre 9 (8420654) - mosaic & stained glass, Tue 7.30 10wk, €130

Cabinteely Community School Johnstown Rd 18 (2857455) - handmade greeting cards, 7.30 Mon 10 wks €95

Coolmine Community School Clonsilla 15 (8214583) - mosaic magic, Mon 10 wks €80/ mosaic blitz workshop Sat 7 Oct 10am-1 €25

Hartstown Community School Clonsilla 15 (8209863) - sewing & craftwork,10wks, €85 each/ stained glass skills, 10 wks, €95; beading & jewellery making 10 wks €88

Holy Family Community School Rathcoole (4580766)

KLEAR Grange Park View Kilbarrack 5 (8671845) - creative crafts, day

Old Bawn Community School Tallaght 24 (4526137) - beginners, original handbag making, Tue/ beginners handmade cards, etc, Thurs: each 7.30-9.30, 10wks €95

St Tiernan's Community School Parkvale Balally 16 (2953224) - mosaics for home or garden, Wed, 7.30-9.30pm, 10 wks, €95

Yellow Brick Road 8 Bachelors Walk 1 (8730177) - 8 wk jewellery making course, all materials included, 7.30-9.30, €250 (commence: Sept/Jan/Mar)/ 1 night workshops excluding materials, 7-9.30, €25 - separate workshops for wire work, netting & chips, organza necklace, mesh embellishment

CREATIVE LIVING
Jean Strong (2892323) - unlock creativity - 'The Artist's Way': Mon, Tue 14 wks €250

Roebuck Counselling Centre 59 Rathgar Rd 6 (4971929) - creativity - creative arts course, 1 day wkend monthly 12 mths / educational drama, Thurs eve, ongoing

CREATIVE TEXTILES
Quilt Art Workshops 4 Mill Wood Naas (045-876121) - classes & workshops, SAE for info

CREATIVE THINKING
Newpark Adult Education Centre, Newtownpark Ave Blackrock (2884376 / 2883725) - enhance creativity: The Artist's Way, Mon 7.30 10 wks €120

UCD Adult Education Centre Belfield (7167123) - creative thinking and problem solving, Sat 1 day

Walmer College & Holistic Centre First Floor, River Hse Raheny Shopping C 5 (8329645) - ' The Artist's Way'

CREATIVE WRITING see also Writing, creative
Ballsbridge CFE,, Shelbourne Rd 4 (6684806) - Tues, 6pm & 7.45 10 wks €60

Bray Institute of FE, Novara Ave Bray (2866111 / 2829668) - beginners Mon / intermediate Tue: 7.30 10 wks, €85 each

Coláiste Dhúlaigh CFE, Barryscourt Rd Coolock 17 (8481337) - Mon, 8 wks, 7.15-9.15/ Fri 11.30-1, 10 wks

Donahies Community School Streamville Rd 13 (8482217) - Mon 7.30-9.30 10 wks, €95

Greendale Community School Kilbarrack 5 (8322735) - Tue, 7.30 10 wks €95

Hartstown Community School Clonsilla 15 (8209863) - 10 wks, €85

Irish Writers' Centre 19 Parnell Sq 1 (8721302)

KAIES-Knocklyon Community Centre, 16 (4931213) - Fri 9.45am 8 wks €80

KLEAR Grange Park View Kilbarrack 5 (8671845) day only

Lucan Community College Esker Drive (6282077) - Tue 7.30-8.30 8 wks €104

Malahide Community School Malahide (8460949) - 7.30pm 10 wks €80

Old Bawn Community School Tallaght 24 (4526137) - informal, Tues, 7.30-9.30pm, 10 wks €90

Our Lady's Hospice Harold's Cross 6 (4068806 4068810) - for use in bereavement or loss, 1 day workshop 22 Jan07 9-4.30pm €100 incl lunch

Palmerstown CS - Pobailscoil Iosolde, Kennelsfort Rd 20 (6260116) - Tues 7.30-9.30 10 wks €100

Plunket College Swords Rd, Whitehall 9 (8371689) - Tues, 10 wks, €90

Pobalscoil Rosmini Adult Ed Grace Pk Rd 9 (8371015) - beginners - your first story skills, Wed 7.30-9.30 €120

Stillorgan CFE, Old Road Stillorgan (2880704) -Thur 7.30-9.30 8 wks €104

UCD Adult Education Centre Belfield (7167123) - 10 week courses: the creative edge; discovering and channelling creativity; editing techniques; enjoy writing; literature history and romance; unblocking the block - creative writing for beginners; write that novel; writers workshop in children's fiction; development workshop in children's fiction; writing fiction the short story & beyond, also, module 2; writing for radio/ the business of writing, 1 Sat spring / writing for the screen, Sat 2 day

CRIME / CRIMINOLOGY see also Law

Marino College 14-20 Marino Mart 3 (8332100) - crime & punishment in modern Ireland 8pm Thurs 10 wks €65

Pobalscoil Rosmini Adult Ed Grace Pk Rd 9 (8371015) - intro to criminology & the law, tue 7-8.30pm €90

Trinity College 2 (8961000) - (8968589) crime & punishment in Ireland & Europe, 1500-1950, eve 9 wks €60

UCD Adult Education Centre Belfield (7167123) - Crime and Criminality, Tues 10 wks

CROATIAN Serbo-Croatian

Ballsbridge CFE, Shelbourne Rd 4 (6684806) - beginners, Thurs 6-7.30pm 10 wks €80

Marino College 14-20 Marino Mart 3 (8332100) - Tuesday, 6.30, 10 wks €65

Sandford Language Institute Milltown Pk Sandford Rd 6 (2601296) - Croatian/ Serbian/ Bosnian/ Slovene: all levels subject to demand, 15 wks €350

CROCHET see also Crafts

Ballymun Trinity CS, Adult Ed Centre 9 (8420654) - & hand knitting, embroidery, all stages: Mon 7pm 10wk, €90

Donahies Community School Streamville Rd 13 (8482217) - & knitting Wed 7.30 10 wks €85

St Tiernan's Community School Parkvale Balally 16 (2953224) - Tue 7.30 10 wks €95

CULTURAL STUDIES see also Folklore / Irish / Popular

KLEAR Grange Park View Kilbarrack 5 (8671845) - know your world, 26 wks - day/ western Europe made easy, 26 wks, day

National College of Ireland Mayor St IFSC 1 (4060500/ 1850 221721) - Foundation

Certificate in Cultural Studies, 1 year, €950

Trinity College 2 (8961000) - (8968589) images of power: propaganda and ideology in the ancient world, 9 wks €60/ Egypt of the Pharaohs in imagination & reality, 9 wks €80/ the history of the book 3000BC-2000AD, eve 9 wks €60/ the middle ages & the renaissance, eve (6082686)

UCD Adult Education Centre Belfield (7167123) - international development: Key issues and challenges; the history of the Palestinian-Israeli conflict each 10 wks

CURRENT AFFAIRS see also Political Studies

DATE Centre CFE, Dundrum 14 (2964322 (9.30am-12pm)) - politics & curent affairs, 11am 8 wks, €57

KLEAR Grange Park View Kilbarrack 5 (8671845) - day

People's College for Continuing Education & Training 32 Parnell Sq 1 (8735879) - politics, €40

CURTAIN MAKING see also Sewing / Soft Furnishing

Tallaght Community School Balrothery 24 (4515566) - 10wk, 7.30-9.30 €80

CUSTOMER SERVICE & CUSTOMER CARE

CTA Computer Training Academy, St James's Tce Malahide (8454070) - reception & customer care skills

DIT Faculty: Tourism & Food Cathal Brugha St 1 (4023000) - communications and customer excellence, 12 wks €235

FAS Training Centres: Loughlinstown Wyattville Rd, DL (2043600) - sales rep & customer care, 10 wks; Tallaght Cookstown Indl Est 24 (4045200)

Palmerstown CS - Pobailscoil Iosolde, Kennelsfort Rd 20 (6260116) - Mon 8-9.30 10 wks €80 FETAC 5

Training Options Plus 6-8 Wicklow St 2 (6717787) - 1 day, cert

CYCLING see also Adventure Sports

Corporate Club 24 Elmcastle Green Tallaght 24 (4610935)

Network Club 24 Elmcastle Green Tallaght 24 (4524415)

CZECH Languages

Sandford Language Institute Milltown Pk Sandford Rd 6 (2601296) - & Slovak: : all levels subject to demand, 15 wks €350

Trinity College 2 (8961000) (8961896) beginners / lower intermediate: ea 24 wks €320

DANCE see also Aerobics / Ballet / Ballroom / Belly / Contemporary / Disco / Folk / Irish / Jive / Latin American / Line / Modern / Old Time / Tap / Waltz / Set

Ballyfermot CFE, Ballyfermot Rd 10 (6269421) - modern mix, Wed 8-9pm 10 wks

Brooks Academy 15 Henrietta St 1 (8730093) - set dancing, Sept-May Mon & Thurs 8-10pm

Coiscéim Dance 14 Sackville Pl 1 (8780558) - for adults: contemporary dance, ballet & jazz, city centre studio, beginners welcome: Mon Tues & Thurs, 6.15 & 7.45, 8 wks €100

Dance Club Rathmines & Rathgar (2893797)

Dance Theatre of Ireland Bloomfields Centre, Lr George St Dún Laoghaire (2803455) - modern/ hip-hop, contemporary, pilates & dance; capoeira; salsa, cardio salsa, yoga, jazz belly dance, body conditioning: all ages, eves, w'ends, also 'dance all day' summer course intensive; also youth dance company based at centre: 10 wks €80

Danzon (087 9172939) - salsa, all levels available: Thurs 8.30pm & Sun 7.15pm, ongoing €9.50 per class, 8-10 Harrington St 2/; also Mon 7pm Wynn's Hotel Lr Abbey St 1/ Wed 7pm St Caitriona's 59 Lr Baggot St

Donahies Community School Streamville Rd 13 (8482217) - for fun, Thurs 7.30, 10 wks €85

Dublin Folk Dance Group 48 Ludford Drive Ballinteer 16 (2987929) - adult sets /figure/solo (step)/ step for beginners/international dances

Dublin School of Dance 13 Stamer St Portobello 8 (4755451) - adult beginners eve/ various

Hartstown Community School Clonsilla 15 (8209863) - latino & salsa, 10 wks €60

Hollywood Academy Dublin 13-14 Sackville Pl 1 (8786909) - from 4-8pm: Hip-hop, salsa, street, ballet, freestyle, breakdance: 11 mths €75 per mth, cert

Ingrid Nachstern (2600663) - ballet, beginners, 10wk, Tues, Sandymount

Just Dance (8273040 087 8473518) - all dance types. all levels, venues Dublinwide, for fitness & fun

Killester CFE, Collins Ave 5 (8337686) - salsa & cha-cha, beginners Mon 7pm/8.30 10 wks €50 ea

Knocklyon Youth & Community Centre, 16 (4931213) - social dancing, beginners 11.30am/ advanced 9.45am, Mon 8 wks €80/ beginners, Thurs 8.15pm 8 wks €90

Marino College 14-20 Marino Mart 3 (8332100) - swing dancing (Big band 30s 40s). improvers: thurs 6.30/8pm €65 each

Morosini-Whelan School of Dancing 46 Parnell Sq W 1 (8303613) - ballroom/ waltz/ rock 'n roll/ quickstep/ swing/ salsa/ Argentinian/Tango - also private lessons by appointment

Parnell School of Music & Performing Arts 13-14 Sackville Pl 1 (8786909) - from 4-8pm, cert

Pobalscoil Rosmini Adult Ed Grace Pk Rd 9 (8371015) - ballroom/ salsa/ Latin American/ set dancing

Ringsend Technical Institute Cambridge Rd 4 (6684498) - hip hop; swing; salsa & Latin American beginners: each 10 wks €70

TACT St Dominic's School St Dominic's Rd Tallaght 24 (4596757)

Taney Parish Centre Taney Rd Dundrum 14 (2985491) - hip hop, Fri (2986309)/ Irish, Thurs 086 8170292

DANISH see also Languages

Sandford Language Institute Milltown Pk Sandford Rd 6 (2601296) - all levels, 15 wks €285

DATA INPUT COURSES see Keyboarding

DATABASES see also computer training

BCT Institute, Institute 30 Fitzwilliam St 2 (6616838 /891) - oracle9i introduction SQL, Thurs 6.45-9pm 12; database administration I, Tue 6.45-9pm 14 wks/ introduction to PHP & MySQL, Mon, 6.45-9pm 11 wks

CTA Computer Training Academy, St James's Tce Malahide (8454070) - access: 2 days, day/eve/sat

Dorset College 64 Lr Dorset St/ 8 Belvedere Pl 1 (8309677)

Dún Laoghaire CFE, 17 Cumberland St Dún Laoghaire (2809676) - oracle SQL fundamentals, Tue 20 wks 7-9pm €300

Eden Computer Training Rathfarnham 16 & 1 Green St 7 (4953155)

FAS Training Centre Loughlinstown Wyattville Rd, DL (2043600) - MOS access core, 10 wks

Fitzwilliam Institute Ltd Temple Court Temple Rd Blackrock (2834579) - dip in oracle database programming, ICM, 10 wk - 2 eve wkly, Tue & Thurs, 6.30-9.30pm, €1265 incl exam fees; city centre; accredited by ICM

Pitman Training Centre 6-8 Wicklow St 2 (6768008) - ms access, day eve sats, cert

DEAFNESS see also Sign Language

National Assoc for Deaf People 35 Nth Frederick St 1 (8175700 /fax 8723816) - deaf adults with acquired hearing loss - hearing help & lipreading, day & eve, 8 wk-term, 2 yr prog, €15 subsidised; completion cert

Trinity College 2 (8961000) - (cdsinfo@tcd.ie) deaf studies introduction, 18 wks €270

DEGREE & POST-GRADUATE COURSES

Dublin Business School 13/14 Aungier St 2 (4177500) - Accounting & Finance; Business Studies; Business Management; Financial Services; Marketing & Event Management; Management & Information Systems; Psychology; Social Science; Counselling & Psychotherapy; HRM / Law / Accounting / Marketing; Marketing; Media & Marketing Studies; General Arts - (Economics, Psychoanalysis & Philosophy, Cultural Studies, Media Studies, Literature & Drama) / MA International Accounting & Finance

Irish Academy of Public Relations (2780802) - courses at UCD, Belfield: graduate diploma in public relations, HETAC, 1 yr 2 evs, €4600

National College of Ireland Mayor St IFSC 1 (4060500/ 1850 221721) - in business/ computers/ software sys/ elearning/ learning technologies/ management. finance/ HRH/ industrial relations/ personnel etc

The Open University Enquiry/Advice Centre Holbrook House, Holles St 2 (6785399) - BA/BSc degrees/ dips/ postgrad degrees/ progs in management, education, health & social welfare

DESIGN see also Computer Aided Design / Dress / Engineering / Graphic / Interior / Printing / Web

Coláiste Dhúlaigh CFE,Barryscourt Rd Coolock 17 (8481337) - art,design & craft, Fetac 3 Wed 2-5pm 20 wks

DIT Faculty: Built Environment Bolton St 1 (4023000) - p/time design studies higher cert, 2 yr 2 eve weekly, €1400pa/ signwork, advanced, 1 & 2, 28 wks, each €730

Institute of Art Design & Technology Dún Laoghaire (2414631) - various courses

Irish Academy of Computer Training 98 St Stephen's Green 2 (4347662) - IACT webmaster 12 wks dip/ desktop pub 20 wks cert; also day/ quarkxpress; corel draw; ms pub; adobe photoshop & illustrator; framemaker: ea 8 wks cert/ powerpoint; freelance graphics: 4 wks each cert: all, day/eve

St Kevin's College, Clogher Rd Crumlin 12 (4536397) - & art, 1yr, day

DESK-TOP PUBLISHING

Adelaide Computers 14 Pembroke Lane Ballsbridge 4 (2696213)

Ashfield Computer Training Main St Templeogue 6W (4926708) - Quark, Photoshop, Illustrator, Publsiher, Acrobat; Digital Photog; all courses offered morns, eves and accelerated

Ballyfermot CFE, Ballyfermot Rd 10 (6269421) - Fetac 5 Mon 7-9.30 22 wks

Bray Institute of FE, Novara Ave Bray (2866111 / 2829668) - with photoshop, Tue 7.30-9.30 10 wks €170

Coláiste Dhúlaigh CFE, Barryscourt Rd Coolock 17 (8481337) - Tue 7-9.30, 10 wks

Dorset College 64 Lr Dorset St/ 8 Belvedere Pl 1 (8309677) - incl quark express, photoshop, illustrator, acrobat, Mon & Wed 6.30-9.30pm, 12 wks FETAC

Dún Laoghaire CFE, 17 Cumberland St Dún Laoghaire (2809676) - Wed 20 wks 7-9pm €300

Eden Computer Training Rathfarnham 16 & 1 Green St 7 (4953155)

FAS Training Centre Ballyfermot 10 (6055900); Cabra Bannow Rd 7 (8821400) - level 1 10 wks; Jervis St 1 (8044600) - levels 1 & 2: 6-9pm 10 wks each; Cookstown Indl Est 24 (4045200)

Greenhills College Limekiln Ave Walkinstown 12 (4507779/4507863) - word processing and DTP, Tue, 20 wks €292 FETAC cert

Irish Academy of Computer Training 98 St Stephen's Green 2 (4347662) - dtp course 24 wks, cert/ quarkxpress; corel draw; ms pub; adobe photoshop & illustrator; framemaker: ea 8 wks, cert/ IACT webmaster in web design, 12 wks, dip; day/eve

Moresoft Computers Ltd 44 Lr Lesson St 2 (2160902) - DTP master, 12 wks 6-9pm

Plunket College Swords Rd, Whitehall 9 (8371689) - DTP, FETAC level 5, Tues 25 wks, €287

DEVELOPMENT STUDIES see also Third World Studies

Ballsbridge CFE, Shelbourne Rd 4 (6684806) - Latin-American development issues - LASC, Tues, 6.30-8.30pm 20 wks

Comhlamh 10 Upr Camden St 2 (4783490) - global issues

Kimmage Development Studies Centre Holy Ghost College Whitehall Rd 12 (4064386/4064380) - MA / Grad Dip & BA, in development studies: 9- 12 months, day / Understanding Development, eve, 20 wks €200 cert

Saor-Ollscoil na hÉireann 55 Prussia St 7 (8683368)

DIET see also Nutrition / Food / Health

Holistic Healing Centre 38 Dame St 2 (6710813)

Kilroy's College Wentworth House Grand Canal Street Lr 2 (6620538 1850-700700) - tutor supported home study: fitness, health, nutrition, dip

Rathmines CFE - Senior College, Town Hall 6 (4975334) - health & alternative nutrition - effects of diet, Tue 7-9pm €90

Taney Centre Taney Rd Dundrum 14 (2985491) - weightwatchers, Mon/Thurs, also day

Tony Quinn Centre 66/67 Eccles St 7 (8304211) - 1 yr diploma holistic dietetics & nutrition; also nutrition clinic

DIGITAL ELECTRONICS & MICRO PROCESSORS see also Computer Maintenance

Hi-Tech Training 4 Nth Gt George's St 1 (1850-759759) - digital electronics levels 1-3, 50% practical hands-on, 1 eve wkly 7-10pm, level 1 & 3, 15 wks each, level 2 10 wks; C&G cert

Kilroy's College Wentworth House Grand Canal Street Lr 2 (6620538 1850-700700) - home study: PC Assembly & A+

DIGITAL IMAGING see also Photography, Computers, Graphic
FAS Training Centre Cabra Bannow Rd 7 (8821400) - 10 wks; Finglas Jamestown Rd 11 (8140200) - digital imaging with photoshop, 6.30 10 wks; Loughlinstown Wyattville Rd, DL (2043600) - with photoshop 10 wks

DISABILITY STUDIES see also Carers / Caring
Ballyfermot CFE, Ballyfermot Rd 10 (6269421) - intellectual disability, Fetac 5 22 wks Wed 7-10/ NUI Maynooth cert, 100 hrs Wed 7-10

College of Progressive Education 27-29 Carysfort Ave Blackrock (4884300) - FETAC level 5 caring for people with disabilities, intellectual and physical disabilities studies, special needs assistant training

Coolmine Community School Clonsilla 15 (8214583) - caring for people with disabilities, Tue 7-9.45 FETAC 5 (Coll of Prog Ed course) €600

Dún Laoghaire CFE, 17 Cumberland St Dún Laoghaire (2809676) - NUI cert disability studies, Tue 25 wks 7-10pm, €1200 (+4 Sats 9-4pm)

Inchicore CFE, Emmet Rd 8 (4535358) - in sports & leisure, 2 yr FETAC/ BTEI higher dip in social care

Maynooth NUI Adult & Community Ed Dept (7084500) - disability studies, CIL Carmichal House 7 (8730455); Dún Laoghaire CFE (2809676) Tue 7-10pm; Beaufort College Navan (046 9028915)

DISCO-DANCING see also Dance / Keep-Fit
DISTANCE LEARNING see also Teachers
College of Progressive Education 27-29 Carysfort Ave Blackrock (4884300) - childcare:

foundation & advanced studies in childcare/dip in crêche management ILM/ cert in childcare & crêche work / foundation in montessori method / cert in classroom assistants training / child psychology / business skills of running a crêche / FETAC level 5 & 6 cert in special needs assistants training, classroom assistant conversion to special needs / FETAC level 5 caring for children 0-6, early childhood education, child development, after school care, and caring for people with disabilities/ health care: providing home care/ introduction to caring/ FETAC level 5 introduction to nursing; care of the older person

DIT Faculty: Engineering Bolton St 1 (4023000) - motor vehicle parts personnel cert GCLI, €750

Dublin Institute of Design 25 Suffolk St 2 (6790286) - Interior Design, online cert, timeable to suit your lifestyle

FAS Net College (2043732 ecollegeinfo@fas.ie) - variety of courses online: personal development; business; health & safety; apprenticeships; computer applications; ecdl; networks; web design; programming; databases; etc

Fitzwilliam Institute Ltd Temple Court Temple Rd Blackrock (2834579) - dip in event management (with PR module), €1395 incl exam fee; accredited by ICM

Institute of Public Administration 57-61 Lansdowne Rd 4 (2403600) - public management & business studies degree & dip courses/ one yr part-time cert

International Foundation of Adult Education PO Box 93 Eglinton St Cork (022-29358 / 0818 365305) - social studies/psychology/anthropology/sociology: IFAE-Netherlands

Irish Academy of Public Relations (2780802) - intro to PR, cert/ practical journalism, cert, 1 yr, €390 / €440 each by email or correspondence

Irish Computer Society / ICS Skills Crescent Hall, Mount St Crescent 2 (6447820) - health informaiton/ information technology/ teacher courses/ training/ sales

Irish Payroll Association (IPASS) IPASS Hse, Centerpoint Business Pk Oak Rd 12 (4089100) - nationally recognised payroll or VAT qualification. Certified Payroll Technician or Certified VAT Technician

Kilroy's College Wentworth House Grand Canal Street Lr 2 (6620538 1850-700700) - tutor supported

Marketing Institute Sth Co Business Pk, Leopardstown 18 (2952355) - marketing / selling, cert 2 yrs, dip 3 yrs, graduateship 4 yrs, by distance learning €700 for 1st module, then €350 ea additional module within same acad yr

Milltown Institute Milltown Pk 6 (2776331) - Carmelite spirituality, by corresp, 2 yr (2776334)/ online modules: testament/ general theology & sacraments: €270 or €510 for 2 & €710 for 3 courses

Montessori Education Centre 41-43 Nth Gt George's St 1 (8780071) - distance learning
Montessori teacher training

National College of Communications Park Hse Cabinteely Vlg 18 (2898236) -
various courses

National College of Ireland Mayor St IFSC 1 (4060500/ 1850 221721)

National Training Authority ITEC Hse Cornelscourt 18 (2070597)

New Media Technology College, 13 Harcourt St 2 (4780905) - interactive media
production, electronic media, 1 yr dip EBU credit

Oscail - National Distance Education Centre DCU 9 (7005481)

Sales Institute of Ireland, The 68 Merrion Sq 2 (6626904) - selling skills, cert, online

Saor-Ollscoil na hÉireann 55 Prussia St 7 (8683368) - environmental studies/ peace
& conflict studies

TEFL Training Institute of Ireland 38 Harrington St 8 (4784035) - TEFL: max 40 wks,
€500; for abroad

The Open University Enquiry/Advice Centre Holbrook House, Holles St 2 (6785399)
- BA/BSc degrees/ dips/ postgrad degrees/ prof training progs in management,
education, health & social welfare

DIVING see also Adventure Sports / Scuba Diving

National Aquatic Centre Snugborough Rd Blanchardstown 15 (6464300) - all levels

DIVORCE see also MARRIAGE

Donahies Community School Streamville Rd 13 (8482217) - life after separation &
divorce, Tue €135

DIY COURSES

Bray Institute of FE, Novara Ave Bray (2866111 / 2829668) - home maintenance, Tue
10wks, €90

Cabinteely Community School Johnstown Rd 18 (2857455) - beginners, 6wk, €65

Hartstown Community School Clonsilla 15 (8209863) - home maintenance, 10wks, €85

Kylemore College Kylemore Rd 10 (6265901) - diy with woodwork, 12 wks Fri 9.30-
12.30pm/ caretakers & maintenance, wed 1.30-4pm/Fri 9.30-12.30, 12 wks ea

Newpark Adult Education Centre Newtownpark Ave Blackrock (2884376 / 2883725) - 10wks, €125, home maintenance, Tue 7.30-9.45pm

Pobalscoil Rosmini Adult Ed Grace Pk Rd 9 (8371015) - elementary DIY about the home, Mon & & 8.30pm €100 each/ beginners, Mon 7.30 €90

Ringsend Technical Institute Cambridge Rd 4 (6684498) - house maintenance Thurs 7-9pm 10 wks, €90

DOG TRAINING

Dublin West Dog Training Club Cathy McGuinness (8388869)

Hartstown Community School Clonsilla 15 (8209863) - clicker training for your dog 10 wks €85

DOMESTIC HEATING ENGINEERING

DIT Faculty: Built Environment Bolton St 1 (4023000) - oil fired, 10 wks €250 / gas installation & safety, 1 yr

DRAMA see also Acting / Literature / Personal Development / Speech and Drama / Theatre / Voice

Abbey School of Music 9b Lr Abbey St 1 (8747908) - Kathleen Yeates

Betty Ann Norton Theatre School 11 Harcourt St 2 (4751913) - acting dip / adult foundation course

DIT Faculty: Applied Arts Aungier St 2 (4023000) - drama in education intro/ intermediate each 1 yr €495

Gaiety School of Acting Sycamore St Temple Bar 2 (6799277) - 2 yr full time acting course/ 1 yr courses: performance, adv. performance, performance theatre company/ 10 wk courses: intro to drama / page to stage / acting for camera / comedy improv / stage combat / stagecraft / audition technique / dramatic writing/ wkend workshops: voice / stage combat / make a 'short' short/ young gaiety & youth theatre workshops/ easter & summer courses. Venues: Temple Bar, Bray, Sutton, Cork & Kerry

Marino College 14-20 Marino Mart 3 (8332100) - for beginners, 7.30 Thurs 10 wks €90

Maynooth NUI Adult & Community Ed Dept (7084500) - performance / directing: Kilkenny campus 056 7775910

Network Club 24 Elmcastle Green Tallaght 24 (4524415)

New Media Technology College 13 Harcourt St 2 (4780905) - performing arts, 1 yr FETAC 5 cert; also part-time eve/ intro to acting, 8 wks eve

Newpark Adult Education Centre Newtownpark Ave Blackrock (2884376 / 2883725) - beginners, workshop, 10wks, €120, Tue 7.30-9.45

Pobalscoil Rosmini Adult Ed Grace Pk Rd 9 (8371015) - 'playschool for adults' Wed 7.30-9.30 €120

St Kevin's College Clogher Rd Crumlin 12 (4536397) - 10 wks

Tallaght Community School Balrothery 24 (4515566) - 10wk, 7.30-9.30 €70

Taney Centre Taney Rd Dundrum 14 (2985491) - Encore, Mon 087 9085913; Tues, Thurs 2987641

UCD Adult Education Centre Belfield (7167123) - from Text To Theatre 1, 2 & 3 Weds/ Staging Imagination Mon: each 10 wks

DRAUGHTS

Corporate Club & Network Club 24 Elmcastle Green Tallaght 24 (4524415)

DRAUGHTSMANSHIP
FAS Training Centre Cabra Bannow Rd 7 (8821400) - 2D CAD 30 wks/ autocad 10 wks
FAS Training Centre Tallaght Cookstown Indl Est 24 (4045200)
Pearse College Clogher Rd Crumlin 12 (4536661/4541544) - architectural/ CAD 1 &
  2: FETAC 2/ C&G CAD 3 certs: 2yr €150/€170

DRAWING / FROM LIFE / STILL LIFE
Ballsbridge CFE,, Shelbourne Rd 4 (6684806) - Mon 6-9pm 10 wks €150
Bray Institute of FE, Novara Ave Bray (2866111 / 2829668) - Tue & Wed: 7.30 10 wks €95
Brian Byrnes Art Studio 3 Upr Baggot St 4 (6671520 / 6711599) - 8wk, €150, also day
Cabinteely Community School Johnstown Rd 18 (2857455) - beginners/improvers,
  10wk, €95
Gallery Art Centre The Mill, Celbridge Co Kildare (6276206) - life drawing, am/pm
  9 wks €100
Hartstown Community School Clonsilla 15 (8209863) - 10wks, €85
National Gallery of Ireland Merrion Sq W 2 (6615133) -drawing studies in 3 terms,
  10 wks (autumn, winter, spring): season ticket autumn & winter, €150; spring €135
NCAD Centre for Continuing Educ 100 Thomas Street 8 (6364214) - drawing &
  painting from life, intro & intermediate/ drawing with pastels/ 2D work studio, intro
  & intermediate / 'seeing is believing'/ drawing intermediate / the human figure,
  intro: each c 22 wks
UCD Adult Education Centre Belfield (7167123) - the key to drawing and painting,
  Tue 10 wks Airfield Hse

DRAWING AND PAINTING see also Art / Landscape / Oil Painting / Pastel /
Portrait / Sketching / Water Colours
Ballyfermot CFE, Ballyfermot Rd 10 (6269421) - Mon 7-9.30 12 wks
Brian Byrnes Art Studio 3 Upr Baggot St 4 (6671520 / 6711599) - 8wk, €150, also day
Coláiste Dhúlaigh CFE, Barryscourt Rd Coolock 17 (8481337) - intermediate, Wed
  12.30-2.30/ for all, Mon 11-1pm: each 10 wks
DATE Centre CFE, Dundrum 14 (2964322 (9.30am-12pm)) - watercolours &
  drawing, 10 wks €97
Greendale Community School Kilbarrack 5 (8322735) - and sketching, Tue, Thurs
  7.30 10 wks €95
Inchicore CFE, Emmet Rd 8 (4535358)
Kilternan Adult Education Centre Ballybetagh Rd Kilternan 18 (2952050) - Fri
  12-2pm 10 wks €130
Kylemore College Kylemore Rd 10 (6265901) - beginners FETAC 1 13 wks Thurs
  7-9pm/ Improvers, Mon, intermediate Wed: each 16 wks Mon 7-9pm
Lucan Community College Esker Drive (6282077) - drawing sketching, watercolours
  beginners, Mon/ improvers Tue 7.30-8.30 10 wks €130
Marysha Old National School Dunboyne Co Meath (8222929 087 6853452) -
  drawing & painting for children, Mon 4.30-6.30, throughout year
Meridian Art Group c/o St Paul's College Raheny 5 (8310688)
NCAD Centre for Continuing Educ 100 Thomas Street 8 (6364214) - from life/ 2D
  work studio intro/ intermediate drawing, c.22wk each
Newpark Adult Education Centre, Newtownpark Ave Blackrock (2884376 / 2883725)

- watercolour Mon/Thurs; oils Mon; painting & drawing Tue

Rathmines CFE - Senior College, Town Hall 6 (4975334) - beginners/ improvers, Mon & Wed 20 wks €180 ea/ Tue, 7pm 25 wks, €205

Ringsend Technical Institute Cambridge Rd 4 (6684498) - drawing and visual exploration, 10 wks €90 Wed 7-9pm

St Kevin's College, Clogher Rd Crumlin 12 (4536397) - NCVA, 20wks

DREAMS & DREAM INTERPRETATION

Irish School of Shamanism 54 South William St 2 (4577839) - dreamweavery & drumquest, 12 wk

Old Bawn Community School Tallaght 24 (4526137) - Thurs, 7.30-9.30 €90

Our Lady's Hospice Harold's Cross 6 (4068806 4068810) - Dream Tending, 14 & 20 July07 1 day workshops 10am-4pm €100 incl lunch

Paul Bradley (Psychotherapist) Main St Kilcock Co Kildare (6284673/ 087 9598840) - Dream Analyst - eve, wkends seminars, Dublin/ Kildare venues

DRESSMAKING see also Patternmaking / Sewing

Ballsbridge CFE,, Shelbourne Rd 4 (6684806) - Fri, 2.30-4.30pm, 10 wks €90

Bray Institute of FE, Novara Ave Bray (2866111 / 2829668) - beginners Wed/ intermediate Mon: 10 wks €85 ea

Crumlin College of FE, Crumlin Rd 12 (4540662) - Mon/ also for beginners Wed: each 10 wks 7.30-9.30

Grafton Academy of Dress Designing 6 Herbert Place 2 (6763653) - make up commercial patterns, 10 or 20 classes, Wed/Thurs 7-9, Fri 6- 8.30: €270 or €498/ summer courses 1 wk €260, 2 wk f/time €470

Kilroy's College Wentworth House Grand Canal Street Lr 2 (6620538 1850-700700) - tutor supported home-study dip courses

Marino College 14-20 Marino Mart 3 (8332100) - Tues, 5.30/7.30; thurs improvers 5.30: 10 wks €90 ea

Ringsend Technical Institute Cambridge Rd 4 (6684498) - beginners/ improvers, Tue 6.30 & 8pm10wks, €70

St MacDara's CC, Wellington Lane Templeogue 6W (4566216) - Mon, 7.30-9.30pm, 8 wks, €104

DRIVING

Ballyfermot CFE, Ballyfermot Rd 10 (6269421) - intro to, Mon 7-9pm

Bray Institute of FE, Novara Ave Bray (2866111 / 2829668) - driver education with steer clear, Tue 7.30-9.30 10 wks €450, SC cert

FAS Training Centre Ballyfermot 10 (6055900) - delivery driver, 13 wks/ heavy goods vehicle 4 wks: day

KLEAR Grange Park View Kilbarrack 5 (8671845) - rules of the road, day

Malahide Community School (8460949) - driver education, 7.30-9.30 10 wks €350

NIFAST Liberty Risk Services 46 Airways Industrial Estate Santry 17 (8424333) - advanced driving courses

DRIVING INSTRUCTOR TRAINING

Colliers Driving Instructor College Finglas E, Raheny & Blanchardstown (8340329)

National Register of Driving Instructors Road Safety House 50 Nore Rd, Dublin Ind Estate Glasnevin 11 (8308481) - examination & monitoring of driving instructors, cert

DRUGS & ALCOHOL ABUSE see also Family Relationships

Hanly Centre Eblana Ave Dún Laoghaire (2807269) - counselling for alcoholics & other addicts

Trinity College 2 (8961000) - (8961163) problems in contemporary Ireland, 10 wks €100

DRUMS see also Music / Percussion

Hartstown Community School Clonsilla 15 (8209863) - 10 wks €85

Hollywood Academy Dublin 13-14 Sackville Pl 1 (8786909) - from 4-8pm: 11 mths €75 per mth, cert

Liberties College Bull Alley St 8 (4540044) - African Drumming, Wed 7-9pm 10 wks €90

Melody School of Music 178E Whitehall Rd W Perrystown 12 (4650150) - also day; 12 wks

Parnell School of Music & Performing Arts 13-14 Sackville Pl 1 (8786909) - from 4-8pm, cert

Ringsend Technical Institute Cambridge Rd 4 (6684498) - West African hand drums, Mon 7-9pm 10 wks €90

Waltons New School of Music 69 Sth Gt George's St 2 (4781884) - also day, see ad page 155

DUBLIN see also History / Archaeology

DUTCH, ELEMENTARY & INTERMEDIATE see also Languages

Marino College 14-20 Marino Mart 3 (8332100) - Tues 6.30 10 wks €65

Sandford Language Institute Milltown Pk Sandford Rd 6 (2601296) - all levels, 15 wks €285

Trinity College 2 (8961000) - (8961373) for beginners, 18 wks €275/ also intermediate (8961862)

WORDS Language Services 44 Northumberland Rd 4 (6610240) - beginners, advanced & commercial, cert, individual tuition only

DYSLEXIA

Dyslexia Association of Ireland 1 Suffolk St 2 (6790276) - group or individual tuition

E-BUSINESS see also Distance Learning, Business, etc

Ballyfermot CFE, Ballyfermot Rd 10 (6269421) - Fetac 2 Weds 22 wks

Coláiste Dhúlaigh CFE,Barryscourt Rd Coolock 17 (8481337) - international trade & ebusiness, dip IIT 22 wks Mon, Tue 6.45-9.15

Dublin Business School 13/14 Aungier St 2 (4177500) - Higher Dip in Business Studies - E-Business, 2 eves per wk 6.15-9.30pm, 16 mths

Export Edge Training Ltd 57 Merrion Square 2 (6619544) - prof dip in global trade & e-business, eve 1 yr, 60% Fás funded

National College of Ireland Mayor St IFSC 1 (4060500/ 1850 221721) - H.Dip in Business in eBusiness, 1 year, 2 eve, €3,000

Pearse College Clogher Rd Crumlin 12 (4536661/4541544) - 2 yr dip in international trade & ebusiness 1 & 2 €150/€294

E-LEARNING see also Distance Learning / Online / Correspondence

New Media Technology College, 13 Harcourt St 2 (4780905) - EBU dip in electronic media, modular (digital - imaging, video prod, amimation, web development, 3D animation) 1 yr/ FETAC cert - interactive media prod; IT; business studies admin/ various short courses: on flash; dreamweaver; adobe; HTML etc

ECDL (modules include: basic concepts, access, excel, powerpoint, managing files, internet, word processing) see also Computer Training

Ballsbridge CFE, Shelbourne Rd 4 (6684806) - foundation, Mon, 6-9pm 10 wks €180/ ECDL Mon /Tue 20 wks: 6pm

Balymun Comprehensive School Adult Ed Centre 9 (8420654) - complete, Sat 10am-3.30, 10 wks €500/ advanced: word Wed 7pm;/ excel 8.40: €270 each

BCT Institute, Institute 30 Fitzwilliam St 2 (6616838 /891) - ECDL Fri 6.45-9pm 11 wks

Coláiste Dhúlaigh CFE, Barryscourt Rd Coolock 17 (8481337) - ECDL 7 modules, Mon 7.15pm; Thurs 11-1pm: 23 wks/ 4 modules, 12 wks; / ECDL update, Wed 3pm/ pre-ECDL Mon 11-1pm & 6-7.30pm

Coláiste Eanna, Kilkieran Rd Cabra 7 (8389577) - Sept-May, Tue / Thurs 7-9pm 10 wks

Colaiste Ide Cardiffsbridge Rd Finglas W 8443233 11 (8342333) - ECDL, Tues, 7-10pm, cert; 20 wks €400

Connolly House Nth Strand (by 5 Lamps) 1 (8557116) - post-ecdl computer utilities, Wed 6.30 10 wks €105

Crumlin College of FE, Crumlin Rd 12 (4540662) - Tue & Wed, 6.45-9.45 20 wks / MOS core modules, Mon & Tue 6.45, 20 wks

CTA Computer Training Academy, St James's Tce Malahide (8454070) - basic / advanced / workshops: day/eve/Sat

Donahies Community School Streamville Rd 13 (8482217) - Fri, 9.30am-12pm €475, cert

Dorset College 64 Lr Dorset St/ 8 Belvedere Pl 1 (8309677) - all modules, Tue & Thurs 6.30-9pm 15 wks; Sats 9.30-2pm, 15 wks

Dún Laoghaire CFE, 17 Cumberland St Dún Laoghaire (2809676) - ECDL, 25 wks, Mon, Wed, €495 ea

Eden Computer Training Rathfarnham 16 & 1 Green St 7 (4953155)

FAS eCollege (2043732 ecollegeinfo@fas.ie) - online

FAS Training Centre Baldoyle 13 (8167400) - 20 wks; Ballyfermot 10 (6055900); Cabra Bannow Rd 7 (8821400) - 20 wks; Finglas Jamestown Rd 11 (8140200) - 20 wks; Jervis St 1 (8044600) - 6-9pm 10 wks; Tallaght Cookstown Indl Est 24 (4045200); Wyattville Rd, DL (2043600) - 10 wks

I.T. Blanchardstown Rd North 15 (8851000) - 15 wks €500 p/time

Irish Academy of Computer Training 98 St Stephen's Green 2 (4347662) - basic concepts of IT; using computer, managing files; wp; spreadsheets; databases; presentations & drawing; info network services: each 2 wks, cert/ ECDL bootcamp; ECDL multimedia guide: each 10 wks: cert; ECDL advanced - 12 wks/ advanced - word, excel, access, powerpoint, each 4 wks: day/eve

Kilternan Adult Education Centre Ballybetagh Rd Kilternan 18 (2952050) - Thur 10am-1, 10 wks €218.40

Kylemore College Kylemore Rd 10 (6265901) - prep for ecdl, Wed 12 wks 10.30-12.30pm

Lucan Community College Esker Drive (6282077) - for improvers, Mon 7.30-930 10 wks €166

Marino College 14-20 Marino Mart 3 (8332100) - 6-9pm Wed 7 modules 23 wks
€465/ pre-ecdl Thurs 7.30 10 wks €105/ equal skills, Thurs 6pm €115

Moresoft Computers Ltd 44 Lr Lesson St 2 (2160902) - ecdl / ecdl advanced, 6-9pm
16 wks

Newpark Adult Education Centre Newtownpark Ave Blackrock (2884376 / 2883725)
- ECDL, 20wks, €550, Mon 7.30-9.45pm

Palmerstown CS - Pobailscoil Iosolde, Kennelsfort Rd 20 (6260116) - all modules,
Mon/Tue/ Thurs: 10 wks €70 each/ basic concepts €60

Pitman Training Centre 6-8 Wicklow St 2 (6768008) - various courses, cert; day, eve, sats

Plunket College Swords Rd, Whitehall 9 (8371689) - Mon, 24 wks 7-10pm, €456

Pobalscoil Neasáin Baldoyle 13 (8063092) - 4 modules: Tue 8-9.30 12 wks €210/
skills cert €37

Rathmines CFE - Senior College, Town Hall 6 (4975334) - all modules, 6.30, Mon/
Wed: 25 wks/ pre-ECDL 7-9pm Tue 25 wks €185

Ringsend Technical Institute Cambridge Rd 4 (6684498) - ECDL, 25wks Wed
7-10pm, €550-600/ pre-ECDL for absolute beginners 7-9pm 10 wks 140

St Tiernan's Community School Parkvale Balally 16 (2953224) - all modules, 25 wks,
Tue €390

Stillorgan CFE, Old Road Stillorgan (2880704) - Tue 7-10pm 12 wks €475

ECOLOGY see Environment

ECONOMICS see also History / Leaving Cert / Social Studies

Coláiste Eanna, Kilkieran Rd Cabra 7 (8389577) - applied, intro to property economics,
Thurs 10 wks 7-9pm

Kilroy's College Wentworth House Grand Canal Street Lr 2 (6620538 1850-700700)
- home study: & economic history, leaving cert

Plunket College Swords Rd, Whitehall 9 (8371689) - leaving cert, 27 wks, €283

ECUMENICS see also Religion

Irish School of Ecumenics Bea House Milltown Pk 6 (2601144) - (ext.115) Dr
Andrew Pierce/ MLitt & PhD (Ext.126 Prof May, or Ext 111 Christine Houlahan

EDUCATION & TRAINING see also Return to Learning

College of Further Education Main St Dundrum 14 (2951376)

FETAC East Point Plaza East Point Business Park 3 (8659500) - national certification body

I.T. Blanchardstown Rd North 15 (8851000) - level 5 cert in General Studies, 1 yr

Junior Chamber Ireland - email pro@jci-ireland.org for info

UCD Adult Education Centre Belfield (7167123) - your child in secondary school,
Mon 8 wks

ELECTRICAL ENGINEERING

DIT Faculty: Engineering Bolton St 1 (4023000) - electrical systems 1 yr €750/ full
tech dip electrical & electronic eng 3 yrs €700/ BE electrical & electronic
engineering Pt 2, 4 yr €400 per module, project €400/ BTech electrical services eng,
5 yr €1110pa; also higher cert, 3 yr €1110 pa

ELECTRICITY / ELECTRICAL INSTALLATION

DIT Faculty: Engineering Bolton St 1 (4023000) - standards based apprenticeship
updating, phase 4+6, 10 wks per module €290 ea

FAS Training Centres- electrician,10 wks: Baldoyle 13 (8167400); Cabra Bannow Rd 7

(8821400); Finglas Jamestown Rd 11 (8140200); Loughlinstown Wyattville Rd, DL (2043600) - electrician revision 10 wks

ELECTROLYSIS see also Beauty Therapy

Aspen's Beauty Clinic & College of Beauty Therapy 83 Lr Camden St 2 (4751079/ 4751940) - ITEC

Coogan-Bergin Clinic & College of Beauty Therapy Glendenning Hse 6-8 Wicklow St 2 (6794387) - CIBTAC Tue 6.30-9.30 €1795; body electrical treatments 6-9pm Tue & Thurs

Galligan College of Beauty 109 Grafton St 2 (6703933) - ITEC & CIBTAC, Sept - June p/time, 1300

ELECTRONIC ENGINEERING

Institute of Technology Tallaght ITT Dublin, Tallaght 24 (4042101) BEng - Electronic Engineering NFQ Level 7 2 yrs (add on)/ BEng (Hons) - Electronic NFQ Level 8 3 yrs (add on)/ Higher cert in Engineering - Electronic NFQ Level 6 (Flexible Delivery Mode) 3 yrs

ELECTRONICS see also Digital / Computer Maintenance

Coláiste Dhúlaigh CFE, Barryscourt Rd Coolock 17 (8481337) - FETAC & C&G certs, Tue 7-9.15 20 wks

DIT Faculty: Engineering Bolton St 1 (4023000) - degree in electronic & computer systems, 2yrs €1350; also higher cert 3yrs

FAS Training Centres: Baldoyle 13 (8167400) - basic/ intro to programmable logic controllers: 10 wks each; Ballyfermot 10 (6055900); Cabra Bannow Rd 7 (8821400) - basic 10 wks/ programmable logic controllers 10 wks; Finglas Jamestown Rd 11 (8140200) - basic, 10 / programmable logic controllers, 10 wks; Loughlinstown Wyattville Rd, DL (2043600) - wo wks

Hi-Tech Training 4 Nth Gt George's St 1 (1850-759759) - levels 1,2,3, 50% practical hands-on, 1 eve wkly 7-10pm, 15wks each: C&G cert

ELOCUTION see Public Speaking / Speech and Drama

EMAIL see INTERNET & EMAIL

EMBROIDERY / CREATIVE

Ballymun Trinity CS, Adult Ed Centre 9 (8420654) - crochet, handknitting: all stages, Mon 10 wks €90

Grafton Academy of Dress Designing 6 Herbert Place 2 (6763653) - classical beading & embroidery, 6 wks Mon €225/ 2 day workshops / mixed media/ beading/ creative felt: €225 each

Hartstown Community School Clonsilla 15 (8209863) - 10 wks €85

NCAD Centre for Continuing Educ 100 Thomas Street 8 (6364214) - exploring, intro & intermediate, c. 22wk

Old Bawn Community School Tallaght 24 (4526137) - Thurs 7.30-9.30 €90

Quilt Art Workshops 4 Mill Wood Naas (045-876121) - classes & workshops, SAE for info

ENGINEERING see also Computers / Electronic Engineering / Industrial / Management / Mathematics / Telecommunications

DIT Faculty: Engineering Bolton St 1 (4023000) - foundation, 1yr €1200; BE degree, 3 yr p/time €1352; building services, 3 yrs higher cert €250 / BE (Computer Eng)

3 yr €3020 yr 1, €1400 yr 2/ higher cert 3 yr & BEngTech 5 yr in civil engineering, €250 per module

Graduate School of Engineering Studies O'Reilly Institute TCD 2 (8961007) - post-grad dips in: applied building repair & conservation/ construction law & contract admin/ project management/fire safety practice (buildings & other structures) / environmental engineering

Institute of Technology Tallaght ITT Dublin, Tallaght 24 (4042101) - BEng - Manufacturing 2 yrs NFQ Level 7 (add on)/ BEng (Hons) - Manufacturing NFQ Level 8 3 yrs (add on)

Institution of Fire Engineers 77 Ballyroan Road 16 (4943669) - fire safety/ engineering

St Kevin's College, Clogher Rd Crumlin 12 (4536397) - mechanical, all day/electronic, NCVA, 1yr, day

Trinity College 2 (8961000) - (8961007) - environmental, 1yr postgrad dip, 24wks, Fri pm & Sat am/ project management postgrad dip, 1 yr Fri eve+sat morn 24 wks

ENGLISH see also Basic Ed / Creative / Dyslexia / Junior Cert / Languages / Leaving Cert / Literature / Writing

Ballymun Trinity CS,s Adult Ed Centre 9 (8420654) - junior cert, 30wk, €free/ leaving cert, 25wk, €300/ for assylum seekers & refugees, Wed 10 wks, free

Coláiste Dhúlaigh CFE, Barryscourt Rd Coolock 17 (8481337) - basic to Junior cert, 12 classes 9.30-11am, 8 wks/ leaving cert, Wed 11-1pm, 20 wks

Crumlin College of FE, Crumlin Rd 12 (4540662) - junior cert. Tue; leaving cert, Mon, Thurs: eve/ ESOL, Mon, 9.30am-12.30, Thurs 6.45pm 20 wks/ also Wed/Thurs 6.45/7.45

English Language Institute 99 St Stephen's Green 2 (4752965) - for exam prep for KET, PET, IELTS, ACELS, approved school/ part-time: 7.5 hrs per wk €120/ intensive 22.5 hrs €210 per wk/ 3-5pm & 6.30-8.30pm Tue & Thurs €100 for 6 lessons/ also full time courses

Kilroy's College Wentworth House Grand Canal Street Lr 2 (6620538 1850-700700) - tutor supported home study: basic/ leaving cert & junior cert

Kilternan Adult Education Centre Ballybetagh Rd Kilternan 18 (2952050) - Wed 11.45 10 wks €130

KLEAR Grange Park View Kilbarrack 5 (8671845) - junior cert/ leaving cert/ exploring English/ ESOL; day

Park House International Language Institute Ashdale Rd Terenure 6W (4902648) - all levels/ courses for Cambridge, IELTS & TOEFL

People's College for Continuing Education & Training 32 Parnell Sq 1 (8735879) - basic, €15 / as a foreign language, €30

Plunket College Swords Rd, Whitehall 9 (8371689) - leaving cert, 27 wks €425

Ringsend Technical Institute Cambridge Rd 4 (6684498) - leaving cert (O), 2 yr 25wks, €170/ also basic ed second chance LC Mon 7-9pm 2 yr 25 wks free

South Dublin Libraries (4597834-admin only) - classes free: Lucan (6216422), Tallaght (4620073)

TARGET St Kevin's School Newbrook Rd, Donaghmede 13 (8671967) - basic English for adults/ second-chance for those without L Cert / foreign language ESOL

ENGLISH (EFL- as a Foreign Language; ESOL- for speakers of other languages) see also English TEFL / Languages

Aisling Ireland 137 Lr Rathmines Rd 6 (4971902) - business, day/ Cambridge exam prep 11 wks 2 eves 7-9pm

Ballsbridge CFE, Shelbourne Rd 4 (6684806) - lower (Tue 6pm) & higher (Mon 6pm) intermediate; advanced, Tues & Thurs, 6-9pm 10 wks

Bray Institute of FE, Novara Ave Bray (2866111 / 2829668) - learn to speak English, Wed 7.30 10 wks €85

Clondalkin Adult Education Centre, Monastry Rd (4670225) - courses for non-Irish nationals in Clondalkin & Lucan

College of Further Education Main St Dundrum 14 (2951376)

College of Progressive Education 27-29 Carysfort Ave Blackrock (4884300) - how to teach EFL to pre-school children

DATE Centre CFE, Dundrum 14 (2964322 (9.30am-12pm)) - Mon & thurs 10 wks €97, day

Dublin School of English 10-12 Westmoreland St 2 (6773322) - various courses, day, pm, eve; Cambridge, IELTS certs; 24 lessons 1 wk morn; afternoon, eve, 4 wks, 6 lesson wkly / 12 lesson, afternoons, evenings/ also Sat morn classes

Dún Laoghaire CFE, 17 Cumberland St Dún Laoghaire (2809676) - beginners Mon, 10 wks, 6.30-8pm, €95; FCE - first cert in English, Mon 24 wks 8-10pm €290

Finglas Adult Reading & Writing Scheme Colaiste Eoin Cappagh Rd 11 (8340893) - for speakers of other languages ESOL, 10 wks night/ day

Firhouse Community College Firhouse Rd 24 (4525807) - beginners/ intermediate: Mon 7.30-9pm 8 wks €104 ea

Foxrock Institute Kill o' the Grange, Kill Lane Blackrock (4939506) - learn to speak English, Tue eve 8 wks €105

Hartstown Community School Clonsilla 15 (8209863) - 10wks, €85

International Study Centre 67 Harcourt St 2 (478 2766/2845) - general English & exam prep, also day, 2wks-1 yr courses, €30-€170, recog by Dept Ed.

Killester CFE, Collins Ave 5 (8337686) - for beginners, 10 wks Tue 7-8.30 €60

Language Centre NUI Maynooth Co Kildare (7083737) - intermed./adv., 15 wk, €300 cert

Liberties College Bull Alley St 8 (4540044) - Mon, beginners/Wed, intermediate: each 7-9pm 10 wks €55

Lucan Community College Esker Drive (6282077) - - Tue 7.30-8.30 10 wks €130

Malahide Community School Malahide (8460949) - Tue, Thurs 7.30pm 20 wks no fee

Marino College 14-20 Marino Mart 3 (8332100) - for foreign students levels 1,2,3 & Cambridge cert, Tue & Thurs 10 wks, €130 each, / advanced level, Tues 6pm 10 wks €155

National Adult Literacy Agency 76 Lr Gardiner St 1 (8554332) - family literacy/ English as a second language

Plunket College Swords Rd, Whitehall 9 (8371689) - ESOL, for speakers of other languages beginners/ intermediate Tue 10 wks €67

Pobalscoil Neasáin Baldoyle 13 (8063092) - Tue 7.30 10 wks €50

Pobalscoil Rosmini Adult Ed Grace Pk Rd 9 (8371015) - ESOL for speakers of other languages Wed 8.30-9.50 €90

Rathmines CFE - Senior College, Town Hall 6 (4975334) - rep for Cambridge 1st cert/ general/ elementary/ inter/advanced: each 10 wks, €90, Mon, Tue, Wed 7pm

Sandford Language Institute Milltown Pk Sandford Rd 6 (2601296) - all levels 12 wks €350; also day/ IELTS / TOEFL exam prep 12 wks 395/ Phonetics & Pronounciation 12 wks €350; also day

Stillorgan CFE, Old Road Stillorgan (2880704) - Thurs 7.30-9.30 8 wks €104

WORDS Language Services 44 Northumberland Rd 4 (6610240) - individual tuition only

ENGLISH - teaching as a foreign language TEFL Languages

Ballsbridge CFE, Shelbourne Rd 4 (6684806) - Mon 6-9pm, 20 wks €200/ prep for IELTS thurs 6-9pm 10 wks €110

Bray Institute of FE, Novara Ave Bray (2866111 / 2829668) - TEFL, Mon & Wed 7.30 10 wks, €85, cert

Cabinteely Community School Johnstown Rd 18 (2857455) - 10 wks, €95

Clondalkin Adult Education Centre, Monastery Rd (4670225) - TEFL Training Course all levels, ACELS & DES approved. Eve / also at Lucan Inst. FE (6283667)

Dorset College 64 Lr Dorset St/ 8 Belvedere Pl 1 (8309677) - Tues & Thurs + Sat 6-10pm 8 wks

Dublin School of English 10-12 Westmoreland St 2 (6773322) - TEFL part time and full time courses ACELS cert

Hibernian School of English 69 Emmet Road 8 (4540555/ 086-4045205) - all courses & levels, exam prep, one-to-one tuition

Phoenix A.B.C. TEFL Castleknock 15 (8208462)

Stillorgan CFE, Old Road Stillorgan (2880704) - 10 wks €130

TEFL Training Institute of Ireland 38 Harrington St 8 (4784035) - ACELS cert, day/ eve 4 or 6 wks €890, Dept Ed cert / for abroad, Internl cert, day/eve 2 or 4 wks €550

U-Learn 205 New St Mall Malahide (8451619) - TEFL cert, 4wk €890; also day

WORDS Language Services 44 Northumberland Rd 4 (6610240) - by correspondence & e-mail

ENGLISH LITERACY SCHEME see also Adult Educators

Dublin Adult Learning Centre 3 Mountjoy Sq 1 (8787266) - basic English/jnr cert English/leaving cert English

Pearse College Clogher Rd Crumlin 12 (4536661/4541544) - day drop-in centre (4547054)

Southside Adult Literacy Scheme 4 Glenville Tce Dundrum 14 (2964321) - improve your English, day & eve

ENNEAGRAM see also Assertiveness / Personal Development

Cabinteely Community School Johnstown Rd 18 (2857455) - Tues, 10 wks, €95

Firhouse Community College Firhouse Rd 24 (4525807) - Tue 7.30-9pm 4wks €52

Newpark Adult Education Centre, Newtownpark Ave Blackrock (2884376 / 2883725) - intro to personality types, 10 wks, €120, Thurs 7.30-9.45

Old Bawn Community School Tallaght 24 (4526137) - why do I always do that? Thurs, 7.30-9.30, 8 wks €73

Rathmines CFE - Senior College, Town Hall 6 (4975334) - personality types, Wed 10 wks €90

ENTREPRENEURIAL SKILLS see Business, start your own

ENVIRONMENT / Environmental Studies

An Oige 61 Mountjoy Street 7 (8304555) - environmental group

Bray Institute of FE, Novara Ave Bray (2866111 / 2829668) - discover Co Wicklow - 10 wks €85

ECO-UNESCO, 26 Clare St, Dublin 2 (6625491)

ENFO - Information on the Environment 17 St Andrew St 2 (1890 200191) - Dept of the Environment, Heritage & Local Government - free public info service on environmental matters

KLEAR Grange Park View Kilbarrack 5 (8671845) - understanding the landscape, 26 wks -day

People's College for Continuing Education & Training 32 Parnell Sq 1 (8735879) - birds of Ireland, 10 wks €60

Saor-Ollscoil na hÉireann 55 Prussia St 7 (8683368) - environmental studies, Mon

UCD Adult Education Centre Belfield (7167123) - Wet, Wild and Wonderful Bogs and Fens Tue / Our environment, our future, Tue 10 wks

ESPERANTO

Esperanto Assoc of Ireland 9 Templeogue Wood 6W (4945020) - correspondence / monthly meetings, €free

ESTONIAN

Sandford Language Institute Milltown Pk Sandford Rd 6 (2601296) - all levels, subject to demand, 15 wks €350

ETCHING and Related Techniques

NCAD Centre for Continuing Educ 100 Thomas Street 8 (6364214) - etching & printmaking, & dry point techniques, c. 22wk

ETHICS see also ECUMENICS

All Hallows College Gracepark Rd Drumcondra 9 (8373745) - the moral life & specific concerns, Thurs 8.30, 24 wks €390. ECTS credit option

Milltown Institute Milltown Pk 6 (2776331) - higher dip (NUI), foundation in ethics & ethical issues, 7.55 & 8.20, €280 per module

Trinity College 2 (8961000) - (8961927) biomedical ethics: perfecting humanity? 11 wks €150/ ethics, philosophical & theological; approaches to theological ethics: each, 11 wks €150 day

EVENT MANAGEMENT see also Management/ Hospitality

Irish Academy of Public Relations (2780802) - courses at UCD, Belfield: dip in event management, 15 wks 2 evs, €1850.

EXERCISE see also Fitness/ Keep Fit

Bray Institute of FE, Novara Ave Bray (2866111 / 2829668) - to music Mon 6.50-7.50 8 wks €45

Cabinteely Community School Johnstown Rd 18 (2857455) - pilates, Tues, 10 wks, €65

Colaiste Ide Cardiffsbridge Rd Finglas W 8443233 11 (8342333) - nat cert in exercise & fitness (aerobics & gym), 20 wks Tues & Thurs 7-10, NCEF, €500

Greendale Community School Kilbarrack 5 (8322735) - calorie combo, Thurs 7.30pm 10 wks €60/ ladies circuit training Tue 8pm

Irish Yoga Association PO Box 9969 7 (4929213/ 087 2054489) - qualified teachers available all over Ireland/ 4 yr Teacher Training courses

League of Health (Irl) 17 Dundela Pk Sandycove (2807775) - Mary McDaid: exercise to music, morns, 15 wks €88

Motions Health & Fitness Training (087 2808866) - Fitness Instructor training diploma course (ITEC), part-time, 9 hours per week. Venue Citywest Hotel & Leisure Centre, Naas Rd

Newpark Adult Education Centre, Newtownpark Ave Blackrock (2884376 / 2883725) -tai-chi, pilates, yoga - gentle exercise, 10 wks €95, Mon to Thurs

St MacDara's CC, Wellington Lane Templeogue 6W (4566216) - circuit training, Mon 7-8pm 8 wks €52

EXPORT see International Trade

FABRIC PAINTING see BATIK / TIE-DYE/ Silk Painting

FACILITATION SKILLS

Comhlamh 10 Upr Camden St 2 (4783490) - in development ed course

Trinity College 2 (8961000) - (8963885) eve 8 wks €100

FAMILY LAW see Law

FAMILY RELATIONSHIPS

Hanly Centre Eblana Ave Dún Laoghaire (2807269) - adult children of dysfunctional families, modules 1 & 2; 12 steps study series, moldule 3; group therapy, module 4

School of Philosophy & Economic Science 49 Northumberland Rd 4 (6603788) - 10 wks €100

FAMILY TREE see Genealogy

FASHION see also beauty Care / Make Up

Coolmine Community School Clonsilla 15 (8214583) - style coaching, Ms Grant Tue 10 wks €70

Dublin Institute of Design 25 Suffolk St 2 (6790286) - image & styling, 8wks 1 eve, cert

Grafton Academy of Dress Design 6 Herbert Place 2 (6763653) - design, pattern making, assembly, p/time day 4 yr dip €4770 p/time day €3770/ intro to design, pattern making, sewing, 18 or 38 lessons 7-9pm €430 or €860/ also summer holiday courses

Greenhills College Limekiln Ave Walkinstown 12 (4507779/4507863)

Griffith College Dublin Sth Circular Rd 8 (4150400) - BA in fashion design 3 yrs hetac f/t

NCAD Centre for Continuing Educ 100 Thomas Street 8 (6364214) - design & pattern construction, c. 22wk

Portobello School 43 Lr Dominick St 1 (8721277) - fashion merchandising, cert 32 wks eve

FENCING

Bray Institute of FE, Novara Ave Bray (2866111 / 2829668) - Tues 7-9pm 10 wks €70

Hartstown Community School Clonsilla 15 (8209863) - 10wks beginners/ improvers, €70 each

FENG SHUI see also Interior Design

Ballyfermot CFE, Ballyfermot Rd 10 (6269421) - Mon 10 wks

FICTION see also Literature/ Creative / Writing

Dún Laoghaire-Rathdown Co Council Public Library Service - free monthly book clubs; novels discussed, informal, new members welcome: the library at: Blackrock (2888117), Cabinteely (2855363), Dalkey (2855277), Deansgrange (2850860), Dunlaoghaire (2801147), Dundrum (2985000), Sallynoggin (2850127) Shankill (2823081), Stillorgan (2889655)

FIDDLE Music

Clontarf School of Music 6 Marino Mart 3 (8330936 087 8054963) - Irish, 18wk - also day

Comhaltas Ceoltóirí Éireann 32 Belgrave Sq Monkstown (2800295)

Melody School of Music 178E Whitehall Rd W Perrystown 12 (4650150) - all day W/S & Sat; w/ends, Sat-Sun, 12 wks

Na Piobairi Uileann 15 Henrietta St 1 (8730093)

Scoil Shéamuis Ennis, Naul, Co Dublin (8020898 087 7870138)

Waltons New School of Music 69 Sth Gt George's St 2 (4781884) - also day, see ad page 155

FILM / FILM STUDIES / APPRECIATION see also Cinema / Writing, Creative

Ballyfermot CFE, Ballyfermot Rd 10 (6269421) - editing for film & TV, Fetac 5 Wed 7-10pm 22 wks

Coláiste Dhúlaigh CFE,Barryscourt Rd Coolock 17 (8481337) - Tue 7-9pm 9 wks

Digital Film School contact Julianne: (086 8206144) - beginners, recreational film-making

Dún Laoghaire CFE, 17 Cumberland St Dún Laoghaire (2809676) - film studies, Tues 7-9pm 10 wks €110

Film Institute of Ireland Irish Film Centre 6 Eustace St Temple Bar 2 (6795744)

New Media Technology College, 13 Harcourt St 2 (4780905) - digital film production/ Hetac hons degree 4 yr f/time

Newpark Adult Education Centre, Newtownpark Ave Blackrock (2884376 / 2883725) - storytelling on screen, Tue 7.30 10 wks €120

People's College for Continuing Education & Training 32 Parnell Sq 1 (8735879) - film studies, €60

Plunket College Swords Rd, Whitehall 9 (8371689) - film theory & history, The 7-9 10 wks €90

Saor-Ollscoil na hÉireann 55 Prussia St 7 (8683368) - film & theatre studies

St Kevin's College, Clogher Rd Crumlin 12 (4536397) - 10wks

UCD Adult Education Centre Belfield (7167123) - introduction to film studies, 10 wks Mon/ the documentary film: an introduction: Mon 8 wks spring/ elements of film, Wed 8 wks /how to make your own low budget/no budget movie, 2 day Sat spring/ writing for the screen, Sat 2 day

FINANCIAL SERVICES / FINANCE

Ballyfermot CFE, Ballyfermot Rd 10 (6269421) - funds admin, Fetac 2, 22 wks €400

Dublin Business School 13/14 Aungier St 2 (4177500) - BA(Hons) Financial Services, 4 yr; Dip Stockbroking Investment/ Advanced Dip Stockbroking Investment, 1 eve 14 wks/Diploma in Property Investment, 1 eve, 14 weeks: each 6.15-9.30pm / Joint Financial Service Dip, 2 eves, 2 yrs, 6:15-9:30/ Dip Financial Management (ACCA DipFM) 1 eve, 1 yr 6.15-9.45 / Dip International Financial Reporting (ACCA DipIFR, wkends 10am-4pm, 1 yr / MSc International Accounting, 2 yrs / BA (Hons) Accounting & Finance

Institute of International Trade of Ireland 28 Merrion Square 2 (6612182) - documantary credit compliance, 1 day

Institute of Public Administration 57-61 Lansdowne Rd 4 (2403600) - public management & business studies degree & dip courses/ one yr part-time cert

Institute of Technology Tallaght ITT Dublin, Tallaght 24 (4042101) - dip in Financial Management (postgrad) 1 yr ACCA

National College of Ireland Mayor St IFSC 1 (4060500/ 1850 221721) MA in

Finance, 2 years, Fri eve. Sat, 8,900; Masters Qualifying Programme in Finance, 3 Months, €1,295; BA (Hons) in Financial Services, 4 years, Mon, Wed, Thurs eve, €3,285; Foundation Certificate in Financial Services, 1 year, €1,300

UCD Adult Education Centre Belfield (7167123) - finance for non-financial managers, Wed 10 wks spring/ intro to the Stock Market (autumn); and 'the next level' (spring): each 10 wks

Westmoreland College for Management Studies 11 Westmoreland St 2 (6795324/7266) - ACCA dip in financial management

FINE ARTS see also Art Appreciation

Institute of Professional Auctioneers & Valuers 129 Lr Baggot St 2 (6785685) - fine & decorative arts, cert, 15 wks €750

FINNISH see also Languages

Sandford Language Institute Milltown Pk Sandford Rd 6 (2601296) - all levels, 15 wks €285

FIRE FIGHTING

Civil Defence Esplanade Wolftone Qy 7 (6772699) - various centres

FIRE PREVENTION

Institution of Fire Engineers 77 Ballyroan Road 16 (4943669) - fire safety/engineering

FIRST AID

Ballymun Trinity CS, Adult Ed Centre 9 (8420654) - Wed 7.30 10wk, cert, €100

Ballyfermot CFE, Ballyfermot Rd 10 (6269421) - children's first aid, Mon 7-10pm 6 wks

Bray Institute of FE, Novara Ave Bray (2866111 / 2829668) - beginners Order of Malta, Tue 7.30 8 wks, €90, cert

Civil Defence Esplanade Wolftone Qy 7 (6772699) - various centres

Coláiste Dhúlaigh CFE,Barryscourt Rd Coolock 17 (8481337) - Tue 7.30 9 wks

Coláiste Eanna, Kilkieran Rd Cabra 7 (8389577) - dealing with emergencies, 10 wks, Tues, 7-9pm

Colaiste Ide Cardiffsbridge Rd Finglas W 8443233 11 (8342333) - occupational, Thurs 10 wks 7-10, HSA €145

Coolmine Community School Clonsilla 15 (8214583) - basic, Tue 10wk, €80

Dún Laoghaire CFE, 17 Cumberland St Dún Laoghaire (2809676) - Tues, 10 wks, 7.30-9.30pm, €110

FAS Training Centre Loughlinstown Wyattville Rd, DL (2043600) - occupational first aid, 6 wks

Foxrock Institute Kill o' the Grange, Kill Lane Blackrock (4939506) - Tue eve 8 wks €105, Red Cross cert

Greendale Community School Kilbarrack 5 (8322735) - Tues, 7-9pm, 8wks, cert €100

Hartstown Community School Clonsilla 15 (8209863) - cert, 8 wks, €75

Holy Family Community School Rathcoole (4580766)

Irish Red Cross Society 16 Merrion Sq 2 (6765135) - Occupational and private First Aid / also courses in Caring, Therapeutic Hand Care and Skin Camouflage

Kylemore College Kylemore Rd 10 (6265901) - occupational, FETAC 2 12 wks Wed 7-9pm

Malahide Community School (8460949) - Order of Malta, Thurs 7.30pm 10 wks €80

Marino College 14-20 Marino Mart 3 (8332100) - red cross, Tues, 10 wks, €105/ refresher course 8 wks €75

Newpark Adult Education Centre Newtownpark Ave Blackrock (2884376 / 2883725) - Irish Red Cross, 9wks, €120, Mon 7.30-9.30

NIFAST Ltd 46 Airways Industrial Estate Santry 17 (8424333) - occupational, day

Obus School of Healing Therapies, 53 Beech Grove Lucan (6282121) - 1 day €110 cert

Old Bawn Community School Tallaght 24 (4526137) - Irish Red Cross, basic cert, Tues, 10wks, 7.30-9.30

Order of Malta Ambulance Corps St John's House 32 Clyde Rd 4 (6684891) - occupational/ basic/ manual handling: up to 10 wks, cert/ AED training for dip

Palmerstown CS - Pobailscoil Iosolde, Kennelsfort Rd 20 (6260116) - Order of Malta, cert, Mon 8pm 8 wks €90

Plunket College Swords Rd, Whitehall 9 (8371689) - all aspects: Tues, 12 wks, €108 HEA recog.

Pobalscoil Rosmini Adult Ed Grace Pk Rd 9 (8371015) - beginners, techniques & proceedures, Red Cross, Wed 7.30-9.30, cert

Portmarnock Community School Carrickhill Rd (8038056) - civil defence, Tue 7.30 10 wks 7.30-9.20

Saint Finian's Community College Swords (8402623) - Tue, Irish Red Cross, 8 wks

Saint John's Ambulance Brigade 29 Upr Leeson St 4 (6688077) - 9 wks, cert, various venues/ 3 day occupational first aid/ also - basic life support (BLS) and automated external defibrillator (AED) course

Sea & Shore Safety Services Ltd Happy Valley Glenamuck Rd 18 (2955991) - elementary first aid, 1 day €120/ medical, 3 day €195 STCW'95 approved a-VI / 1-3

St Kevin's College Clogher Rd Crumlin 12 (4536397) - REC rescue & emergency care (Ireland), cert

St MacDara's CC, Wellington Lane Templeogue 6W (4566216) - Mon, 7.30-9.30pm, 8 wks, €104, cert

St Tiernan's Community School Parkvale Balally 16 (2953224) - for the home, beginners, Wed 10 wks €95 Order of Malta cert

Stillorgan CFE, Old Road Stillorgan (2880704) - Mon 7.30-9pm 9 wks €89 (Irish Red Cross)

Taney Parish Centre Taney Rd Dundrum 14 (2985491) - Red Cross, Tues (2981117) day

FISHING / Angling

Coolmine Community School Clonsilla 15 (8214583) - fly fishing wed 7.30 10 wks €70

Network Club 24 Elmcastle Green Tallaght 24 (4524415)

FITNESS - HEALTH/LEISURE see also Health / Keep-Fit

Hegarty Fitness Centre 53 Middle Abbey St 1 (8723080) - dynamic health, from €120,home/office/city centre, also day

Irish Yoga Association PO Box 9969 7 (4929213/ 087 2054489) - qualified teachers available all over Ireland/ 4 yr Teacher Training courses

Jackie Skelly's Fitness 42 Clarendon St, 2; Park West, Nangor Rd, 12 & Applewood Village, Swords, & Ashbourne (6770040) - aerobics, spin, toning, taebo, pilates, yoga/ weight-loss courses 10wks

Motions Health & Fitness Training (087 2808866) - Fitness Instructor training diploma course (ITEC), part-time, 9 hours per week. Venue Citywest Hotel & Leisure Centre, Naas Rd

National Training Centre 16a St Joseph's Parade Dorset St 7 (8827777)

Phibsboro Gym 1st Floor, Phibsboro SC 7 (8301849) - body sculpting

Taney Parish Centre Taney Rd Dundrum 14 (2985491) - gentle exercise, League of Health: Mon, Wed, day only, 0404 66423

FLORISTRY COURSE

Crescent Flower Studios 15 Ballyroan Cres 16 (4947507) - start your own floristry business course, Saturdays, private tuition

Crumlin College of FE, Crumlin Rd 12 (4540662) - FETAC course: p/time day 25wks Mon 9.15-1.15pm

Firhouse Community College Firhouse Rd 24 (4525807) - Tue 7.30-9.30pm 8 wks €119

Tallaght Community School Balrothery 24 (4515566) - for beginners, 7.30-9.30 8 wks €70

FLOWER ARRANGING

Ashfield College Main St Templeogue 6W (4900866) - fresh, 7.30-9.30, 8 wks

Ballinteer Community School Ballinteer 16 (2988195)

Ballymun Trinity CS, Adult Ed Centre 9 (8420654) - Tue, 7.30 6wks €75

Bray Institute of FE, Novara Ave Bray (2866111 / 2829668) - Wed 7.30 10 wks, €85

Cabinteely Community School Johnstown Rd 18 (2857455) - 10wk, €95

Coláiste Dhúlaigh CFE, Barryscourt Rd Coolock 17 (8481337) - Thurs 10-12pm 10 wks

Coolmine Community School Clonsilla 15 (8214583) - Mon, 7.30-9.30 10 wks €70

Crumlin College of FE, Crumlin Rd 12 (4540662) - for seasonal & special occasions, Tues, 10 wks 7.30-9.30

Donahies Community School Streamville Rd 13 (8482217) - beginners Tues, 10 wks, €85

Greenhills College Limekiln Ave Walkinstown 12 (4507779/4507863) - beginners/intermediate 10wks, €130

Hartstown Community School Clonsilla 15 (8209863) - 10 wks €85

Killester CFE, Collins Ave 5 (8337686) - Tue 7.30-9.30, 10 wks 70

KLEAR Grange Park View Kilbarrack 5 (8671845) - day

Knocklyon Youth & Community Centre, 16 (4931213) - floral art, Thurs 11.30-1.30 8 wk €85

Lucan Community College Esker Drive (6282077) - Mon beginners/ tue improvers: 7.30-8.30 10 wks €130

Malahide Community School Malahide (8460949) - floral art, 10 wks €90

Marino College 14-20 Marino Mart 3 (8332100) - Thurs 7.30, 10wks, €90/ Wed 1.30-3.30 €85

Newpark Adult Education Centre Newtownpark Ave Blackrock (2884376 / 2883725) - beginners/ improvers, 10 wks, €125 each, Tue/Thurs 7.30-9.45

Old Bawn Community School Tallaght 24 (4526137) - designing with flowers, Thurs, 7.30-9.30pm, 10 wks €95

Palmerstown CS - Pobailscoil Iosolde, Kennelsfort Rd 20 (6260116) - 8 wks Thurs 7.30 €70

Portmarnock Community School Carrickhill Rd (8038056) - Tue, 7.30 10 wks €100

St Finian's Community College Swords (8402623) - 8wks

St Kevin's College, Clogher Rd Crumlin 12 (4536397) - 10wks

St Tiernan's Community School Parkvale Balally 16 (2953224) - Wed 7.30 10 wks €95

TACT St Dominic's School St Dominic's Rd Tallaght 24 (4596757)

TARGET St Kevin's School Newbrook Rd, Donaghmede 13 (8671967) - day 10 wks €80

FLUTE see also Music

Abbey School of Music 9b Lr Abbey St 1 (8747908) - Michael McGrath

Bray Music Centre Florence Rd Bray (2866768)

Comhaltas Ceoltóirí Éireann 32 Belgrave Sq Monkstown (2800295)

Dún Laoghaire Music Centre 130A Lr George's St Dún Laoghaire (2844178)

Leinster School of Music Griffith College Campus South Circular Rd 8 (4150467)

Na Piobairi Uileann 15 Henrietta St 1 (8730093)

Newpark Music Centre Newtownpark Ave Blackrock (2883740) - also day

Scoil Shéamuis Ennis, Naul, Co Dublin (8020898 087 7870138)

Waltons New School of Music 69 Sth Gt George's St 2 (4781884) - classical & trad, also day, see ad page 155

FLYING see Aviation

FOCUSING SKILLS see also STUDY SKILLS

Pobalscoil Neasáin Baldoyle 13 (8063092) - intro to focusing, Tue 7.30, 10 wks €70

UCD Adult Education Centre Belfield (7167123) - Creative Thinking and Problem Solving; Focusing and Personality, 1 day Sat am/pm

FOLK ACTIVITIES/MUSIC see also Singing / Traditional

Dublin Folk Dance Group 48 Ludford Drive Ballinteer 16 (2987929) - adult international dance, ongoing

FOOD SCIENCE see also Nutrition

DIT Faculty: Tourism & Food Cathal Brugha St 1 (4023000) - MSc food safety management, 2yrs €3600 pa/ food product development centre courses 1/2 days each/ dip in meat apprenticeship 3 yrs

FOOTBALL see also Gaelic / Rugby / Soccer

Football Assoc of Ireland 80 Merrion Sq Sth 2 (6766864) - soccer

FORK LIFT TRUCK TRAINING

FACTS Training Damastown Way Damastown Ind Pk 15 (8694700) - forklift driving safety, 8 eve cert €710; 4 eve cert, €395 /day 5 days cert, €710; 2 day cert €395

FAS Training Centre Ballyfermot 10 (6055900)

NIFAST Ltd 46 Airways Industrial Estate Santry 17 (8424333) - day

FRENCH (BEGINNERS to ADVANCED) see also Languages

Aisling Language Services 137 Lr Rathmines Rd 6 (4971902) - beginners, 7.30-9.30 10 wks €160

Alliance Francaise 1 Kildare St 2 (6761632); Alliance-Sud Foxrock Ave 18 (2898760) - groups and one-to-one 32 hrs €285/ conversation classes / dip, cert / workshops

Ashfield College Main St Templeogue 6W (4900866) - beginners & improvers 8wks each 7.30-9.30pm

Balbriggan Community College Pine Ridge Chapel St (8412388/9) - Mon 7.30-9pm 8 wks €78

Ballymun Trinity CS,s Adult Ed Centre 9 (8420654) - beginners/improvers: Tue 7 & 8.30, 10wk, €90

Bray Institute of FE, Novara Ave Bray (2866111 / 2829668) - beginners, Mon/ intermediate, Tue: 10wks €85 each

Cabinteely Community School Johnstown Rd 18 (2857455) - beginners/improvers, 10wk, €95 each

Coláiste Dhúlaigh CFE, Barryscourt Rd Coolock 17 (8481337) - beginners/ intermediate, Mon 6.30 & 7pm, 10 wks/ FETAC cert Mon 1-2pm, 25 wks

Colaiste Ide Cardiffsbridge Rd Finglas W 8443233 11 (8342333) - beginners, Tue 7-10pm 10 wks €150, cert/ for leaving cert Thurs 7-10pm 20 wks €300

College of Further Education Main St Dundrum 14 (2951376) - Tue & Thurs 7-9pm 8 wks €104

Coolmine Community School Clonsilla 15 (8214583) - beginners Mon 10 wks €80/ improvers Tue 20wk €150: 7.30-9.30

Crumlin College of FE, Crumlin Rd 12 (4540662) - beginners, Thurs, 6.45-8.15 20 wks

DATE Centre CFE, Dundrum 14 (2964322 (9.30am-12pm)) - beginners, 10 wks €97/ Le Club, 1 to 4, day/ beginners/ conversational: each 10 wks €97

Donahies Community School Streamville Rd 13 (8482217) - levels 1, 2 & 3: Mon 7.30, 10 wks, €85 each

Dún Laoghaire CFE, 17 Cumberland St Dún Laoghaire (2809676) - levels 1 & 2, Tues, 10 wks, 7.30 & 8.30pm €90

Dún Laoghaire-Rathdown Co Council Public Library Service - Deansgrange lib, Clonkeen Dr (2850860) - Fr/Eng - informal sessions, Thurs 10.30-12 morn

Firhouse Community College Firhouse Rd 24 (4525807) - beginners, - Mon, Tue 7.30-9.30pm 8 wks €104

Foxrock Institute Kill o' the Grange, Kill Lane Blackrock (4939506) - beginners/improvers 8wks, €105

Greendale Community School Kilbarrack 5 (8322735) - absolute beginners/ continuation, Tue, 7.30/ 8.30 10 wks, €90 each/ also Thur 11.30am

Greenhills College Limekiln Ave Walkinstown 12 (4507779/4507863) - 10 wks, €130

Hartstown Community School Clonsilla 15 (8209863) - beginners, 10wks, €85 each

Inchicore CFE, Emmet Rd 8 (4535358)

Killester CFE, Collins Ave 5 (8337686) - beginners /improvers: Mon: 7pm/8.30, 10 wks €60 each

Kilternan Adult Education Centre Ballybetagh Rd Kilternan 18 (2952050) - conversation Thur 7.30/ improvers 8.15: 10 wks €65

KLEAR Grange Park View Kilbarrack 5 (8671845) - advanced, day only

Kylemore College Kylemore Rd 10 (6265901) - 10 wks Tues 7-9pm, beg-intermediate

Langtrain International Torquay Rd Foxrock 18 (2893876) - €96 per term

Language Centre NUI Maynooth Co Kildare (7083737) - all levels, 18wk, €350 cert

Lucan Community College Esker Drive (6282077) - beginners Mon/ improvers Tue 7.30-8.30 10 wks €130

Malahide Community School Malahide (8460949) - beginners, Thurs, 10 wks €90

Marino College 14-20 Marino Mart 3 (8332100) - beginners/intermediate, Tue, Thurs 10 wks, €60 each/ 20 wks €130

Newpark Adult Education Centre Newtownpark Ave Blackrock (2884376 / 2883725) - conversation, 10wks / all levels 1-4, €120 each, Mon 7.30-9.30

Old Bawn Community School Tallaght 24 (4526137) - level 1/2, conversation, advanced: 10 wks €90

Palmerstown CS - Pobailscoil Iosolde, Kennelsfort Rd 20 (6260116) - level 1&2, Mon 6.45 & 9.45pm 10 wks €75

People's College for Continuing Education & Training 32 Parnell Sq 1 (8735879) - all levels, €60

Plunket College Swords Rd, Whitehall 9 (8371689) - conversation, beginners Tue/ advanced Mon: 10 wks, €90 each

Pobalscoil Neasáin Baldoyle 13 (8063092) - Tue 10 wks €85

Pobalscoil Rosmini Adult Ed Grace Pk Rd 9 (8371015) - beginners, Mon 7-8.20/ continuation 1, Mon 8.30-9.50/ continuation 2 Wed 7-820: each €90/ advanced, Pt 1 of 20 wk course, Wed 8.30-9.50 €90

Rathmines CFE - Senior College, Town Hall 6 (4975334) - beginners, Mon, 20 wks €175/ intermediate/advanced, Tue & Wed, 25 wks, €165, 6 & 7.30pm

Ringsend Technical Institute Cambridge Rd 4 (6684498) - beginners/ improvers,

TRINITY COLLEGE
The University of Dublin

Extramural courses and afternoon/evening/weekend degree and diploma courses 2006-2007

Brochure of all part-time courses available to download from: www.tcd.ie/Admissions

Alternatively, contact the Admissions Office, West Theatre, Trinity College, Dublin 2.

Tel: 01-896 3664/01-896 1532/ 01-896 1072

Mon 7 & 8.30: 10wks, €70

Saint Finian's Community College Swords (8402623) - 8 wks

Sandford Language Institute Milltown Pk Sandford Rd 6 (2601296) - all levels, 15 wks €240; also day

St MacDara's CC, Wellington Lane Templeogue 6W (4566216) - Mon, beginners: 7.30-9.30pm, 8 wks, €104

St Tiernan's Community School Parkvale Balally 16 (2953224) - absolute beginners, Mon 7.30 10 wks €95

Sth Dublin Co Libraries (4597834-admin only) - classes free: Ballyroan (4941900), Castletymon (4524888)

Clondalkin (4593315), Lucan (6216422), Tallaght (4620073).

Stillorgan Senior College Old Road Stillorgan (2880704)

Tallaght Community School Balrothery 24 (4515566) - basic conversation, 10 wks 7.30-9.00 €70

TARGET St Kevin's School Newbrook Rd, Donaghmede 13 (8671967) - day only, CDVEC , beginners, intermediate, advanced

WORDS Language Services 44 Northumberland Rd 4 (6610240) - individual tuition only

FRENCH - COMMERCIAL / BUSINESS

Alliance Francaise 1 Kildare St 2 (6761632); Alliance-Sud Foxrock Ave 18 (2898760) - business French / also, CORPORATE courses, in-company classes contact Christine Weld for details (6381441)

Sandford Language Institute Milltown Pk Sandford Rd 6 (2601296)

WORDS Language Services 44 Northumberland Rd 4 (6610240) - individual tuition only

FRENCH FOR HOLIDAYS

Holy Family Community School Rathcoole (4580766)

FRENCH POLISHING

Cabinteely Community School Johnstown Rd 18 (2857455) - 10wk, €95

Greendale Community School Kilbarrack 5 (8322735) - & antique repairs, Thurs, 7.30-9.30pm, 10wks, €95

FRENCH, LEGAL

Alliance Francaise 1 Kildare St 2 (6761632); Alliance-Sud Foxrock Ave 18 (2898760) - dip in legal French, from October; contact Louise Stirling for details (6381445)

FUNDING / FINANCE see Banking, Financial Services

FURNISHINGS see Crafts / Curtain Making / House / Soft Furnishings

FURNITURE MAKING

Kylemore College Kylemore Rd 10 (6265901) - veneer & marquetery, FETAC, 18 WKS Thurs 1.30-4.30

FURNITURE RESTORATION see also Antiques

Kilternan Adult Education Group Ballybetagh Rd Kilternan 18 (2952050) - Wed 11.45 10 wks €130

Newpark Adult Education Centre, Newtownpark Ave Blackrock (2884376 / 2883725) - antiques, Mon/Thurs 7.30-9.45 10 wks €125

St Kevin's College, Clogher Rd Crumlin 12 (4536397) - 10wks

GAELIC GAMES (Football, Hurling & Handball) Camogie

Cumann Camogaiochta na nGael Pairc an Chrocaigh St Joseph's Ave 3 (8364619)

GARDA EXAMS

Kilroy's College Wentworth House Grand Canal Street Lr 2 (6620538 1850-700700) - home-study, preparation/ stages 1 & 2

GARDENING

Ashfield College Main St Templeogue 6W (4900866) - creative gardening, 7.30-9.30 8 wks

Ballymun Trinity CS, Adult Ed Centre 9 (8420654) - all aspects of gardening, Tue 7.30 10 wks €100

BASE Ballyboden Adult Social Education Whitechurch Library Taylor's Lane 16 (4935953) - 10 wks

Cabinteely Community School Johnstown Rd 18 (2857455) - design & flair, 10wk, €95

Coolmine Community School Clonsilla 15 (8214583) - practical, 9wk, Mon €70

DATE Centre CFE, Dundrum 14 (2964322 (9.30am-12pm)) - the autumn garden, 9.30am 10 wks €97

Dublin Institute of Design 25 Suffolk St 2 (6790286) - BTEC higher dip in garden design, 2 eves wkly, 2 yr; f-time 2 yrs/ cert in garden design, 1 eve 12 wks

Dublin School of Horticulture 28 Spencer Villas Dún Laoghaire (2148469) - RHS cert courses/ correspondence

Dún Laoghaire CFE, 17 Cumberland St Dún Laoghaire (2809676) - design, Mon, 7.30-9.30pm, 10 wks, €110

FAS Training Centre Ballyfermot 10 (6055900)

Foxrock Institute Kill o' the Grange, Kill Lane Blackrock (4939506) - garden design, Mon eve 8 wks €105

Greendale Community School Kilbarrack 5 (8322735) - & horticulture, Tues, 7.30-9.30pm, 8wks, €95

Hartstown Community School Clonsilla 15 (8209863) - & design, 10wks, €85

Killester CFE, Collins Ave 5 (8337686) - for fun, tue 7.30 10 wks €90

Kilternan Adult Education Group Ballybetagh Rd Kilternan 18 (2952050) - autumn garden, Tue 11.45-1pm 12 wks 497

Kylemore College Kylemore Rd 10 (6265901) - horticulture, practical 1 & 2, FETAC 12 wks Tue & Thurs 10.30-1pm

Newpark Adult Education Centre Newtownpark Ave Blackrock (2884376 / 2883725) - Tues 7.30-9.45pm, 10wks, €120/ flora & fauna Thurs 10 wks €120

Old Bawn Community School Tallaght 24 (4526137) - beginners, planning a garden, Tues / garden design, Thurs: each 7.30-9.30, 10wks €95

Palmerstown CS - Pobailscoil Iosolde, Kennelsfort Rd 20 (6260116) - and garden design, Mon 7.30, 10 wks €70

People's College for Continuing Education & Training 32 Parnell Sq 1 (8735879) - 10 wks €60

Stillorgan CFE, Old Road Stillorgan (2880704) - Mon 7.30 10 wks €130

TACT St Dominic's School St Dominic's Rd Tallaght 24 (4596757)

Taney Parish Centre Taney Rd Dundrum 14 (2985491) - Tues (2809602/086 8920859), day only

The Garden School (094 9649943) - by correspondence, RHS cert

Trinity College 2 (8961000) - (8961274) - extra mural, practical garden skills 2007 mid-June 1 wk €150

UCD Adult Education Centre Belfield (7167123) - the ecological gardener in the organic kitchen, Sat 1 day spring/ ecological gardening, Thurs 10 wks

GENEALOGY

Newpark Adult Education Centre, Newtownpark Ave Blackrock (2884376 / 2883725) - family history & research, Tues, 7.30-9.45 10 wks €120 -

UCD Adult Education Centre Belfield (7167123) - Genealogy/Family History, module 1&2 (10 wks each); Family history, levels 2-3 (20 wks each) cert ; level 4 (30 wks) dip/ Irish Demography, 1650 - 1911: sources and methodologies 10 wks, spring

GEOGRAPHY see also Surveying

KLEAR Grange Park View Kilbarrack 5 (8671845) - Western Europe made easy

Plunket College Swords Rd, Whitehall 9 (8371689) - leaving cert, 27 wks, €425

GEOLOGY

Trinity College 2 (8961000) - a brief history of life on earth, eve 6 wks €60 (islanders@tcd.ie)

GERMAN see also Languages / Leaving Cert

Ashfield College Main St Templeogue 6W (4900866) - beginners stage 1 / improvers stage 2 7.30-9.30 8 wks each

Bray Institute of FE, Novara Ave Bray (2866111 / 2829668) - beginners, Mon 7.30 10 wks €85

Coláiste Dhúlaigh CFE, Barryscourt Rd Coolock 17 (8481337) - beginners/improvers, Tues 10 wks/ FETAC cert 25 wks, Mon 1-2pm; 7-9.30pm

College of Further Education Main St Dundrum 14 (2951376) - beginners, Tue 7-9pm 8 wks €104

DATE Centre CFE, Dundrum 14 (2964322 (9.30am-12pm)) - beginners/ Level 2: each 10 wks €97 day

Donahies Community School Streamville Rd 13 (8482217) - Tue 7.30 10 wks €95

Dún Laoghaire CFE, 17 Cumberland St Dún Laoghaire (2809676) - levels 1 & 2, Mon, 10 wks, 7&8.30pm, €95

Dún Laoghaire-Rathdown Co Council Public Library Service - Deansgrange lib, Clonkeen Dr (2850860) - Ger/Eng - informal sessions, Wed 10.30-12 morn

Goethe Institut 62 Fitzwilliam Sq 2 (6801110) - beginners/intermediate/advanced, 16wks/ also special courses/ diploma & cert courses 16wks/ summer courses 2-6 wks eve

Greendale Community School Kilbarrack 5 (8322735) - conversation, level 1, Thurs, 7-8.30pm, 10 wks, €85

Hartstown Community School Clonsilla 15 (8209863) - 10 wks €85

Holy Family Community School Rathcoole (4580766)

Inchicore CFE, Emmet Rd 8 (4535358)

Langtrain International Torquay Rd Foxrock 18 (2893876) - €96 per term

Language Centre NUI Maynooth Co Kildare (7083737) - 18wk, €350 cert

Marino College 14-20 Marino Mart 3 (8332100) - beginners, €65/intermediate, €90, Tues 10 wks

Newpark Adult Education Centre Newtownpark Ave Blackrock (2884376 / 2883725) - 2 levels, Mon 10wks, €120 7.30-9.30pm

People's College for Continuing Education & Training 32 Parnell Sq 1 (8735879)

Plunket College Swords Rd, Whitehall 9 (8371689) - conversation, beginners, Tues, 10 wks, €90

Pobalscoil Rosmini Adult Ed Grace Pk Rd 9 (8371015) - beginners, Mon 7-8.20pm €90

Sandford Language Institute Milltown Pk Sandford Rd 6 (2601296) - all levels, 15 wks €240; also day

St Finian's Community College Swords (8402623) - 8 wks

Sth Dublin Co Libraries (4597834-admin only) - conversation classes, Ballyroan (4941900) free

Tallaght Community School Balrothery 24 (4515566) - basic conversation, 10 wks 7.30-9.30 €70

WORDS Language Services 44 Northumberland Rd 4 (6610240) - individual tuition only

GERMAN CULTURE

Goethe Institut 62 Fitzwilliam Sq 2 (6801110) - literature, conversation German, 16wks/ cultural events

pobalscoil iosolde

Palmerstown, Dublin 20. Tel: **6260116**

Email: **info@adulted.ie**   **www.adulted.ie**

Enrol: Sept 4-7 & Sept 11-14: 10am-12 & 2 - 4 pm

Eve Enrol: Sept 7 & 11: 7-8.30pm

GERMAN FOR HOLIDAYS
WORDS Language Services 44 Northumberland Rd 4 (6610240) - individual tuition only

GERMAN, COMMERCIAL
Goethe Institut 62 Fitzwilliam Sq 2 (6801110) - banking, finance, legal 16 wks/ diploma courses, guest speakers 16 wks

WORDS Language Services 44 Northumberland Rd 4 (6610240) - individual tuition only

GLIDING
Dublin Gliding Club (087 9025023)

GLOBALISATION & TRADE see also Development Studies
Comhlámh 10 Upr Camden St 2 (4783490) - courses on issues in development and on trade

GOLF CLASSES
Ballinteer Community School Ballinteer 16 (2988195)

Bray Institute of FE, Novara Ave Bray (2866111 / 2829668) - Mon 8.30 8 wks €95

Cabinteely Community School Johnstown Rd 18 (2857455) - beginners & improvers, limited class size, 10wk, €95 each

Corporate Club 24 Elmcastle Green Tallaght 24 (4610935)

Dominick Reilly PGA, Foxrock 18 (087 6487543)

Donahies Community School Streamville Rd 13 (8482217) - Mon, Wed 7.30 & 8.30pm, 5 wks œ110

Dún Laoghaire CFE, 17 Cumberland St Dún Laoghaire (2809676) - Tues, beginners, 7.30/ improvers, 8.45, €125 each

Elmgreen Golf Course Castleknock 15 (8200797)

Foxrock Institute Kill o' the Grange, Kill Lane Blackrock (4939506) - beginners/improvers, 8wks, €110 each

Greendale Community School Kilbarrack 5 (8322735) - clinic at driving range, Tues/Thurs, 10 wks, €90 each

Hartstown Community School Clonsilla 15 (8209863) - beginners/intermediate, advanced, 6wks, €90 each

Holy Family Community School Rathcoole (4580766)

Knocklyon Youth & Community Centre, 16 (4931213) - beginners/ improvers, Wed 10am/11am, 10 wks €95/ 7pm/8pm, 8 wks €85

Malahide Community School Malahide (8460949) - 7wks, Tues & Thurs, €95ea

Network Club 24 Elmcastle Green Tallaght 24 (4524415)

Old Bawn Community School Tallaght 24 (4526137) - beginners/improvers: morn & eve €120/ advanced, evenings €145; ea 10 wks

Palmerstown CS - Pobalscoil Iosolde, Kennelsfort Rd 20 (6260116) - beginners/ improvers, Tues 7&8pm 8 wks €90 each

Physio-Extra 4 Oliver Bond St 8 (087 7818300 6685048) - golf solution: prof approved muscle & spinal improvement method, morn, day, eve 10 hrs

Pobalscoil Neasáin Baldoyle 13 (8063092) - Tue 3 classes 10 wks €90

Portmarnock Community School Carrickhill Rd (8038056) - beginners/ improvers, Mon 10 wks €100

St Tiernan's Community School Parkvale Balally 16 (2953224) - beginners, Tue 10am & 7pm, 8 wks €130/ improvers, Tue 11.15am & 7pm, 8 wks €130

GOLF COURSES & DRIVING RANGES

Corballis Public Golf Course Donabate (8436583) - 18 hole links

Elmgreen Golf Course Castleknock 15 (8200797)

Leopardstown Golf Centre Foxrock 18 (2895341)

Open Golf Centre Newtown Hse St Margaret's (8640324) - tuition available

Spawell Golf Range Templeogue 6W (4907990) - beginners, improvers, day/eve 6 wks €80

GOLF, PSYCHOLOGY OF

Kilroy's College Wentworth House Grand Canal Street Lr 2 (6620538 1850-700700) - tutor supported home study

GORGE WALKING

Clondalkin Sports & Leisure Centre Nangor Rd Clondalkin 22 (4574858)

GRAPHIC DESIGN

Adelaide Computers 14 Pembroke Lane Ballsbridge 4 (2696213) - photoshop, dreamweaver, quark express, illustrator

Ballyfermot CFE, Ballyfermot Rd 10 (6269421) - Fetac 5 Wed 7-10pm 22 wks

CITAS Computer & I.T. Training 54 Middle Abbey St 1 (8782212) - QuarkXpress, photoshop, illustrator, 6 wks Thurs 6-9pm €600

Coláiste Dhúlaigh CFE, Barryscourt Rd Coolock 17 (8481337) - with portfolio, Fetac Mon, Tue, 20 wks

Crumlin College of FE, Crumlin Rd 12 (4540662) - advertising & graphic design, f/time day

Eden Computer Training Rathfarnham 16 & 1 Green St 7 (4953155)

FAS Training Centre Tallaght Cookstown Indl Est 24 (4045200)

Griffith College Dublin Sth Circular Rd 8 (4150400) - Photoshop/ Quarkexpress, GCD cert: each p/t end-user 1 eve wkly

Irish Academy of Computer Training 98 St Stephen's Green 2 (4347662) - dtp course 24 wks, cert/ quarkxpress; corel draw; ms pub; adobe photoshop & illustrator; framemaker: ea 8 wks, cert/ frontpage 4 wks cert / also day

New Media Technology College, 13 Harcourt St 2 (4780905) - 3D studio Max/ adobe photoshop/ macromedia flash: each, , 8 wks eve 6.30-9.30 or Sat 10-1 or 2-5pm

Portobello School 43 Lr Dominick St 1 (8721277) - Autocad, C&G cert 6.30-9.30, 32 wks

Ringsend Technical Institute Cambridge Rd 4 (6684498) - photoshop, begin. 10 wks €125

Senior College Dún Laoghaire, CFE Eblana Ave Dún Laoghaire (2800385) - cert in computer imaging, FETAC, €310/ cert in web authoring, FETAC, €310

GRAPHOLOGY (Handwriting Analysis)

Institute of Graphology 22 Forest Hill Drogheda Co Louth - by correspondence (send SAE for details)

GREEK - CLASSICAL & MODERN see also Languages

Sandford Language Institute Milltown Pk Sandford Rd 6 (2601296) - modern & aencient - all levels subject to demand, 15 wks €285

Trinity College 2 (8961000) - (8968589) - extra mural, beginners modern Greek, €150/intermediate, €80, 22wks each

GROOMING & MAKE-UP see also Beauty Care

College of Further Education Main St Dundrum 14 (2951376)

Colour Connections B Egan 4 (087 6288582) - make-up & skin care, small classes

Foxrock Institute Kill o' the Grange, Kill Lane Blackrock (4939506) - colour, image & style, 6wks, €105

Newpark Adult Education Centre Newtownpark Ave Blackrock (2884376 / 2883725) - beauty therapy, Thurs 7.30-9.45 10 wks €120

Tallaght Community School Balrothery 24 (4515566) - make-up & skin care 10 wks 7.30-9.30 €70

GUITAR see also Music

Abbey School of Music 9b Lr Abbey St 1 (8747908) - Kevin Robinson ALCM / Electric guitar / bass - Trea Breazeale

Ballymun Men's Centre Lift Shaft 4 Shangan Rd Ballymun 9 (8623117) - Beginners to advanced, guitars provided, Thurs afternoon

Ballymun Trinity CS, Adult Ed Centre 9 (8420654) - Mon 7.30-9.30 10 wks €100

Bill Brady School of Guitar 92 Pecks Lane Castleknock 15 (8210466 / 8220611)

Bray Institute of FE, Novara Ave Bray (2866111 / 2829668) - beginners/improvers, Tues 7.00/ 8.30 10wks, €85

Bray Music Centre Florence Rd Bray (2866768)

Cabinteely Community School Johnstown Rd 18 (2857455) - folk, beginners/improvers, 10wk, €50 each

Carl Alfred 6 Palmerston Villas, Basement Fl 2 off Upr Rathmines Rd 6 (4972095) - hear-feel method popular-guitar course. Free preview

Clontarf School of Music 6 Marino Mart 3 (8330936 087 8054963) - acoustic/Irish trad/jazz /electric/ classical, 18wk - also day / group & private

Coláiste Dhúlaigh CFE, Barryscourt Rd Coolock 17 (8481337) - beginners, Tue 6-7.20pm 10 wks

Coláiste Eanna, Kilkieran Rd Cabra 7 (8389577) - beginners, recreation & folk, 10wks, Thurs 7-9pm

Coolmine Community School Clonsilla 15 (8214583) - beginners, improvers, advanced: Mon, Tue, Wed : 7, 8 & 9pm 10 wks €60 ea

Dublin School of Guitar 36/37 Harrington St 8 (4053848) - all styles, individual tuition, grades/dips; junior / leaving cert, 10wk, €200; also day

Dún Laoghaire Music Centre 130A Lr George's St Dún Laoghaire (2844178)

Dundrum Family Recreation Centre Meadowbrook 16 (2984654)

Firhouse Community College Firhouse Rd 24 (4525807) - cont, Tue 7.30-9.30pm 8 wks €104

Foxrock Institute Kill o' the Grange, Kill Lane Blackrock (4939506) - 8wks, €105

Greendale Community School Kilbarrack 5 (8322735) - beginners Thurs, 10 wks, €90

Greenhills College Limekiln Ave Walkinstown 12 (4507779/4507863) - beginners/improvers, 10 wks, €130

Hartstown Community School Clonsilla 15 (8209863) - 10wks, €60

Hollywood Academy Dublin 13-14 Sackville Pl 1 (8786909) - from 4-8pm: 11 mths €75 per mth, cert

Holy Family Community School Rathcoole (4580766)

John Murphy Guitar Studio 38 Dellbrook Pk Ballinteer Rd Dundrum 16 (2962797) - group lessons, beginners Tue & Wed 10 wks

John Ward 5 Tibradden Drive Walkinstown 12 (4520918) - popular & classical preparation for TCL grade exams - also day

Kilternan Adult Education Group Ballybetagh Rd Kilternan 18 (2952050) - beginners/ improvers 7 & 8pm 10 wks €75

Knocklyon Youth & Community Centre, 16 (4931213) - Wed 8-9.30 8 wks €85

Kylemore College Kylemore Rd 10 (6265901) - beg-improvers, 10 wks 7-9pm

Leinster School of Music Griffith College Campus South Circular Rd 8 (4150467)

Lucan Community College Esker Drive (6282077) - Tue 7&8 10 wks €130/ also improvers 9pm

Marino College 14-20 Marino Mart 3 (8332100) - beginners/intermediate, 6.30/8pm Tues, 10wks, €65 each

Melody School of Music 178E Whitehall Rd W Perrystown 12 (4650150) - also day; 12 wks

Newpark Adult Education Centre Newtownpark Ave Blackrock (2884376 / 2883725) - beginners, 10 wks, €95, Thurs 7pm or 8.30pm

Newpark Music Centre Newtownpark Ave Blackrock (2883740) - jazz guitar, also day

Old Bawn Community School Tallaght 24 (4526137) - beginners, tHURS/improvers, Tue: each 10 wks €95

Palmerstown CS - Pobailscoil Iosolde, Kennelsfort Rd 20 (6260116) -beginners/ improvers, Tues 7pm 10 wks, €70 each

Parnell School of Music & Performing Arts 13-14 Sackville Pl 1 (8786909) - from 4-8pm, cert

People's College for Continuing Education & Training 32 Parnell Sq 1 (8735879) - classical, €60

Plunket College Swords Rd, Whitehall 9 (8371689) - beginners, Tues, 10 wks, €90

Pobalscoil Rosmini Adult Ed Grace Pk Rd 9 (8371015) - beginners 1 & 2: Mon, 7pm & 8.30, €90 each

Portmarnock Community School Carrickhill Rd (8038056) - Tue 7.30, beginners/ advanced 8.30: 10 wks €80

Ringsend Technical Institute Cambridge Rd 4 (6684498) - beginners/ improvers,

10wks, €90 each Mon 7& 8.30

Scoil Shéamuis Ennis, Naul, Co Dublin (8020898 087 7870138)

St Finian's Community College Swords (8402623) - 8 wks

St MacDara's CC, Wellington Lane Templeogue 6W (4566216) - beginners Tue: 7.30 8 wks €104

St Tiernan's Community School Parkvale Balally 16 (2953224) - introductory, 10 wks Wed 7.30 €95

Tallaght Community School Balrothery 24 (4515566) - beginners / intermediate, 10 wks 7.30-9pm €70 each

Waltons New School of Music 69 Sth Gt George's St 2 (4781884) - classical, acoustic, electric, spanish/flamenco, jazz, bass, also day, see ad page 155

GYMNASTICS

Clondalkin Sports & Leisure Centre Nangor Rd Clondalkin 22 (4574858)

Pearse College Clogher Rd Crumlin 12 (4536661/4541544) - ITEC dip in gym instruction, day

HAIRDRESSING see also Beauty Care

Ballyfermot CFE, Ballyfermot Rd 10 (6269421) - eatensions/ eyelashes: each AINT cert 10 wks Wed 7-9pm

Coláiste Dhúlaigh CFE,Barryscourt Rd Coolock 17 (8481337) - hair extension technician cert 10 wks, permanent eyelash extension cert 5 wks: Mon 7-9pm/ 3rd & 4th yr apprentices, Mon, 2nd yr Tue, 1st yr Wed, all 9.00-2.30, each 25 wks cert/ basic hair care, Mon 7-9.15 8 wks

Crumlin College of FE, Crumlin Rd 12 (4540662) - day release, beginners thurs 9.15 & 4.30 / junior trade exam class; senior trade exam class (advanced practical & theory); master dip for qual. hairdressers (2 yrs) Mon 6.45/ barbershop techniques (Unisex) Mon 10 wks 7.30; cutting & styling (unisex), Tue 4.45/ refresher courses in latest techniques (various dates)

Greenhills College Limekiln Ave Walkinstown 12 (4507779/4507863) - hair care, Tue, 10 wks €130

Hartstown Community School Clonsilla 15 (8209863) - & hair care, weds, 10wks, €85

People's College for Continuing Education & Training 32 Parnell Sq 1 (8735879) - & theatrical wig, €60

Tallaght Community School Balrothery 24 (4515566) - haircutting, beginners 8 wks 7.30-9.30 €70

HAND CARE (Therapeutic)

Irish Red Cross Society 16 Merrion Sq 2 (6765135) - Therapeutic Hand Care and Skin Camouflage

HARMONICA

Waltons New School of Music 69 Sth Gt George's St 2 (4781884) - also day, see ad page 155

HARP

Bray Music Centre Florence Rd Bray (2866768)

Comhaltas Ceoltóirí Éireann 32 Belgrave Sq Monkstown (2800295)

Waltons New School of Music 69 Sth Gt George's St 2 (4781884) - also day, see ad page 155

Courses:–

temple bar natural healing centre
2, temple lane, temple bar, dublin, 2.
ph. 01 679 8786 www.meltonline.com info@meltonline.com

one year massage course
BUPA, VHI, VIVAS Approved Therapies
indian head massage workshop – Learn how to relax
through the traditional massage techniques of India –
a weekend workshop. Starting every month.

reflexology workshop – Reflexology helps to balance
and detoxify the body. This weekend workshop covers
all the anatomy and techniques that you will need to
use this therapy on yourself. Please call reception for
starting dates.

Traditional Chinese Medicine and Natural Health Clinic – open seven days a week

HEALING

Bray Institute of FE, Novara Ave Bray (2866111 / 2829668) - energy healing, Mon 7.30-9.30 10 wks €85

Foxrock Institute Kill o' the Grange, Kill Lane Blackrock (4939506) - herbal medicine; reflexology: each 8 wks, €105

Harmony Healing 41 Beneavin Pk Glasnevin 11 (8641768)

Healing House 24 O'Connell Ave Berkeley Rd 7 (8306413) - intro to healing therapies, spiritual healing, hands-on healing, numerology, aromatherapy, massage, indian head massage, reflexology, Australian bush flower essences, kinesiology , 10 wks (or wknd), 8-10pm Tues€200/ healing wkend 23rd/24th Sept €150/ support group - teaching, healing & visualisation, Mon 8-10 €10

Holistic Healing Centre 38 Dame St 2 (6710813) - healing massage ITEC dip

Motions Health & Fitness Training (087 2808866) - Diploma in Holistic Massage (ITEC), part-time course, 3 hours per week. Castleknock, Citywest & Naas

Moytura Healing Centre Rinn Rua Claremont Grove Killiney (2854005) - energy healing, cert, eve: Fri, 10 wks €190/ dip, Fri eve 30 wks €520

National College of Complementary Medical Ed, 16a St Joseph's Parade Off Dorset Street 7 (8827777) - neuromuscular therapy, NMT, one w/end per month, 15 mths, €3520 higher dip, wkends 2yrs €7000

Obus School of Healing Therapies, 53 Beech Grove Lucan (6282121) - aromatherapy, wkends 1 yr €2025, dip

Our Lady's Hospice Harold's Cross 6 (4068806 4068810) - exploring healing, Tue eve 16 wks Sept-June Tue 5.30-7.30 €495/ auricular candle therapy, 28-29 April07 10-5pm €175 incl lunch/ touch for healing 2 March07; 19 October07: 10-4pm €100 incl lunch

Physio Extra 37 Upr Grand Canal St 4 (087 7818300 6685048 6685048) - spineright: yoga with pilates

Shiatsu Ireland classes at 44 Adelaide Rd 2 (2962839) - shiatsu & massage - beginners & advanced

T'ai Chi Energy Centre Milltown Pk Conference Centre Sandford Rd Ranelagh 6 (4961533) - t'ai chi/qi gong - & wkend workshops

TACT St Dominic's School St Dominic's Rd Tallaght 24 (4596757)

Tony Quinn Centre 66/67 Eccles St 7 (8304211) - twice weekly, Tue+Thurs 12 & 6.30; €30 per wk, 2 sessions

HEALTH AND SAFETY see also Stress / Food Science

Coláiste Dhúlaigh CFE,Barryscourt Rd Coolock 17 (8481337) - Tue 7-9.15pm 20 wks

College of Progressive Education 27-29 Carysfort Ave Blackrock (4884300) - FETAC level 5 safety and health at work

DIT Faculty: Tourism & Food Cathal Brugha St 1 (4023000) - hygiene & safety in
services industry, 12 wks 1 eve €130/ MSc in environmental health safety
management, 2 yr €2000 pa

Dorset College 64 Lr Dorset St/ 8 Belvedere Pl 1 (8309677) - in childcare

Dún Laoghaire CFE, 17 Cumberland St Dún Laoghaire (2809676) - occupational
h & s (NISO) Wed 12 wks 7-9pm €460

FAS eCollege (2043732 ecollegeinfo@fas.ie) - online courses

FAS Training Centre Baldoyle 13 (8167400) - Safepass, 1 wk; Cabra Bannow Rd 7
(8821400) - Safe Pass 1 wk/ safety health & welfare at work 10 wks; Finglas Jamestown
Rd 11 (8140200) - Safe Pass 1 wk/ health & safety at work 10 wks; Loughlinstown
Wyattville Rd, DL (2043600) - Safe Pass 1 wk/ safety health welfare at work 10 wks

Institute of International Trade of Ireland 28 Merrion Square 2 (6612182) - dangerous
goods safety awareness advisor (road, sea air) 4 days

Keytrainer Ireland Ltd 6W (4922223) - tailored courses

NIFAST Ltd 46 Airways Industrial Estate Santry 17 (8424333) - various courses, day

Palmerstown CS - Pobailscoil Iosolde, Kennelsfort Rd 20 (6260116) - safe pass, Sats
10-5pm day €80

Plunket College Swords Rd, Whitehall 9 (8371689) - in the work place, Wed, 7-9.30 €90

Westmoreland College for Management Studies 11 Westmoreland St 2
(6795324/7266) - ICM cert in health & safety at work

HEALTH CARE & SOCIAL CARE see also Carers / Child Care

College of Progressive Education 27-29 Carysfort Ave Blackrock (4884300) - FETAC
level 5 full time health care support DHSXX part time care of the older person, care
support, safety and health at work, care skills, communications, work experience,
nutrition, introduction to nursing, intellectual and physical disability studies, caring
for people with disabilities

Dorset College 64 Lr Dorset St/ 8 Belvedere Pl 1 (8309677) - healthcare studies, -
FETAC level 5, Mon-thurs 9.30-2.30pm 1 yr

Inchicore CFE, Emmet Rd 8 (4535358) - support worker, 1 yr

HEALTH EDUCATION see also Aromatherapy / Bereavement / Diet / Mental Health / Nutrition / Personal Development / Self-Awareness / Stress

Alexander Technique Postural Re-education Frank Kennedy 35 Callary Rd Mt Merrion (2882446) - alexander technique/ stress management - also day

Coláiste Dhúlaigh CFE,Barryscourt Rd Coolock 17 (8481337) - human growth & development, Tue 7-9.20 20 wks/ mental health, Fetac, Tue 7-9.15 20 wks

Dún Laoghaire CFE, 17 Cumberland St Dún Laoghaire (2809676) - chi-kung health preservation, Wed 10 wks 8.30-9.30 €80

Health Promotion Unit Dept of Health Hawkins House 2 (6354000) - info, booklets, leaflets

Holistic Healing Centre 38 Dame St 2 (6710813)

Holy Family Community School Rathcoole (4580766)

Irish Computer Society / ICS Skills Crescent Hall, Mount St Crescent 2 (6447820) - health informatics sys HITS (6447848), online foundation course, 20 hrs, ICS & HISI cert, B Altranais approved: €250

Irish T'ai Chi Ch'uan Assoc St Andrew's Resource Centre 114 Pearse St 2 (6771930) - chi kung class, weekly, Sat; drop-in also

Irish Yoga Association PO Box 9969 7 (4929213/ 087 2054489) - qualified teachers available all over Ireland/ 4 yr Teacher Training courses

KAIES-Knocklyon Community Centre, 16 (4931213) - total well-being, Thurs 10am 8 wks €80

Kilroy's College Wentworth House Grand Canal Street Lr 2 (6620538 1850-700700) - tutor supported home study: diet, fitness, health, nutrition, dip

KLEAR Grange Park View Kilbarrack 5 (8671845) - health awareness, day

Margaret Macken Yoga Stephen's Gr/Adelaide Rd/Clontarf (8332954) - Iyengar Yoga, 6 wk course; also relaxation, stress management and meditation

Motions Health & Fitness Training (087 2808866) - Fitness Instructor training diploma course (ITEC), part-time, 9 hours per week. Venue Citywest Hotel & Leisure Centre, Naas Rd

Palmerstown CS - Pobailscoil Iosolde, Kennelsfort Rd 20 (6260116) - safe food for life, Mon 7-9pm 10 wks €80, cert

Pearse College Clogher Rd Crumlin 12 (4536661/4541544) - holistic health, aromatherapy, massage, reflexology, health studies - day

Pobalscoil Rosmini Adult Ed Grace Pk Rd 9 (8371015) - positive approach, Wed 7-9pm €120

St John Ambulance Brigade of Ireland 29 Upr Leeson St 4 (6688077) - basic life support (BLS) and automated external defibrillator (AED) course; also first aid courses

T'ai Chi Energy Centre Milltown Pk Conference Centre Sandford Rd Ranelagh 6 (4961533) - t'ai chi/qi gong - & wkend workshops

Taney Parish Centre Taney Rd Dundrum 14 (2985491) - voluntary stroke scheme, Weds (4941052)

The Open University Centre Holbrook House, Holles St 2 (6785399) - & social welfare

Trinity College 2 (8961000) - (8962182) - health informatics, 1yr postgrad dip, 24wks/ MSc, 1 further yr

Westmoreland College for Management Studies 11 Westmoreland St 2 (6795324/7266) - ICM dip health services management/ICM health & safety at work

HEALTH FOOD & COOKERY

Dún Laoghaire CFE, 17 Cumberland St Dún Laoghaire (2809676) - health & alternative nutrition, 10 wks, Wed 7.30pm, €110 natural foods, cooking, 10 wks Wed 7pm €150

Time Out (4591038) - also wkend

HEBREW see also Bible / Languages

Sandford Language Institute Milltown Pk Sandford Rd 6 (2601296) - modern & biblical - all levels subject to demand, 15 wks €350

HERBS & HERBALISM

Bray Institute of FE, Novara Ave Bray (2866111 / 2829668) - herbal medicine, Wed 10 wks €85

Dún Laoghaire CFE, 17 Cumberland St Dún Laoghaire (2809676) - herbal medicine, Mon 7-9pm 10 wks €130

Newpark Adult Education Centre, Newtownpark Ave Blackrock (2884376 / 2883725) - herbal medicine, Wed 7.30 10 wks €120

National University of Ireland Maynooth

DEPARTMENT OF ADULT AND COMMUNITY EDUCATION
Continuing Education 2006 - 2007

Undergraduate Courses

Course Title	Contact
Addiction Studies	01 708 4500
Adult & Community Education	01 708 4500
Community Arts for Community Development	01 708 4500
Community Development and Leadership	01 708 4500
Counselling Skills	01 708 3784
Directing (New)*	056 7775910
Disabilities Studies	01 708 4500
Group Work Theory & Practice	01 708 4500
Heritage Management (New)*	056 7775910
Local History	01 708 4500
Performance (New)*	056 7775910
Psychology	01 708 4500
Race and Ethnic Studies	01 708 4500
Return To Learning	01 708 4500
Social and Human Studies	01 708 4500
Women's Studies	01 708 4500
Youth Studies	01 708 4500

Professional Development Courses

Adult Guidance Theory & Practice	01 708 3757
Communication & Group Skills for Managers (New)*	01 708 4500
Equality Studies in Training & Development	042 9322399
Integrating Literacy	01 708 4500
Training & Continuing Education	01 821 0016
Diploma In Training & Development	
(For Socially Inclusive Workplaces)	01 708 3683
Diploma in Arts (Local & Community Studies)	01 708 4500
Diploma in Rural Development by Distance Learning	01 708 3590

Degree Programmes

BA in Local Studies	01 708 4587
BA in Community Studies	01 708 4587
BSc in Rural Development by Distance Learning	01 708 3590

To request a brochure please contact
Department for Adult and Community Education, NUI Maynooth
Tel: 01 708 4500   Fax 01 708 4687   Email:adcomed@nuim.ie
Website: http://adulteducation@nuim.ie

HERITAGE STUDIES
Maynooth NUI Adult & Community Ed Dept (7084500) - heritage management, Kilkenny Campus

Saor-Ollscoil na hÉireann 55 Prussia St 7 (8683368) - heritage studies, celtic studies

HIKING & HILL WALKING see also Adventure Sports
An Oige 61 Mountjoy Street 7 (8304555) - also young hill walkers' club

Corporate Club & Network Club 24 Elmcastle Green Tallaght 24 (4524415)

HINDI Languages
Sandford Language Institute Milltown Pk Sandford Rd 6 (2601296) - all levels, 15 wks €350

HIP HOP see MODERN DANCE
Dundrum Family Recreation Centre Meadowbrook 16 (2984654)

Just Dance (8273040 087 8473518) - for children & adults, Dublinwide, for fitness & fun

Marino College 14-20 Marino Mart 3 (8332100) - Tue 5-6pm wks €45

HISTORY see also Archaeology / Architecture / Art / Classical
All Hallows College Gracepark Rd Drumcondra 9 (8373745) - church history 1&2, Tue 6.50 24 wks, €390; ECTS credits option

Ballymun Trinity CS, Adult Ed Centre 9 (8420654) - jun cert level, Wed 7.30 30 wks free

Coláiste Eanna, Kilkieran Rd Cabra 7 (8389577) - Irish history 1800-86, Thurs 10 wks 7-9

Kilroy's College Wentworth House Grand Canal Street Lr 2 (6620538 1850-700700) - tutor supported home study: leaving cert

KLEAR Grange Park View Kilbarrack 5 (8671845) - understanding history, day

Old Dublin Society The Secretary c/o Pearse St Library 2 (6602735 Hon Sec; 8333089) - lectures, visits, tours: €30 pa: Oct, Nov, Feb, Mar at 138-144 Pearse St 2 on weds 7.30

People's College for Continuing Education & Training 32 Parnell Sq 1 (8735879) - €60

Plunket College Swords Rd, Whitehall 9 (8371689) - leaving cert, 27 wks, €425/ 1916-and the writers, Tue 7.30 10 wks €90

Saor-Ollscoil na hÉireann 55 Prussia St 7 (8683368) - Irish History Local & Maritime

Trinity College 2 (8961000) - (8968589) contesting history, opposing voices, eve 16 wks €320/ the experience of the 1st world war; the history of the book 3000BC-2000AD: 9 wks €60 each/ the rise of the west & origins of the modern world 9 wks €120

UCD Adult Education Centre Belfield (7167123) - 17th century england/ 1916 in context/ a history of ideas in Europe/ a history of Ireland from plantation to peace process/ a history of us foreign policy / a history of women in Europe/ establishing a university: from Newman to UCD/ Henry VIII/ Ireland and the history of polar exploration/ seventeenth century Ireland/ international development/ the history of the Palestinian-Israeli conflict: each 10 wks. introduction to Greece and Rome/ Italy: from the Medici to Mussolini/ the rise and fall of the British Empire: each 20 wks

HISTORY, LOCAL
Ballyfermot CFE, Ballyfermot Rd 10 (6269421) - Fetac 5 Wed 7-10pm 22 wks

Bray Institute of FE, Novara Ave Bray (2866111 / 2829668) - discover co Wicklow, Tue 10 wks €88

Greenhills College Limekiln Ave Walkinstown 12 (4507779/4507863) - Mon 5 wks €65

Malahide Community School Malahide (8460949) - NUI Maynooth cert, 25 wks, eve

Maynooth NUI Adult & Community Ed Dept (7084500) - NUI Maynooth campus; also at Malahide CS (8460949) Tues; St Peter's Coll Dunboyne, Tue 7-10pm

(8252552); Dunshaughlin Community College (8259137)

UCD Adult Education Centre Belfield (7167123) - History of Dublin through Walks & Talks; More Walks & Talks (spring), Thurs, 5 wks each

HOCKEY

Irish Hockey Association 6a Woodbine Pk Blackrock (2600028)

Women's Morning Hockey Rathfarnham 14 (2835296) - Thurs am

HOLISTIC HEALTH / MEDICINE/ THERAPY - see also Healing

Irish Yoga Association PO Box 9969 7 (4929213/ 087 2054489) - qualified teachers available all over Ireland/ 4 yr Teacher Training courses

Motions Health & Fitness Training (087 2808866) - Diploma in Holistic Massage (ITEC), part-time course, 3 hours per week. Castleknock, Citywest & Naas

Pearse College Clogher Rd Crumlin 12 (4536661/4541544) - complimentary & holistic therapies 2 yr course: yr 1 €495; yr 2 €845: day; FETAC & ITEC certs / diplomas

Rathmines CFE - Senior College, Town Hall 6 (4975334) - holistic lifestyle, Tue, Wed 10 wks €90

Walmer College & Holistic Centre First Floor, River Hse Raheny Shopping C 5 (8329645) - holistic studies, ITEC dip, full time 1 yr

HOME NURSING see also First Aid

HOMOEOPATHY

Balbriggan Community College Pine Ridge Chapel St (8412388/9) - Tue 8 wks 7.30-9.30, €104

Old Bawn Community School Tallaght 24 (4526137) - Thurs, 7.30-9.30 €122 (incl remedy kit)

Ringsend Technical Institute Cambridge Rd 4 (6684498) - in the home, Mon 7-9pm 10 wks €90

The Irish School of Homoeopathy Milltown Pk College Ranelagh 6 (8682581) - regular wkend workshops -'get started', €120/ short course - 6 wkends 'the power of homoeopathy' - €480/ practitioner's professional training, 4yr, part-time weekends course (courses also in Cork city)

HORSE CARE / EQUESTRIAN

National College of Complementary Medical Ed, 16a St Joseph's Parade Off Dorset Street 7 (8827777) - equine neuromuscular therapy, cert

HORSE RIDING

Brennanstown Riding School Hollybrook Kilmacanogue Co Wicklow (2863778) - eve & day; 10 wks €255

Broadmeadows Equestrian Centre Bullstown, Ashbourne Co Meath (8351633)

Callaighstown Riding Centre Rathcoole (4588322) - also day/ holiday courses/ BHS exams

Corporate Club 24 Elmcastle Green Tallaght 24 (4610935)

Killegar Stables The Scalp Enniskerry (2860919) - evening lessons for adults

Network Club 24 Elmcastle Green Tallaght 24 (4524415)

Thornton Pk Equestrian Centre Killsallaghan, Swords (8351164) - beginners & advanced /c. 25 mins from city centre/in & outdoor arenas/group concessions/ intermediate to advanced equitation & stable management, eve 14 wks €285 BHS stage 1 cert

HORTICULTURE see also Gardening

Dublin School of Horticulture 28 Spencer Villas Dún Laoghaire (2148469) - RHS cert courses/ correspondence

I.T. Blanchardstown Rd North 15 (8851000) - landscape & garden management, 1 yr 1400/ landscape design, 1 yr €1400/ BSc in Horticulture workbased, 3 yrs p/time

Kilroy's College Wentworth House Grand Canal Street Lr 2 (6620538 1850-700700) - tutor supported home study: gardening, dip

Kylemore College Kylemore Rd 10 (6265901) - practical gardening, FETAC 1 & 1 Tue & thurs 12 wks 10.30-12.30

Pearse College Clogher Rd Crumlin 12 (4536661/4541544) - amenity horticulture, landscape construction, nursery stock production, etc - day €150 FETAC 2 cert

Portmarnock Community School Carrickhill Rd (8038056) - intro, gardening, Mon 7.30 10 wks €100

HOSPITAL AND HEALTH SERVICES ADMINISTRATION

Westmoreland College for Management Studies 11 Westmoreland St 2 (6795324/7266) - ICM dip health services management/ICM cert health & safety at work

HOSPITALITY MANAGEMENT

DIT Faculty: Tourism & Food Cathal Brugha St 1 (4023000) - hospitality services management, 2 yrs €810pa, higher cert/ MSc in hospit management, 2 yr €1900pa / revenue management, 12 wks €235

Griffith College Dublin Sth Circular Rd 8 (4150400) - BA in International Hospitality management, 3 yr HETAC NTU f/time

HOSTELLING

An Oige 61 Mountjoy Street 7 (8304555)

HOTEL AND CATERING

DIT Faculty: Tourism & Food Cathal Brugha St 1 (4023000) - hotel management (IHCI), 3 yr 1 day wkly, €810pa/ BA in hotel & restaurant management, 3 yrs €810pa

HOUSE FURNISHINGS & CRAFTS see Crafts / DIY

HOUSE MAINTENANCE & IMPROVEMENTS see also Building Construction / DIY / Interior Design / Plumbing

Newpark Adult Education Centre Newtownpark Ave Blackrock (2884376 / 2883725) - DIY, 10wks, €125 Tue 7.30-9.45pm

Ringsend Technical Institute Cambridge Rd 4 (6684498) - Thurs 7-9pm 10 wks €90

HUMANITIES STUDIES see also Liberal Arts

UCD Adult Education Centre Belfield (7167123) - access to arts & humanities, Tue/Thurs, 20 wks

HUMOUR

Ringsend Technical Institute Cambridge Rd 4 (6684498) - 'Every joke is a tine revolution', Mon 7-8.30 10 wks €70

HUNGARIAN

Sandford Language Institute Milltown Pk Sandford Rd 6 (2601296) - all levels, 15 wks €350

HYPNOTHERAPY / HYPNOSIS

IICH Education 118 Stillorgan Road 4 (2017422) - workshops; certs; diplomas in hypnotherapy, NLP, counselling skills, life coaching

Institute of Clinical Hypnotherapy & Psychotherapy Therapy Hse 6 Tuckey St Cork (021-4273575) - theory dip by correspondence, advanced practical dip/workshops in Dublin & Cork - prospectus & demo cassette free

Plunket College Swords Rd, Whitehall 9 (8371689) - intro to, Mon 7.30 10 wks €67

INDIAN LANGUAGES Hindi, Urdu

Sandford Language Institute Milltown Pk Sandford Rd 6 (2601296) - Hindi, Urdu, etc, - all levels subject to demand, 15 wks €350

INDUSTRIAL RELATIONS

National College of Ireland Mayor St IFSC 1 (4060500/ 1850 221721) - BA (Hons) in Industrial Relations and HRM (CIPD), 4 years, €3,285

INDUSTRIAL SAFETY see Health & Safety

INFORMATION CENTRES see also Community / Consumer / Library / Youth

Youth Info Centres - info on youth activities: education, training, jobs, rights & entitlements, travel sport & leisure: Main St, Blanchardstown (8212077) Monastery Rd, Clondalkin (4594666) Bell Tower, Dún Laoghaire (2809363); Main Rd, Tallaght

INFORMATION TECHNOLOGY Computers

BCT Institute, Institute 30 Fitzwilliam St 2 (6616838 /891)

CTA Computer Training Academy, St James's Tce Malahide (8454070)

DIT Faculty: Science Kevin St 8 (4023000) - BSc in IT: Ord/Hons/Dip, 5 yrs €450 per module - mature students welcome

INFORMATION TECHNOLOGY (contd)

Dorset College 64 Lr Dorset St/ 8 Belvedere Pl 1 (8309677)

Dublin Business School 13/14 Aungier St 2 (4177500) - Microsoft Office Specialist (MOS) Master - incorporating Sage, 1 eve wk, 1 yr 6:15-9:30/ JEB Teachers Dip in IT, 2 eves - 10 wks, 6.15-9.30pm 16 wks / Higher Dip in Business Studies - IT, 2 eves per wk 6.15-9.30pm, 16 mths / Dip in Web Design/ Advanced Dip in Web Development, 1 eve wk, 6:15-9:30

Eden Computer Training Rathfarnham 16 & 1 Green St 7 (4953155)

I.T. Blanchardstown Rd North 15 (8851000) - BSc in computing in IT support, 2 yrs €1700 pa, p/time

Institute of Technology Tallaght ITT Dublin, Tallaght 24 (4042101) - European Certification for Informatics Professionals 1 yr EUCIP

Irish Academy of Computer Training 98 St Stephen's Green 2 (4347662) Intro to Computer & to Programming, 8 wks/ Word; Spreadsheets; Databases (Access and SQL Server); Programming (Intro; C, C++, VC++, VB, Java, Visual J++, Access); Operating Systems - Linux, Windows 2003 Administrator, Windows XP Pro; Networking with Windows XP, Linux; Graphics; DTP: all 6 wks/ Presentation Tools 8 wks; CCNA 20 wks; A+ / Network+ CompTIA 24 wks cert; day/eve

Irish Computer Society / ICS Skills Crescent Hall, Mount St Crescent 2 (6447820) - Euro cert Infomatics professionals EUCIP, competence development for professionals & undergrads, cert. 150 hrs lecture+ 150 lab/project €1600: at various 3rd level venues

Kilroy's College Wentworth House Grand Canal Street Lr 2 (6620538 1850-700700) - tutor supported home study: PC repair, assembly & A+, ECDL, MOUS, networking, visual basic 6.0

National College of Ireland Mayor St IFSC 1 (4060500/ 1850 221721) - BSc (Hons) in Business Information Systems, 4 years, €3,600/ MSc in Learning Technologies, 2 years, Tues, Thurs eve, €3,000

New Media Technology College 13 Harcourt St 2 (4780905) - cert, 1 yr f/time

Pearse College Clogher Rd Crumlin 12 (4536661/4541544) - fast-track to IT courses/

BTEI initiative - basic computers/ ecdl/ return to learning/ reception & IT/ English for speakers of other languages/ book-keeping

School of Computer Technology 21 Rosmeen Gdns Dún Laoghaire (2844045) - unix/linux LPI cert, €825/ java; C++; visual basic: C&G certs/ SQL; perl; PHP; website design: all 36 hrs, €750 ea/ also day

Senior College Dún Laoghaire, CFE Eblana Ave Dún Laoghaire (2800385) - teachers' dip in IT skills, JEB €795

The Open University Enquiry/Advice Centre Holbrook House, Holles St 2 (6785399)

Trinity College 2 (8961000) - (8961039/2003) - info systems, dip, 2yr, 24wks/ BSc 4yr, 24wks per yr/ IT & learning, MSc, 2 yrs, 24 wks per yr (8962182)

INSTRUCTOR TRAINING see also Teaching/Teachers Courses

Fingall Sailing School Malahide (8451979)

Irish Academy of Computer Training 98 St Stephen's Green 2 (4347662) - train the trainer/ MOS master instructor: cert / day, eve

Litton Lane Studios PO Box 9853 Dunshaughlin Co Meath (8728044) - leisure & recreational studies, Instructor courses, venue DCU - 30 wks, 2 eves per week, all courses begin mid Sept

Motions Health & Fitness Training (087 2808866) - Fitness Instructor training diploma course (ITEC), part-time, 9 hours per week. Venue Citywest Hotel & Leisure Centre, Naas Rd

National Training Centre 16a St Joseph's Parade Dorset St 7 (8827777) - 18 wks part-time €1935

INSURANCE see also Law

Pearse College Clogher Rd Crumlin 12 (4536661/4541544) - insurance business & computer studies, day, 1 yr €323, FETAC/Insurance Inst of Ireland

Plunket College Swords Rd, Whitehall 9 (8371689) - foundation cert, pt 1 & pt 2: 25 wks tue 7-9pm €262 IIF cert

Senior College Dún Laoghaire, CFE Eblana Ave Dún Laoghaire (2800385) - Insurance Institute of Ireland (III) course, €650

INTERIOR DESIGN & DECOR see also Painting and Decorating / Retail / Garden / Comp[uter Aided / Graphic

Ashfield College Main St Templeogue 6W (4900866) - prelim/improvers, 7.30-9.30, 8 wks / AssOciate dip 1 yr p/time, from Oct

Ballsbridge CFE,, Shelbourne Rd 4 (6684806) - Mon & Tue, 10 wks, 7pm €100

Ballyfermot CFE, Ballyfermot Rd 10 (6269421) - Fetac 5 22 wks Wed 7-10pm

Ballymun Trinity CS,s Adult Ed Centre 9 (8420654) - Mon 7.30, 10wk, €100

Bray Institute of FE, Novara Ave Bray (2866111 / 2829668) - interior design Mon 7.30 10 wks €85

Cabinteely Community School Johnstown Rd 18 (2857455) - 10wk, €95

Coláiste Dhúlaigh CFE, Barryscourt Rd Coolock 17 (8481337) - Tues, 10 wks, 7.30

Colour Connections B Egan 4 (087 6288582) - small classes

Coolmine Community School Clonsilla 15 (8214583) - Limperts Academy dip, Mon 7-9.30 €1265/ workshop, an introduction, Sat 7 Oct 10am-1, €25

Crumlin College of FE, Crumlin Rd 12 (4540662) - Limperts Academy Dip, Mon 6.45-9.45 20 wks

Dorset College 64 Lr Dorset St/ 8 Belvedere Pl 1 (8309677) - Limperts dip in interior design, Wed 6.30-9.30, 1 yr/ higher dip in interior design & architecture (BTEC HND, Tue & thurs 6.30-9, 1 yr

Dublin Institute of Design 25 Suffolk St 2 (6790286) - your designer home, foundation course, 1 eve or morn 8 wks/ Rhodec Assoc dip, 14 wks 1 day or 25 wks 1 eve or morn/ BETC Higher Nat Dip, 2 eve or 1 day wkly, 2 yrs; f-time day 2 yr/ also, Online certificate - timetable to suit your lifestyle

Dún Laoghaire CFE, 17 Cumberland St Dún Laoghaire (2809676) - Wed, 10 wks 7.45pm €110

FAS Training Centre Cabra Bannow Rd 7 (8821400) - 10 wks; Finglas Jamestown Rd 11 (8140200) - 10 wks; Loughlinstown Wyattville Rd, DL (2043600) - 10 wks

Foxrock Institute Kill o' the Grange, Kill Lane Blackrock (4939506) - 6ks, €99

Greendale Community School Kilbarrack 5 (8322735) - introduction, Tue 10 wks €95

Greenhills College Limekiln Ave Walkinstown 12 (4507779/4507863) - 10wks, €130

Griffith College Dublin Sth Circular Rd 8 (4150400) - BA in design & interior architecture, 3 yr HETAC p/time 2-3 eve per wk; BA (Hons) 1 yr add-on Hetac f/time / GCD dip in interior design 2 yr f/time; 2 yr p/time 2 eves per wk/ BA in fashion design 3 yrs hetac f/t

Harcourt Business School HSI 89 Harcourt St 2 (4763975) - dip in interior design

Hartstown Community School Clonsilla 15 (8209863) - 10wks, €85

Holy Family Community School Rathcoole (4580766)

Killester CFE, Collins Ave 5 (8337686) - Tues 7.30-10pm, 10 wks €75/ Fri 10am-12pm, 10 wks €65

Malahide Community School Malahide (8460949) - introductory, 10 wks €80

Marino College 14-20 Marino Mart 3 (8332100) - Tue 7.30pm, 10wks, €90

Newpark Adult Education Centre Newtownpark Ave Blackrock (2884376 / 2883725) - 10wks, €120, Tue 7.30-9.45

Old Bawn Community School Tallaght 24 (4526137) - Thurs, 7.30-9.30pm, 10 wks €95

Palmerstown CS - Pobailscoil Iosolde, Kennelsfort Rd 20 (6260116) - Thurs 7pm, 10wks €80

Plunket College Swords Rd, Whitehall 9 (8371689) - intro, Tues, 10 wks, €90/ Limpérts Academy of Design Dipl, Tue 7-10pm, 30 wks €665+€345

Pobalscoil Rosmini Adult Ed Grace Pk Rd 9 (8371015) - introductory, Wed 7.30pm €100

Portmarnock Community School Carrickhill Rd (8038056) - foundation, Tue 10 wks 7.30 €100

Portobello School 43 Lr Dominick St 1 (8721277) - residential dip 32 wks/ residential & commercial dip, 2 yrs / C&G cert

Rathmines CFE - Senior College, Town Hall 6 (4975334) - intro, 10 wks, €90, Mon 7-9pm

Senior College Dún Laoghaire, CFE Eblana Ave Dún Laoghaire (2800385) - cert in interior design, C&G RAFA, €450

St Finian's Community College Swords (8402623) - 8 wks

St Kevin's College, Clogher Rd Crumlin 12 (4536397) - 10wks

St MacDara's CC, Wellington Lane Templeogue 6W (4566216) - Tue, 7.30-9.30pm, 8 wks, €104

St Tiernan's Community School Parkvale Balally 16 (2953224) - brighten your home, Tue 7.30-9.30 10 wks, €95

Walmer College & Holistic Centre First Floor, River Hse Raheny Shopping C 5 (8329645)

INTERNATIONAL TRADE & MARKETING

Coláiste Dhúlaigh CFE, Barryscourt Rd Coolock 17 (8481337) - dip in international trade & e-Business, 20 wks, Mon & Tues, 6.45pm

Institute of International Trade of Ireland 28 Merrion Square 2 (6612182) - prof. dip in Global Trade / documentary credit compliance, 1 day/ customs compliance,

2 day/ dangerous goods safety awareness & advisor; various locations

Pearse College Clogher Rd Crumlin 12 (4536661/4541544) - & business studies, day, 2 yr dip €150/ yr 2 €294

UCD Adult Education Centre Belfield (7167123) - International Trade and Export Practice, Tue 10 wks

Westmoreland College for Management Studies 11 Westmoreland St 2 (6795324/7266) - ICM dip marketing, advertising & PR

INTERNET & E-MAIL

Adelaide Computers 14 Pembroke Lane Ballsbridge 4 (2696213)

Ballsbridge CFE, Shelbourne Rd 4 (6684806) - beginners, Thurs, 6pm, 10 wks, €110

Ballymun Trinity CS, Adult Ed Centre 9 (8420654) - for beginners, Tue 7pm 10 wks €120

Bray Institute of FE, Novara Ave Bray (2866111 / 2829668) - Mon 7.30 10 wks €95

Cabinteely Community School Johnstown Rd 18 (2857455) - 7-8.25, 10wks €110

Coláiste Dhúlaigh CFE, Barryscourt Rd Coolock 17 (8481337) - computers & the internet, beginners Mon 10 wks, 11am-1 or 6-7.45pm

College of Further Education Main St Dundrum 14 (2951376) - iintro, Tue & Thurs 7-9pm 8 wks €140

CTA Computer Training Academy, St James's Tce Malahide (8454070) - basic, 9 hrs: day/eve/Sat

Dorset College 64 Lr Dorset St/ 8 Belvedere Pl 1 (8309677) - ecitizen, Sat 10-1pm 8 wks

Dublin Public Libraries Admin Hq, 138-144 Pearse St 2 (6744800) - internet facilities in city branch libraries, free, booking essential; contact local branch

Dún Laoghaire-Rathdown Co Council Public Library Service - free internet & email access: the library at: Blackrock (2888117), Cabinteely (2855363), Dalkey (2855277), Deansgrange (2850860), Dún Laoghaire (2801147), Dundrum (2985000), Sallynoggin (2850127), Shankill (2823081), Stillorgan (2889655); free internet training at many libraries ongoing

Eden Computer Training Rathfarnham 16 & 1 Green St 7 (4953155)

FAS Training Centres: Baldoyle 13 (8167400); Cabra Bannow Rd 7 (8821400); Finglas Jamestown Rd 11 (8140200); Loughlinstown Wyattville Rd, DL (2043600); Tallaght Cookstown Indl Est 24 (4045200);: each - intro: 2 wks/ 5 wks

Fingal Co Libraries County Hall Main St Swords (8905520) - internet access/ self-learning: Balbriggan: 8411128; Baldoyle: 906793; Blanchardstown: 8905563; Howth: 8322130; Malahide: 8452026; Swords: 8404179; Skerries: 8491900; Mobile Library HQ: 8221564; Schools Library:8225056; Housebound Service: 8604290

Grange Community College Grange Abbey Rd Donaghmede 13 (8471422) - intro to, improve skills, 8.30-10pm 10 wks

Greenhills College Limekiln Ave Walkinstown 12 (4507779/4507863) - introduction, 10 wks €166

Irish Academy of Computer Training 98 St Stephen's Green 2 (4347662) - IACT's webmaster in web design, 12 wk dip/ intro to e-commerce & web marketing 6wk; intro to internet & HTML, 6wk; webmaster web design 12 wk; web develpoment & HTML 6 wk; design with frontpage 6wk; intro to frontpage, HTML 6 wk; Java 10 wk; Java primer 10wk; visual basic 8wk; ms publisher 8wk: each cert, day/eve

Kylemore College Kylemore Rd 10 (6265901) - Sat 10 wks 10.30-12.30pm

Old Bawn Community School Tallaght 24 (4526137) - introduction to, 5 wks €52

Palmerstown CS - Pobailscoil Iosolde, Kennelsfort Rd 20 (6260116) - for beginners, Thurs 6.45-7.45pm 10 wks €70/ Ecdl Mon 8.45pm

Pitman Training Centre 6-8 Wicklow St 2 (6768008) - day eve sats, cert

Pobalscoil Neasáin Baldoyle 13 (8063092) - getting to know, morns, 10 wks

Pobalscoil Rosmini Adult Ed Grace Pk Rd 9 (8371015) - e-citizen, Mon 7pm & 8.30 €160 ICS cert/

Rathmines CFE - Senior College, Town Hall 6 (4975334) - beginners, 6-7.30 10 wks Tue €95

St Tiernan's Community School Parkvale Balally 16 (2953224) - levels 1 & 2: Wed 6 wks €110 each

Stillorgan CFE, Old Road Stillorgan (2880704) - Mon 7.30-9.30 8 wks €140

The Open University Enquiry/Advice Centre Holbrook House, Holles St 2 (6785399)

INTERVIEWING / INTERVIEWS

Communication & Personal Development 30/31 Wicklow St 2 (6713636/ 6613225)

CTA Computer Training Academy, St James's Tce Malahide (8454070) - preparation

Eden Computer Training Rathfarnham 16 & 1 Green St 7 (4953155)

Enriching Careers 38 Clonliffe Rd 3 (6589091)

Leinster School of Music & Drama Griffith College Campus South Circular Rd 8 (4150467) - interview preparation

MD Communications 38 Spireview Lane off Rathgar Rd 6 (4975866)

Plunket College Swords Rd, Whitehall 9 (8371689) - preparing for, Tues 7.30-9.30 8 wks €90

IRELAND, LEARN ABOUT see also Irish Culture / History / Music

Old Bawn Community School Tallaght 24 (4526137) - introducing Ireland for people new to living here, Thurs 730-9.30pm

IRISH (GAEILGE) All Levels See also Basic / Leaving Cert / Languages

Ballymun Trinity CS,s Adult Ed Centre 9 (8420654) - beginners Tue 7pm, 10wk, €70

Bray Institute of FE, Novara Ave Bray (2866111 / 2829668) - re-discover Irish, tue 7.30 10 wks, €85

Coláiste Dhúlaigh CFE, Barryscourt Rd Coolock 17 (8481337) - beginners, Mon 10 wks 6.30-8pm/ also: beginners 12.55-2pm; intermediate 11.15am; rdrang Tue 9.30-11am: 25 wks each; venue also at Pobalscoil Neas n, Mon & Weds

College of Further Education Main St Dundrum 14 (2951376) - beginners, Tue, Thurs, 7-9pm 8 wks €104

Comhaltas Ceoltóirí Éireann 32 Belgrave Sq Monkstown (2800295) - conversation

Conradh na Gaeilge 6 Sr Fhearchair (Harcourt St) BAC 2 (4757401) - for adults, Tues/Wed/Thurs, 7 levels; Leaving Cert classes - all commence last wk Sept

DATE Centre CFE, Dundrum 14 (2964322 (9.30am-12pm)) - beginners/ improvers/ conversation/ ciorcal cainte: each day 10 wks €97

Dún Laoghaire CFE, 17 Cumberland St Dún Laoghaire (2809676) - refresher course, Mon 10 wks 7-8pm €75

Dún Laoghaire-Rathdown Co Council Public Library Service - - Irish/Eng informal sessions, Tue 10.30am-12, Deansgrange lib, Clonkeen Dr (2850860); Mon 11am-12 Dundrum lib (2985000)

Gael Linn 35 Dame St 2 (6751200) - classes held @35 Dame St 2

GaelChultúr Ltd Filmbase Building (Level 2) Curved St, Temple Bar 2 (7653658/ 085 7076182) - for adults, all levels year round, city centre

Greenhills College Limekiln Ave Walkinstown 12 (4507779/4507863) - beginners only, 10 wks, €130/ conversation, Tue, 10wks, €130/ leaving cert 20 wks €130

Hartstown Community School Clonsilla 15 (8209863) - beginners, 10wks, €85

Killester CFE, Collins Ave 5 (8337686) - conversation, Mon 7.30-9, 10 wks €60

Kilternan Adult Education Group Ballybetagh Rd Kilternan 18 (2952050) - conversation, Thur 9.30-11am 10 wks €97

KLEAR Grange Park View Kilbarrack 5 (8671845) - conversation - beginners, improvers, advanced, day only

Language Centre NUI Maynooth Co Kildare (7083737) - 18wk, €350 cert

Marino College 14-20 Marino Mart 3 (8332100) - language, Thurs 10 wks, €65

Newpark Adult Education Centre, Newtownpark Ave Blackrock (2884376 / 2883725) - for absolute beginners only, Thurs 10 wks, €120

Old Bawn Community School Tallaght 24 (4526137) - beginners & improvers, basic conversation, Thurs, 10 wks ea €90

Palmerstown CS - Pobailscoil Iosolde, Kennelsfort Rd 20 (6260116) - for everyone, Tues 7pm, 10 wks €70

People's College for Continuing Education & Training 32 Parnell Sq 1 (8735879) - €45

Plunket College Swords Rd, Whitehall 9 (8371689) - leaving cert, 27 wks, €425

Pobalscoil Rosmini Adult Ed Grace Pk Rd 9 (8371015) -adults 1, 7pm/ adults 2, 8.30: each: Mon €90

Sandford Language Institute Milltown Pk Sandford Rd 6 (2601296) - all levels subject to demand, 15 wks €285/ also Irish for teaching / for business & professional

Saor-Ollscoil na hÉireann 55 Prussia St 7 (8683368) - Mon

Scoil Shéamuis Ennis, Naul, Co Dublin (8020898 087 7870138) - for beginners, intermediate and teenagers in: Irish (Conversation) on Wednesday eve

South Dublin Co Libraries (4597834-admin only) - classes free: Ballyroan (4941900), Clondalkin (4593315), Lucan (6216422), Tallaght (4620073).

TARGET St Kevin's School Newbrook Rd, Donaghmede 13 (8671967) - conversation beginners, improvers, day only, CDVEC

UCD Adult Education Centre Belfield (7167123) - RTE's Turas Teanga 1 & 2, Wed 10 wks each

IRISH CULTURE see Folklore / Traditional Music

IRISH DANCING - CEILI/FIGURE

Brooks Academy 15 Henrietta St 1 (8730093) - set dancing, Sept-May Mon & Thurs 8-10pm

Comhaltas Ceoltóirí Éireann 32 Belgrave Sq Monkstown (2800295) various venues, sets & ceili

Corporate Club 24 Elmcastle Green Tallaght 24 (4610935)

Dublin Folk Dance Group 48 Ludford Drive Ballinteer 16 (2987929) - adult set dancing various centres, ongoing

Dundrum Family Recreation Centre Meadowbrook 16 (2984654)

Network Club 24 Elmcastle Green Tallaght 24 (4524415)

Scoil Shéamuis Ennis, Naul, Co Dublin (8020898 087 7870138)

St Kevin's College Clogher Rd Crumlin 12 (4536397) - set, 10wks

IRISH HISTORY see History

IRISH TRADITIONAL MUSIC see also Music / Accordian/ Fiddle/ Tin Whistle etc

Cor Duibhlinne, Foras Na Gaeilge 7 Merrion Sq 2 (086 3948492) - choir/ choral singing in Irish, Mon eves ongoing €5 per night

Greendale Community School Kilbarrack 5 (8322735) - tin whistle, Thurs 7pm 10 wks €85

Scoil Shéamuis Ennis, Naul, Co Dublin (8020898 087 7870138) - for beginners / improvers in: Pipes; Flute; Whistle; Fiddle Guitar; Button Accordion; Concertina on Mon, Wed & Thurs eves and on Saturdays (subject to demand)

IT see Information Technology / Computer / Internet / Teaching

ITALIAN FOR HOLIDAYS

Malahide Community School Malahide (8460949) - beginners - designed to enable visitor communicate effectively, 10 wks €80

ITALIAN LANGUAGE & CULTURE Languages

Aisling Ireland 137 Lr Rathmines Rd 6 (4971902) - all levels, 7.30-9.30 10 wks €160

Ashfield College Main St Templeogue 6W (4900866) - beginners 1, 6.30-8pm, 10 wks / improvers 2, 8-9.30, 10 wks

Balbriggan Community College Pine Ridge Chapel St (8412388/9) - Wed 7.30-9pm 8 wks €78

Ballsbridge CFE, Shelbourne Rd 4 (6684806) - beginners Mon 6pm & 7.45 10 wks €80

Bray Institute of FE, Novara Ave Bray (2866111 / 2829668) - beginners, Wed 7.30 /stage 2 Mon 7.30: 10wks, €85 each

Cabinteely Community School Johnstown Rd 18 (2857455) - beginners, 10wk, €95

Coláiste Dhúlaigh CFE, Barryscourt Rd Coolock 17 (8481337) - FETAC cert, Tue, 22 wks, beginners / improvers

Coláiste Eanna, Kilkieran Rd Cabra 7 (8389577) - beginners conversation, Thurs 6.30-8/ improvers 7.30-9: 10 wks each

College of Further Education Main St Dundrum 14 (2951376) - beginners/ continuation: Tue & Thurs 7-9pm 8 wks €104

RANGANNA GAEILGE DO DHAOINE FÁSTA

Coolmine Community School Clonsilla 15 (8214583) - beginners Mon €150/ improvers Tue: €150: 20wk each/ beginners Wed 10 wks €80

DATE Centre CFE, Dundrum 14 (2964322 (9.30am-12pm)) - beginners, level 1-3, each10 wks, day €97

Donahies Community School Streamville Rd 13 (8482217) - begin., Mon 7.30 10 wks €85

Dún Laoghaire CFE, 17 Cumberland St Dún Laoghaire (2809676) - levels 1&2: each 10 wks, Wed, 7 & 8.30 €95

Dún Laoghaire-Rathdown Co Council Public Library Service - Deansgrange lib, Clonkeen Dr (2850860) - Ital/Eng - informal sessions, Mon 10.30-12 morn;

Foxrock Institute Kill o' the Grange, Kill Lane Blackrock (4939506) - beginners/for fun, 8 wks, €105 each

Greendale Community School Kilbarrack 5 (8322735) - conversation, Mon 10 wks 7&8.30 pm €90

Hartstown Community School Clonsilla 15 (8209863) - 10wks, €85

Inchicore CFE, Emmet Rd 8 (4535358)

Italian Alternative, The 45 Leeson St 4 (4978465) - language: beginners/ intermediate/ advanced: 16 wks 32 hrs €280 each, Tue, Wed eve 6.30-8.30

Killester CFE, Collins Ave 5 (8337686) - beginners/ improvers, Mon 7pm/8.30, 10 wks €60 ea

Kylemore College Kylemore Rd 10 (6265901) - 10 wks 7-9pm, beg-intermediate

Langtrain International Torquay Rd Foxrock 18 (2893876) - €96 per term

Bray Institute of Further Education

web: www.bife.ie • email: Braynightschool@Hotmail.com
nightschool@bife.ie

Co. Wicklow
V.E.C.

Full range of daytime or evening courses
tel: (01) 2866 111 / 2829 668 • fax: 2760 653

Language Centre NUI Maynooth Co Kildare (7083737) - beginners/intermediate, 18wk, €350 cert

Marino College 14-20 Marino Mart 3 (8332100) - beginners/ intermediate, 10-20 wks, €65/€130

Newpark Adult Education Centre Newtownpark Ave Blackrock (2884376 / 2883725) - all levels, 10wks/also conversation; Mon/Tue 7.30-9.30 €120 each

Old Bawn Community School Tallaght 24 (4526137) - conversation for beginners, Tues, improvers, Thurs/ advanced Tues: each €90

Palmerstown CS - Pobailscoil Iosolde, Kennelsfort Rd 20 (6260116) - levels 1&2, Thur, 6.45&8.15pm 10wks €75

People's College for Continuing Education & Training 32 Parnell Sq 1 (8735879) - language classes, €60

Pobalscoil Rosmini Adult Ed Grace Pk Rd 9 (8371015) - beginners, for holidays: 1: Tue 7pm & 2: 8.30pm, each €90

Rathmines CFE - Senior College, Town Hall 6 (4975334) - various levels, Mon 7-9pm €175/ Tue, Wed: 6 & 730pm 20 wks €165/ 7-9pm 25 wks €205

Ringsend Technical Institute Cambridge Rd 4 (6684498) - conversational, beginners/improvers 10 wks €70, Wed 7&8.30

Sandford Language Institute Milltown Pk Sandford Rd 6 (2601296) - all levels, 15 wks €240; also day

UCD Adult Education Centre Belfield (7167123) - Italian for Beginners 20 wks Wed/ Spoken Italian Workshop Wed 10 wks

WORDS Language Services 44 Northumberland Rd 4 (6610240) - individual tuition only

JAPANESE Language & Culture see also Languages

Aisling Language Services 137 Lr Rathmines Rd 6 (4971902) - beginners to intermediate, 7.30-9.30 10 wks €200

The Asian Institute, Nova UCD, Belfield 4 (2899608) - all levels, conversational, native-speaking teacher 10 wks €200+book; also, for practical business use, on-site

Bray Institute of FE, Novara Ave Bray (2866111 / 2829668) - Mon 7.30 10 wks, €85

Sandford Language Institute Milltown Pk Sandford Rd 6 (2601296) - all levels, 15 wks €285; also day

Trinity College 2 (8961000) - (8961560) - extra mural, intro to language & culture/ post-beginners/ intermediate: 24wks, €365 each

JAZZ

Dance Theatre of Ireland Bloomfields Centre, Lr George St Dún Laoghaire (2803455) - Thurs, 8.30-9.30, beginners, 10 wks €80

Dún Laoghaire Music Centre 130A Lr George's St Dún Laoghaire (2844178)

Newpark Music Centre Newtownpark Ave Blackrock (2883740) - improvisation

Waltons New School of Music 69 Sth Gt George's St 2 (4781884) - improvisation/ ensemble, also day, see ad page 155

JAZZ DANCE / BALLET see also Ballet

Coiscéim Dance 14 Sackville Pl 1 (8780558) - for adults: city centre studio, beginners welcome: Thurs 7.45, 8 wks €100

JET SKI

Irish Sailing Assoc 3 Park Rd Dún Laoghaire (2800239) -beginners - intermediate/ personal watercraft handling: apply for provider list

JEWELLERY

Ballymun Trinity CS, Adult Ed Centre 9 (8420654) - bead & wire jewellery making, Wed 8.30pm, 10 wks €90

Cormac Cuffe Craft Jewellery School Monkstown Rd Blackrock (2846037; 087 6887722) - silver jewellery, design & make, morn/ eve 4 wks; also intensive course, 3 day 9.15-3.15; summer holiday course 9.30-4.15

Dún Laoghaire CFE, 17 Cumberland St Dún Laoghaire (2809676) - making jewellery, Tues 6 wks 7.70-9.30pm €100

FAS Training Centre: - stone setting, 12 wks: Baldoyle 13 (8167400); Cabra Bannow Rd 7 (8821400); Finglas Jamestown Rd 11 (8140200); Loughlinstown Wyattville Rd, DL (2043600)

Foxrock Institute Kill o' the Grange, Kill Lane Blackrock (4939506) - jewellery making, Wed 8 wks €105

Killester CFE, Collins Ave 5 (8337686) - make jewellery, tue 7.30pm 10 wks €70

Liberties College Bull Alley St 8 (4540044) - Mon 7-9pm, 10 wks €90

Marino College 14-20 Marino Mart 3 (8332100) - & beadmaking, 7.3-pm Tue 10wks, €90

NCAD Centre for Continuing Educ 100 Thomas Street 8 (6364214) - intro & all levels, c22 wks /art jewellery & metalwork, c. 22wk

Newpark Adult Education Centre, Newtownpark Ave Blackrock (2884376 / 2883725) - and bead design, Mon 7.30 10 wks €120

Ringsend Technical Institute Cambridge Rd 4 (6684498) - beadmaking 10 wks €70, Tue 6.30

Senior College Dún Laoghaire, CFE Eblana Ave Dún Laoghaire (2800385) - making, €120

Stillorgan CFE, Old Road Stillorgan (2880704) - making, Thurs 10 wks €130

Yellow Brick Road 8 Bachelors Walk 1 (8730177) - 8 wk jewellery making course, all materials included, 7.30-9.30, €250 (commence: Sept/Jan/Mar)/ 1 night workshops excluding materials, 7-9.30, €25 - separate workshops for wire work, netting & chips, organza necklace, mesh embellishment

JIVE - Rock 'n' Roll Dance

Dance Club Rathmines & Rathgar (2893797)

JOB-SEEKING SKILLS see also Interviewing

CTA Computer Training Academy, St James's Tce Malahide (8454070) - CV skills, 3 hrs

Eden Computer Training Rathfarnham 16 & 1 Green St 7 (4953155) - cv prep

Enriching Careers 38 Clonliffe Rd 3 (6589091)

Kilroy's College Wentworth House Grand Canal Street Lr 2 (6620538 1850-700700) - home study: interview techniques, aptitude & intelligence tests

JOINERY see Woodwork

JOURNALISM see also Broadcasting / Communications / Media

Ballyfermot CFE, Ballyfermot Rd 10 (6269421) - print journalism, Fetac 5 Wed 7-10pm 22 wks

Coláiste Dhúlaigh CFE,Barryscourt Rd Coolock 17 (8481337) - Tue 7.15-9.30, 10 wks

Communications & Management Institute Regus Hse, Harcourt Rd 2 (4927070) - and media studies, dip: Tue 1 yr €1350/ journalism dip Tue 1 yr €1350/ broadcast journalism cert; print journalism cert: Tue 10 wks €750 each

Dublin Business School 13/14 Aungier St 2 (4177500) - Dip in Journalism & Media Studies, 2 eves ,1 yr / Dip in Sports Journalism, 1 eve 10 wks: each 6.15-9.30pm

Griffith College Dublin Sth Circular Rd 8 (4150400) - dip & higher dip in journalism & media communications, 18 mths, GCD dip, p/t, 3 eves per wk/ cert in journalism (print & radio) 1 yr, p/t, 2 eves per wk/ BA in journalism & visual media, 3 yr HETAC f/time/ BA in journalism 3 yr f/time

Harcourt Business School HSI 89 Harcourt St 2 (4763975) - intro to sports journalism

Irish Academy of Public Relations (2780802) - courses at UCD, Belfield: dip in journalism, 1 yr 2 evs, €1850; cert in journalism and print, 12 wks 1 ev €730; practical journalistic writing skills, by email or corresp, €390/€440

Killester CFE, Collins Ave 5 (8337686) - intro to, Tue 8.30, 10 wks €60

Kilroy's College Wentworth House Grand Canal Street Lr 2 (6620538 1850-700700) - tutor supported home study: freelance

Pearse College Clogher Rd Crumlin 12 (4536661/4541544) - dip in media techniques 2 yr course: FETAC media production award; C&G media techniques dip: 1 €150/ 2 €250

Pitman Training Centre 6-8 Wicklow St 2 (6768008) - day eve sats, dip

Plunket College Swords Rd, Whitehall 9 (8371689) - intro to, Tue 7-10, 10 wks €135

Stillorgan CFE, Old Road Stillorgan (2880704) - Thurs

Westmoreland College for Management & Business 11 Westmoreland St 2 (6795324/7266) - ICM dip in journalism & media

JUDO

Portmarnock Sports & Leisure Club Blackwood Lane Carrickhill Portmarnock (8462122)

JUGGLING

Hartstown Community School Clonsilla 15 (8209863) - 10 wks €85

JUNIOR CERT for Adults

Ashfield College Main St Templeogue 6W (4900866) - higher, English, Business, French, German, Irish, Maths, Science, p/time

Ballymun Trinity CS, Adult Ed Centre 9 (8420654) - maths, cert optional: Mon 7.30 30 wks free

Clontarf School of Music 6 Marino Mart 3 (8330936 087 8054963) - musicianship, day & eve 17 wks

Coláiste Dhúlaigh CFE, Barryscourt Rd Coolock 17 (8481337) - history(o); Spanish(o); Maths(o); metal work (o): Mon, Tues eves

Dublin Adult Learning Centre 3 Mountjoy Sq 1 (8787266) - English, maths

Dún Laoghaire Music Centre 130A Lr George's St Dún Laoghaire (2844178) - music

Finglas Adult Reading & Writing Scheme Colaiste Eoin Cappagh Rd 11 (8340893) - maths 30 wks ord level, Tues/ englsih, ord level 30 wkls thurs 9.30-11.30; Tues 7-9pm

Institute of Education 82/85 Lr Leeson St 2 (6613511)

Kilroy's College Wentworth House Grand Canal Street Lr 2 (6620538 1850-700700) - tutor supported home study: Maths, English, Irish

KLEAR Grange Park View Kilbarrack 5 (8671845) - English, day only

Kylemore College Kylemore Rd 10 (6265901) - music, Thurs 6.390-8.30

Pearse College Clogher Rd Crumlin 12 (4536661/4541544) - 1yr, for adults, day/ also individual subjects

Plunket College Swords Rd, Whitehall 9 (8371689) - junior cert for adults: English, Maths, history, art, CSPE: Mon, Tue morns, 25 wks each

Southside Adult Literacy Scheme 4 Glenville Tce Dundrum 14 (2964321) - maths FETAC 1

St Kevin's College, Clogher Rd Crumlin 12 (4536397) - day

KARATE see also Martial Arts / Self-Defence

Clondalkin Sports & Leisure Centre Nangor Rd Clondalkin 22 (4574858)

Dublin Shotokan Karate International (Dublin SKI) St Paul's College Sybil Hill Road 5 (085 7267840) - Mon & Thurs 6.30-8.30/ also St Vincent's & St Joseph's Shotokan Clubs 087 8197785/ 8570353, Mon, Thurs, Fairview & Marino/ 087 2215685, Brian/ 087 2389159, Tom

Portmarnock Sports & Leisure Club Blackwood Lane Carrickhill Portmarnock (8462122) - kenpo karate

Rathgar Kenpo Karate Studios Garville Rd Rathgar 6 (8423712) - Mon, Wed, Fri: 8-9.30pm

St Vincent's Shotkan Karate Club St Vincent's GAA Club Malahide Road Marino 3 (8570353/ 087 8197785) - Mon, Tue (Juniors), Thurs; also at St Joseph's PS, Marino Mart, Fairview

Taney Centre Taney Rd Dundrum 14 (2985491) - Fri (2986046)

KEEP FIT CLASSES see also Aerobics/ Exercise, etc

Cabinteely Community School Johnstown Rd 18 (2857455) - taebo (with kickboxing techniques), mon 7.30-8.30, 10wks €50/ ultimate fat burning class, tues, 1hr 10wks €50

Cabinteely Community School Johnstown Rd 18 (2857455) - Taebo / total body conditioning: Mon, 1 hr, 10 wks €50 each; ultmate fat-burning class: Tue 1 hr 10 wks €50

Clondalkin Sports & Leisure Centre Nangor Rd Clondalkin 22 (4574858) - Khai-bo/ combination work-out/total fitness/ - also day

Greendale Community School Kilbarrack 5 (8322735) - circuit training, women Tue 8pm: 10 wks €60

Greenhills College Limekiln Ave Walkinstown 12 (4507779/4507863) - women, salsa fit, 10 wks, €65

Inchicore CFE, Emmet Rd 8 (4535358)

Irish Yoga Association PO Box 9969 7 (4929213/ 087 2054489) - qualified teachers available all over Ireland/ 4 yr Teacher Training courses

Jackie Skelly's Fitness 42 Clarendon St, 2; Park West, Nangor Rd, 12 & Applewood Village, Swords, & Ashbourne (6770040) - gym membership incls classes - keep fit, step, pump, aerobics, spin, toning

League of Health (Irl) 17 Dundela Pk Sandycove (2807775) AT: Ballinteer-2988550; Blackrock/ Booterstown-2896162; Bray-2807775; Clondalkin-087 9385777; Clontarf-086 8863917; Dalkey-2807775; Donnybrook-2888761; Dundrum-4927887; Dún Laoghaire-2814931; Enniskerry-2824463; Glasnevin-2888761; Glenageary-2841187; Greystones -2896162; Kill o' the Grange 2858588/2894079; Lucan 086 8863917/ Malahide 8363186; Monkstown 2896162; Mount Merrion 2888761; Newbridge 087 9385777/ Raheny 2852255; Rathgar 2988550; Rathmichael 2824463; Rathmines 2988550; Sandymount 086 8863917; Santry-8363186; Templeogue-2988576; Terenure-2988550; Wicklow, 087 4195474

Motions Health & Fitness Training (087 2808866) - Fitness Instructor training diploma course (ITEC), part-time, 9 hours per week. Venue Citywest Hotel & Leisure Centre, Naas Rd

Newpark Adult Education Centre Newtownpark Ave Blackrock (2884376 / 2883725) - pilates, yoga, t'ai chi: €95

Phibsboro Gym 1st Floor, Phibsboro SC 7 (8301849) - & boxercise

Portmarnock Sports & Leisure Club Blackwood Lane Carrickhill Portmarnock (8462122) - also fully equipped gym

Saint Anthony's House St Lawrence Rd 3 (8335300) - League of Health, 15wks, also day

Taney Parish Centre Taney Rd Dundrum 14 (2985491) - pilates, Wed (086 6638467)

Tony Quinn Centre 66/67 Eccles St 7 (8304211) - weight training & body build. (8304998)

KEYBOARD SKILLS see also Computers / Typing / Word Processing

Ballymun Trinity CS, Adult Ed Centre 9 (8420654) - learn to type, Tue 7pm 10 wks, €90

Cabinteely Community School Johnstown Rd 18 (2857455) - & typing, 10wk, €95

Coláiste Dhúlaigh CFE, Barryscourt Rd Coolock 17 (8481337) - 'step O', Mon 10 wks, 6-8pm

Crumlin College of FE, Crumlin Rd 12 (4540662) - Mon, 10 wks, 6.45-8.45

CTA Computer Training Academy, St James's Tce Malahide (8454070) - typing, 15 hrs: day/eve/Sat

Grange Community College Grange Abbey Rd Donaghmede 13 (8471422) - computers/typing 7.30-9pm 10wks

Irish Academy of Computer Training 98 St Stephen's Green 2 (4347662) - becoming computer literate/ word for windows: each 4 wks, cert/ e-Citizen ECDL skills 6 wks/ day/eve

Newpark Adult Education Centre Newtownpark Ave Blackrock (2884376 / 2883725) - typewriting, €125 Tue 7.30-9.45

Pitman Training Centre 6-8 Wicklow St 2 (6768008) - speed/ audio data entry, 16-20 hrs, cert

Rathmines CFE - Senior College, Town Hall 6 (4975334) - cert in keyboarding, typing and wp: Mon 7-9pm, 20 wks, €145

St Tiernan's Community School Parkvale Balally 16 (2953224) - Mon 6 wks 7.39 €100

Tallaght Community School Balrothery 24 (4515566) - & typing skills, beginners & improvers, 10wk, €80

KEYBOARDS (Tuition) see also Music

Abbey School of Music 9b Lr Abbey St 1 (8747908) - John Hunter

Clontarf School of Music 6 Marino Mart 3 (8330936 087 8054963)

Dún Laoghaire Music Centre 130A Lr George's St Dún Laoghaire (2844178)

Hartstown Community School Clonsilla 15 (8209863) - 10wks, €85

Hollywood Academy Dublin 13-14 Sackville Pl 1 (8786909) - from 4-8pm: 11 mths €75 per mth, cert

John Ward 5 Tibradden Drive Walkinstown 12 (4520918) - prep for RIAM grade exams/ also day

Melody School of Music 178E Whitehall Rd W Perrystown 12 (4650150) - also day; also w/ends Sat-Sun, 12 wks

Nolan School of Music 3 Dean St 8 (4933730) - also day

Waltons New School of Music 69 Sth Gt George's St 2 (4781884) - also day, see ad page 155

KICK BOXING

Cabinteely Community School Johnstown Rd 18 (2857455) - Tues 10 wks 7.30-9pm €75

Dundrum Family Recreation Centre Meadowbrook 16 (2984654)

Lucan Community College Esker Drive (6282077) - khai bo, 1 & 2: Tue 7.15/8.15 10 wks €65

Palmerstown CS - Pobailscoil Iosolde, Kennelsfort Rd 20 (6260116) - Tues 7pm 10 wks €80

Phibsboro Gym 1st Floor, Phibsboro SC 7 (8301849) - all levels

Ringsend Technical Institute Cambridge Rd 4 (6684498) -tae bo, Wed 6.30 10 wks €50

KINESIOLOGY see also Health Education

Kinesiology Institute 84 Cappaghmore Clondalkin 22 (4571183) - dip course, Sept 06 to June 07: 13 w/end workshops, practices, exams, fees: €195 per w/end or €2,475

KNITTING / MACHINE KNITTING

Grafton Academy of Dress Design 6 Herbert Place 2 (6763653) - machine, basic/ advanced, 25 hr €598

Marino College 14-20 Marino Mart 3 (8332100) - and crochet Thurs 8pm 10 wks €65

KNOW YOUR RIGHTS see Consumer Education / Law

KOREAN see also Languages

The Asian Institute, Nova UCD, Belfield 4 (2899608) - 10 wks, for practical business use, on-site

KUNG FU

Yang's Martial Arts Assoc Blackrock (2814901) - Yang's Martial Arts Association/ white crane & long fist, all levels

LANDSCAPE PAINTING see also Art / Painting

Brian Byrnes Art Studio 3 Upr Baggot St 4 (6671520 / 6711599) - 8wk, €140, also day

UCD Adult Education Centre Belfield (7167123)

LANGUAGES see also Translators Course and under individual languages

Aisling Ireland 137 Lr Rathmines Rd 6 (4971902)

The Asian Institute, Nova UCD, Belfield 4 (2899608) - 10 wk courses in Mandarin Chinese, Cantonese, Korean, Japanese; also practical business courses on-site

Dublin Public Libraries Admin Hq, 138-144 Pearse St 2 (6744800) - central library Ilac Centre, D1 (8734333) or Library HQ for details (6744800), self-learning €free: including: Afrikaans, Amharic, Arabic, Bulgarian, Cambodian, Chinese - Mandarin/ Cantonese, Czech, Danish, Dutch, English Incl English As A Second Language, Finnish, French, German, German, Commercial, Greek-classical & modern, Hausa, Hebrew, Hindi, Hungarian, Icelandic, Indonesian, Irish (All Levels), Italian , Japanese, Korean, Lakota, Latin, Lithuanian, Malay, Norwegian, Persian, Polish, Portuguese, Romanian, Russian, Scots Gaelic, Serbo-Croatian, Somali, Spanish & Latin American Spanish,, Swahili, Swedish, Thai, Turkish, Ukranian, Urdu, Vietnamese, Welsh, Zulu

Dún Laoghaire-Rathdown Co Council Public Library Service - free self-learning language facilities: the library at: Blackrock (2888117), Cabinteely (2855363), Dalkey (2855277), Deansgrange (2850860), Dún Laoghaire (2801147), Dundrum (2985000), Sallynoggin (2850127), Shankill (2823081), Stillorgan (2889655)

Esperanto Assoc of Ireland 9 Templeogue Wood 6W (4945020) - Esperanto correspondence course, €free

Fingal Co Libraries County Hall Main St Swords (8905520) - self-learning, free, Ballbriggan: 8411128; Baldoyle: 8906793; Blanchardstown: 8905563; Howth: 8322130; Malahide: 8452026; Swords: 8404179; Mobile Library HQ: 8221564; Skerries 8491900; Schools Library Service: 8225056; Housebound Services: 8604290

Foxrock Institute Kill o' the Grange, Kill Lane Blackrock (4939506) - French/ Italian/ Spanish, 8 wks, €105

GaelChultúr Ltd Filmbase Building (Level 2) Curved St, Temple Bar 2 (7653658/ 085 7076182) - Irish, for adults, all levels year round, city centre

Goethe Institut 62 Fitzwilliam Sq 2 (6801110) - German, all levels; also commercial and legal

Greenhills College Limekiln Ave Walkinstown 12 (4507779/4507863) - French, Irish, Spanish, 10 wks, €87 each

Hartstown Community School Clonsilla 15 (8209863) - French, beginners/ Irish, beginners/ Italian, beginners, intermediate/ Spanish beginners, intermediate: 10 wks, €85 each

Kilroy's College Wentworth House Grand Canal Street Lr 2 (6620538 1850-700700) home study: Spanish, German, Irish, French, Italian

Newpark Adult Education Centre, Newtownpark Ave Blackrock (2884376 / 2883725) - Chinese, French, German, Irish, Italian, Polish, Spanish, 10 wks €120 ea, 7.30-9.30pm

Park House International Language Institute Ashdale Rd Terenure 6W (4902648) - Spanish, English

Pearse College Clogher Rd Crumlin 12 (4536661/4541544) - for business & tourism, French, German, Spanish - 1 yr day€350 FETAC

Taney Parish Centre Taney Rd Dundrum 14 (2985491) - Macdus, Sat (2883992; 4905679)

The Open University Enquiry/Advice Centre Holbrook House, Holles St 2 (6785399)

WORDS Language Services 44 Northumberland Rd 4 (6610240) - individual tuition in various languages

LATIN

Sandford Language Institute Milltown Pk Sandford Rd 6 (2601296) - all levels subject to demand, 15 wks €350; also day/ also for professional purposes

UCD Adult Education Centre Belfield (7167123) - Latin for beginners, Mon / improvers, Wed: ea 20 wks, cert

LATIN AMERICAN DANCE see also Dance

Cabinteely Community School Johnstown Rd 18 (2857455) - samba, cha cha, rumba & jive, 10wk, €50

Dance Club Rathmines & Rathgar (2893797)

Morosini-Whelan School of Dancing 46 Parnell Sq W 1 (8303613) - Salsa, Mon & Wed, 7-8pm, Argentinian, Tango, 8-9pm €8

LATVIAN

Sandford Language Institute Milltown Pk Sandford Rd 6 (2601296) - all levels subject to demand, 15 wks €350

LAW & LEGAL STUDIES see also Industrial Relations / Legal Aid / Secretarial

Coláiste Dhúlaigh CFE, Barryscourt Rd Coolock 17 (8481337) - know your rights, Tue 7.30-9.30, 7 wks/ employment legislation intro, 10 wks Tue

Crumlin College of FE, Crumlin Rd 12 (4540662) - legal studies cert: constitutional law Mon & sources of law-Irish legal system, Tue/ legal studies diploma: contract (Mon) & tort & criminal law, Wed/ 2 yr course, ICM exam

DIT Faculty: Applied Arts Aungier St 2 (4023000) - BA (Ord) in Law, 2 yr p/time, €1090 pa/ - foundations in civil & or criminal law litigation, 1 eve weekly, €645, cert/ continuing professional development, cert €315 per subject/ MA in criminology, 2 yrs €2500/ BSc in business & legal studies, modu lar, €1555

Study Languages@DIT

Evening Language Classes

Would you like to improve your language skills for fun, travel, or to enhance your career prospects?

Languages:	French/Chinese/German/Irish/Italian/Spanish
Levels:	Beginners, Intermediate, Advanced Level
Course Duration:	2 hours x 12 weeks (evenings)
Fees:	€225 (per semester)

English as a Foreign Language

Would you like to communicate through English successfully and with ease? Students interested in preparing for internationally recognised exams in English as a foreign language will find these courses very helpful.

Levels:	Intermediate, Upper Intermediate, Advanced Level
Course Duration:	2 hours x 12 weeks (evenings)
Fees:	€225 (per semester)

Online Translation Course: French, German, Spanish

This distance learning course offers you the opportunity to learn and practice translation skills using your own computer. If you are interested in preparing for the **Institute of Linguists' Diploma in Translation**, you will find this online course very helpful.

Requirements:	University degree or equivalent in French, German or Spanish.
Essential:	Internet Connection and Basic Computer Skills
Course Duration:	27 weeks
Fee:	€600

Students, of all the above courses, will receive a DIT Certificate on completion.

For further information & registration details contact:
DIT School of Languages
Kevin Street, Dublin 8
T: 01 402 46 73/ 28 43 E: languages@dit.ie
www.dit.ie/DIT/appliedarts/languages/index.html

www.dit.ie   DIT – It's a step closer to the real world.

135

Dorset College 64 Lr Dorset St/ 8 Belvedere Pl 1 (8309677) - cert/dip in legal studies, Mon & Wed, 6.30-9.30pm, 1-2yrs

Dublin Business School 13/14 Aungier St 2 (4177500) - Dip in Legal Studies/ Advanced Dip in Legal Studies, 2 eves a wk, 6.15-9.30pm, 1 yr / BA in Business Management (Law) 4 yrs / Dip in Employment Law; Dip in Family Law: each 1 eve, 10 wks, 6.15-9.30

Griffith College Dublin Sth Circular Rd 8 (4150400) - BA in legal studies, 3 yrs, HETAC f/t/ IILEX cert & dip in professional legal studies, 1 yr 2 eves wkly/ LLB in Irish Law, 3 yrs, f/t, mon to fri; also 3 eves per wk/ BA Law with Business, 4 yrs, HETAC, f/t / BA Business & Law, 3yr, 3 eve per wk; also f/time/ Law Soc prep exams, 13 wk 2 eve wkends/ Kings Inns entrance exams, 3 mths 1 eve, wkends/ New York Bar, 8-10 wks corresp course/ qualified lawyers transsfer test, 2 sittings pa

Harcourt Business School HSI 89 Harcourt St 2 (4763975) - dip in employment law

Inchicore CFE, Emmet Rd 8 (4535358) - business admin with legal studies, day

Palmerstown CS - Pobailscoil Iosolde, Kennelsfort Rd 20 (6260116) - legal studies FETAC 5, Thurs 7pm 10 wks €90

Pitman Training Centre 6-8 Wicklow St 2 (6768008) - legal, cert, day eve sats/ legal secretarial, full/pt-time, dip; day eve sats

Plunket College Swords Rd, Whitehall 9 (8371689) - employment law intro, Tue 7.30 10wks €90

Pobalscoil Rosmini Adult Ed Grace Pk Rd 9 (8371015) - introductory for beginners, contract, criminal, tort, property, EU: Mon 7pm & 8.30, €90 each

The Open University Enquiry Centre Holbrook House, Holles St 2 (6785399) - English

Trinity College 2 (8961000) - (8961007) - construction law & contract admin, postgrad dip, 24wks, also Sat

Westmoreland College for Management Studies 11 Westmoreland St 2 (6795324/7266) - ICM dip legal studies

LAW FOR THE LAY PERSON

DIT Faculty: Applied Arts Aungier St 2 (4023000) - foundation courses in law: contract/ property/ tort/ EU law/ equity/ criminal/ constitutional/ company/ family / employment/ human rights/ immigration/ civil, criminal foundations: 1 eve or morn wkly, €345 ea

Hartstown Community School Clonsilla 15 (8209863) - know your rights, tues, 10wks, €85

Saor-Ollscoil na hÉireann 55 Prussia St 7 (8683368) - legal studies

UCD Adult Education Centre Belfield (7167123) - Irish family law, 10 wks cert/ understanding human rights 9 wks/ Crime and Criminality 10 wks/ Last Will and Testament in Irish Society Wed 5 wks

LEADERSHIP see also Community / Management/ Youth

Junior Chamber Ireland - email pro@jci-ireland.org for info

LEAVING CERTIFICATE / PRE-LEAVING for Adults

Ashfield College Main St Templeogue 6W (4900866) - choice of subjects, p/time higher, lower /taking an extra subject / intensive summer language courses

Bray Institute of FE, Novara Ave Bray (2866111 / 2829668) - maths(o) Mon 7.30 20 Wks€170

Clontarf School of Music 6 Marino Mart 3 (8330936 087 8054963) - musicianship, day & eve 17 wks

Coláiste Dhúlaigh CFE, Barryscourt Rd Coolock 17 (8481337) - art; English; history; maths; music; Spanish: all Mondays 20/22 wks eve

Colaiste Ide Cardiffsbridge Rd Finglas W 8443233 11 (8342333) - French, Thurs 7-10pm 20 wks €300

Conradh na Gaeilge 6 Sr Fhearchair (Harcourt St) BAC 2 (4757401) - Irish

Crumlin College of FE, Crumlin Rd 12 (4540662) - English, Geography, History, Irish, Maths ord level/also LC prep in Maths: 6.15. 7.15, 8.15pm

DATE Centre CFE, Dundrum 14 (2964322 (9.30am-12pm)) - English (o) (BTEI)/ English (h) / classical studies/ history (BTEI)

Dublin Adult Learning Centre 3 Mountjoy Sq 1 (8787266) - English

Dún Laoghaire Music Centre 130A Lr George's St Dún Laoghaire (2844178) - music

Finglas Adult Reading & Writing Scheme Colaiste Eoin Cappagh Rd 11 (8340893) - English ord level Wed 9.30-11.30am; Tues 7-9pm/ maths 30 wks ord level tues 7-9pm

Goethe Institute 62 Fitzwilliam Sq 2 (6801110) - pre-leaving cert German, 16wks/ intensive 2 wk day summer courses

Grange Community College Grange Abbey Rd Donaghmede 13 (8471422) - maths ord level 16wks

Greenhills College Limekiln Ave Walkinstown 12 (4507779/4507863) - maths (O)/ Irish: 20wks, €130 each

Institute of Education 82/85 Lr Leeson St 2 (6613511)

Kilroy's College Wentworth House Grand Canal Street Lr 2 (6620538 1850-700700) - tutor supported home study, all major subjects/ full rapid revision courses

KLEAR Grange Park View Kilbarrack 5 (8671845) - English, day only

Kylemore College Kylemore Rd 10 (6265901) - second chance 1 yr courses, account-ing/ business/ english/ geography/ maths/ music yr1 & 2: all 7-9pm/ history Sat 10.30-12.30pm

Pearse College Clogher Rd Crumlin 12 (4536661/4541544) - 2yr for adults/ also repeat - day/ also individual subjjects: €220/ €70 with med card

Plunket College Swords Rd, Whitehall 9 (8371689) - 27 wks, most subjects, €283-425 per subject/ business org, Tues 7-9pm 27 wks €283

Rathmines CFE - Senior College, Town Hall 6 (4975334) - Maths, 25 wks, Mon 7pm/ life drawing Tue 6pm, 10 wks, €55

Ringsend Technical Institute Cambridge Rd 4 (6684498) - LC English, Maths

Southside Adult Literacy Scheme 4 Glenville Tce Dundrum 14 (2964321) - English

St Kevin's College, Clogher Rd Crumlin 12 (4536397) - also post-jnr, day

TACT St Dominic's School St Dominic's Rd Tallaght 24 (4596757)

Waltons New School of Music 69 Sth Gt George's St 2 (4781884) - music, also day, see ad page 155

LEISURE & RECREATIONAL STUDIES

Inchicore CFE, Emmet Rd 8 (4535358) - leisure & recreation management; leisure & disability studies; travel & tourism management; (post-LC courses)

Litton Lane Studios PO Box 9853 Dunshaughlin Co Meath (8728044) - exercise & fitness instructor course - 20wks, €1950

LETTERING see Calligraphy / Signwriting
LIBERAL ARTS / STUDIES
Saor-Ollscoil na hÉireann 55 Prussia St 7 (8683368)
The Open University Enquiry/Advice Centre Holbrook House, Holles St 2 (6785399)
LIBRARIES see also Information Centres / Music Library
Central Library Ilac Centre 1 (8734333)
Dublin City Council Public Libraries Admin Hq, 138-144 Pearse St 2 (6744800) - central library Ilac Centre, D1, (8734333) or Library HQ for details (6744800)- self-learning €free
Dún Laoghaire-Rathdown Co Council Public Library Service - Dún Laoghaire-Rathdown Public Library Service - free monthly book clubs; novels discussed, informal, new members welcome: the library at: Blackrock (2888117), Cabinteely (2855363), Dalkey (2855277), Deansgrange (2850860), Dunlaoghaire (2801147), Dundrum (2985000), Sallynoggin (2850127) Shankill (2823081), Stillorgan (2889655)
Fingal Co Libraries County Hall Main St Swords (8905520) - internet access/ self-learning: Balbriggan: 8411128; Baldoyle: 906793; Blanchardstown: 8905563; Howth: 8322130; Malahide: 8452026; Skerries: 8491900; Swords: 8404179; Mobile Library HQ: 8221564; Schools Library:8225056; Housebound Service: 8604290
National Library of Ireland Kildare St 2 (6030200) - various exhibitions, lectures
South Dublin Co Libraries (4597834-admin only) - self learning /also language & computer classes. free: Ballyroan (4941900), Castletymon (4524888)
Clondalkin (4593315), Lucan (6216422), Tallaght (4620073).
LIFE DRAWING & PAINTING see also Drawing / Painting
Gallery Art Centre The Mill, Celbridge Co Kildare (6276206) - life drawing, am/pm 9 wks €100
Rathmines CFE - Senior College, Town Hall 6 (4975334) - beginners, 10 wks Tue 6-7pm €55
LIFE SAVING see Water Safety
LIFE SKILLS / COACHING see also Personal Development, Coaching
Cabinteely Community School Johnstown Rd 18 (2857455) - life changes & success, Tue 10 wks €95
Communication & Personal Development 30/31 Wicklow St 2 (6713636/ 6613225)
Dún Laoghaire CFE, 17 Cumberland St Dún Laoghaire (2809676) - intro to life coaching, 10 wks Wed 7pm €110
Enriching Careers 38 Clonliffe Rd 3 (6589091)
Foxrock Institute Kill o' the Grange, Kill Lane Blackrock (4939506) - live your dream 8 wks €189
IICH Education 118 Stillorgan Road 4 (2017422) - workshops; certs; diplomas
Killester CFE, Collins Ave 5 (8337686) - energise your life, 10 wks Tue 7.30 €70
KLEAR Grange Park View Kilbarrack 5 (8671845) - for positive living, day
Lucan Community College Esker Drive (6282077) - Tue 7.30-8.30 10 wks €130
Malahide Community School Malahide (8460949) - intro to, 10 wks €80
Newpark Adult Education Centre, Newtownpark Ave Blackrock (2884376 / 2883725) - become your own life coach, 10 wks €120: Mon/ Tue: 7.30-9.45
Portmarnock Community School Carrickhill Rd (8038056) - Mon 7.30 10 wks €100

Positive Success Group Applewood Med Centre Swords (8956820) - emotional intelligence

Ringsend Technical Institute Cambridge Rd 4 (6684498) - boost self confidence, Tue 7.30-9.30 8 wks €70

St Finian's Community College Swords (8402623) - 8 wks

St Tiernan's Community School Parkvale Balally 16 (2953224) - Mon 7.30 10 wks €80

LINE DANCING see Dancing

LINGUISTICS - Applied

UCD Adult Education Centre Belfield (7167123) - Languages, Dialects and Accents, Mon 10 wks

LIP-READING

National Assoc for Deaf People 35 Nth Frederick St 1 (8175700 /fax 8723816) -deaf adults with acquired hearing loss - hearing help & lipreading, day & eve, 8 wk-term, 2 yr prog, €15 subsidised; completion cert

LITERACY (BASIC) see also English Literacy

Hartstown Community School Clonsilla 15 (8209863) - for adults, improve spelling, 10 wks, €40

National Adult Literacy Agency 76 Lr Gardiner St 1 (8554332) - no courses; org Tutor training via local literacy schemes/ family literacy/ English as a second language

South Dublin Learning Centre 4 Glenville Tce Dundrum 14 (2964321)

LITERATURE see also German Culture / Book Club / Writing

Children's Books Ireland 17 North Great George's St 1 (8727475) - seminars/ workshops for adults on books for young readers; also quarterly magazine, *Inis*

DATE Centre CFE, Dundrum 14 (2964322 (9.30am-12pm)) - enjoying English lit (19th cent & contemporary), Thurs 9.30 & 11.10am 10 wks €97

Dún Laoghaire-Rathdown Co Council Public Library Service - free monthly book clubs; novels discussed, informal, new members welcome: the library at: Blackrock (2888117), Cabinteely (2855363), Dalkey (2855277), Deansgrange (2850860) Dún Laoghaire (2801147), Dundrum (2985000), Sallynoggin (2850127), Shankill (2823081), Stillorgan (2889655)

Grange Community College Grange Abbey Rd Donaghmede 13 (8471422) - 7-9pm Mon 10 wks appreciation

James Joyce Centre 35 Nth Gt George's St 1 (8788547) - Reading Joyce, Sept - May

Kilroy's College Wentworth House Grand Canal Street Lr 2 (6620538 1850-700700) - tutor supported home study: English, dip

People's College for Continuing Education & Training 32 Parnell Sq 1 (8735879) - €40

Plunket College Swords Rd, Whitehall 9 (8371689) - crime fiction, Tue 7.30 10wks €67/ 1916-and the writers, Tue 7.30 10 wks €90

Pobalscoil Neasáin Baldoyle 13 (8063092) - UCD course modules 1 & 2, 10 wks Tue morns

Saor-Ollscoil na hÉireann 55 Prussia St 7 (8683368) - European

Trinity College 2 (8961000) - (6082885) - English lit/ poetry & politics: 9 wks €40 each

UCD Adult Education Centre Belfield (7167123) - 10 week courses: 20th Century Anglo-Irish Literature/ Appreciating Poetry/ Forensic Fiction/ Jane Austen's Men/ Languages, Dialects and Accents/ Literature, History and Romance/ Modern Classics 1& 2/ Monsters and Misfits in Film and Literature/ Sexual and Economic Politics in novels/ Talking about novels, memoirs, histories and biographies (4wks)/ The Detective Novel: Does It Matter Whodunnit?/ Victorian Literature in Ireland (new texts)/ Yeats: Life & Works (8wks, NLI)

LITERATURE FOR CHILDREN

UCD Adult Education Centre Belfield (7167123) - fairytales in contemporary culture & literature, Tue 10 wks/ writers workshop in children's fiction, 10 wks/ development workshop in children's fiction

Children's Books Ireland 17 North Great George's St 1 (8727475) - seminars/ workshops for adults on books for young readers; also quarterly magazine, *Inis*

LITHUANIAN

Sandford Language Institute Milltown Pk Sandford Rd 6 (2601296) - all levels subject to demand, 15 wks €350

LITURGY
All Hallows College Gracepark Rd Drumcondra 9 (8373745) - liturgy 1, Mon 6.50, 24 wks €200 / Liturgy 2 Tue 8.30pm 12 wks: €200. ECTS credits option

LOBBYING SKILLS
Comhámh 10 Upr Camden St 2 (4783490)

LONE PARENT see Parenting

MAKE-UP (for Stage, Television and Film)
Ballyfermot CFE, Ballyfermot Rd 10 (6269421) - 15 wks Mon 7-10pm

Bray Institute of FE, Novara Ave Bray (2866111 / 2829668) - fashion, theatre, make-up, special effects, 25 wks €500 - ptime modular dy course

Inchicore CFE, Emmet Rd 8 (4535358) - costume design & wardrobes, day

Portobello School 43 Lr Dominick St 1 (8721277) - facial make-up, ITEC cert, 6.30pm 16 wks/ special effects make-up 6.30, 32 wks dip/ make-up artistry, 6.30, 32 wks ITEC dip / fashion, theatre & media make-up, dip ITEC

School of Stage, TV & Film: 1000 Faces Stage, TV & Film 9 (8368201/ 087 2261479) - fashion, special effects, airbrushing costume, etc, diploma course

MANAGEMENT see also Business / Computer / Financial / Industrial Relations / Personnel / Supervision / Teamwork
Ballyfermot CFE, Ballyfermot Rd 10 (6269421) - group skills for managers, NUI Maynooth cert, 100 hrs x 2 yrs, Wed 7-10pm

Bray Institute of FE, Novara Ave Bray (2866111 / 2829668) - supervisory, IMI cert,

2nd yr Mon: €380 / frontline management IMI cert 1st yr, Tue 7-10 25 wks €400 IMI members; €460 non-members

Communications & Management Institute Regus Hse, Harcourt Rd 2 (4927070) - event management dip: Wedf 20 wks €1350/ event mangement + PR, cert, Wed 10 wks €750/ mamagement cert, Tue €750/ management dip, Wed eve 9 mths €1950/ graduate dip in management, Tue 9mths €1950

Coolmine Community School Clonsilla 15 (8214583) - NCI dip in first-line management: 2 yrs, Mon 7-9.30 €1150

DIT Faculty: Business Aungier St 2 (4023000) - MSc in strategic management, 2yr ptime €2808 pa

DIT Faculty: Tourism & Food Cathal Brugha St 1 (4023000) - becoming a more effective manager, 12 wks €235, cert/ meat managememnt; bar management dip, each, 2 yrs €550pa / performance management skills, 12 wks €235/ management principles 1 & 2, each 12 wks €130

Dorset College 64 Lr Dorset St/ 8 Belvedere Pl 1 (8309677) - ILM cert: project management; risk management/ dip in level 4 management/ dip in project management

Dublin Business School 13/14 Aungier St 2 (4177500) - BA (Hons) Management; BA (Hons) Marketing & Event Management; BA (Hons) Management & Information Systems: each 6.15-9.30pm 4 yrs / Dip Management Studies 1 year Oct , 17 wks Feb; Dip in Selling & Sales Management; Dip Event Management 1 eve 14 wks; Dip Project Management 14 wks;Advanced Diploma in Project Management; Dip Tourism Management & Marketing, 1 eve 1 yr, Dip in Coaching for Performance, 1 eve, 10 wks: all 6.15-9.30pm

Eden Computer Training Rathfarnham 16 & 1 Green St 7 (4953155)

FAS Training Centres:- 10 wks, intro, ILM cert: Baldoyle 13 (8167400); Ballyfermot 10 (6055900):Cabra Bannow Rd 7 (8821400); Finglas Jamestown Rd 11 (8140200); Loughlinstown Wyattville Rd, DL (2043600); Tallaght Cookstown Indl Est 24 (4045200) / Jervis St 1 (8044600) - ICM cert, intro: 6-9pm 10 wks

Fitzwilliam Institute Ltd Temple Court Temple Rd Blackrock (2834579) - dip in event management (with PR module), 14 wks - 2 eves weekly 6.30-9.30, Mon & Wed, €1395 incl exam fees; city centre; accredited by PRII

Griffith College Dublin Sth Circular Rd 8 (4150400) - International Bus Management: MBA, 2 yr p/t or 1 yr f/t, both with 2 yr work experience/ MSc, NTU or 2yr p/time; also 1 yr f/t / Grad Dipl, 4 semesters p/t 3 eve wkly/ post-graduate cert, 2 semesters p/time; or 1 semester f/t/ professional cert, 1 semester f/t

Harcourt Business School HSI 89 Harcourt St 2 (4763975) - dip in event management

I.T. Blanchardstown Rd North 15 (8851000) - project management 1 yr, p/time €2325

Institute of Public Administration 57-61 Lansdowne Rd 4 (2403600) - BA (NUI cert) / dip in public management, 2 yrs part-time

Institute of Public Administration 57-61 Lansdowne Rd 4 (2403600) - public management & business studies degree & dip courses/ one yr part-time cert

Institute of Technology Tallaght ITT Dublin, Tallaght 24 (4042101) - BBusiness, Management NFQ Level 7 3 yrs/ (Hons) Management NFQ Level 8 1 yr (add on) / BA Technology Management NFQ Level 7 1 yr/ BSc (Hons) Technology Management NFQ Level 8 1 yr (add on)

Irish Academy of Public Relations (2780802) - courses at UCD, Belfield: dip in event management, 15 wks 2 evs, €1850.

Irish Management Institute Sandyford Rd 16 (2078400) - Henley Diploma in management, 18mth prog

Kilroy's College Wentworth House Grand Canal Street Lr 2 (6620538 1850-700700) - tutor supported home study: basic, business

Malahide Community School (8460949) - project management Tue 7.30 10 wks €95/ BA in business management, NCI course, Tue & Thurs 2 yrs, €2500 pa

Maynooth NUI Adult & Community Ed Dept (7084500) - communication & group skills for managers: NUI Maynooth campus; also Ballyfermot CFE (6269421)

National College of Ireland Mayor St IFSC 1 (4060500/ 1850 221721) - - Certificate in Managing Teams (online), 12 weeks, €915/ see also Personnel Managment HRH

Old Bawn Community School Tallaght 24 (4526137) - first-line management, 2 yr dip, 6.30-9pm, 24 wks - National College of Ireland (4498534) - also 1 yr dip, 1.30-6pm

Palmerstown CS - Pobailscoil Iosolde, Kennelsfort Rd 20 (6260116) - NCI dip in 1st line management, 2yr, Mon 7-9.30 €980

Pobalscoil Rosmini Adult Ed Grace Pk Rd 9 (8371015) - crisis intervention & management, introductory, Wed 7-8.20 €90

Tallaght Community School Balrothery 24 (4515566) - transport management cert, CPC, 30wk, €550 (payable €275 x 2)

Trinity College 2 (8961000) - (8961007) - project, 1yr postgrad dip, 24wks, Fri pm Sat am

UCD Adult Education Centre Belfield (7167123) - management techniques, Mon 10 wks; finance for non-financial managers, Wed 10 wks

Westmoreland College for Management Studies 11 Westmoreland St 2 (6795324/7266) - ICM dip health services management/ ICM dipcorporate management/ ICM grad dip management/ ICM dip HR management/ Adv dip in project management

MANDOLIN see also Music

Comhaltas Ceoltóirí Éireann 32 Belgrave Sq Monkstown (2800295)

Waltons New School of Music 69 Sth Gt George's St 2 (4781884) - also day, see ad page 155

MANICURE & PEDICURE

Aspen's College of Beauty Therapy 83 Lr Camden St 2 (4751079/ 4751940) - ITEC / also, nail technology/ short courses: gel nail; acrylic nail

Ballyfermot CFE, Ballyfermot Rd 10 (6269421) - gel nail technician AINT dip, 20 wks 7-9pm

Bray Institute of FE, Novara Ave Bray (2866111 / 2829668) - nail technician's cert,

Mon & Wed 7-9pm 10 wks €480/ manicure, pedicure & airbrush tanning cert, Tue 7-9pm 10 wks €300

Coláiste Dhúlaigh CFE,Barryscourt Rd Coolock 17 (8481337) - nail training prof dip, Mon 6.15-9.30 12 wks

Irish Academy of Training 33 Monkstown Lawns, Clondalkin 22 (4640126) - ITEC cert, Thurs eve from Oct06

Portobello School 43 Lr Dominick St 1 (8721277) - ITEC cert eve 32 wks

MARINE TECHNOLOGY

Cabinteely Community School Johnstown Rd 18 (2857455) - marine engine maintenance, 10wk, €95

Ringsend Technical Institute Cambridge Rd 4 (6684498) - engine maintenance, 10wks, €115, Tue 7pm

MARKETING see also Sales

Bray Institute of FE, Novara Ave Bray (2866111 / 2829668) - MII cert in marketing skills, Mon+Wed 7-10pm 25 wks €450

Communications & Management Institute Regus Hse, Harcourt Rd 2 (4927070) - marketing, PR, advertising & sales dip, Tue 1 yr €1550/ marketing cert, Tue 10 wks €750/ marketing dip Tue & thurs 20 wks €1450

DIT Faculty: Business Aungier St 2 (4023000) - foundation MI cert, 2 yrs €777pa/ MI dip, 1 yr €682/ MI graduateship, 1 yr, €777

DIT Faculty: Tourism & Food Cathal Brugha St 1 (4023000) -intro to for hospitality sector, 12 wks €130

Dorset College 64 Lr Dorset St/ 8 Belvedere Pl 1 (8309677) - dip marketing, advertising & PR, Mon & Wed, 6.30-9.30 1yr

Dublin Business School 13/14 Aungier St 2 (4177500) - BA (Hons) Marketing, 6.15-9.30pm, 4 yrs / Dip in Marketing, Advertising, Sales & PR, 2 eves, 6.15-9.30pm, Oct 1 yr, Feb 14 wks /Diploma in Internet Marketing, 1 eve, 10 weeks / MA in Marketing, 2 eve 6.15 1 yr, 14 wks

Dún Laoghaire CFE, 17 Cumberland St Dún Laoghaire (2809676) - ICM dip, 20wks, Mon + Wed, 7-10pm €585

Griffith College Dublin Sth Circular Rd 8 (4150400) - dipl in marketing, advertising & sales, 4-8 mths, 2 eve per wk, ICM, p/time/ BA 3yr HETAC f/time / management studies 4-8 mth ICM dip 2 eve wkly

Harcourt Business School HSI 89 Harcourt St 2 (4763975) - dip in marketing, advertising, PR & sales

Institute of Technology Tallaght ITT Dublin, Tallaght 24 (4042101) - Business - Marketing NFQ Level 7 3 yrs/ (Hons) - Marketing Management NFQ Level 8 1 yr (add on)

Irish Academy of Public Relations (2780802) - courses at UCD, Belfield: cert in marketing and advertising, 12 wks 1 ev, €730

Marketing Institute Sth Co Business Pk, Leopardstown 18 (2952355) - marketing / selling cert 2yrs, dip 3 yrs, graduateship 4 yrs by attending / certificate in mkt skills 1yr, by attending college, MII reg fee €275 + exam fee c €130

Pitman Training Centre 6-8 Wicklow St 2 (6768008) - marketing & PR, full/pt-time, dip; day eve sats

Portobello School 43 Lr Dominick St 1 (8721277) - marketing advertising & PR, 1

yr, 1 eve per wk, ICM dip/ ICM subject cert

Senior College Dún Laoghaire, CFE Eblana Ave Dún Laoghaire (2800385) - MII cert/dip, stages 1-3, yr €420 / graduateship stage 4, €500

UCD Adult Education Centre Belfield (7167123) - Export Marketing, Tue (spring) 10 wks

Westmoreland College for Management Studies 11 Westmoreland St 2 (6795324/7266) - ICM dip marketing, advertising & PR

MARRIAGE and RELATIONSHIP COUNSELLING

ACCORD (Catholic Marriage Care Service) 39 Harcourt St 2 (4780866) - appointments & drop-in service

Donahies Community School Streamville Rd 13 (8482217) - life after separation & divorce, Tue €135

MARRIAGE incl Marriage Preparation see also Family / Parents / Counselling / Personal Development

Clanwilliam Institute 18 Clanwilliam Tce 2 (6761363) - marital & family therapy: foundation, 1yr/ professional, 3yrs

MARTIAL ARTS see also Aikido / Judo / Kung-Fu / Karate / Tae-Kwon-Do / T'ai Chi / Self Defence

Aikido Federation of Ireland 1, Park Lane East Pearse St 2 (6718454) - all levels

Irish Martial Arts Commission The Base, 23 York St 2 (4783831) - nationwide info service, 350 affiliated instructors

Irish T'ai Chi Ch'uan Assoc St Andrew's Resource Centre 114 Pearse St 2 (6771930) - Chinese Kung Fu, 8wks, competition standard, forms, weapons

Natural Health Training Centre 1 Park Lane E Pearse St 2 (6718454) - all levels

St Vincent's Shotkan Karate Club St Vincent's GAA Club Malahide Road Marino 3 (8570353/ 087 8197785) - Mon, Tue (Juniors), Thurs; also at St Joseph's PS, Marino Mart, Fairview

Taekwon-Do Centre 10 Exchequer St 2 (6710705)

Yang's Martial Arts Assoc Blackrock (2814901) - Yang's Martial Arts Association/ white crane & long fist kung fu & yang style t'ai chi ch'uan, all levels

MASSAGE

Aspen's College of Beauty Therapy 83 Lr Camden St 2 (4751079/ 4751940) - ITEC holistic body massage

Balbriggan Community College Pine Ridge Chapel St (8412388/9) - Indian head massage, Mon 7.30 €104

Ballyfermot CFE, Ballyfermot Rd 10 (6269421) - Indian head massage

Ballymun Men's Centre Lift Shaft 4 Shangan Rd Ballymun 9 (8623117) - back & head massage, Tue Afternoons

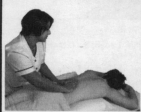

Ballymun Comprehensive School Adult Ed Centre 9 (8420654) - oils & how to, Wed 10 wks €130

BASE Ballyboden Adult Social Education Whitechurch Library Taylor's Lane 16 (4935953) - for relaxation, 10 wks

Berni Grainger 21 Grangemore Ave 13 (8472943/ 086 2694214) - holistic body/Indian head, w/end, €180

Bray Institute of FE, Novara Ave Bray (2866111 / 2829668) - basic threapeutic Mon 7.30, 8 wks €70

Bronwyn Conroy Beauty School Temple Hall, Temple Rd Blackrock (2107848) - anatomy & physiology

Colaiste Ide Cardiffsbridge Rd Finglas W 8443233 11 (8342333) - intro to healing massage, Sat, 10-1.30pm, 10 wks €100, cert

Crumlin College of FE, Crumlin Rd 12 (4540662) - CIBTAC dip, indian head massage, 13 wks, Mon & Wed 6.45-9.45

Foxrock Institute Kill o' the Grange, Kill Lane Blackrock (4939506) - indian head, Wed eve 8 wks €105

Galligan College of Beauty 109 Grafton St 2 (6703933) - ITEC & CIBTAC,Sept - June p/time, €1000

Harmony Healing 41 Beneavin Pk Glasnevin 11 (8641768)

Harmony Yoga Ireland 233 St James Rd Walkinstown 12 (087 8263778) - pregnancy massage dip, 4 day/ massge in schools, 2 day

Hartstown Community School Clonsilla 15 (8209863) - massge therapy, 10 wks €85

Hazel Byrne (087-2843079) - baby massage classes

Healing House 24 O'Connell Ave Berkeley Rd 7 (8306413) - healing massage basic intro, w/end workshop €150/ Indian Head massage intro €175 cert att/ Indian head massage ITEC dip w/ends €750 / ITEC dip Holistic massage, Tue/Thurs 7-10pm or mthly w/ends €1750

Holistic Healing Centre 38 Dame St 2 (6710813) - ITEC dip in: Indian head massage; sports massage; healing massage

Irish Academy of Massage & Complementary Therapies 33 Monkstown Lawns, Clondalkin 22 (4640126) - ITEC dip: holistic massage €1600/ Indian head massage, €500

Irish Health Culture Association 66 Eccles St 7 (8304211) - diploma in ki-massage therapy, 10 wkends from 14 October, €2850/ and concentrated courses

KLEAR Grange Park View Kilbarrack 5 (8671845) - Shiatsu, Indian head massage, day only

Litton Lane Training PO Box 9853 Dunshaughlin Co Meath (8728044) - ITEC massage course, 20 wks €1550

Lucan Community College Esker Drive (6282077) - Indian head, Mon 7.30-8.30 6 wks €78

Marino College 14-20 Marino Mart 3 (8332100) - & aromatherapy for women, Tue 6-8pm €90/ 8pm mixed, €65: 10wks each

Melt, Temple Bar Natural Healing Centre 2 Temple Ln 2 (6798786) - 1 year massage course/ Indian head massage, w/end, €180, cert/ on-site chair techniques for therapists 1 day €120/ flat stone, for therapists w/end €140/ BUPA, VHI, VIVAS approved therapies

Motions Health & Fitness Training (087 2808866) - Diploma in Holistic Massage (ITEC), part-time course, 3 hours per week. Castleknock, Citywest & Naas

Moytura Healing Centre Rinn Rua Claremont Grove Killiney (2854005) - dip, Fri eve & Sat, 10 wks €810

National College of Complementary Medical Ed, 16a St Joseph's Parade Off Dorset Street 7 (8827777) - nat qual, day, eve ptime, €3520

Newpark Adult Education Centre Newtownpark Ave Blackrock (2884376 / 2883725) - basic for women, Mon / basic for men, Thurs: each 10wks €120

Obus School of Healing Therapies, 53 Beech Grove Lucan (6282121) - aromatherapy, 1yr, dip, Leixlip; stone massage, wkend 2 day €200; indian head masage wkend 3 day €250

Our Lady's Hospice Harold's Cross 6 (4068806 4068810) - 2 day workshops: Indian head: 24-25 March07 / seated on-site, 9-10 June07: each 10-5pm €175 incl lunch

Palmerstown CS - Pobailscoil Iosolde, Kennelsfort Rd 20 (6260116) - Indian head, Thurs 7pm 10 wks €70

Pearse College Clogher Rd Crumlin 12 (4536661/4541544) - ITEC dip, day - massage, sports massage, indian head

Plunket College Swords Rd, Whitehall 9 (8371689) - holistic massage, Mon 7.30 10wks €67

Pobalscoil Rosmini Adult Ed Grace Pk Rd 9 (8371015) - Indian head massage, mon 7-8.20 €90

Portobello School 43 Lr Dominick St 1 (8721277) - sports massage / holistic massage/ Indian head massage; stone therapy massage: each 32 wks eve

Seamus Lynch 19 St Patrick's Cresc Monkstown Farm Dún Laoghaire (2846073) - Indian head, w/end, 13.5 hrs, €180, cert of completion

Senior College Dún Laoghaire, CFE Eblana Ave Dún Laoghaire (2800385) - dip in anatomy, physiology & body massage, CIBTEC, €720/ intro to aromatherapy & massage, €120

Shiatsu Ireland classes at 44 Adelaide Rd 2 (2962839) - shiatsu, beginners & advanced

TACT St Dominic's School St Dominic's Rd Tallaght 24 (4596757)

Tallaght Community School Balrothery 24 (4515566) - intro to massage & aromatherapy, 7.30-9.30 10 wks €60

Tony Quinn Centre 66/67 Eccles St 7 (8304211) - ki massage, etc Diploma €2850 (14 Oct)

Walmer College & Holistic Centre First Floor, River Hse Raheny Shopping C 5 (8329645) - sports massage

Walmer College & Holistic Centre First Floor, River Hse Raheny Shopping C 5 (8329645) - holistic massage, ITEC dip/ sports massage ITEC dip/ Indian head, ITEC dip / hydrotherm, ITEC dip/ massage introduction/ infant massage

Walmer College & Holistic Centre
Tel:8329645/8329648
1st Floor, River House,
Raheny SC, Raheny, Dublin 5

ITEC Diploma Courses: Holistic Massage, Aromatherapy, Diet & Nutrition. Indian Head Massage, Sports Massage (August 2006), Beauty Specialist (Sept 2006) **Workshops:** Angels, Colour Therapy, Reiki, Expand Your Strokes, Yoga, Life Skills, Onsite Seated Massage, Food Mood & Emotion, Harley Body Wrap - and loads more!

To browse visit: www.walmer.ie   Email: info@walmer.ie

Clinic: Acupuncture; Chiropractor; Colonics; Osteopath; Hypnosis; Holistic Massage; Craniosacral; Energy Healing; Reiki Medium; Sports Injury; Beauty Treatments; Astrology; Allergy Vega Testing.

MATHEMATICS see also Basic Education / Junior Cert / Leaving Cert / Parents

Ballymun Trinity CS, Adult Ed Centre 9 (8420654) - numeracy, Mon 7.30 10 wk, €free/ Maths Wed 7-10 25 wks €300/ maths for everyday living, Mon 7.30 10 wks free

Coláiste Dhúlaigh CFE, Barryscourt Rd Coolock 17 (8481337) - Junior cert(O), Leaving cert(O)

Coláiste Eanna, Kilkieran Rd Cabra 7 (8389577) - for electrical apprentices Thurs 10 wks 7-9pm/ leaving cert maths, Tue 10 wks 7-9pm

DIT Faculty: Science Kevin St 8 (4023000) - MSc applied maths & theoretical physics, 3 yr p/time, €760 per module €850 thesis/ BSc mathematics 6 yrs (higher cert 2 yrs; Ord 2 yrs; Hons 2 yrs) €900pa

Dublin Adult Learning Centre 3 Mountjoy Sq 1 (8787266) - jnr cert/ basic

Grange Community College Grange Abbey Rd Donaghmede 13 (8471422) - leaving cert ord level, 16 wks

Greenhills College Limekiln Ave Walkinstown 12 (4507779/4507863) - leaving cert(O), 20 wks, €130

Kilroy's College Wentworth House Grand Canal Street Lr 2 (6620538 1850-700700) - tutor supported basic arithmetic for adults, also junior & leaving cert, home-study

KLEAR Grange Park View Kilbarrack 5 (8671845) - discovering maths, dau / foundation maths Thurs eve

National Adult Literacy Agency 76 Lr Gardiner St 1 (8554332) - national referral service for adults to get help with reading, writing & maths

Old Bawn Community School Tallaght 24 (4526137) - what is Mathematics? Thurs 7.30-9.30 €90

Plunket College Swords Rd, Whitehall 9 (8371689) - leaving cert (H&O), 27 wks, €425

Ringsend Technical Institute Cambridge Rd 4 (6684498) - leaving cert (O), 2 yr 25wks, second chance ed, free

South Dublin Learning Centre 4 Glenville Tce Dundrum 14 (2964321) - basic junior cert

The Open University Enquiry/Advice Centre Holbrook House, Holles St 2 (6785399)

MECHANICAL ENGINEERING see also Engineering

DIT Faculty: Engineering Bolton St 1 (4023000) - BEngTech 5yr, €400 per module/ pneumatics; hydraulics; mechanical power transmission, cert; maintenance org; CNC advanced parts prog: cert, €550 ea

St Kevin's College, Clogher Rd Crumlin 12 (4536397) - engineer technician, NCVA, 1yr, day

MEDIA see also see Broadcasting / Communications / Journalism / Print / Television / Writing / Video / Film / Public Relations

Coláiste Dhúlaigh CFE, Barryscourt Rd Coolock 17 (8481337) - media analysis, Mon 7-9.15, 20 wks

Comhlamh 10 Upr Camden St 2 (4783490) - media skills

DIT Faculty: Applied Arts Aungier St 2 (4023000) MA in media studies/ MA in digital media technoligies: ea 2 yr p/time €2500

Dublin Business School 13/14 Aungier St 2 (4177500) - BA (film studies, lit & drama) 4 yrs 6.15-9.30pm / BA Media & Cultural studies, 4 yrs

Griffith College Dublin Sth Circular Rd 8 (4150400) - dipl in media techniques, TV & video, 1 yr, CGLI, f/t ; 1 yr p/t, 2 eve per wk/ higher dip in journalism & media communications 18 mths p/time; also f/time 1 yr; also, diploma, 18mths GCd 3 eves per wk

Harcourt Business School HSI 89 Harcourt St 2 (4763975) - TV presenters course

Irish Academy of Public Relations (2780802) - practical journalism, cert, 12 wks, €390/€440 by email or correspondence

New Media Technology College, 13 Harcourt St 2 (4780905) - digital video production & online broadcasting/ interactive media production/ electronic media EBU dip

Pearse College Clogher Rd Crumlin 12 (4536661/4541544) - dip in media techniques 1 €150; 2 €250/ & production skills dip; radio, video, journalism - day. Yr 1 FETAC certs/ yr 2 C&G dip

Saor-Ollscoil na hÉireann 55 Prussia St 7 (8683368) - media studies, Weds

St Kevin's College Clogher Rd Crumlin 12 (4536397) - production, Higher National Dip, 2yrs, day

UCD Adult Education Centre Belfield (7167123) mass communications

Westmoreland College for Management & Business 11 Westmoreland St 2 (6795324/7266) - ICM dip in journalism & media

MEDICAL RECORDS ADMINISTRATION

DIT Faculty: Science Kevin St 8 (4023000) - records & patient services management, 1 yr Tue & Thurs €760, cert

Pitman Training Centre 6-8 Wicklow St 2 (6768008) - medical, 40 hrs, day eve sats/ medical secretarial dip, full/pt-time; dayeve sats

MEDICINE

DIT Faculty: Science Kevin St 8 (4023000) - MSc in molecular pathology, 2ye ptime €4124/ intro to cellular pathology & histology, 12 wk €315/ BSc in clinical measurement, 2yr p/time €920

Dún Laoghaire CFE, 17 Cumberland St Dún Laoghaire (2809676) - herbal, Mon 7-9pm 10 wks €130

Saint Anthony's House St Lawrence Rd Clontarf 3 (8335300) - Parkinson's association

MEDITATION see also Buddhism / Yoga / Reiki/ Spirituality

Brahma Kumaris WSU Raja Yoga Centres 5 Leeson Pk Ave 6 (6687480) - 7wk free

Bray Institute of FE, Novara Ave Bray (2866111 / 2829668) - angels, spirituality, healing, Wed 10 wks €85

Classical Hatha Yoga 5 Leeson Pk Ave 6 (6687480) - peace & clarity, 4 wks + life long, free, self-rulership - also day

Coláiste Eanna, Kilkieran Rd Cabra 7 (8389577) - stress/ tension relief, 10wks, Tues, 7.30-9pm

Divine Rainbow Centre Marino 3 (8333640)

Dublin Buddhist Centre 42 Lr leeson St (Basement) 2 (6615934) - 5wk, €150 waged, €95 unwaged

Holistic Healing Centre 38 Dame St 2 (6710813)

Irish School of Shamanism 54 South William St 2 (4577839)

Irish T'ai Chi Ch'uan Assoc St Andrew's Resource Centre 114 Pearse St 2 (6771930) - t'ai chi prep, level 1-4 breathing/relaxation/stretching/meditation, 2mths

Irish Yoga Association PO Box 9969 7 (4929213/ 087 2054489) - qualified teachers available all over Ireland/ 4 yr Teacher Training courses

Margaret Macken Yoga Stephen's Gr/Adelaide Rd/Clontarf (8332954) - Iyengar Yoga, 6 wk course; also relaxation, stress management and meditation

Melt, Temple Bar Natural Healing Centre 2 Temple Ln 2 (6798786) - Tibetan meditation, Sun 10am €50.00

Milltown Institute Milltown Pk 6 (2776331) - the art of stillness, Wed 10.25am-12.15, or 7-9pm 12 wks

Obus School of Healing Therapies, 53 Beech Grove Lucan (6282121) - morns & eves, 6wks €110

Pobalscoil Rosmini Adult Ed Grace Pk Rd 9 (8371015) - basic practices Wed 4-5pm €100

Rigpa Tibetan Buddhist Meditation Centre 12 Wicklow St, 3rd Floor 2 (6703358) - intro to meditation, a basis in practice, teachings of Sogyal Rinpoche: 10 wks

Sam Young Howth area (8322803) - 'The Power of Now' (Tolle) 12 wks, morn & eve

T'ai Chi Energy Centre Milltown Pk Conference Centre Sandford Rd Ranelagh 6 (4961533) - t'ai chi/qi gong - & wkend workshops

TACT St Dominic's School St Dominic's Rd Tallaght 24 (4596757)

Tara Buddhist Centre 18 Long Lane 8 (7078809) - ongoing: €8 per class, Tues, Thurs 7.30; also at Melt, Temple Lane Mon 6.45-8, €6, and Adult Ed Centre, Sion Hill Tues 8pm €8

The Sanctuary Stanhope Street 7 (6705419) - the art of being still 7wks €70

MEN, COURSES/ACTIVITIES FOR

Ballymun Men's Centre Lift Shaft 4 Shangan Rd Ballymun 9 (8623117) - day trips, various courses, information sessions, daytime drop-in centre

Paul Bradley (Psychotherapist) Main St Kilcock Co Kildare (6284673/ 087 9598840) - seminars for men, eve/wkend, Dublin/ Kildare venues

METAL WORK see also Art Metal Work

Coláiste Dhúlaigh CFE,Barryscourt Rd Coolock 17 (8481337) - junior cert o level, 25 wks

DIT Faculty: Engineering Bolton St 1 (4023000)

Newpark Adult Education Centre Newtownpark Ave Blackrock (2884376 / 2883725) - Tue/ Thurs: metalcraft, 10 wks, €150

MILLINERY

Grafton Academy of Dress Design 6 Herbert Place 2 (6763653) - felt & straw hats, Tues, 7-9pm, €275

MIME see also Acting

Betty Ann Norton Theatre School 11 Harcourt St 2 (4751913)

MODEL ENGINEERING

St Kevin's College, Clogher Rd Crumlin 12 (4536397) - 10wks

MODERN DANCE

Dance Theatre of Ireland Bloomfields Centre, Lr George St Dún Laoghaire (2803455) - hip-hop Mon & Wed 8-9pm; also Saturdays for adults, teen-to-adult, young people at various times between 11.15am-4.15: 10 wks €80

MONEY MANAGEMENT / PERSONAL ACCOUNTS

Donahies Community School Streamville Rd 13 (8482217) - how to make the most of your money, Wed 7.30-9.30 5 wks €50

Newpark Adult Education Centre, Newtownpark Ave Blackrock (2884376 / 2883725) - the knowledgeable investor: saving, pensions & investment, Thurs 7.30 10 wks €135

Pobalscoil Rosmini Adult Ed Grace Pk Rd 9 (8371015) - from debt to wealth, Mon 7pm & 8.30 5 wks €100 each

MONTESSORI COURSE

College of Further Education Main St Dundrum 14 (2951376) - intro to, NCVA level 2

College of Progressive Education 27-29 Carysfort Ave Blackrock (4884300) - FETAC level 6 montessori method of education full or part time / foundation studies by distance learning

Montessori Education Centre 41-43 Nth Gt George's St 1 (8780071) - Montessori teacher training dip: course (1 nursery) 0-6 yrs, eve 9 mths Mon & Tue 6.30-8.30 €2100; also by distance learning; (2 junior) 6-9 yrs, (3 primary) 9-12 yrs: by distance learning, 10 mths, €1500, dip

Old Bawn Community School Tallaght 24 (4526137) - Montessori foundation dip, St Nicholas Montessori College Ireland, Tues & Thurs, 6.45-9.45pm, 30 wks

Portobello School 43 Lr Dominick St 1 (8721277) - FETAC Competency Cert, 1 eve per wk, 32 wks

MORRIS DANCING

Dublin City Morris Dancers c/o Alan Corsini 38 Meadow Mount 16 (2985068)

MOTOR BOAT TRAINING

Irish Sailing Assoc 3 Park Rd Dún Laoghaire (2800239) - motorboat handling coastal, offshore; powerboat inland, coastal: apply for provider list

MOTOR CYCLE MAINTENANCE

DIT Faculty: Engineering Bolton St 1 (4023000) - motor cycle studies, 3yrs 2 eve wkly, €830

Kylemore College Kylemore Rd 10 (6265901) - garage workshoip Tue, Wed 10 wks 7-9pm

Pobalscoil Rosmini Adult Ed Grace Pk Rd 9 (8371015) - beginners, Tue 7.39-9.30 €120

MOTOR INDUSTRY MANAGEMENT see also Garage Management

DIT Faculty: Engineering Bolton St 1 (4023000) - industry cert/ dip: management, legislation, finance, admin, project: yr 1 €850 / yrs 2&3 €950pa

MOTOR MAINTENANCE - Know Your Car, NTC

Ballymun Trinity CS,s Adult Ed Centre 9 (8420654) - NCT oriented Wed 10wk, €120

Cabinteely Community School Johnstown Rd 18 (2857455) - 10wk, €95

Coláiste Dhúlaigh CFE,Barryscourt Rd Coolock 17 (8481337) - car test, mechanic, Wed 2.15-3.30pm/ motor vehicle theory & practice, Wed 11.45-2pm 20 wks

Coolmine Community School Clonsilla 15 (8214583) - 7.30-9.30, 10 wks, €80, Mon & Tue/ workshop Sat 7 Oct 10am-1 €25

DIT Faculty: Engineering Bolton St 1 (4023000) - vehicle parts personnel, distance learning prog, €750/ technological cert in auto engineering: elementary, intermediate, advanced, 1 yr each €950 per stage

Firhouse Community College Firhouse Rd 24 (4525807) - Mon 7.30-9.30pm 8 wks €104

Greendale Community School Kilbarrack 5 (8322735) - 10wks, Tues, 7.30-9.30pm, €95

Greenhills College Limekiln Ave Walkinstown 12 (4507779/4507863) - 10 wks, €130

Hartstown Community School Clonsilla 15 (8209863) - beginners/intermediate, 10wks, €85 each

Kylemore College Kylemore Rd 10 (6265901) - NCT check Mon 8 wks 7.30-9.30pm

Newpark Adult Education Centre Newtownpark Ave Blackrock (2884376 / 2883725) - 10wks, €120, 7.30-9.45pm

Palmerstown CS - Pobailscoil Iosolde, Kennelsfort Rd 20 (6260116) - Mon 8-9.30 10 wks €75

Plunket College Swords Rd, Whitehall 9 (8371689) - beginners, Tues, 10 wks, €90

Pobalscoil Rosmini Adult Ed Grace Pk Rd 9 (8371015) - Mon 7.30-9.30 €125

Ringsend Technical Institute Cambridge Rd 4 (6684498) - 10wks €105, Thurs 7pm

Saint Finian's Community College Swords (8402623) - 8 wks

Stillorgan CFE, Old Road Stillorgan (2880704) - Thurs 7.30 8 wks €104

MOTOR SPORTS

Motor Cycle Union of Ireland Linn-comm House Stephenstown Bus Pk Balbriggan (8834885) - motor cycling

Taney Centre Taney Rd Dundrum 14 (2985491) - model car racing, Sat (4944345)

MULTIMEDIA

Crumlin College of FE, Crumlin Rd 12 (4540662) - design in multimedia computing, f/time day VTOS

MUSIC see also Music Appreciation and under individual instruments, Orchestra

Abbey School of Music 9b Lr Abbey St 1 (8747908)

Bray Music Centre Florence Rd Bray (2866768)

Carl Alfred 6 Palmerston Villas, Basement Fl 2 off Upr Rathmines Rd 6 (4972095) - hear-feel method popular-guitar course. Free preview

Clontarf School of Music 6 Marino Mart 3 (8330936 087 8054963) - courses in guitar, piano, singing, fiddle, violin, theory, tin-whistle/ also making music for 3-6 and 7-12 year olds

Coláiste Dhúlaigh CFE,Barryscourt Rd Coolock 17 (8481337) - appreciation & history, Tue 7.30-9.30 10 wks

DIT Faculty: Applied Arts Aungier St 2 (4023000) - individual & or class tuition instrumental/ vocal: incl most instruments: at DIT Rathmines (4023513)

Dún Laoghaire Music Centre 130A Lr George's St Dún Laoghaire (2844178)

Hollywood Academy Dublin 13-14 Sackville Pl 1 (8786909) - singing, dance, piano, guitar, drums, dancing, eves & Sats, 11 mths €75 per mth, cert/ band workshops, demos etc

Leinster School of Music Griffith College Campus South Circular Rd 8 (4150467) - music diplomas

Melody School of Music 178E Whitehall Rd W Perrystown 12 (4650150) - wkend courses in piano, keyboard, violin: Sat & Sun, 12 wk

Merriman School of Singing and Music Bel Canto House 21 North Great George's St 1 (874 2034)

Metropolitan College of Music 59 Lr Baggot St 2 (4540753) - private, all instruments, 30wks

Na Piobairi Uilleann 15 Henrietta St 1 (8730093) - see various instruments/ also recitals Sat nights

Rachel Dempsey Global Harmonies Smithfield 7 (086 3097232) - singing for personal development/ voice work/ vocal jamming/ intercultural understanding through music: each 8 wks various venues €100

Waltons New School of Music 69 Sth Gt George's St 2 (4781884) - also day, see ad above

MUSIC APPRECIATION

DATE Centre CFE, Dundrum 14 (2964322 (9.30am-12pm)) - 11am, 10 wks, €97 day

Newpark Adult Education Centre Newtownpark Ave Blackrock (2884376 / 2883725) - Mozart, Thurs 10 wks 7.30-9.45pm €120

People's College for Continuing Education & Training 32 Parnell Sq 1 (8735879) - €60

UCD Adult Education Centre Belfield (7167123) - Mon: Between Midnight and Day/ Tue: introducing Opera/ Thurs: Wolfgang Amadeus Mozart/ Opera in the Romantic Age: each 10 wks

Waltons New School of Music 69 Sth Gt George's St 2 (4781884) - also day, see ad above

MUSIC BUSINESS see also Music Technology / Sound Engineering etc
Sound Training Centre Temple Bar Music Centre Curved Street Temple Bar 2 (6709033)
MUSIC LIBRARY
Central Library Ilac Centre 1 (8734333)
MUSIC TECHNOLOGY
Balbriggan Community College Pine Ridge Chapel St (8412388/9) - computer electronic music, for beginners: 6 modules - software, bets, bass, melody, song structures, sound effects (no musical knowledge necessary) 8 wks Weds 7.30-9.30 €140
Dún Laoghaire Music Centre 130A Lr George's St Dún Laoghaire (2844178)
Griffith College Dublin Sth Circular Rd 8 (4150400) - dip in music tech & studio operations, 1 yr CGLI p/t 2 eve per wk; also 1 yr f/t
Hollywood Academy Dublin 13-14 Sackville Pl 1 (8786909) - computer based
Kylemore College Kylemore Rd 10 (6265901) - Wed 10 wks 7-9pm
Marino College 14-20 Marino Mart 3 (8332100) - music prod uning PC technology, Tue 10 wks 6.30, €65
New Media Technology College, 13 Harcourt St 2 (4780905) - for recording or making music, 18 wks 6.30-9.30 C&G cert
Sound Training Centre Temple Bar Music Centre Curved Street Temple Bar 2 (6709033) - sound engineering & music technology C&G 1&2 34 weeks €4500 ftime - €3300 ptime / sound engineering lighting & stage production C&G1&2 34 wks €4500 ftime / music & media technology C&G3 34 wks €4500 Sept/ advanced mixed media programme / electronic music production STC cert 15 wks €1000 Oct & Mar / dj'ing & music production STC cert 15 wks €1000 Oct & Mar / intro to dj'ing & music production STC cert 1 wk €500 summer course
Waltons New School of Music 69 Sth Gt George's St 2 (4781884) - also day, see ad page 155
MUSIC THEATRE see also Music Business
Dún Laoghaire Music Centre 130A Lr George's St Dún Laoghaire (2844178)
Waltons New School of Music 69 Sth Gt George's St 2 (4781884) - see ad page 155
MUSIC THEORY & HARMONY
Abbey School of Music 9b Lr Abbey St 1 (8747908) - Kevin Robinson
Bray Music Centre Florence Rd Bray (2866768)
Clontarf School of Music 6 Marino Mart 3 (8330936 087 8054963)
Dún Laoghaire CFE, 17 Cumberland St Dún Laoghaire (2809676) - musicianship, Wed 7-9pm 10 wks €110
John Ward 5 Tibradden Drive Walkinstown 12 (4520918) - prep for Assoc board grade exams - also day
Metropolitan College of Music 59 Lr Baggot St 2 (4540753) - private, 30wks
Newpark Music Centre Newtownpark Ave Blackrock (2883740)
Waltons New School of Music 69 Sth Gt George's St 2 (4781884) - also day, see ad page 155
MUSICAL INSTRUMENT REPAIR
Na Piobairi Uilleann 15 Henrietta St 1 (8730093) - reed making classes
NATURAL HISTORY / NATURE STUDY see also Ornithology / Wildlife/ Zoo
Dublin Naturalists Field Club Fridolin Kerr, Membership Sec. 31 Cherrywood Pk

Clondalkin 22

UCD Adult Education Centre Belfield (7167123) - a guide to Ireland's seashore communities, Wed 8 wks

NAVIGATION

Ballsbridge CFE, Shelbourne Rd 4 (6684806) - yachtmaster coastal, Mon 6.15pm 20 wks

Bray Sailing Club The Harbour Bray (2860272) - evening classes

Glenans Irish Sailing Club 5 Lr Mount St 2 (6611481) - coastal cert

Irish Sailing Assoc 3 Park Rd Dún Laoghaire (2800239) - navigation & pilotage courses, all levels, apply for provider list

Newpark Adult Education Centre, Newtownpark Ave Blackrock (2884376 / 2883725) - yachtmaster offshore cert, advanced, Thurs 20 wks, €360, 7.30-9.45pm

Ringsend Technical Institute Cambridge Rd 4 (6684498) - coastal & offshore, Mon 7pm 20 wks €270 ISA cert

Sea-Craft 3 Newcourt Ave Bray (2863362) - ISA Yachtmaster coastal, 21 wk €435, cert; Yachtmaster offshore, 21 wks €485 cert; yachtmaster ocean, 20 wks €500 ISA RYA cert/ RYA MCA SRC DSC radio courses, eve+day, Irish 1.5 days €189, Dept Marine cert, also 1 day, €129, RYA MCA DSC cert

NEEDLEWORK / CRAFT

KLEAR Grange Park View Kilbarrack 5 (8671845) - day

NEGOTIATION SKILLS

Hartstown Community School Clonsilla 15 (8209863) - 10 wks, €85

NEUROLINGUISTIC PROGRAMMING

Ballsbridge CFE, Shelbourne Rd 4 (6684806) - foundation NLP, Mon 7-9pm 10 wks €90

Cabinteely Community School Johnstown Rd 18 (2857455) - introduction to NLP, Mon 10 wks €95

IICH Education 118 Stillorgan Road 4 (2017422) - workshops; certs; diplomas

Marino College 14-20 Marino Mart 3 (8332100) - 6.30 Thurs 10 wks €65

Success Partners Compass Hill Kinsale Co Cork (021 4772564 087 6142980) - accelerated NLP practitioner & master practitioner cert: 4 courses pa, venue Mount Herbert hotel

NORWEGIAN

Sandford Language Institute Milltown Pk Sandford Rd 6 (2601296) - all levels, 15 wks €285

NUMEROLOGY

Healing House 24 O'Connell Ave Berkeley Rd 7 (8306413) - charts, w/end workshop €150

NURSERY TRAINING see also Childcare / Montessori

Hazel Byrne (087-2843079) - baby massage classes

Inchicore CFE, Emmet Rd 8 (4535358)

NURSING STUDIES

Ballyfermot CFE, Ballyfermot Rd 10 (6269421) - intro to nursing, Fetac 5, 22 wks Wed 7-10pm

College of Progressive Education 27-29 Carysfort Ave Blackrock (4884300) - FETAC level 5 introduction to nursing

Crumlin College of FE, Crumlin Rd 12 (4540662) - ITEC holistic massage dip in anatomy & physiology & body massage, for registered nurses, Mon & Wed 6.45

Dorset College 64 Lr Dorset St/ 8 Belvedere Pl 1 (8309677) - FETAC level 5, Mon-thurs 9.30-2.30pm 1 yr

Inchicore CFE, Emmet Rd 8 (4535358) - pre-nursing studies/ nursery studies & child care

Kilroy's College Wentworth House Grand Canal Street Lr 2 (6620538 1850-700700) - home-study: entrance exam

Our Lady's Hospice Harold's Cross 6 (4068806 4068810) Palliative Care: conference "moving points in palliative care" / intro to for registered nurses (1 wk) / palliative care for care assistants (1 day) / symptom management in (1 day) / providing spiritual care within palliative care (1 day) / professional update for experienced palliative care nursing (1 wk) / interdisciplinary intro to (1 wk) / syringe driver work-shop (3 hrs) / artificial hydration in (3 hrs): courses repeated regularly / hospice approach to care of the older person for registered nursing (3 days) or care assistants (1 day) / reminiscence therapy (2 days) / gerontology conference (1 day) / rheumatology for nurses (2 days) / rheumatology conference (1 day)./ h dip courses - palliative, gerontology, and rheumatology nursing: contact 01 7165578 / 01 7167341 /general courses: struggle against restraint (1 day) / reminiscence ther-apy (1 day) / social issues (1 day) / writing skills - essay assignments h.dip students (1 day) / research for beginners (1 day) / assertiveness skills for health professionals (1 day) / complementary therapies within healthcare settings (summer school) / multicultural Ireland '05-'06 cultures & faith for healthcare professionals (1 day). Courses repeated regularly - phone for brochure

NUTRITION see also Diet / Food Science / Health

College of Progressive Education 27-29 Carysfort Ave Blackrock (4884300) - FETAC level 5 nutrition

Dún Laoghaire CFE, 17 Cumberland St Dún Laoghaire (2809676) - FETAC, Wed 7-9.20 20 wks €300

Holistic Healing Centre 38 Dame St 2 (6710813)

Irish Health Culture Association 66 Eccles St 7 (8304211) - diploma in holistic dietetics & nuitrition, 7 wkends + 1 wk seminar, €2850

Kilroy's College Wentworth House Grand Canal Street Lr 2 (6620538 1850-700700) - tutor supported home study

KLEAR Grange Park View Kilbarrack 5 (8671845) - day

Old Bawn Community School Tallaght 24 (4526137) - bodywise nutritional course, Thurs 7.30-9.30 €95

Portobello School 43 Lr Dominick St 1 (8721277) - & diet, ITEC dip, eve 32 wks

Rathmines CFE - Senior College, Town Hall 6 (4975334) - health & alternative nutrition - effects of diet, Tue 7-9pm €90

Senior College Dún Laoghaire, CFE Eblana Ave Dún Laoghaire (2800385) - intro to, FETAC €150

Time Out (4591038) - & food intolerances, also wkend

Walmer College & Holistic Centre First Floor, River Hse Raheny Shopping C 5 (8329645) - & diet, ITEC dip

OFFICE SKILLS / PROCEDURES / TECHNOLOGY Secretarial / Computer Training / ECDL etc

Coláiste Dhúlaigh CFE,Barryscourt Rd Coolock 17 (8481337) - Fetac, Tue 10-12pm 20 wks

Colaiste Ide Cardiffsbridge Rd Finglas W 8443233 11 (8342333) - cert of professional competence, Tues & Thurs, 7.30-10, 13 wks €470 CILT

CTA Computer Training Academy, St James's Tce Malahide (8454070)

Irish Academy of Computer Training 98 St Stephen's Green 2 (4347662) - MOUS master - ms office user specialist 20 wks, cert/ MOS/MOUS master boot camp, 10 wks, cert

Kilroy's College Wentworth House Grand Canal Street Lr 2 (6620538 1850-700700) - tutor supported home study, typing, book-keeping & accounts, computer skills

Kylemore College Kylemore Rd 10 (6265901) - basic, with word processing, tue 12 wks 10.30-12.30 FETAC

Pitman Training Centre 6-8 Wicklow St 2 (6768008) - advanced dip in office technology, full/pt-time; day eve sats

Training Options Plus 6-8 Wicklow St 2 (6717787) - meetings & minutes, 1 day, cert

OIL BURNER SERVICING

DIT Faculty: Built Environment Bolton St 1 (4023000) - domestic oil fired, 10 wks €250

FAS Training Centre Ballyfermot 10 (6055900)

FAS Training Centre Cabra Bannow Rd 7 (8821400) - 10 wks

OIL PAINTING see also Art / Drawing / Painting

Ashfield College Main St Templeogue 6W (4900866) - 7.30-9.30, 8 wks

Bray Institute of FE, Novara Ave Bray (2866111 / 2829668) - Wed 7.30 10wks, €85

Brian Byrnes Art Studio 3 Upr Baggot St 4 (6671520 / 6711599) - 8wk, €150 also day

Cabinteely Community School Johnstown Rd 18 (2857455) - beginners/improvers, 10wk, €95 each

Coláiste Eanna, Kilkieran Rd Cabra 7 (8389577) - intro to, Thur 10 wks 7-9pm

Coolmine Community School Clonsilla 15 (8214583) - oil & acrylic Tue & Wed 10 wks 7.30 €80/ workshop Sat 7 Oct 10am-1 €25

DATE Centre CFE, Dundrum 14 (2964322 (9.30am-12pm)) - 10 wks, €97 day 9.30 & 11.30

Donahies Community School Streamville Rd 13 (8482217) - Tues, Wed, 7.30 10 wks, €85 ea

Foxrock Institute Kill o' the Grange, Kill Lane Blackrock (4939506) - Wed & Sat 8wks €105 ea

Gallery Art Centre The Mill, Celbridge Co Kildare (6276206) - 9 wks €130 materials supplied

Holy Family Community School Rathcoole (4580766)

Jean Strong (2892323) - ongoing, beginners, improvers, 10 wks €170/also day:- Blackrock & Dundrum

Kilternan Adult Education Group Ballybetagh Rd Kilternan 18 (2952050) - acrillics Mon, Tue 9.30am; 7.30pm/ Wed 9.30am: 10 wks €130

Kylemore College Kylemore Rd 10 (6265901) - beg-improvers, 10 wks Thurs 7-9pm

Lucan Community College Esker Drive (6282077) - Tue 7.30-8.30 10 wks €130

Marino College 14-20 Marino Mart 3 (8332100) - & watercolours, Thurs, beginners €90/ intermediate €65, 10wks ea/ wed 1.30pm €85

Meridian Art Group c/o St Paul's College Raheny 5 (8310688)

NCAD Centre for Continuing Educ 100 Thomas Street 8 (6364214) - aspects of, introductory & intermediate, 21wk

Newpark Adult Education Centre, Newtownpark Ave Blackrock (2884376 / 2883725) - Mon 10 wks €120, 7.30-9.45pm

Newpark Adult Education Centre, Newtownpark Ave Blackrock (2884376 / 2883725) - Mon 10 wks

Pobalscoil Neasáin Baldoyle 13 (8063092) - wed 2-4pm, 10 wks €170

Pobalscoil Rosmini Adult Ed Grace Pk Rd 9 (8371015) - beginners & improvers, wed 7.30-9.20 €95

OLD-TIME DANCING see also Ballroom / Dance

Dance Club Rathmines & Rathgar (2893797)

ONLINE EDUCATION see also Distance Learning

FAS Net College (2043732 ecollegeinfo@fas.ie) - variety of courses online: personal development; business; health & safety; apprenticeships; computer applications; ecdl; networks; web design; programming; databases; etc

OPERA

UCD Adult Education Centre Belfield (7167123) - Mon: Between Midnight and Day/ Tue: introducing Opera/ Thurs: Wolfgang Amadeus Mozart/ Opera in the Romatic Age: each 10 wks

ORCHESTRA

Waltons New School of Music 69 Sth Gt George's St 2 (4781884) - see ad page 155

ORIENTEERING see also Adventure Sports

Corporate Club & Network Club 24 Elmcastle Green Tallaght 24 (4524415)

ORNITHOLOGY

Birdwatch Ireland Rockingham Hse Newcastle Co Wicklow (2819878) - wildlife activities

People's College for Continuing Education & Training 32 Parnell Sq 1 (8735879) - birds of Ireland, 10 wks €60

UCD Adult Education Centre Belfield (7167123) - Irish birds, Thur 10 wks

OUTDOOR EDUCATION

St Kevin's College Clogher Rd Crumlin 12 (4536397) - BTEC dip, day, ICU/BTEC, 2yr, day

PA & EXECUTIVE see also Business Skills

Training Options Plus 6-8 Wicklow St 2 (6717787) - Executive PA skills, 1 day, cert

PAIN MANAGEMENT / BACKPAIN see HEALING

Bray Institute of FE, Novara Ave Bray (2866111 / 2829668) - energy healing, Mon 7.30-9.30 10 wks €85

Foxrock Institute Kill o' the Grange, Kill Lane Blackrock (4939506) - herbal medicine; reflexology: each 8 wks, €105

Harmony Healing 41 Beneavin Pk Glasnevin 11 (8641768)

Healing House 24 O'Connell Ave Berkeley Rd 7 (8306413) - intro to healing therapies, spiritual healing, hands-on healing, numerology, aromatherapy, massage, indian head massage, reflexology, Australian bush flower essences, kinesiology , 10 wks (or wkend), 8-10pm Tues€200/ healing wkend 23rd/24th Sept €150/ support group - teaching, healing & visualisation, Mon 8-10 €10

Holistic Healing Centre 38 Dame St 2 (6710813) - healing massage ITEC dip

Motions Health & Fitness Training (087 2808866) - Diploma in Holistic Massage (ITEC), part-time course, 3 hours per week. Castleknock, Citywest & Naas

Moytura Healing Centre Rinn Rua Claremont Grove Killiney (2854005) - energy healing, cert, eve: Fri, 10 wks €190/ dip, Fri eve 30 wks €520

National College of Complementary Medical Ed, 16a St Joseph's Parade Off Dorset Street 7 (8827777) - neuromuscular therapy, NMT, one w/end per month, 15 mths, €3520 higher dip, wkends 2yrs €7000

Obus School of Healing Therapies, 53 Beech Grove Lucan (6282121) - aromatherapy, wkends 1 yr €2025, dip

Our Lady's Hospice Harold's Cross 6 (4068806 4068810) - exploring healing, 16 wks Sept-June Tue 5.30-7.30 €495/ auricular candle therapy, 28-29 April07 10-5pm €175 incl lunch/ touch for healing 2 March07; 19 October07: 10-4pm €100 incl lunch

Physio Extra 37 Upr Grand Canal St 4 (087 7818300 6685048) - spineright: yoga with pilates, beginner & intermediate levels; morn, day, eve

Shiatsu Ireland classes at 44 Adelaide Rd 2 (2962839) - shiatsu & massage - beginners & advanced

T'ai Chi Energy Centre Milltown Pk Conference Centre Sandford Rd Ranelagh 6 (4961533) - t'ai chi/qi gong - & wkend workshops

TACT St Dominic's School St Dominic's Rd Tallaght 24 (4596757)

Tony Quinn Centre 66/67 Eccles St 7 (8304211) - twice weekly, Tue+Thurs 12 & 6.30; €30 per wk, 2 sessions

PAINTING see also Acrylics / Art / Art History / Drawing / Landscape / Oil Painting / Pastel / Portrait / Sketching / Watercolour

Bray Institute of FE, Novara Ave Bray (2866111 / 2829668) - & sketching, Mon, Tue 7.30: 10wks, €85

Brian Byrnes Art Studio 3 Upr Baggot St 4 (6671520 / 6711599) - water colour, oil, 8wk, €150, also day

DATE Centre CFE, Dundrum 14 (2964322 (9.30am-12pm)) - and drawing Wed, 11.10am/ Fri 9.30am 10 wks €97 ea

Foxrock Institute Kill o' the Grange, Kill Lane Blackrock (4939506) - watercolours for pleasure, 8wks, €105

Gallery Art Centre The Mill, Celbridge Co Kildare (6276206) - painting made simple, day/ eve, 9 wks €110

Greendale Community School Kilbarrack 5 (8322735) - Tue 7.30 10 wks €95

Jean Strong (2892323) - ongoing, beginners-improvers, 10wks, €170/also day:- Blackrock & Dundrum

Killester CFE, Collins Ave 5 (8337686) - beginners, Mon & improvers, Tue: 10 wks
7.30 €80 ea

Kilternan Adult Education Centre Ballybetagh Rd Kilternan 18 (2952050) - painting
to music Wed 2-4pm 8 wks €104

KLEAR Grange Park View Kilbarrack 5 (8671845) - painting & drawing 1, day

Kylemore College Kylemore Rd 10 (6265901) - beginners Tue 7-9pm 10 wks

NCAD Centre for Continuing Educ 100 Thomas Street 8 (6364214) - from life/new
perspectives, intermediate/ painting the figure/ portrait painting

Newpark Adult Education Centre Newtownpark Ave Blackrock (2884376 / 2883725)
- & drawing/ watercolour painting, 10wks, €120 each 7.30-9.45pm

People's College for Continuing Education & Training 32 Parnell Sq 1 (8735879) - €60

Pobalscoil Rosmini Adult Ed Grace Pk Rd 9 (8371015) - beginners & improvers, wed
1.30-3.30pm €95

Ringsend Technical Institute Cambridge Rd 4 (6684498) - oil & acrillic, Thurs 7-9pm
10 wks €90

St Tiernan's Community School Parkvale Balally 16 (2953224) - intro to acrillic, Mon
7.30 10 wks €95

PAINTING AND DECORATING see Interior Design

PALMISTRY

Catherine Woods - Prof Tarot Card Reader 12 Church St E East Wall 3 (8552799) -
1 day workshops, 12-5pm €75

PARENTS & PARENTING see also Child / Drugs / Family / Pre-School / Psychology

Ballyfermot CFE, Ballyfermot Rd 10 (6269421) - parenting skills, Mon 7-9.30 12 wks

Firhouse Community College Firhouse Rd 24 (4525807) - parenting teens, Tue 7.30-
9.30pm 8 wks €104

KLEAR Grange Park View Kilbarrack 5 (8671845) - parent to parent/ day

National College of Ireland Mayor St IFSC 1 (4060500/ 1850 221721) - NCI Diploma
in Parenting Mentoring, 1 year, €2,650

Newpark Adult Education Centre, Newtownpark Ave Blackrock (2884376 / 2883725)
- life skills for parents, teen physical/mental health, Mon 7.30 10 wks €120

Nurture Institute of Further Education for Parents 140 Meadow Grove, Dundrum 16
(2963795) - parenting course 0-18yr: changing role of parenting, 7.30-9.30pm,
30 wks €350

Portmarnock Community School Carrickhill Rd (8038056) - teen parenting programme, 6 wks 7.30-9.20 €80

Saint Anthony's House St Lawrence Rd Clontarf 3 (8335300) - mother & toddler group

School of Philosophy & Economic Science 49 Northumberland Rd 4 (6603788) -
parenting, age 0-10 yr./ age 10-21 yrs: each course, 9 wks €100

Taney Parish Centre Taney Rd Dundrum 14 (2985491) - parenting, Tues (2832141)

TARGET St Kevin's School Newbrook Rd, Donaghmede 13 (8671967) - day only, HSE

Transactional Analysis in Ireland (4511125) - in everyday situations, mthly wkshop, donation

PASTELS: PAINTING & DRAWING

Jean Strong (2892323) - ongoing, beginners, improvers, 10 wks €170/also day:-
Blackrock & Dundrum

NCAD Centre for Continuing Educ 100 Thomas Street 8 (6364214) - drawing with, c. 22wk

PASTORAL CARE
All Hallows College Gracepark Rd Drumcondra 9 (8373745) - pastoral education 2,
Wed 6.50 24 wks €390; ECTS credits/ pastoral use of scripture, Johannine writings,
Tue 8.30, 24 wks €390
Milltown Institute Milltown Pk 6 (2776331) - pastoral studies, day 1 yr
PATCHWORK & QUILTING
Ballymun Trinity CS,s Adult Ed Centre 9 (8420654) - 3D coupage & Mountmellick
lace-making, Mon, 10 wks €90
Quilt Art Workshops 4 Mill Wood Naas (045-876121) - classes & wkshops, SAE for info
St Tiernan's Community School Parkvale Balally 16 (2953224) - make quilts, covers,
cushions, Wed, 7.30-9.30pm, 10 wks, €95
PAYE, VAT & WAGES see also Book-Keeping / Business Studies / Taxation
Bray Institute of FE, Novara Ave Bray (2866111 / 2829668) - book-keeping for paye,
prsi, vat, Tues 7.30-9.30 10wks €85
CTA Computer Training Academy, St James's Tce Malahide (8454070)
Marino College 14-20 Marino Mart 3 (8332100) - Thurs 8pm 10 wks €65
PAYROLL / ACCOUNTS
Ballyfermot CFE, Ballyfermot Rd 10 (6269421) - payroll technician, IPASS cert,
stage 1 10 wks/ stage 2 2007 10 wks: Wed 7-9.30
CTA Computer Training Academy, St James's Tce Malahide (8454070)
Dorset College 64 Lr Dorset St/ 8 Belvedere Pl 1 (8309677) -manual & computerised,
Sat 10am 12 wks

Dún Laoghaire CFE, 17 Cumberland St Dún Laoghaire (2809676) - Tue 12 wks 5-7pm €200

Eden Computer Training Rathfarnham 16 & 1 Green St 7 (4953155)

Irish Payroll Association (IPASS) IPASS Hse, Centerpoint Business Pk Oak Rd 12 (4089100) - nationally recognised qualification: Certified Payroll Technician, 1 night per week, 10 weeks for both Stage 1 and Stage 2. Diploma in Payroll Management, 4 modules, 2 days training per module. Venues: City Centre, Griffith Avenue, Swords, Blanchardstown, Ballyfermot, Lucan, Tallaght, Dún Laoghaire, Sandyford, Bray, Rathmines, Mount St, Sth Circular Rd (Sat morns)

Palmerstown CS - Pobailscoil Iosolde, Kennelsfort Rd 20 (6260116) - manual & computerised: Tue 8.15, 10 wks €90 FETAC 5

Pearse College Clogher Rd Crumlin 12 (4536661/4541544) - 80 hour BTEI course, 20 wks FETAC 2

Senior College Dún Laoghaire, CFE Eblana Ave Dún Laoghaire (2800385) - Sage, cert in payroll, FETAC, €160

PC REPAIR, ASSEMBLY see also COMPUTER MAINTENANCE

FAS Training Centre Loughlinstown Wyattville Rd, DL (2043600) - 10 wks

Irish Academy of Computer Training 98 St Stephen's Green 2 (4347662) - pc troubleshooting & repair, 8 wks cert/ A+ in troubleshooting cert, 20 wks / also day

Palmerstown CS - Pobailscoil Iosolde, Kennelsfort Rd 20 (6260116) - Tue 7.30 10 wks €70

PEACE STUDIES see also POLITICAL STUDIES

Irish School of Ecumenics (TCD) Bea House Milltown Pk 6 (2601144) - (Ext.110) Dr Iain Atack; or Ext. 113 Mary Priestman / Postgrad dip in conflict & dispute resolution studies (Ext.113 Mary Priestman)

PEDICURE see Manicure

PERCUSSION see also Music

Waltons New School of Music 69 Sth Gt George's St 2 (4781884) - African/Latin percussion/drum kit, also day, see ad page 155

PERSONAL DEVELOPMENT see also Assertiveness / Creative Living / Enneagram / Self-Awareness / Beauty Care / Teamwork / Life Skills

Ballymun Trinity CS,s Adult Ed Centre 9 (8420654) - Tue, 10wk, €90

Blue Sky Meditation Centre 42 Leeson St Lr 2 (6615934) - mindfulness for stress, Tue eve 8 wks €290 / unwaged €180

Brahma Kumaris WSU Raja Yoga Centres 5 Leeson Pk Ave 6 (6687480) - 7wk, day free

Bray Institute of FE, Novara Ave Bray (2866111 / 2829668) - Mon, 10 wks €85/ how to worry less, Mon 7.30 10 wks €85

Cabinteely Community School Johnstown Rd 18 (2857455) `- unlocking your creative potential, Tues, 10wks, €95/ life-coaching Tue 10 wks €95

Centre for Professional & Personal Development 44 Westland Row 2 (6612291) - career course, eve, w/end, 6 wks, €420, cert

Communication & Personal Development 30/31 Wicklow St 2 (6713636/ 6613225) - confidence building & personal development for women

Corporate Club 24 Elmcastle Green Tallaght 24 (4610935)

Donahies Community School Streamville Rd 13 (8482217) - Tue 7.30-9.30 8 wks €75/ life after separation & divorce, Tue €135

Eden Computer Training Rathfarnham 16 & 1 Green St 7 (4953155)

Finglas Adult Reading & Writing Scheme Colaiste Eoin Cappagh Rd 11 (8340893)

Foxrock Institute Kill o' the Grange, Kill Lane Blackrock (4939506)

Geraldine Brand Style Image Consultant City Centre (8327332) - courses for men, women; image/style workshop, morns 1 wk June/July 14-19 yr old girls €250

Hartstown Community School Clonsilla 15 (8209863) - intro/continuing/life enrichment - 10wks, €85 each

Hegarty Fitness Centre 53 Middle Abbey St 1 (8723080) - yogametrics, also home/office/city centre, from €480

Holistic Healing Centre 38 Dame St 2 (6710813)

Junior Chamber Ireland - email pro@jci-ireland.org for info

KLEAR Grange Park View Kilbarrack 5 (8671845) - self-esteem, group facilitation & advanced facilitation/ confidence building/ mindpower; day

Marino College 14-20 Marino Mart 3 (8332100) - dress with confidence, Tue 10 wks 8pm €90

Milltown Institute of Theology & Philosophy Milltown Pk 6 (2776331) - the art of stillness, Wed 10.25am-12.15, or 7-9pm 12 wks/ adult ed dip in spirituality - overview of key issues, Mon 7.30-10pm; Six Sats: €820; also at An Croi Centre, Ashbourne

Network Club 24 Elmcastle Green Tallaght 24 (4524415)

Newpark Adult Education Centre, Newtownpark Ave Blackrock (2884376 / 2883725) - life skills/ Louise L Hay workshop/ journey into freedom Wed 7.30-9.45, Wed 10 wks €120 / soul mates - human relationships, Tue 7.30 10 wks €120

Old Bawn Community School Tallaght 24 (4526137) - psychic development, Tues 10 wks €137/ creating personal relatioinships - skills to transform personal, social and professional relationships, Thurs 7pm €95 / past life regression, Thurs 10 wks €137

Our Lady's Hospice Harold's Cross 6 (4068806 4068810) - workshops & courses: why do bad things happen to good people; grieving; assertiveness & listening; exploring healing; reminiscence therapy

Palmerstown CS - Pobailscoil Iosolde, Kennelsfort Rd 20 (6260116) - Mon 7.30-9, 10wks €70

Paul Bradley (Psychotherapist) Main St Kilcock Co Kildare (6284673/ 087 9598840) - seminars for men, Dublin/ Kildare venues

People's College for Continuing Education & Training 32 Parnell Sq 1 (8735879) - meditation & relaxation

Pobalscoil Rosmini Adult Ed Grace Pk Rd 9 (8371015) - mental self defence, Wed 8.30-9.50 €90/ weqr life like a loose garment, Tue 7pm & 8.30 €90 ea

Quantum Communications Ken McCready 39 Emerald Sq, Dolphin's Barn 8 (086 1502604) - empowerment training, at Teachers Centre, 36 Parnell Sq 1, 6 wks €239

Rachel Dempsey Global Harmonies Smithfield 7 (086 3097232) - singing for personal development, creativity & stress release, 8 wks various venues €100

Rathcoole Community School Rathcoole (4580766)

Rathmines CFE - Senior College, Town Hall 6 (4975334) - & assertiveness, Mon, 10 wks, €90

Rigpa Tibetan Buddhist Meditation Centre 12 Wicklow St, 3rd Floor 2 (6703358) - intro to meditation, a basis in practice, teachings of Sogyal Rinpoche: 10 wks

Ringsend Technical Institute Cambridge Rd 4 (6684498) - boost self confidence, Tue 7.30-9.30 8 wks €65 / lime management, Wed 7.30 10 wks €130 cert

Roebuck Counselling Centre 59 Rathgar Rd 6 (4971929) - life change: life tutoring courses, Wed, 25 wks/ creativity - creative arts course, 1 day wkend monthly 12 mths; also Wed eve/ educational drama Thurs eve ongoing/ relationships & personal dev training for men, Thurs eve ongoing

Sam Young Howth area (8322803) - 'The Power of Now' (Tolle) 12 wks, morn & eve

St Kevin's College Clogher Rd Crumlin 12 (4536397) - social workplace relationship skills, 1 yr, NCVA 2, NUI, cert Maynooth

TACT St Dominic's School St Dominic's Rd Tallaght 24 (4596757)

The Professional Training and Coaching Consultancy (087 6379765/ 045 865783) - assertiveness / confidence building/ achieving your goals: 6 wks, Terenure / Lucan / Dundrum

The Sanctuary Stanhope Street 7 (6705419) - finding sanctuary, 6 wks

Tony Quinn Centre 66/67 Eccles St 7 (8304211) - relaxation & stress management

Training Options Plus 6-8 Wicklow St 2 (6717787) - assertiveness, communications skills, job seeking skills, day, cert

Transactional Analysis in Ireland (4511125) - in everyday situations, mthly workshop, donation

UCD Adult Education Centre Belfield (7167123) - career planning and personal development/ creative thinking and problem solving; focusing and personality; what are you doing the rest of your life?/ work life balance each 1 day, Sat am/pm

Walmer College & Holistic Centre First Floor, River Hse Raheny Shopping C 5 (8329645)

PERSONNEL PRACTICE / MANAGEMENT / HR MANAGEMENT see also Management

Coláiste Dhúlaigh CFE,Barryscourt Rd Coolock 17 (8481337) - management & employee relations, Tue 7-9.30 20 wks

Colaiste Ide Cardiffsbridge Rd Finglas W 8443233 11 (8342333) - CIPD cert in personnel practice, Tues & Thurs, 7-10pm, 20 wks, €700

DIT Faculty: Business Aungier St 2 (4023000) - BSc in human resource management, 4 yrs p/time €1525 pa/ CIPD cert in personnel practice, 1 yr €819

Dorset College 64 Lr Dorset St/ 8 Belvedere Pl 1 (8309677) - CIPD cert, day 24 wks/ CIPd cert training practice Tue & Thurs6.30-9.30pm 24 wks

Griffith College Dublin Sth Circular Rd 8 (4150400) - dipl in HRM, 4-8 mths, 2 eve per wk, ICM, p/time

Harcourt Business School HSI 89 Harcourt St 2 (4763975) - dip in human resources management

Institute of Technology Tallaght ITT Dublin, Tallaght 24 (4042101) - Cert in Personnel Practice 1 yr CIPD/ Cert in Employment Relations, Law & Practice 1 yr CIPD

Malahide Community School Malahide (8460949) - BA in HR management, NCI degree Tue & Thurs 2 yrs 42500 pa

National College of Ireland Mayor St IFSC 1 (4060500/ 1850 221721) - Certificate in Personnel Practice (CIPD), 1 year, €1,750; Certificate in Personnel Practice (fast track) (CIPD), 15 Saturdays, Sat, €1,750/ MA in Human Resource Management, 2 years, Fri eve, Sat, 8,900; H.Dip in Business in Human Resource Management, 1 year, 4,990; BA (Hons) in Human Resource Management, 1 year, Tue, Thurs eve, €3,285; BA in Human Resource Management (CIPD), 3 years, €3,285; Bachelor of Business in Human Resource Management, 1 year, Mon, Wed eve,10 Sat, €2,950

Old Bawn Community School Tallaght 24 (4526137) - NCI Bachelor in Business in HRM, Tues & Thurs 6.30-9.30+10 Sats €2950

Plunket College Swords Rd, Whitehall 9 (8371689) - HR for small & medium enterprises, Mon 7.30 10 wks €90

Westmoreland College for Management Studies 11 Westmoreland St 2 (6795324/7266) - ICM dip corporate management/ ICM dip health services management/ ICM grad dip management/ ICM dip HR management/ Adv dip in project management

PERSONNEL/ HUMAN RESOURCES

Dublin Business School 13/14 Aungier St 2 (4177500) - Dip in Human Resource Management, 1 eve per wk, 1 yr Oct, 14 wks Feb / Hgher Dip in Business Studies - HR Management, 2 eves 6.15pm, 16 months / BA (Hons) Business Management (Human Resource Management) 4 yrs, 6.15:9:30pm / MA, 2 yrs

Pitman Training Centre 6-8 Wicklow St 2 (6768008) - full/pt-time dip; day eve sats

PHARMACY

DIT Faculty: Science Kevin St 8 (4023000) - MSc pharmaceutical quality assurance, 4 yr p/t, 12 modules

Institute of Technology Tallaght ITT Dublin, Tallaght 24 (4042101) - Higher Cert in Science - Good Manufacturing Practice and Technology NFQ Level 6 2 yrs/ BSc Pharmaceutical Technology - a follow on to higher cert Science GMP and

Technology NFQ Level 6 1.5 yrs (add on)/ Higher Dip, Pharmaceutical Production NFQ Level 8, 1.5 yrs/ MSc - Pharmaceutical Production NFQ Level 9 1 yr

St Kevin's College Clogher Rd Crumlin 12 (4536397) - pharmaceutical & toxicological services, 2 yr day, FETAC, BETEC, Nct Dipl

PHILOSOPHY see also Buddhism / Religion

All Hallows College Gracepark Rd Drumcondra 9 (8373745) - philos of religion, Mon 6.50, 24 wks €390 / logic: philosophical anthropology & intro to psychology, Mon 7.45, 24 wks €590 / theory of knowledge, Thurs, 6.50 ; contemporary philosophy, Thurs 8.30: each 24 wks €390: / historical intro to philos, Thurs 6.50, €390/ metaphysics, Thurs 6.50, 24 wks €390. ECTS credits

Brahma Kumaris WSU Raja Yoga Centres 5 Leeson Pk Ave 6 (6687480) - 5wk,Yoga philosophy free

Coláiste Dhúlaigh CFE,Barryscourt Rd Coolock 17 (8481337) - Fri 10am-11.30 10 wks

DATE Centre CFE, Dundrum 14 (2964322 (9.30am-12pm)) - wed 11.10am 10 wks €97

Greendale Community School Kilbarrack 5 (8322735) - inrto Thurs 10 wks €95

Irish T'ai Chi Ch'uan Assoc St Andrew's Resource Centre 114 Pearse St 2 (6771930) - taoist tao te ching, 2mths

Killester CFE, Collins Ave 5 (8337686) - intro to, Tues 7.30, 10 wks €60

Kilternan Adult Education Centre Ballybetagh Rd Kilternan 18 (2952050) - hist of western philos, Tues 9.30-11.30 10 wks 4130

Kylemore College Kylemore Rd 10 (6265901) - Thurs 10 wks 7-9pm

Milltown Institute of Theology & Philosophy Milltown Pk 6 (2776331) - NUI dip, Tue & Thurs 6.30 & 8.20pm, 2yrs, modular €1800 pa or €240 per module

Newpark Adult Education Centre, Newtownpark Ave Blackrock (2884376 / 2883725) - intro to philos past & present, Tue 10 wks €120, 7.30-9.45

Rathmines CFE - Senior College, Town Hall 6 (4975334) - intro to existance, God, being, right & wrong: ue 7-9pm 10 wks €90

Saor-Ollscoil na hÉireann 55 Prussia St 7 (8683368) - Mon

School of Philosophy & Economic Science 49 Northumberland Rd 4 (6603788) - practical philosophy, introductory course 12 wks 7.30, €125 also Sat

TACT St Dominic's School St Dominic's Rd Tallaght 24 (4596757)

Trinity College 2 (8961000) - (8961529) philosophers in dialogue, 9 wks €50/ modern intro to mental science, day 5 wks €80

UCD Adult Education Centre Belfield (7167123) - 10 week courses: conspiracy theories/ ethics and political philosophy/ further philosophical explorations/ philosophical explorations/ philosophy and the person/ philosophy in the matrix (5wks)/ what is philosophy?

PHOTOGRAPHY Film & Digital

An Oige 61 Mountjoy Street 7 (8304555) - group

Ashfield Computer Training Main St Templeogue 6W (4926708) - digital photography, morns, eves and accelerated

Ballsbridge CFE, Shelbourne Rd 4 (6684806) - digital beginners Mon, Thurs 6pm/ improvers Mon 7.45: 10 wks €90

Ballymun Trinity CS, Adult Ed Centre 9 (8420654) - digital, Mon 7-8.30 10 wks €100

Bray Institute of FE, Novara Ave Bray (2866111 / 2829668) - digital, Tue, Wed 7.30: 10wks, €85

Photography Classes for Beginners

AT THE DUBLIN CAMERA CLUB

Two comprehensive 10-week courses in the basics of Digital and Film based Photography, starting Wednesday September 20, 2006 , and Wednesday January 24, 2007. Further information from:

Telephone 01-6624464 / www.dublincameraclub.ie

As accommodation at these classes is limited early enrolment is advised

---

Cabinteely Community School Johnstown Rd 18 (2857455) - beginners, 10wk, €95

Coláiste Dhúlaigh CFE, Barryscourt Rd Coolock 17 (8481337) - introduction, Mon 7.15-9.30pm 20 wks/ digital for beginners, Tue: 7.30-9.30, 9 wks

Connolly House Nth Strand (by 5 Lamps) 1 (8557116) - SLR / digital: each Wed 6pm 10 wks €90/€95

Coolmine Community School Clonsilla 15 (8214583) - digital, Tue, Wed 7.30, 10 wks €80/ workshop, 'the basics' Sat 7 Oct 10am-1 €25

Crumlin College of FE, Crumlin Rd 12 (4540662) - digital (own camera necessary) with photoshop, Wed 6.45 10 wks

Donahies Community School Streamville Rd 13 (8482217) - intro to manual & digital, Mon 7.30, 10 wks €85/ digital, Tue 7.30 10 wks €110

Dublin Camera Club 10 Lr Camden St 2 (6624464) - beginners, Wed 6.30/ 8.30, 10 wks

Dún Laoghaire CFE, 17 Cumberland St Dún Laoghaire (2809676) - beginners, Tue+Wed/ intermediate, Tue: each 10 wks, 7.30, €110/ portfolio course, Mon, 24 wks, 7.30pm, €300/ digital photo & image processing, Tue+Wed, 10wks €170

FAS Training Centre Loughlinstown Wyattville Rd, DL (2043600) - digital darkroom - retouch techniques, 10 wks

Firhouse Community College Firhouse Rd 24 (4525807) - 35mm film, - Mon 7.30-9.30pm 8 wks €104

Gallery of Photography Meeting House Square 2 (6714654) - black & white (beginners/ advanced)/ refresher courses/ studio portraiture/ digital photography. Also Sats/ creative approaches

Greenhills College Limekiln Ave Walkinstown 12 (4507779/4507863) - Mon, 10wks, €130

Griffith College Dublin Sth Circular Rd 8 (4150400) - cert, 2 yr, CGLI, p/t, 2 eves per wk

Hartstown Community School Clonsilla 15 (8209863) - 10wks, €90

Holy Family Community School Rathcoole (4580766)

KAIES-Knocklyon Community Centre, 16 (4931213) - digital photog, Wed 8-9.30pm/ 11am, each 8 wks €90

Killester CFE, Collins Ave 5 (8337686) - improvers Tue 7-10pm 10 wks €120/

digital, for beginners Mon 7-10pm 10 wks €120

Kilroy's College Wentworth House Grand Canal Street Lr 2 (6620538 1850-700700) - tutor supported home study: practical, dip

Kilternan Adult Education Centre Ballybetagh Rd Kilternan 18 (2952050) - digital camera course, Thur 6.45 & 8.15 8wks each €65

Kylemore College Kylemore Rd 10 (6265901) - digital wihtphotoshop, thurs 8 wks 7-9pm

Lucan Community College Esker Drive (6282077) - amateur photog + intro to digital, Mon 7.30-8.30 10 wks €130

Malahide Community School Malahide (8460949) - digital camera, 10 wks €90

Moresoft IT Institute 44 Lr Lesson St 2 (2160902) - digital photog, 6-9pm 5 wks

NCAD Centre for Continuing Educ 100 Thomas Street 8 (6364214) - intro/ intermediate, c 22wk each

New Media Technology College, 13 Harcourt St 2 (4780905) - FETAC 5 1yr f/time; also p/time eve/ traditional b/w photography & 35mmSLR: 8 wks eves 6.30-9.30 or Sat 10-1 or 2-5pm

Newpark Adult Education Centre Newtownpark Ave Blackrock (2884376 / 2883725) - beginners, Mon 10wks, €120/ digital, beginners, improvers: Mon, Tue Wed, Thurs, 7.30-9.45pm

Old Bawn Community School Tallaght 24 (4526137) - beginners, 35mm SLR, b/w, Thurs 10 wks €95/ digital photography beginners & advanced, 10 wks Tue & Thurs €95

Palmerstown CS - Pobailscoil Iosolde, Kennelsfort Rd 20 (6260116) - digital, for beginners/ advanced: Thurs 6.45&8.15, 10 wks €100 ea

People's College for Continuing Education & Training 32 Parnell Sq 1 (8735879) - €60

Plunket College Swords Rd, Whitehall 9 (8371689) - beginners incl digital, 10 wks, €90

Pobalscoil Rosmini Adult Ed Grace Pk Rd 9 (8371015) - digital, Mon 7pm & 8.30/ Tue 7pm & 8.30: each €150

Portmarnock Community School Carrickhill Rd (8038056) - 35mm; digital; flash: landscape & portrait: Tue 10 wks €100

Rathmines CFE - Senior College, Town Hall 6 (4975334) - digital imaging for home photography, Wed 6.30-9 €140

Ringsend Technical Institute Cambridge Rd 4 (6684498) - SLR camera: beginners €90 / digital for beginners Mon €140: 10 wks each

Senior College Dún Laoghaire, CFE Eblana Ave Dún Laoghaire (2800385) - digital photography intro, €120

St Kevin's College, Clogher Rd Crumlin 12 (4536397) - media production & digital imaging, NCVA, 1yr, day

St MacDara's CC, Wellington Lane Templeogue 6W (4566216) - 35mm, Mon/ digital, Tue: 7.30 8 wks €104

St Tiernan's Community School Parkvale Balally 16 (2953224) - digital camera techniques, 10 wks Wed 7.30 €120

Stillorgan CFE, Old Road Stillorgan (2880704) - Mon 7.30 10 wks €130/ digital, Tue 7.30 8 wks €140

Tallaght Photographic Society 26 Alderwood green Springfield 24 (4517431) - beginners, 10 wks €65

PHYSICAL EDUCATION see Aikido / Body / Keep Fit / Weight Training

PHYSICS

DIT Faculty: Science Kevin St 8 (4023000) - MSc applied math & theoretical physics, 3 yr p/time €760 per module €840 thesis

PHYSIOLOGY see also Nursing

Colaiste Ide Cardiffsbridge Rd Finglas W 8443233 11 (8342333) - ITEC dip in anatomy, physiology & body massage, 20 wks Tue & Thurs 7-10 €500

Coogan-Bergin Clinic & College of Beauty Therapy Glendenning Hse 6-8 Wicklow St 2 (6794387) - anatomy, physiology & massage, CIBTAC, Thurs 6-9pm, €1795

Trinity College 2 (8961000) - (8962723) - extra mural, exercise physiology & fitness evaluation, 10wks, €200

Walmer College & Holistic Centre First Floor, River Hse Raheny Shopping C 5 (8329645) - & anatomy, ITEC dip

PIANO see also Keyboards / Music

Abbey School of Music 9b Lr Abbey St 1 (8747908) - Linda Butler, John Hunter

Bray Music Centre Florence Rd Bray (2866768)

Clontarf School of Music 6 Marino Mart 3 (8330936 087 8054963) - classical & modern, 18wk - also day

Dún Laoghaire Music Centre 130A Lr George's St Dún Laoghaire (2844178)

Hollywood Academy Dublin 13-14 Sackville Pl 1 (8786909) - from 4-8pm: 11 mths €75 per mth, cert

John Ward 5 Tibradden Drive Walkinstown 12 (4520918) - prep for RIAM grade exams - also day

Leinster School of Music Griffith College Campus South Circular Rd 8 (4150467)

Melody School of Music 178E Whitehall Rd W Perrystown 12 (4650150) - also day; also w/ends Sat-Sun, 12 wks

Newpark Music Centre Newtownpark Ave Blackrock (2883740) - also day

Parnell School of Music & Performing Arts 13-14 Sackville Pl 1 (8786909) - from 4-8pm, cert

Waltons New School of Music 69 Sth Gt George's St 2 (4781884) - also day, see ad page 155

PICTURE FRAMING

Newpark Adult Education Centre, Newtownpark Ave Blackrock (2884376 / 2883725) - Mon, 10 wks €130

PILATES see also KEEP-FIT

Alan Pelly Mercy College Coolock 5 (8476440 / 087 2749011) - at St Brigid's Parish Resource Cntr, Killester, Wed 7 & 8pm: each 8 wks €90

Ballymun Trinity CS, Adult Ed Centre 9 (8420654) - Wed 7pm 10 wks €90

Bray Institute of FE, Novara Ave Bray (2866111 / 2829668) - Stott pilates, Tue 7 & 8.15: 10 wks €150 ea

Cabinteely Community School Johnstown Rd 18 (2857455) - Mon/Tue/Wed: 7, 8- &9pm, 10 wks €65

Centre Studios 15 Upr Rathmines Rd 2 (4066812) - 8 wks €125; also day / yoga pilates fusion 8 wks €125/ pre-natal 8wks €125

Crumlin College of FE, Crumlin Rd 12 (4540662) - 10 wks Thurs 6.45 & 8.15

Dundrum Family Recreation Centre Meadowbrook 16 (2984654)

Firhouse Community College Firhouse Rd 24 (4525807) - pure pilates, - Mon 7.30pm 8 wks €52

Foxrock Institute Kill o' the Grange, Kill Lane Blackrock (4939506) - Mon 8wks €105

Greendale Community School Kilbarrack 5 (8322735) - Tue 8pm 10 wks €90/ cont 9pm

Healing House 24 O'Connell Ave Berkeley Rd 7 (8306413) - foundation & advanced, 6 wk: Mon, Tue; Fri; also lunchtimes

KAIES-Knocklyon Community Centre, 16 (4931213) - Thurs 10-11am, 8 wks €80

Killester CFE, Collins Ave 5 (8337686) - 10 wks Mon 7 & 8.30 €60 each

KLEAR Grange Park View Kilbarrack 5 (8671845) - day

Malahide Community School Malahide (8460949) - Tue, Thurs 7.30pm 8 wks

Marino College 14-20 Marino Mart 3 (8332100) - Thur 6.30 & 8pm 10 wks €65

Melt, Temple Bar Natural Healing Centre 2 Temple Ln 2 (6798786) - 1&2: postural classes, 6 wks €75

Newpark Adult Education Centre, Newtownpark Ave Blackrock (2884376 / 2883725) - Tue, Wed, Thurs 10 wks €95

Obus School of Healing Therapies, 53 Beech Grove Lucan (6282121) - morns & eves, 6wks €110

Old Bawn Community School Tallaght 24 (4526137) - improve posture & spine, Tue & Thurs 10 wks, 7.20 & 8.30 €80

Palmerstown CS - Pobailscoil Iosolde, Kennelsfort Rd 20 (6260116) - beginners/ intermediate: Tue 7 & 8pm 10 wks €70

Phibsboro Gym 1st Floor, Phibsboro SC 7 (8301849)

Physio Extra 37 Upr Grand Canal St 4 (087 7818300 6685048) - yoga with pilates

Pilates Institute (NTC) 16a St Joseph's Parade 7 (8827777)

Portmarnock Community School Carrickhill Rd (8038056) - for all, 8 wks 7.30-8.30 €80/ also stage 2, 8.30-9.30pm

Ringsend Technical Institute Cambridge Rd 4 (6684498) - Tue / Wed , 7.30-8.30 10 wks €50

St Kevin's College Clogher Rd Crumlin 12 (4536397) - 10 wks

St Tiernan's Community School Parkvale Balally 16 (2953224) - Tue 7.30 10 wks €80

TACT St Dominic's School St Dominic's Rd Tallaght 24 (4596757)

The Sanctuary Stanhope Street 7 (6705419) - 8 wks €95

Valerie Ward, Yoga Teacher city centre & southside (087 2852293) - body sculpting pilates

Walmer College & Holistic Centre First Floor, River Hse Raheny Shopping C 5 (8329645)

PITCH AND PUTT see also Golf

Corporate Club 24 Elmcastle Green Tallaght 24 (4610935)

Elmgreen Golf Course Castleknock 15 (8200797)

Network Club 24 Elmcastle Green Tallaght 24 (4524415)

Spawell Golf Range Templeogue 6W (4907990)

PITMANSCRIPT see Shorthand

PLANNING

DIT Faculty: Built Environment Bolton St 1 (4023000) - MSc in planning & development, 2 yr p/time, €3200 pa/ MSc in spacial planning, 2.5 yrs p/time, yr 1 €1600, yrs 2&3 €3200

Trinity College 2 (8961000) - (8961007) physical planning, post-grad dip 1 yr

PLASTERING

DIT Faculty: Built Environment Bolton St 1 (4023000) - decorative plasterwork, 30 wks €550

PLAY GROUPS see also Pre-School / Child Care

College of Progressive Education 27-29 Carysfort Ave Blackrock (4884300) - creative activities for children / FETAC level 6 therapeutic play

Firhouse Community College Firhouse Rd 24 (4525807) - play & the developing child IPPA, Tue 7.30-9.30pm 10 wks €130

PLUMBING

DIT Faculty: Built Environment Bolton St 1 (4023000) - advanced plumbing, mechanical services, 12 modules, 2 yr €700pa

Newpark Adult Education Centre Newtownpark Ave Blackrock (2884376 / 2883725) - beginnners, 10wks, €130, Thurs 7.30-9.45

POETRY see also CREATIVE / WRITING

Ballymun Trinity CS, Adult Ed Centre 9 (8420654) - learn about the great poets & their work, Tue 10 wks free

UCD Adult Education Centre Belfield (7167123) - appreciating poetry 10 wks/ Yeats: Life and Works (8 wks NLI)

POLISH see also Languages

Language Centre NUI Maynooth Co Kildare (7083737) - for beginners, 18wk, €350 cert

Newpark Adult Education Centre, Newtownpark Ave Blackrock (2884376 / 2883725) - Wed 7.30-9.30 10 wks €120

Pobalscoil Rosmini Adult Ed Grace Pk Rd 9 (8371015) - beginners, Tue 7-8.20 €90

Polish Social & Cultural Society 20 Fitzwilliam Pl 2 (2954058) - all levels, cert, 12wks, €155

Ringsend Technical Institute Cambridge Rd 4 (6684498) - conversational beginners Tue 7-8.30 10 wks €70

Sandford Language Institute Milltown Pk Sandford Rd 6 (2601296) - all levels, 15 wks €285

St Tiernan's Community School Parkvale Balally 16 (2953224) - beginners, 10 wks Mon 7.30 €90

Trinity College 2 (8961000) - (8961896) - extra mural, beginners €590/ intermediate; advanced: each €320: 24wks

POLITICAL STUDIES / POLITICS see also Current Affairs / European Studies

A Pamphlet: *Step Together - From Pillar to Spire: A Proposal for Citizens Day* available €3.00 post-free The OtherWorld Press, 68 Mountjoy Square 1

Coláiste Dhúlaigh CFE,Barryscourt Rd Coolock 17 (8481337) - politics & international relations, tue 7.15-9.15 9 wks

Coláiste Eanna, Kilkieran Rd Cabra 7 (8389577) - inrto to politics, Thurs 10 wks 7-9pm

DATE Centre CFE, Dundrum 14 (2964322 (9.30am-12pm)) - current issues, 8 wks, day

Saor-Ollscoil na hÉireann 55 Prussia St 7 (8683368) - politics/ peace & world order, Weds

UCD Adult Education Centre Belfield (7167123) - politics - becoming a player, Mon 8wks/ current affairs 10 wks spring

PONY TREKKING see Horse Riding

POPULAR CULTURE see also Cultural Studies

Irish Institute for Popular Culture 30/31 Wicklow St 2 (6713636)

PORTFOLIO PREPARATION

Ballyfermot CFE, Ballyfermot Rd 10 (6269421) - art portfolio, Fetac 5 Mon/Wed 7-10pm 15 wks

Meridian Art Group c/o St Paul's College Raheny 5 (8310688)

NCAD Centre for Continuing Educ 100 Thomas Street 8 (6364214) - pre-third level, 16 wks

St Kevin's College, Clogher Rd Crumlin 12 (4536397) - 20wks

TACT St Dominic's School St Dominic's Rd Tallaght 24 (4596757)

PORTRAIT PAINTING / SKETCHING see also Art

Brian Byrnes Art Studio 3 Upr Baggot St 4 (6671520 / 6711599) - 8wk, €150, also day/ pen & ink, 8wk, €150

Dún Laoghaire CFE, 17 Cumberland St Dún Laoghaire (2809676) - drawing & painting, Tues 7.30-9.30 10 wks €120

NCAD Centre for Continuing Educ 100 Thomas Street 8 (6364214) - portrait painting intermediate/ human figure/ painting the figure

PORTUGUESE see also Languages

Cabinteely Community School Johnstown Rd 18 (2857455) - beginners & improvers, practical & conversation, Tue 10 wks €95

Language Centre NUI Maynooth Co Kildare (7083737) - for beginners, 18wk, €350 cert

Marino College 14-20 Marino Mart 3 (8332100) - beginners, Tues 6&8pm 10 wks €90

Pobalscoil Rosmini Adult Ed Grace Pk Rd 9 (8371015) - beginners, Tue 7-8.20 €90

Sandford Language Institute Milltown Pk Sandford Rd 6 (2601296) - Portugal / Brrazil: each also day: all levels, 15 wks €285

WORDS Language Services 44 Northumberland Rd 4 (6610240) - beginners, advanced, commercial, individual tuition only

POTTERY, PORCELAIN, CERAMICS see also Art / Crafts

Balbriggan Community College Pine Ridge Chapel St (8412388/9) - make your own, Wed 7.30-9pm 8 wks €104

Bray Institute of FE, Novara Ave Bray (2866111 / 2829668) - pottery, ceramics, Mon, Tue, Wed: 10 wks, €95

Cabinteely Community School Johnstown Rd 18 (2857455) - 10wk, €115

Ceramic Forms Michelle Maher 9 Fernleigh Cl Castleknock 15 (6405614 087-2047695) - pottery/ ceramic hand building, 6 wk (all mats) €150; Mon, Tue, Wed 7.30/ also Tues 10.30-12.30am; ongoing; also wkend workshops & corporate groups

Grange Community College Grange Abbey Rd Donaghmede 13 (8471422) - 7-9pm Mon 10 wks

Greendale Community School Kilbarrack 5 (8322735) - incl. raw materials, Thurs, 7.30-9.30pm, €85

Liberties Vocational School Bull Alley St 8 (4540044) - pottery, Mon 7-9pm 10 wks €90

Lucan Community College Esker Drive (6282077) - Mon 7.30-8.30 10 wks €130

Malahide Community School Malahide (8460949) - Wed 3.15-5.15pm 10 wks €90

Newpark Adult Education Centre Newtownpark Ave Blackrock (2884376 / 2883725) - pottery, ceramics, Tue/ Thurs: 10wks, €135, 7.30-9.45pm

Palmerstown CS - Pobailscoil Iosolde, Kennelsfort Rd 20 (6260116) - beginners advanced, Thurs 7pm, 10wks €80

Plunket College Swords Rd, Whitehall 9 (8371689) - hand pottery, beginners, 10 wks, €90

Ringsend Technical Institute Cambridge Rd 4 (6684498) - level 1&2, 10 wks, €90 each

Saint Tiernan's Community School Parkvale Balally 16 (2953224) - pottery, Mon, 7.30-9.30pm, 10 wks, €120

Tracy Miley Cabinteely venue 18 (086 8485394) - hand built ceramics, beginners, improvers, 7.30-9.30pm 8 wks, €140, materials supplied, day

POWERPOINT see COMPUTER TRAINING

PRE-MARRIAGE / MARRIAGE EDUCATION

ACCORD (Catholic Marriage Care Service) 39 Harcourt St 2 (4780866) - marriage preparation courses, 1 wkend, €120/ inter-church marriage preparation, 1 wkend, €120 / marriage enrichment, 5 nights

PRE-RETIREMENT

Retirement Planning Council of Ireland 27/29 Lr Pembroke St 2 (6613139) - mid-career (35-50 yrs) courses; senior executive courses; planning for retirement courses, Dublin, Dundalk and countrywide: details on request

PRE-SCHOOL / PLAY SCHOOL see also Childcare / Montessori / Parents

College of Further Education Main St Dundrum 14 (2951376)

Greenhills College Limekiln Ave Walkinstown 12 (4507779/4507863) - IPPA cert, 10wks, €130

Hartstown Community School Clonsilla 15 (8209863) - play & the developing child, cert, 10wks, €85

IPPA - the Early Childhood Org, Unit 4 Broomhill Business Complex, 24 (4630010) - various short courses, IPPA, FETAC, C&G certs

Saint Finian's Community College Swords (8402623) - IPPA play & the developing child, cert, 10wk

Tallaght Community School Balrothery 24 (4515566) - IPPA cert, 10wk, 7.30-9.30 €80

PRE-THIRD LEVEL COURSES see also Return to Learning / Pre-University

FETAC East Point Plaza East Point Business Park 3 (8659500) - national certification body

Pearse College Clogher Rd Crumlin 12 (4536661/4541544) - uni access course, mature students, day/ third-level foundation; access to Trinity; FETAC liberal studies cert

Pearse College Clogher Rd Crumlin 12 (4536661/4541544) - university foundation PLC €150

PRE-UNIVERSITY EDUCATION see Return to Learning, etc

PREGNANCY see also Yoga / Pilates

Harmony Yoga Ireland 233 St James Rd Walkinstown 12 (087 8263778) - pergnancy yoga 4 day / pregnancy massage, dip 4 day

PRESENTATION SKILLS

Communication & Personal Development 30/31 Wicklow St 2 (6713636/ 6613225)

CTA Computer Training Academy, St James's Tce Malahide (8454070) -

ms powerpoint, 1 day: day/eve/Sat

Marino College 14-20 Marino Mart 3 (8332100) - for business Tue 10 wks 8-9.30 €65

Pitman Training Centre 6-8 Wicklow St 2 (6768008) - ms powerpoint, day eve sats, cert

PRIMARY SCHOOL see also Teachers

Alliance Francaise 1 Kildare St 2 (6761632); Alliance-Sud Foxrock Ave 18 (2898760) - tuition in ps, contact Aude Japy at Alliance for details (6381449)

PRINT / PRINTING & BOOK PRODUCTION see also Publishing

Irish Academy of Public Relations (2780802) - courses at UCD, Belfield: cert in journalism and print production, 12 wks 1 ev, €730

PSYCHOANALYSIS

Trinity College 2 (8961000) - (2722928) inside modern psychoanalysis, 9 wks €130

PSYCHOLOGY see also Counselling / Personal Development / Sports / Golf

All Hallows College Gracepark Rd Drumcondra 9 (8373745) - logic: philosophical & psychological anthropology, Wed 7.45, 24 wks €590. ECTS credit option

Ann Faherty 8 Grey's Lane Howth (8321255; 086 2312684) - NUI Maynooth, cert: 25wks, 7-10pm+5 Sats: at Coolmine, The Donahies & Palmerstown

Ballymun Trinity CS,s Adult Ed Centre 9 (8420654) - various topics, Mon 8wk, €90

Brahma Kumaris WSU Raja Yoga Centres 5 Leeson Pk Ave 6 (6687480) - 3wk, Yoga psychology free

Bray Institute of FE, Novara Ave Bray (2866111 / 2829668) - NUI cert, Wed 6-9.30pm 25 wks €850

Coláiste Dhúlaigh CFE,Barryscourt Rd Coolock 17 (8481337) - intro to, Mon 7.15-9.15, 10 wks

College of Progressive Education 27-29 Carysfort Ave Blackrock (4884300) - certificate in child psychology (FROEBEL)

Communications & Management Inst Regus Hse, Harcourt Rd 2 (4927070) - diploma, eve, wkends 9 mths €1750

Coolmine Community School Clonsilla 15 (8214583) - NUI cert, Mon 7-10pm, €1100

DATE Centre CFE, Dundrum 14 (2964322 (9.30am-12pm)) - psy of gifted development, tue 9.30am

Donahies Community School Streamville Rd 13 (8482217) - NUI Maynooth cert, Tue, €1110

Dorset College 64 Lr Dorset St/ 8 Belvedere Pl 1 (8309677) - dip in psy, Tues & Thurs/ child psychology, Fri, 12 wks/ forensic psy cert, Fri 12 wks: all 6.30-9.30pm

Dublin Business School 13/14 Aungier St 2 (4177500) - BA (Hons) Psychology, 2 eves 6.15:9:30pm, 4 yrs / Dip in Popular Psychology, 10 wks, 1 eve, 6:15-9:30pm / Dip in Psychology, 1yr, 1 eve, 6.15-9:30pm / Dip in Child Psychology, 1 eve, 6.15-9.30pm, 10 wks / Dip in Popular Forensic Psychology, 1 eve 6.15-9.30, 10 wks / Higher Dip in Psychoanalytic studies, 1 yr / Dip in Sports Psycholog y, 1 eve 10 wks

Dún Laoghaire CFE, 17 Cumberland St Dún Laoghaire (2809676) - NUI cert, psychology, 25wks: Mon 7-10pm +4 Sats, €1200

Harcourt Business School HSI 89 Harcourt St 2 (4763975) - dip in psychology

International Foundation for Adult Education PO Box 93 Eglinton St Cork

(022-29358 / 0818 365305) - dip, distance learning, IFAE-Netherlands

Killester CFE, Collins Ave 5 (8337686) - introduction to, Mon 7pm 10 wks €65

KLEAR Grange Park View Kilbarrack 5 (8671845) - day

Kylemore College Kylemore Rd 10 (6265901) - & criminology, Thurs 10 wks 7-9pm/ human growth & development - child/adloescent/adult, Mon; behavioural studies, Thurs: each FETAC, 18 wks 7-9pm

Malahide Community School Malahide (8460949) - introduction, Mon 10 wks €90

Maynooth NUI Adult & Community Ed Dept (7084500) - NUI cert: Bray Inst FE (2866111); Clane (045-893243); Coolmine (8214583); Crumlin (4536397) 10.15am-12.15; Donaghies 13 (8473522); Dunlaoghaire (2809676); Leixlip (6246420); Newbridge VTOS (045 434297); Navan VEC day (046 9021680); Old Bawn (4526137); Palmerstown (6260116); St Andrew's St Pearse St D2 (6771930) 10am-1; Trim (046 9438000); Wicklow (0404 64023)

Newpark Adult Education Centre, Newtownpark Ave Blackrock (2884376 / 2883725) - intro to, 10 wks €120 7.30-9.45pm

Old Bawn Community School Tallaght 24 (4526137) - NUI Maynooth, cert, course in Old Bawn, 1yr, 100hrs, Thurs

Our Lady's Hospice Harold's Cross 6 (4068806 4068810) - why do bad things happen to good people, 1 day workshops 29 Nov; 14 Feb07; 13 June07; 1 day €100 incl lunch/ reminiscence therapy, 11-12 Dec06; 10-11 Feb07; 11-12 May07: 2-day workshops €250 10-4pm incl lunch/ reminiscence through drama, 1 day 30 Sept06 10-4.30 €100 incl lunch

Palmerstown CS - Pobailscoil Iosolde, Kennelsfort Rd 20 (6260116) - NUI cert 1 yr Thurs 7pm 20 wks €850

Pobalscoil Rosmini Adult Ed Grace Pk Rd 9 (8371015) - for everyone, beginners, Wed 7-8.20 €75

Portmarnock Community School Carrickhill Rd (8038056) - intro to, Mon 7.30 10 wks €100

Rathmines CFE - Senior College, Town Hall 6 (4975334) - for everyday life, UCD module 1, 10 wks €250 cert, or special interest, €190: Mon 10 wks 6.30/ module 2 spring Mon 10 wks

Saor-Ollscoil na hÉireann 55 Prussia St 7 (8683368) - Wed

TACT St Dominic's School St Dominic's Rd Tallaght 24 (4596757)

Tallaght Community School Balrothery 24 (4515566) - intro, 10wk, 7.30-9.30 €80

Transactional Analysis in Ireland (4511125) - in everyday situations, mthly workshop, donation

Trinity College 2 (8961000) - (8961886) psychology: the science of behaviour and mind, 22 wks €300/ applied behaviour analysis (for professionals in disability services or child & adolecsence care services: (6082431) day Sats + one Fri eve mthly €3445

UCD Adult Education Centre Belfield (7167123) - intro to forensic psychology/ psychology of happiness: each 10 wks/ sense of self (3 Sats)/ introduction to psychology (3 Sats) / psychology in everyday life; and, how the mind works (Rathmines Senior College)

PSYCHOTHERAPY see also Counselling

Dublin Business School 13/14 Aungier St 2 (4177500) - BA (Hons) in Counselling & Psychotherapy, 6.15-9.30pm, 4 yrs ; Higher Dip in Counselling & Psychotherapy 6:15-9:30, 1 yr; MSc Counselling & Psychotherapy, 6:15- 9:30pm, 2 yrs

Irish Association of Holistic Medicine 66 Eccles St 7 (8500493) - diploma in holistic psychotherapy & counselling, 2 yr over 6 wkends + 6day module per yr, €2850pa

Irish Institute for Integrated Psychotherapy 26 Longford Tce Monkstown (2809313)

Roebuck Counselling Centre 59 Rathgar Rd 6 (4971929) - dip in counselling & psychotherapy, 3 yrs, Fri 4-10pm; Sat 8am-2pm

PUBLIC ADMINISTRATION see Administration

PUBLIC RELATIONS

Communications & Management Institute Regus Hse, Harcourt Rd 2 (4927070) - PR, advertising, marketing & sales dip, Tue 1 yr €1550/ PR cert, Thurs 10 wks €750

Dorset College 64 Lr Dorset St/ 8 Belvedere Pl 1 (8309677) - dip marketing advertising & pr, Mon & Wed, 6.30-9 1yr

Dublin Business School 13/14 Aungier St 2 (4177500) - Dip in Marketing,

Advertising, Sales & Public Relations, 2 eves, 6.15-9.30pm, 1 yr Oct, 14 wks Feb; Dip in Event Management & Public Relations, 1 eve, 14 weeks

Dún Laoghaire CFE, 17 Cumberland St Dún Laoghaire (2809676) - intro to, Wed 7-9pm 10 wks €140

Fitzwilliam Institute Ltd Temple Court Temple Rd Blackrock (2834579) - dip in PR, 2 eves weekly Sept-May, 6.30-9.30 €1945; city centre; accredited by PRII

Irish Academy of Public Relations (2780802) - courses at UCD, Belfield: Grad dip in pr, HETAC, 1 yr 2 evs, €4600; dip in pr, advertising & marketing, 1 yr 2 evs, €1850; dip in event management, 15 wks 2 evs, €1850; cert in pr and pr writing skills, 12 wks 1 ev, €730; Intro to PR, by email /corresp €390/€440

Lucan Community College Esker Drive (6282077) - foundation, Tue 7.30-8.30 10 wks €130

Portobello School 43 Lr Dominick St 1 (8721277) - marketing advertising & PR, ICM dip, 1 yr 2 eve per wk/ ICM subject cert, 32 wks

Westmoreland College for Management & Business 11 Westmoreland St 2 (6795324/7266) - ICM dip, marketing, advertising & PR

PUBLIC SPEAKING see also Debating

Cabinteely Community School Johnstown Rd 18 (2857455) - Mon 10 wks €95

Communication & Personal Development 30/31 Wicklow St 2 (6713636/ 6613225)

Coolmine Community School Clonsilla 15 (8214583) - before an audience (Toastmasters) Mon 10wk, €70

Hartstown Community School Clonsilla 15 (8209863) - presentation skills, 10 wks €85

Holy Family Community School Rathcoole (4580766)

Leinster School of Music Griffith College Campus South Circular Rd 8 (4150467)

Lucan Community College Esker Drive (6282077) - Mon 7.30-8.30 10 wks €97

Marino College 14-20 Marino Mart 3 (8332100) - Tue 6pm 10 wks €65

Newpark Adult Education Centre, Newtownpark Ave Blackrock (2884376 / 2883725) - confidence in, 10 wks €120, Mon 7.30-9.45

People's College for Continuing Education & Training 32 Parnell Sq 1 (8735879) - €60

Peoples College Debating Society 32 Parnell Sq 1 (8735879) - and debating

Plunket College Swords Rd, Whitehall 9 (8371689) - beginners, 10 wks

Pobalscoil Rosmini Adult Ed Grace Pk Rd 9 (8371015) - Wed 7-8.20 €75

St Tiernan's Community School Parkvale Balally 16 (2953224) - preparing speeches & public speaking, 10 wks Mon 7.30 €95

Toastmasters International Clubs (2860718 / 087 3542277 - call ans) - Clubs in greater Dublin area: AIB (Ballsbridge), Bray, Castleknock, Clondalkin, Drogheda, Dublin, Dún Laoghaire, East Coast, Eblana, ESB Engineers, Fingal, Glasnevin, Greystones, Hellfire, , Iarnrod Éireann, Lucan, Malahide, Naas, Navan, PRII, Rathfarnham Society, Swords, Tara

UCD Adult Education Centre Belfield (7167123) - speak with confidence, Fri/sat 1 day

PUBLISHING see also Desk-Top / Printing

BookConsulT 68 Mountjoy Square 1 - book publishing consultancy / editorial reports & assessment / writing

Cle, Irish Book Publishers Assoc 25 Denzille Lane 2 (6394868) - trade association/ occasional courses

SPI Society of Publishers in Ireland - for people in book publishing and related activities

Trinity College 2 (8961000) - (8968589) history of the book: writing, reading and printed word 3000BC-2000AD, eve 9 wks €60

UCD Adult Education Centre Belfield (7167123) - the business of writing (1 Day) 1 day / getting published 1 day workshop, Blackrock

PURCHASING & MATERIALS MANAGEMENT/ SUPPLY CHAIN

Coláiste Dhúlaigh CFE, Barryscourt Rd Coolock 17 (8481337) - supply chain management, 20 wks: 1st yr cert, Mon 7-9.30/ 2nd yr Tue 15 wks

Colaiste Ide Cardiffsbridge Rd Finglas W 8443233 11 (8342333) - dip, 3 yrs, Tues & Thurs, 6.30-10pm each yr, 25 wks, IIPMM, €500 per yr/ dip research assign 10 wks €250 IIPMM

Crumlin College of FE, Crumlin Rd 12 (4540662) - IIPMM courses: foundation cert in Supply Chain Management/ graduateship in purchasing & materials management (strategy, operations, storage & distribution, commercial relationships)/ dip part 3 (marketing, supply chain, business law, research assignment) eves 6.45-9.45

DIT Faculty: Business Aungier St 2 (4023000) - purchasing & materials management, cert/ advanced cert: / diploma: 2 yrs €811 ea

Dún Laoghaire CFE, 17 Cumberland St Dún Laoghaire (2809676) - IIPMM cert in supply chain management yr 1/also graduateship professional stage 1 yr 2: each 22 wks, Mon+Wed, 7-10pm, €525

FAS Training Centre Cabra Bannow Rd 7 (8821400) - best practice procurement,

10 wks/ manul handling 2 wks

FAS Training Centre Finglas Jamestown Rd 11 (8140200) - manual handling 2 wks

FAS Training Centre Loughlinstown Wyattville Rd, DL (2043600) - manual handling, 2 wks

Qi GONG

Dún Laoghaire CFE, 17 Cumberland St Dún Laoghaire (2809676) - chi-kung & health preservation, Wed 10 wks 8.30-9.30 €80

Irish College of Traditional Chinese Medicine ICTCM House Merchants Road 3 (8559000) - health-giving: 1 day/ 5 day workshops, cert/ CPD credits/ medical: PT Licentiate in medical qigong and traditional chinese medicine, 3 yrs 12 weekends pa Lic.MQG recognized by Guangzhou Uni of TCM; post graduate cert for practitioners of acupuncture

Melt, Temple Bar Natural Healing Centre 2 Temple Ln 2 (6798786) - exercise Sun 11am ongoing €75

Obus School of Healing Therapies, 53 Beech Grove Lucan (6282121) - morns & eves, 6 wks €100

QUALITY CONTROL

DIT Faculty: Engineering Bolton St 1 (4023000) - quality management, cert & dip: each 1 yr €545

Institute of Technology Tallaght ITT Dublin, Tallaght 24 (4042101) - Higher Cert in Science - Good Manufacturing Practice and Technology NFQ Level 6 2 yrs/ BSc Pharmaceutical Technology - a follow on to higher cert Science GMP and Technology NFQ Level 6 1.5 yrs (add on)/ Higher Dip, Pharmaceutical Production NFQ Level 8 1.5 yrs/ MSc - Pharmaceutical Production NFQ Level 9 1 yr

Trinity College 2 (8961000) - (8961768) - quality improvement, 1yr postgrad dip, 24wks

QUILTING Patchwork

Quilt Art Workshops 4 Mill Wood Naas (045-876121) - classes & workshops, SAE for info

RACE ISSUES / ANTI-RACISM see also Conflict/ Peace

Maynooth NUI Adult & Community Ed Dept (7084500) - race & ethnic studies, NUI cert: Old Bawn Tallaght, (4526137); beaufort College Navan (046 9028915); St Kilian's Bray (2864646)

Old Bawn Community School Tallaght 24 (4526137) - in Irish & globel contexts, NUI cert, Thurs 6.45-9.45+some Sats, €90

Trinity College 2 (8961000) - (8962766) - theories of race & ethnicity, 10 wks €150

RADIO - AMATEUR

Blind & Disabled Amateur Radio Group c/o Joseph Dillon IRTS PO Box 462 9 (8390812) - ham radio theory, B licence / inquiries for Dublin and countrywide

Nth Dublin Radio Club Artane Beaumont Rec Centre Coolock 5 (8313267) - ham radio, theory, B licence/Morse Class, A licence (with theory), €35 each, Oct to May

RADIO AND TV see also Broadcasting

St Tiernan's Community School Parkvale Balally 16 (2953224) - intro to community radio, 10 wks Wed 7.30 €95

RADIO SERVICING / PRODUCTION

Ballyfermot CFE, Ballyfermot Rd 10 (6269421) - radio production, Fetac 5 Wed 7-10pm 22 wks

Dún Laoghaire CFE, 17 Cumberland St Dún Laoghaire (2809676) - radio production techniques, Tue 10 wks, 7-10pm, €260

Sea-Craft 3 Newcourt Ave Bray (2863362) - DSC SCR radio, dept marine, eve + day, 1.5 days €189, dept marine cert; UK DSC radio, 1 day €129, RYA MCA DSC cert;

READING see also Basic Education / English Literacy Scheme / Dyslexia

National Adult Literacy Agency 76 Lr Gardiner St 1 (8554332) - national referral service for adults to get help with reading, writing & maths

RECEPTIONIST Office Procedure / Secretarial Courses

CTA Computer Training Academy, St James's Tce Malahide (8454070) - telephone, reception area, 1 day

FAS Training Centre Loughlinstown Wyattville Rd, DL (2043600) - clerical receptionist skills, 10 wks

Pearse College Clogher Rd Crumlin 12 (4536661/4541544) - reception & IT skills, 25 wks FIT fast-track course

Pitman Training Centre 6-8 Wicklow St 2 (6768008) - telephone reception skills, 1 day, cert/

Training Options Plus 6-8 Wicklow St 2 (6717787) - telephone & reception, 1 day, cert

RECORDER see also Music

Abbey School of Music 9b Lr Abbey St 1 (8747908) - Michael McGrath

Bray Music Centre Florence Rd Bray (2866768)

Dún Laoghaire Music Centre 130A Lr George's St Dún Laoghaire (2844178)

Leinster School of Music Griffith College Campus South Circular Rd 8 (4150467)

Newpark Music Centre Newtownpark Ave Blackrock (2883740) - also day

Nolan School of Music 3 Dean St 8 (4933730) - also day

Waltons New School of Music 69 Sth Gt George's St 2 (4781884) - also day, see ad page 155

REFEREEING

Basketball Ireland National Basketball Arena Tallaght 24 (4590211)

Football Assoc of Ireland 80 Merrion Sq Sth 2 (6766864)

REFLEXOLOGY

Aspen's Beauty Clinic & College 83 Lr Camden St 2 (4751079/ 4751940) - ITEC

Ballymun Trinity CS, Adult Ed Centre 9 (8420654) - Tue 7pm, 8 wks, €90

Beaumont Institute of Complementary Therapies Sr Brega (Member Inst Reflexology 6 (8571327) - course starts early Oct, 1 yr;

Berni Grainger 21 Grangemore Ave 13 (8472943/ 086 2694214) - intro, w/end, €180

Colaiste Ide Cardiffsbridge Rd Finglas W 8443233 11 (8342333) - Sat, 2-4.30pm, 10 wks, €100, cert

SUAIMHNEAS REFLEXOLOGY

Day and evening classes begin Sept. and April
Internationally recognized diploma course *(AoR, ITEC and IRI)*
Venue: Walmer Holistic College, Raheny Shopping Centre, D.5.
***Principal:* Carol Donnelly** BN, MAR, MIRI, ITEC, Cert. Ed.
tel. 8329645 / 087-6849790 or email carol@suaimhneas.com

Coolmine Community School Clonsilla 15 (8214583) - Tue 7.30-9.30, 8 wks €70

Foxrock Institute Kill o' the Grange, Kill Lane Blackrock (4939506) - 8 wks, €105

Galligan College of Beauty 109 Grafton St 2 (6703933) - ITEC & CIBTAC, Sept - June p/time, 41200

Hartstown Community School Clonsilla 15 (8209863) - 8 wks, €85

Healing House 24 O'Connell Ave Berkeley Rd 7 (8306413) - ITEC qualification, Wed 7-10 or wkends mthly, 1 yr €1750; also graduate course/ introductory foot massage 1 day workshop €90

Holistic Healing Centre 38 Dame St 2 (6710813) - ITEC dip

KLEAR Grange Park View Kilbarrack 5 (8671845) - day

Lucan Community College Esker Drive (6282077) - Mon 7.30-8.30 10 wks €130

Marino College 14-20 Marino Mart 3 (8332100) - Thurs, 10wks, €90

Melt, Temple Bar Natural Healing Centre 2 Temple Ln 2 (6798786) - wk/end €180 cert

Pearse College Clogher Rd Crumlin 12 (4536661/4541544) - ITEC dip, day

Pobalscoil Rosmini Adult Ed Grace Pk Rd 9 (8371015) - beginners, Mon 8.30-9.50 €90

Portobello School 43 Lr Dominick St 1 (8721277) - ITEC & AoR dip, eve 32 wks

Senior College Dún Laoghaire, CFE Eblana Ave Dún Laoghaire (2800385) - dip in reflexology, CIBTAC, €660

Suaimhneas Reflexology c/o Walmer Holistic College 1st Floor River Hse Raheny Shopping Centre 5 (8329645) - dip, 52wks, €1825

Time Out (4591038) - also wkend

Walmer College & Holistic Centre First Floor, River Hse Raheny Shopping C 5 (8329645) - ITEC dip

REFRIGERATION AND AIR CONDITIONING

DIT Faculty: Built Environment Bolton St 1 (4023000) - advanced level, 1 yr €550

REIKI see also Healing, Health Education

Ballymun Trinity CS, Adult Ed Centre 9 (8420654) - levels 1& 2: Mon 6.30 & 8.15: 10 wks, €120/ €150

Bray Institute of FE, Novara Ave Bray (2866111 / 2829668) - Tue 7.30 10 wks €85

Christine Courtney 53 Beech Grv Lucan (6282121) - levels 1, 2 & 3, cert, day - 1:€95, 2:€95, 3:€330

Coolmine Community School Clonsilla 15 (8214583) - workshop Sat 7 Oct 10am-1 €25

Donahies Community School Streamville Rd 13 (8482217) - I & II, MOn 7pm/8.30: 8 wks €95 ea cert

Foxrock Institute Kill o' the Grange, Kill Lane Blackrock (4939506) - 6 wks €95

Grange Community College Grange Abbey Rd Donaghmede 13 (8471422) - 7-8.30pm 8 wks €78

Greendale Community School Kilbarrack 5 (8322735) - Tue 7pm 10 wks €90

Greenhills College Limekiln Ave Walkinstown 12 (4507779/4507863) - 10 wks €130

Hartstown Community School Clonsilla 15 (8209863) - mon, 10wks, €85

Obus School of Healing Therapies, 53 Beech Grove Lucan (6282121) - day courses, Lucan

Old Bawn Community School Tallaght 24 (4526137) - fun & relaxation with angels, level 1& 2, Tue & Thurs, 10 wks each €95

Palmerstown CS - Pobailscoil Iosolde, Kennelsfort Rd 20 (6260116) - level 1& 2(cert), Thurs 5.45/7.45: 10 wks €80

Pobalscoil Rosmini Adult Ed Grace Pk Rd 9 (8371015) - level 1: Wed 7-8.20pm €120

Portmarnock Community School Carrickhill Rd (8038056) - level 1 cert, 8 wks 7.30 €100

Ringsend Technical Institute Cambridge Rd 4 (6684498) - Wed 7.30-9.30 10 wks €130 cert

School of Reiki Ivy House Sth Main St Naas (045 898243 086 3084657) - reiki 1, 2 & 3 to master level, cert/ wkend workshops

RELAXATION see also Meditation / Stress / Yoga

Brahma Kumaris WSU Raja Yoga Centres 5 Leeson Pk Ave 6 (6687480) - 3wk free

Classical Hatha Yoga 5 Leeson Pk Ave 6 (6687480) - peace & clarity, 4 wks + life long, free - also day

Forde Clinic 316 Howth Road Raheny 5 (8339902) - mind yoga for stress management (breathing, relaxation, meditation, visualistion - no exercise), Tues, 8-9.30, 6wks, €80

Hartstown Community School Clonsilla 15 (8209863) - through art, 10 wks €85

Holistic Healing Centre 38 Dame St 2 (6710813)

Irish T'ai Chi Ch'uan Assoc St Andrew's Resource Centre 114 Pearse St 2 (6771930) - t'ai chi prep, level 1-4, 2mths/beginners /advanced, chi-kung & t'ai-chi movement 10 wks, various centres

Margaret Forde Yoga (8339902) - venues: Raheny, St Paul's College, Sybil Hill, 6 wks Mon & Wed, 7.30/ Baggot St 2: 12.30pm € 5.30pm/ also pregnancy & birth yoga classes

Margaret Macken Yoga Stephen's Gr/Adelaide Rd/Clontarf (8332954) - Iyengar Yoga, 6 wk course; also relaxation, stress management and meditation

Newpark Adult Education Centre, Newtownpark Ave Blackrock (2884376 / 2883725) - stress, yoga, tai chi, pilates: 10 wks €95 each

T'ai Chi Energy Centre Milltown Pk Conference Centre Sandford Rd Ranelagh 6 (4961533) - t'ai chi/qi gong - & wkend workshops

Tony Quinn Centre 66/67 Eccles St 7 (8304211) - & stress management & personal development; also Dún Laoghaire (2809891)

RELIGION see also Pastoral Care / Philosophy / Scripture

Catholic Youth Care 20-23 Arran Qy 7 (8725055) - Catholic Religious Education - School of Faith for 18-23 yr old

Milltown Institute of Theology & Philosophy Milltown Pk 6 (2776331) - various degree, cert & dip courses in theology, philosophy and spirituality

Trinity College 2 (8961000) - (8961297) decoding Da Vinci, eve 8 wks €65/ Israel & ancient near East; New Testament- Synoptic Gospels & Johannine writings; election, covenant, kingship in Israel; Paul & early christianity; prophecy &

apocalypse in Israel; history of christianity in Europe & Ireland : each 22 wks €259
day/ traditions of christian thinking - intro to theology/ pluralist & post-secular?
contemporary contitions of faith; the question of God; religion & sceince; Islam an
intro: each 11 wks €150

RESCUE TECHNIQUES see also Adventure Sports
Civil Defence Esplanade Wolftone Qy 7 (6772699) - various centres
Sea & Shore Safety Services Ltd Happy Valley Glenamuck Rd 18 (2955991) -
personal survival techniques, 1 day €165/ safety & social responsibility, 1 day €100/
elementary fire fighting; crowd management; crisis management:each, half-day
€100/ fast rescue boat, 2 days €2000: all STWC'95 approved

RETAIL STUDIES see also Sales Persons
Consumers Association of Ireland 43-44 Chelmsford Rd Ranelagh 6 (4978600) -
professional skills development, CAIRS course, 1 day €425, cert
DIT Faculty: Business Aungier St 2 (4023000) - retail management, 2 yrs €744pa
Dublin Institute of Design 25 Suffolk St 2 (6790286) - retail interiors, cert, 1 eve or
morn 15 wks / visual merchandising cert, 1 eve 6 wks

RETURN TO LEARNING see also Basic Education/ VTOS
Coláiste Eanna, Kilkieran Rd Cabra 7 (8389577) - access to arts & social sciences,
UCD, 10 wks Tue / Thurs 7-9pm
FETAC East Point Plaza East Point Business Park 3 (8659500) - national certification body
Greendale Community School Kilbarrack 5 (8322735) - office/ nat cert in community
care & health/ post-leaving cert (8322735)
Inchicore CFE, Emmet Rd 8 (4535358) - various subjects, post leaving cert course/
also VTOS
Maynooth NUI Adult & Community Ed Dept (7084500) - NUI cert, Maynooth Campus
Old Bawn Community School Tallaght 24 (4526137) - access to arts & human
sciences programme: English lit, politics, study/writing skills, educ guidance, IT &
tutorials, Tue & Thurs eves 20 wks €739 (some assistance available)
Plunket College Swords Rd, Whitehall 9 (8371689) - junior cert for adults: 25 wk
courses
Pobalscoil Neasáin Baldoyle 13 (8063092) - UCD course, 20 wks, day
Roebuck Counselling Centre 59 Rathgar Rd 6 (4971929) - assistance with learning at
3rd level for adults, Tues eve ongoing
UCD Adult Education Centre Belfield (7167123) - access to arts & humanities/ access
commerces/ access science & engineering: outreach courses

ROCK CLIMBING see also Adventure Sports / Mountaineering
Clondalkin Sports & Leisure Centre Nangor Rd Clondalkin 22 (4574858)
Kylemore College Kylemore Rd 10 (6265901) - indoor climbing wall, Mon 10 wks 7-9pm

ROCK MUSIC see also Sound Engineering
Abbey School of Music 9b Lr Abbey St 1 (8747908) - Trea Breazeale
Waltons New School of Music 69 Sth Gt George's St 2 (4781884) - also music
technology, see ad page 155

ROMANIAN see also Languages
Sandford Language Institute Milltown Pk Sandford Rd 6 (2601296) - all levels, 15
wks €285

RUGBY

Irish Rugby Football Union 62 Lansdowne Rd 4 (6473800)

RUSSIAN see also Languages

Aisling Language Services 137 Lr Rathmines Rd 6 (4971902) - beginners, 7.30-9.30 10 wks €200

Bray Institute of FE, Novara Ave Bray (2866111 / 2829668) - beginners, Mon/ intermediate, Wed: 7.30, 10 wks €85 ea

Coolmine Community School Clonsilla 15 (8214583) - for beginners Mon 7.30 10 wks €80

Greendale Community School Kilbarrack 5 (8322735) - conversation intro, Tue 10 wks €90

Marino College 14-20 Marino Mart 3 (8332100) - Thurs, 10 wks €65

Ringsend Technical Institute Cambridge Rd 4 (6684498) - conversational beginners, Tue 8.30 10 wks €70

Sandford Language Institute Milltown Pk Sandford Rd 6 (2601296) - all levels, 15 wks €285

Trinity College 2 (8961000) - (8961896) - extra mural, beginners, 24wk, €590/ lower intermediate 24 wks €590/ intermediate; advanced: each 24 wks, €320/ heritage speaker & near-native speaker group, eve 24 wks €590

WORDS Language Services 44 Northumberland Rd 4 (6610240) - individual tuition only

SAILING AND SEAMANSHIP see also Adventure Sports / Navigation / Yachtmaster's Cert

Bray Sailing Club The Harbour Bray (2860272) - sail boat / power boat; advanced power boat / safety boat

Corporate Club 24 Elmcastle Green Tallaght 24 (4610935) - sailing

Fingall Sailing School Malahide (8451979)

Glenans Irish Sailing Club 5 Lr Mount St 2 (6611481)

Irish National Sailing School W Pier Dún Laoghaire (2844195) -basic & improving skills, eve & day, 1/2 wks, RYA/ISA cert, €479

Irish Sailing Assoc 3 Park Rd Dún Laoghaire (2800239) - sailing - dinghies, open dingies keelboats, catamarans; costal & offshore & ocean cruising yachtmaster courses: beginner to advanced, all yr, apply for provider list

Network Club 24 Elmcastle Green Tallaght 24 (4524415) - sailing

Sea & Shore Safety Services Ltd Happy Valley Glenamuck Rd 18 (2955991) - efficient deck hand, fast craft, 5 days €400 UK cert/ passenger cargo & hull integrity, day & eve, hald-day €100 STCW'95 A-V/2/ VHF, eve & day 2 days €240, Dept Marine cert

Sea-Craft 3 Newcourt Ave Bray (2863362) - ISA Yachtmaster coastal, 21 wk €435, cert; ISA Yachtmaster offshore, 21 wks €485; ISA yachtmaster ocean, 20 wks €500: ISA & RYA certs

Surfdock Grand Canal Dockyard Sth Dock Rd Ringsend 4 (6683945) - beginner sailing / also wkend/corporate groups

Trisailing Ltd (4525368) - trisailing, trimaran for beginners

SALES PERSONS / SELLING TECHNIQUES

Communications & Management Institute Regus Hse, Harcourt Rd 2 (4927070) - sales management dip, Wed 20 wks €1450/ sal;es practice cert, Tue 10 wks €750

Crumlin College of FE, Crumlin Rd 12 (4540662) - selling & sales management, f/time day

DIT Faculty: Business Aungier St 2 (4023000) - MI cert in selling, 2 yrs

FAS Training Centre Loughlinstown Wyattville Rd, DL (2043600) - sales rep & customer care, 10 wks

FAS Training Centre Tallaght Cookstown Indl Est 24 (4045200)

Irish Computer Society / ICS Skills Crescent Hall, Mount St Crescent 2 (6447820) - cert in selling skills, workshop & distance learning format, 20 hrs + 95 hrs project work, ICS/SII cert

Pearse College Clogher Rd Crumlin 12 (4536661/4541544) - retail management & business studies, day €150

Rathmines CFE - Senior College, Town Hall 6 (4975334) - sales & marketing management, Mon 7-9, 20 wks €145

Sales Institute of Ireland, The 68 Merrion Sq 2 (6626904) - selling skills, cert, online

SALSA see also DANCE

Coláiste Dhúlaigh CFE,Barryscourt Rd Coolock 17 (8481337) - with Colette Kirwan, Tue 7.30-8.45 10 wks

Coláiste Eanna, Vocational School Kilkieran Rd Cabra 7 (8389577) - beginners, Tues, 10 wks, 7-8 & 8-9pm

Dance Club Rathmines & Rathgar (2893797)

Dance Theatre of Ireland Bloomfields Centre, Lr George St Dún Laoghaire (2803455) - Tues, 7.45-9pm / cardio salsa, 6.30 & 7.30, 10 wks €80

Danzon (087 9172939) - salsa, all levels available: Thurs 8.30pm & Sun 7.15pm, ongoing €9.50 per class, 8-10 Harrington St 2/; also Mon 7pm Wynn's Hotel Lr Abbey St 1/ Wed 7pm St Caitriona's 59 Lr Baggot St

Foxrock Institute Kill o' the Grange, Kill Lane Blackrock (4939506) - salsa 8 wks €105

Just Dance (8273040 087 8473518) - salsa / jive / samba, venues Dublinwide, for fitness & fun

Killester CFE, Collins Ave 5 (8337686) - salsa & cha-cha, beginners Mon 7pm/8.30 10 wks €50 ea

Kylemore College Kylemore Rd 10 (6265901) - Wed 10 wks 7-9pm

Malahide Community School Malahide (8460949) - 10 wks €90

Marino College 14-20 Marino Mart 3 (8332100) - Tues 7*8.15pm 10wks, €50

Morosini-Whelan School of Dancing 46 Parnell Sq W 1 (8303613)

Newpark Adult Education Centre, Newtownpark Ave Blackrock (2884376 / 2883725) - salsa & latin American, beginners, Thurs 10 wks, €95

Palmerstown CS - Pobailscoil Iosolde, Kennelsfort Rd 20 (6260116) - dancing, Tues 7pm/ salsa, cha-cha, latino 8.15pm: ea 10 wks €70

Plunket College Swords Rd, Whitehall 9 (8371689) - Mon 7-8pm 10 wks €67

Pobalscoil Neasáin Baldoyle 13 (8063092) - Tue, 7.30 10 wks

Pobalscoil Rosmini Adult Ed Grace Pk Rd 9 (8371015) - & Latin American, beginners 1, Mon 7pm; 2, 8.30 each €90

Ringsend Technical Institute Cambridge Rd 4 (6684498) - and Latin American, Thurs 7 & 8.30 10 wks €70

St MacDara's CC, Wellington Lane Templeogue 6W (4566216) - Mon 7.30-9, 8 wks

€78/ Tue cardio-salsa, 7.30-9 €78

St Tiernan's Community School Parkvale Balally 16 (2953224) - Tue 7.30 10 wks €95 (partner not necessary)

Stillorgan CFE, Old Road Stillorgan (2880704) - Tue 7.30 8 wks €65

SAXOPHONE see also Music

Abbey School of Music 9b Lr Abbey St 1 (8747908) - Ronan O'Sullivan

Bray Music Centre Florence Rd Bray (2866768)

Dún Laoghaire Music Centre 130A Lr George's St Dún Laoghaire (2844178)

Newpark Music Centre Newtownpark Ave Blackrock (2883740) - also day

Nolan School of Music 3 Dean St 8 (4933730) - also day

Waltons New School of Music 69 Sth Gt George's St 2 (4781884) - also day, see ad page 155

SCIENCE see also Biology / Chemistry / Computer / Geology / Natural History / Physics

Dublin Zoo Education Dept Phoenix Pk 8 (4748932) - conservation & wildlife

Institute of Technology Tallaght ITT Dublin, Tallaght 24 (4042101) Higher Cert in Science - Good Manufacturing Practice and Technology NFQ Level 6 2 yrs/ BSc Pharmaceutical Technology - a follow on to higher cert Science GMP and Technology NFQ Level 6 1.5 yrs (add on)/ Higher Dip, Pharmaceutical Production NFQ Level 8, 1.5 yrs/ MSc - Pharmaceutical Production NFQ Level 9 1 yr

St Kevin's College, Clogher Rd Crumlin 12 (4536397) - applied laboratory, NCVA, 1yr

The Open University Enquiry/Advice Centre Holbrook House, Holles St 2 (6785399)

Trinity College 2 (8961000) - (8962182) - polymer science & technology, post-grad dip, 6 mths/ religion & science 11 wks day €150

UCD Adult Education Centre Belfield (7167123) - Access Science, 20 wks

SCREENWRITING see also WRITING, CREATIVE

Ballyfermot CFE, Ballyfermot Rd 10 (6269421) - Mon 7-9pm 12 wks

SCRIPTURE STUDY see also Bible Study / Religion

All Hallows College Gracepark Rd Drumcondra 9 (8373745) - introduction to scripture, Tue 6.40, 24 wks €390 / pastoral use of & Johannine writings, Tue 8.30, 24 wks, €390/ the prophets & Pauline writings, Wed 8.30, 24 wks €390. ECTS credits option

SCUBA DIVING

Irish Underwater Council 78a Patrick St Dún Laoghaire (2844601) - info on local clubs

Portmarnock Sub-Aqua Club Colin Murray Diving Instructor (087 2428575)

SCULPTURE see also Art

Ceramic Forms Michelle Maher 9 Fernleigh Cl Castleknock 15 (6405614 087-2047695) - clay modelling, 7.30-9.30pm, also Tues 10.30-12.30, 6 wks €150, incl materials

Marino College 14-20 Marino Mart 3 (8332100) - beginners, Tue 7.30 10 wks €95

NCAD Centre for Continuing Educ 100 Thomas Street 8 (6364214) - modelling from life, intro, c22wk

SECONDARY SCHOOL LEVEL COURSES

Alliance Francaise 1 Kildare St 2 (6761632); Alliance-Sud Foxrock Ave 18 (2898760) - pre-teen 6th class / secondary 1st & 2nd, Junior cert, 5th yr, Leaving cert

SECRETARIAL COURSES see also Business / Computers / Keyboards / OfficeSkills / Receptionist / Shorthand / Typing / Word Processing

CTA Computer Training Academy, St James's Tce Malahide (8454070)

Kilroy's College Wentworth House Grand Canal Street Lr 2 (6620538 1850-700700) - tutor supported home study: computer skills, keyboard & typing, dip

Pitman Training Centre 6-8 Wicklow St 2 (6768008) - legal secretarial, secretarial dip / intro to office skills, cert/ executive PA dip : all full/pt-time/ day eve Sat

SECURITY

Crumlin College of FE, Crumlin Rd 12 (4540662) - security studies. f/time day

Dún Laoghaire CFE, 17 Cumberland St Dún Laoghaire (2809676) - security skills, Mon & Wed 7-9pm 5 wks €290

SELF-AWARENESS / REALISATION see also Personal Development

Brahma Kumaris WSU Raja Yoga Centres 5 Leeson Pk Ave 6 (6687480) - 7wk free

Divine Rainbow Centre Marino 3 (8333640)

Holistic Healing Centre 38 Dame St 2 (6710813)

Irish Yoga Association PO Box 9969 7 (4929213/ 087 2054489) - qualified teachers available all over Ireland/ 4 yr Teacher Training courses

KLEAR Grange Park View Kilbarrack 5 (8671845) - self-esteem, day

Paul Bradley (Psychotherapist) Main St Kilcock Co Kildare (6284673/ 087 9598840) - seminars for men, Dublin/ Kildare venues

SELF-DEFENCE see also Karate / Judo / Martial Arts

Clondalkin Sports & Leisure Centre Nangor Rd Clondalkin 22 (4574858)

Hartstown Community School Clonsilla 15 (8209863) - 8 wks, €85

Holy Family Community School Rathcoole (4580766)

Irish T'ai Chi Ch'uan Assoc St Andrew's Resource Centre 114 Pearse St 2 (6771930) - Chin Na (joint locking & pressure point strikes) self defence, 8wks/ also, push hands & applications class, weekly, Sat; drop-in also.. All styles welcome

Rathgar Kenpo Karate Studios Garville Rd Rathgar 6 (8423712) - Mon, Wed, Fri: 8-9.30pm

Taekwon-Do Centre 10 Exchequer St 2 (6710705)

Yang's Martial Arts Assoc Blackrock (2814901) - white crane & long fist kung fu

SELF-EMPLOYED see Business Small / Entrepreneurial Skills

SERBO-CROATIAN see also Languages

Sandford Language Institute Milltown Pk Sandford Rd 6 (2601296) - all levels subject to demand, 15 wks €350

SET DANCING

Brooks Academy 15 Henrietta St 1 (8730093) - Sept-May Mon & Thurs 8-10pm

Corporate Club 24 Elmcastle Green Tallaght 24 (4610935)

Crossroads Set Dancers Scoil Aine, Raheny 5 (8420662 / 6601898) - Tue, 8.30-10.30

Dublin Folk Dance Group 48 Ludford Drive Ballinteer 16 (2987929) - adult set dancing

Dundrum Family Recreation Centre Meadowbrook 16 (2984654)

Kilternan Adult Education Group Ballybetagh Rd Kilternan 18 (2952050) - Mon beginners 7-8pm €30/ improvers: 8p-10pm €60: 10 wks ea

Na Piobairi Uileann 15 Henrietta St 1 (8730093) Thurs, begin.; Mon & Wed, intermediate

Pobalscoil Rosmini Adult Ed Grace Pk Rd 9 (8371015) - beginners 1 & 2: 7pm & 8.30, each €90

St Kevin's College Clogher Rd Crumlin 12 (4536397) - 10wks

SEWING see also Dressmaking

Donahies Community School Streamville Rd 13 (8482217) - sewing & craftwork, Tue 10 wks, €85

Hartstown Community School Clonsilla 15 (8209863) - sewing & craftwork, 10wks, €85

St MacDara's CC, Wellington Lane Templeogue 6W (4566216) - creative sewing for the home, Tue 7.30 8 wks €104

SHAMANISM

Irish School of Shamanism 54 South William St 2 (4577839) - dreamweavery & drumquest, 12 wk

Karen Ward Classes, Dublin 4 (6704905) - as seen on RTE TV's 'The Health Squad'; also workshops; shamanism wkends & holidays with yoga

SHIATSU

Dún Laoghaire CFE, 17 Cumberland St Dún Laoghaire (2809676) - shiatzy massage training, Tues, 10 wks, 7.30-9.30pm, €110

Irish School of Shiatsu c/o 9 Lauderdale Tce Bray (2865997) - beginner & practitioner training, eve, wkends, 1 dat/ 8wk/ 3 yr p/time: city centre & Monkstown venues

Killester CFE, Collins Ave 5 (8337686) - Tue 7-9pm €70

KLEAR Grange Park View Kilbarrack 5 (8671845) - day

Old Bawn Community School Tallaght 24 (4526137) - deep finger pressure masasge, Thurs 8 wks €73

Shiatsu Ireland classes at 44 Adelaide Rd 2 (2962839) - beginners & advanced

TARGET St Kevin's School Newbrook Rd, Donaghmede 13 (8671967) - theraputic art from Japan, introductory, 10 wks

SHOOTING

East Coast Shooting Club (087 2243829) - also, target rifle shooting

SHORTHAND see also Secretarial

Pitman Training Centre 6-8 Wicklow St 2 (6768008) - 60 hrs, cert

SIGHT SINGING/EAR TRAINING

Waltons New School of Music 69 Sth Gt George's St 2 (4781884) - see ad page 155

SIGN LANGUAGE see also Deafness

Ballymun Trinity CS, Adult Ed Centre 9 (8420654) - beginners Tue €90/advanced Wed €90: 10wk each

Bray Institute of FE, Novara Ave Bray (2866111 / 2829668) - beg., Tue 7.30 10wks, €85

Coláiste Dhúlaigh CFE, Barryscourt Rd Coolock 17 (8481337) - part 1 cert, Mon 7.30-9.30 10 wks

Coláiste Eanna, Kilkieran Rd Cabra 7 (8389577) - beginners, 10 wks, Tues, 7-9pm

Donahies Community School Streamville Rd 13 (8482217) - level 1 Tue 7.30/ intermediate 8.15: 10 wks €75 each

Firhouse Community College Firhouse Rd 24 (4525807) - Tue 7.30-9.30pm 8 wks €104

Foxrock Institute Kill o' the Grange, Kill Lane Blackrock (4939506) - 8 wks, €105

Hartstown Community School Clonsilla 15 (8209863) - 10 wks, €85

Lucan Community College Esker Drive (6282077) - Mon 7.30-8.30 10 wks €130

Marino College 14-20 Marino Mart 3 (8332100) - 6pm 10wks Thurs €65/ level 1 &2 SLAI cert 20 wks €130

National Assoc for the Deaf 35 Nth Frederick St 1 (8175700 /fax 8723816) - beginners, starts Mon 9 Oct-to April: 6.30-8pm/ Wed 11th Oct 7.30-9pm/ Thurs 2 Oct 7-8.30/ advanced, Tue 10th Oct, 7.30-9pm €190 cert

Newpark Adult Education Centre, Newtownpark Ave Blackrock (2884376 / 2883725) - level 1 beginner, 10 wks Thurs 7.30-9.45, €120

Old Bawn Community School Tallaght 24 (4526137) - Tues 7.30-9.30pm: cert, level 1, Thurs 20 wks €150/ cert, level2, 20 wks €170/ Level 3 Tues

Palmerstown CS - Pobailscoil Iosolde, Kennelsfort Rd 20 (6260116) - Tue 7.30pm 10 wks €70

Plunket College Swords Rd, Whitehall 9 (8371689) - Tues 7-8.30 10 wks, €67

Pobalscoil Rosmini Adult Ed Grace Pk Rd 9 (8371015) - beginners 1 & 2: Mon 7pm & 8.30 €90 each

Ringsend Technical Institute Cambridge Rd 4 (6684498) - Irish sign language, beginners, 7-8.30 10 wks €70

Tallaght Community School Balrothery 24 (4515566) - beginners 10 wks 7.30-9.30, €70

Trinity College 2 (8961000) - (cdsinfo@tcd.ie) - extra mural, Irish Sign Language: beginners / post-beginners / intermediate, 24 wks, €360 each / intro to Irish Sign Language (ISL) 10 wks €150/ intro to Deaf Studies, 18 wks €270

SILK PAINTING

Jean Strong (2892323) - ongoing, beginners-improvers, 10wks, €170/also day:- Blackrock & Dundrum

Plunket College Swords Rd, Whitehall 9 (8371689) - Wed 7.30-9.30 10 wks €90

St Tiernan's Community School Parkvale Balally 16 (2953224) - Wed 7.30 10 wks €120

SINGING see also Music / Voice

Abbey School of Music 9b Lr Abbey St 1 (8747908) - Conor Farren (8747909)

Bel Canto School of Singing Bel Canto House 21 Nth Gt George's St 1 (8742460/ 8740184) - vocal analysts/ coaches, all fields of singing, modern and classical

Bray Music Centre Florence Rd Bray (2866768)

Clontarf School of Music 6 Marino Mart 3 (8330936 087 8054963)

Comhaltas Ceoltóirí Éireann 32 Belgrave Sq Monkstown (2800295) - traditional

Donahies Community School Streamville Rd 13 (8482217) - for 'non-singers', Wed 7.30 10 wks, €85

Dublin Airport Singers (8403539) - at St Vincent De Paul girls school, Griffith Ave, Tues 8pm: light; sacred; Irish; light classical; carols; vocal technique; music theory; sight-reading sheet music; membership open

Dún Laoghaire Music Centre 130A Lr George's St Dún Laoghaire (2844178)

Edwin Williamson School of Singing Bel Canto House 21 Nth Gt George's St 1 (874 2034) - singing teacher, vocal analysis & coaching, all fields of singing, modern and classical

Hollywood Academy Dublin 13-14 Sackville Pl 1 (8786909) - all styles, from 4-8pm: 11 mths €75 per mth, cert

Leinster School of Music Griffith College Campus South Circular Rd 8 (4150467) - group singing for adult beginners, 6 wks/ also individual lessons

Melody School of Music 178E Whitehall Rd W Perrystown 12 (4650150) - also day; 12 wks

Merriman School of Singing and Music Bel Canto House 21 North Great George's St 1 (874 2034)

Newpark Music Centre Newtownpark Ave Blackrock (2883740) - also day

Rachel Dempsey Global Harmonies Smithfield 7 (086 3097232) - for personal development/ free the voice/ vocal jamming: each 8 wks €100 various venues

Waltons New School of Music 69 Sth Gt George's St 2 (4781884) - see ad page 155

SKETCHING see also Art / Drawing / Landscape / Oil Painting / Still Life

DATE Centre CFE, Dundrum 14 (2964322 (9.30am-12pm)) - sketching & drawing, 10 wks, €97 day

Dún Laoghaire CFE, 17 Cumberland St Dún Laoghaire (2809676) - Wed 7.30 10 wks €110

Kylemore College Kylemore Rd 10 (6265901) - Thurs 13 wks 7-9pm

Marino College 14-20 Marino Mart 3 (8332100) - pencil, 7.30 Tue, 10wks €90

SKIING

Ski Club of Ireland Kilternan (2955658)

SKIN CARE see also Beauty Care

Coláiste Dhúlaigh CFE, Barryscourt Rd Coolock 17 (8481337) - & make up, Tues, 8 wks, 7.15

Crumlin College of FE, Crumlin Rd 12 (4540662) - CIBTAC dip, ptime day 20 wks

Donahies Community School Streamville Rd 13 (8482217) - make up & skin care skills, Mon 7.30 10 wks €85

Holy Family Community School Rathcoole (4580766)

Killester CFE, Collins Ave 5 (8337686) - Tue 7.30 10 wks €70

Old Bawn Community School Tallaght 24 (4526137) - and beauty theraph, Thurs 10 wks

SLIMMING

Dundrum Family Recreation Centre Meadowbrook 16 (2984654) - weightwatchers, ladies/ men

Hegarty Fitness Centre 53 Middle Abbey St 1 (8723080) - cellulite removal/ slimming/figure therapy, 4-10 wks, €28 ea, also day

Saint Anthony's House St Lawrence Rd Clontarf 3 (8335300) - also day

Tony Quinn Centre 66/67 Eccles St 7 (8304211) - nutrition clinic 6pm

SLOVENE

Sandford Language Institute Milltown Pk Sandford Rd 6 (2601296) - all levels subject to demand, 15 wks €350

SNOOKER

Network Club 24 Elmcastle Green Tallaght 24 (4524415)

SOCCER

Clondalkin Sports & Leisure Centre Nangor Rd Clondalkin 22 (4574858) - indoor; also day/ all weather

Corporate Club 24 Elmcastle Green Tallaght 24 (4610935)

Donahies Community School Streamville Rd 13 (8482217) - indoor football for men, Mon 7.30/ Tues 8pm/ ladies soccer, Wed 7.30: 10 wks €70 each

Football Assoc of Ireland 80 Merrion Sq Sth 2 (6766864)

Network Club 24 Elmcastle Green Tallaght 24 (4524415)

Portmarnock Sports & Leisure Club Blackwood Lane Carrickhill Portmarnock (8462122) - outdoor 5-a-side/ indoor

Women's Football Assoc of Ireland 80 Merrion Sq 2 (7037500)

SOCIAL EVENTS

An Oige 61 Mountjoy Street 7 (8304555)

Ballymun Men's Centre Lift Shaft 4 Shangan Rd Ballymun 9 (8623117) - group outings, theatre, cinema, day trips, weekend residential workshops

Corporate Club 24 Elmcastle Green Tallaght 24 (4610935) - barbecues, treasure hunts, parties, camping, quizes, music groups, dances, cinema, theatre, set dancing, etc

Junior Chamber Ireland - email pro@jci-ireland.org for info

Network Club 24 Elmcastle Green Tallaght 24 (4524415) - barbecues, treasure hunts, parties, camping, quizzes, music groups, dances, cinema, theatre, set dancing

Saint Anthony's House St Lawrence Rd Clontarf 3 (8335300) - club, day

SOCIAL STUDIES/ AFFAIRS see also Law / Psychology / Sociology

Ballyfermot CFE, Ballyfermot Rd 10 (6269421) - NUI (UCC) dip, 100 hrs x 2 yrs, Wed 7-10pm

Dublin Business School 13/14 Aungier St 2 (4177500) BA (Hons) Social Science, 2 eves, 4 years

Hartstown Community School Clonsilla 15 (8209863) - & human studies, cert (NUI Maynooth) 25 wks €1050

I.T. Blanchardstown Rd North 15 (8851000) - BA in applied social studies in social care, 3 yrs €3360 pa p/time

Inchicore CFE, Emmet Rd 8 (4535358) - social studies cert

International Foundation of Adult Education PO Box 93 Eglinton St Cork (022-29358 / 0818 365305) - dip, distance learning, IFAE-Netherlands

Liberties College Bull Alley St 8 (4540044) social studies childcare: FETAC level 5, Mon & Wed, 7-9pm, 10 wks €100

Maynooth NUI Adult & Community Ed Dept (7084500) - NUI cert: Hartstown,15 (8209863); Newbridge (045 434297)

The Open University Enquiry/Advice Centre Holbrook House, Holles St 2 (6785399)

Trinity College 2 (8961000) - alcohol & drug problems in Ireland 10 wks €100 (8961163am)/ facilitation skills 8 wks €100 (8963885)

UCD Adult Education Centre Belfield (7167123) - Conflict Resolution and Mediation Skills, 1 & 2: each Thurs 7 wks

SOCIAL WORKERS SERVICES / AGENCIES see Voluntary

SOCIOLOGY

International Foundation of Adult Education PO Box 93 Eglinton St Cork (022-29358 / 0818 365305) - dip, distance learning, IFAE-Netherlands

Kylemore College Kylemore Rd 10 (6265901) - Mon 16 WKS 7-9pm FETAC 2

Newpark Adult Education Centre Newtownpark Ave Blackrock (2884376 / 2883725) - intro to, Thurs 10 wks 7.30-9.45 €120

Trinity College 2 (8961000) - (8962766) - theories of race & ethnicity - intro, 10 wks €150

UCD Adult Education Centre Belfield (7167123) - Exploring Ethnic Ireland 10 wks spring / The Vexed Question of National Identity, Wed 10 wks

SOFT FURNISHINGS see also Patchwork

Dún Laoghaire CFE, 17 Cumberland St Dún Laoghaire (2809676) - patchwork, dressmaking, Tues, 10 wks, 7.30-9.30pm, €110

SOFTWARE, COMPUTER see Computer entries

SONG WRITING see also Music

Hollywood Academy Dublin 13-14 Sackville Pl 1 (8786909) - wkend courses

SOUND ENGINEERING

Ballyfermot CFE, Ballyfermot Rd 10 (6269421) - Wed 7-10pm 15 wks

Hollywood Academy Dublin 13-14 Sackville Pl 1 (8786909) - recording course/ also home recording course

Kylemore College Kylemore Rd 10 (6265901) - FETAC 2 10 wks Mon 7-9pm

Lucan Community College Esker Drive (6282077) - Mon 7.30-8.30 10 wks €130

Plunket College Swords Rd, Whitehall 9 (8371689) - overview of all aspects, Mon 7.30 10 wks €90/ home PC recordinhg studio, Wed 7.30 10 wks €90

Pulse Recording Studios 67 Pleasants Place 8 (4784045) - C&G 1820 Part 1, Oct-May: Sat, €2300; Part 2 Mon, Wed eves Sept-June €2300; Part 3 Sept-Dec: Tue, Thurs eves, €1500/ Part 1&2 day full time, €4900 /Part 3, +Live Sound post-prod, full time €4900

Sound Training Centre Temple Bar Music Centre Curved Street Temple Bar 2 (6709033) - sound engineering & music technology C&G 1&2 34 weeks €4500 ftime - €3300 ptime / sound engineering lighting & stage production C&G1&2 34 wks €4500 ftime / music & media technology, C&G3 34 wks €4500 Sept/ advanced mixed media programme / electronic music production STC cert 15 wks €1000 Oct & Mar / dj'ing & music production STC cert 15 wks €1000 Oct & Mar / intro to dj'ing & music production STC cert 1 wk €500 summer course

Waltons New School of Music 69 Sth Gt George's St 2 (4781884) - also day, see ad page 155

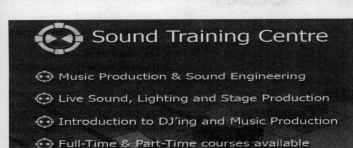
SPANISH see also Languages

Aisling Ireland 137 Lr Rathmines Rd 6 (4971902) - all levels, 7.30-9.30 10 wks €160

Ashfield College Main St Templeogue 6W (4900866) - beginners / improvers 7.30-9.30 8 wks

Balbriggan Community College Pine Ridge Chapel St (8412388/9) - introduction, Tues 8 wks 7-8.30pm €78

Ballinteer Community School Ballinteer 16 (2988195)

Ballsbridge CFE, Shelbourne Rd 4 (6684806) - beginners, Mon 6pm & 7.45; continuation Mon 7.45: 10 wks €80 each

BASE Ballyboden Adult Social Education Whitechurch Library Taylor's Lane 16 (4935953) - beginners/ continuation, all yr

Bray Institute of FE, Novara Ave Bray (2866111 / 2829668) - beginners, Tues 7.30 /intermediate Wed 7.30, 10 wks, €85 each

Cabinteely Community School Johnstown Rd 18 (2857455) - beginners/improvers, 10wk, €95 each

Coláiste Dhúlaigh CFE, Barryscourt Rd Coolock 17 (8481337) - FETAC cert Mon 1-2pm, 24 wks

Colaiste Ide Cardiffsbridge Rd Finglas W 8443233 11 (8342333) - for Gringos, Tue 7-9pm 10 wks €120, cert

College of Further Education Main St Dundrum 14 (2951376) - beginners, Tue & Thurs 7-9pm 8 wks €104

Coolmine Community School Clonsilla 15 (8214583) - beginners, Mon/ improvers, Tue: 20wk, €150 each/ for holidays, Tue-Wed 10 wks €80

Crumlin College of FE, Crumlin Rd 12 (4540662) - beginners, Tues, 6.45/ 8.15 20 wks

DATE Centre CFE, Dundrum 14 (2964322 (9.30am-12pm)) - levels I- IV: beginners/ continuation/ advanced: each 10 wks €97 day

Donahies Community School Streamville Rd 13 (8482217) - levels 1, 2, 3: 7.30 Tue 10 wks €85 each

Dún Laoghaire CFE, 17 Cumberland St Dún Laoghaire (2809676) - levels 1, 2, 3 & 4: each 7.30-8.30 10 wks €95

Dún Laoghaire-Rathdown Co Council Public Library Service - Deansgrange lib, Clonkeen Dr (2850860) - Spanish/Eng - informal sessions, Fri & Sat 10.30-12 morn;

Firhouse Community College Firhouse Rd 24 (4525807) - continued, Mon/ beginners, Tue: 7.30-9.30pm 8 wks €104

Foxrock Institute Kill o' the Grange, Kill Lane Blackrock (4939506) - for fun, 8 wks, €105

Grange Community College Grange Abbey Rd Donaghmede 13 (8471422) - beginners 7-8.30pm 10wks

Greendale Community School Kilbarrack 5 (8322735) - conversation, levels 1 & 2, Tue eve & morn: each 10 wks €90

Greenhills College Limekiln Ave Walkinstown 12 (4507779/4507863) - beginners, 10 wks, €130

Hartstown Community School Clonsilla 15 (8209863) - 10wks, €85

Holy Family Community School Rathcoole (4580766)

Inchicore CFE, Emmet Rd 8 (4535358)

Instituto Cervantes Spanish Cultural Inst 58 Northumberland Rd 4 (6682024)

Killester CFE, Collins Ave 5 (8337686) - beginners/ improvers: Mon: 7.30/ 8.30, 10 wks €60

Kilternan Adult Education Centre Ballybetagh Rd Kilternan 18 (2952050) - conversation, Tue 7.30 10 wks €130

Kylemore College Kylemore Rd 10 (6265901) - 10 wks 7-9pm - beg - advanced

Language Centre NUI Maynooth Co Kildare (7083737) - beginners/intermediate, 18wk, €350 cert

Lucan Community College Esker Drive (6282077) - beginners, Mon/improvers Tue: 7.30-8.30 10 wks €130

Malahide Community School (8460949) - beginners, Tues/improvers, Thurs - 10wks €90 each

Marino College 14-20 Marino Mart 3 (8332100) - beginners/ improvers: Tue & Thurs: 10 wks €65 each/ 1st cert Istituto Cervantes 22 wks tue €170

Newpark Adult Education Centre Newtownpark Ave Blackrock (2884376 / 2883725) - all levels, 10wks, €120, Mon-Thurs 7.30-9.45

Palmerstown CS - Pobailscoil Iosolde, Kennelsfort Rd 20 (6260116) - level 1&2, Thurs 6.45 & 8.15.so 10 wks €75 ea

Park House International Language Institute Ashdale Rd Terenure 6W (4902648) - beginners & improvers

People's College for Continuing Education & Training 32 Parnell Sq 1 (8735879) - €60

Plunket College Swords Rd, Whitehall 9 (8371689) - beginners Tue/ intermediate Wed: conversation, 10 wks, €90 each

Pobalscoil Neasáin Baldoyle 13 (8063092) - Tue 7.30 10 wks

Pobalscoil Rosmini Adult Ed Grace Pk Rd 9 (8371015) - beginners 1 & 2: Tue or Wed, 7pm & 8.30 €90 each

Portmarnock Community School Carrickhill Rd (8038056) - beginners, Tue/ improvers, Mon: 7.30-9.30 10 wks each

Rathmines CFE - Senior College, Town Hall 6 (4975334) - beginners Mon 20 wks €175/improvers, Tues; intermediate Wed: 7pm 25 wks €205; intermediate/ advanced 25 wks €165 ea

Ringsend Technical Institute Cambridge Rd 4 (6684498) - beginners/ intermediate/ advanced, 10wks, €70 each, Mon 7 & 8.30

Saint Finian's Community College Swords (8402623) - 8 wks

Sandford Language Institute Milltown Pk Sandford Rd 6 (2601296) - all levels, 15 wks €240; also day

St MacDara's CC, Wellington Lane Templeogue 6W (4566216) - Mon beginners/ Tue improvers, 7.30-9.30pm, 10 wks, €104 ea

Sth Dublin Co Libraries (4597834-admin only) - classes free: Ballyroan (4941900), Castletymon (4524888)

Clondalkin (4593315), Lucan (6216422), Tallaght (4620073).

Stillorgan Senior College Old Road Stillorgan (2880704) - beginners, Tue 7.30 10 wks €130

TACT St Dominic's School St Dominic's Rd Tallaght 24 (4596757)

TARGET St Kevin's School Newbrook Rd, Donaghmede 13 (8671967) - 10 wks, day only, beginners, improvers

WORDS Language Services 44 Northumberland Rd 4 (6610240) - individual tuition only

SPANISH COMMERCIAL
WORDS Language Services 44 Northumberland Rd 4 (6610240) - individual tuition only

SPANISH CULTURE
Instituto Cervantes Spanish Cultural Inst 58 Northumberland Rd 4 (6682024)

SPANISH FOR HOLIDAYS
Ballymun Trinity CS, Adult Ed Centre 9 (8420654) - Tue 7 & 8.30 €90 ea

Old Bawn Community School Tallaght 24 (4526137) - beginners, Thurs/ improvers & advanced, Tues: 10 wks €90 ea

Rathmines CFE - Senior College, Town Hall 6 (4975334) - Tue 7-9pm 10 wks €90

St Tiernan's Community School Parkvale Balally 16 (2953224) - levels 1-3, Mon, Tue, Wed, 10 wks, €95 each

SPECIAL NEEDS ASSISTANT see Classroom / Child Care / Teachers
SPEECH AND DRAMA see also Drama / Public Speaking / Voice Production
Betty Ann Norton Theatre School 11 Harcourt St 2 (4751913) - all levels, all ages

Leinster School of Music Griffith College Campus South Circular Rd 8 (4150467) - grades / diplomas

Taney Parish Centre Taney Rd Dundrum 14 (2985491) - Thurs (4069758), day only

SPEECH TRAINING see also Public Speaking / Voice Production
MD Communications 38 Spireview Lane off Rathgar Rd 6 (4975866)

SPEED READING
Speed Reading Centre Ranelagh 6 (4975239) - Joe Foyle's modern one-day course

SPIRITUAL DEVELOPMENT / SPIRITUALITY

All Hallows College Gracepark Rd Drumcondra 9 (8373745)

Brahma Kumaris WSU Raja Yoga Centres 5 Leeson Pk Ave 6 (6687480) - free

Divine Rainbow Centre Marino 3 (8333640)

Irish School of Shamanism 54 South William St 2 (4577839)

Milltown Institute of Theology & Philosophy Milltown Pk 6 (2776331) - adult ed dip in spirituality - overview of key issues, Mon 7.30-10; Six Sats: €820; also at An Croi Centre, Ashbourne/ Carmelite spirituality course, by corresp, 2 yr (2776334)/ summer school - soul paths, day 3 wks

Old Bawn Community School Tallaght 24 (4526137) - intro to theory & practice of spiritual intelligence

Paul Bradley (Psychotherapist) Main St Kilcock Co Kildare (6284673/ 087 9598840) - seminars for men, Dublin/ Kildare venues

SPORT / Sport Coaching

Colaiste Ide Cardiffsbridge Rd Finglas W 8443233 11 (8342333) - sport & recreation supervisory management, Tue & Thurs 20 wks 7pm ISRM €550

FAS Training Centre Ballyfermot 10 (6055900) - sports Teic project: coaching- aerobics; swimming assist; badminton; FAI soccer; GAA football & hurling, day 2yr

Inchicore CFE, Emmet Rd 8 (4535358) - 1 yr FETAC 5, day

Irish Amateur Boxing Assoc National Stadium SCR 8 (4533371) - boxing

Irish Squash Sport HQ 13 Joyce Way, Park West 12 (6251145) - squash coaching, wkends

Pearse College Clogher Rd Crumlin 12 (4536661/4541544) -soccer career development course, 1 yr cert

Tennis Ireland Dublin City University Glasnevin 9 (8844010) - coaching levels 1 & 2: mini, midi and full court

SPORTS MASSAGE

Motions Health & Fitness Training (087 2808866) - Diploma in Holistic Massage (ITEC), part-time course, 3 hours per week. Castleknock, Citywest & Naas

National College of Complementary Medical Ed, 16a St Joseph's Parade Off Dorset Street 7 (8827777) - sports massage & remedial therapy, NSSM, 15mths, day, eve wkends, €3520

Portobello School 43 Lr Dominick St 1 (8721277) - ITEC dip, 6.30 32 wks

SPORTS PSYCHOLOGY / THERAPY see also Golf, psychchology of

UCD Adult Education Centre Belfield (7167123) - Sports Psychology Workshop for Golfers, 1 day Sat, am/pm

SPREADSHEETS see also computer training

CTA Computer Training Academy, St James's Tce Malahide (8454070) - excel, basic/ intermediate/ advanced/ ecdl/mos: day/eve/Sat

FAS Training Centre Loughlinstown Wyattville Rd, DL (2043600) - MOS excel core, 10 wks

FAS Training Centre Tallaght Cookstown Indl Est 24 (4045200)

Pitman Training Centre 6-8 Wicklow St 2 (6768008) - ms excel, day eve sats, cert

SQUASH

Dundrum Family Recreation Centre Meadowbrook 16 (2984654)

Irish Squash Sport HQ 13 Joyce Way, Park West 12 (6251145) - coaching, wkends

Portmarnock Sports & Leisure Club Blackwood Lane Carrickhill Portmarnock (8462122)

STAINED GLASS
Ballymun Trinity CS,s Adult Ed Centre 9 (8420654) - & mosaics, Tue 7.30 10wk, €130
Bray Institute of FE, Novara Ave Bray (2866111 / 2829668) - Mon 7.30 10wks, €90
Cabinteely Community School Johnstown Rd 18 (2857455) - glass & equip supplied, 10wk, €115
Hartstown Community School Clonsilla 15 (8209863) - stained glass skills, 10 wks, €95
Killester CFE, Collins Ave 5 (8337686) - making stained glass,Tue 7.30, 10 wks €80
NCAD Centre for Continuing Educ 100 Thomas Street 8 (6364214) - intro/intermediate, c. 22wk
Newpark Adult Education Centre, Newtownpark Ave Blackrock (2884376 / 2883725) - Thurs 7.30 10 wks €120
Ringsend Technical Institute Cambridge Rd 4 (6684498) - workshop, Tue 8-10pm, 10 wks €90
Tracy Miley Cabinteely venue 18 (086 8485394) - beginners, 7.30-9.30 8 wks €140, day
STATISTICS
DIT Faculty: Science Kevin St 8 (4023000) - grad dip of royal statistical society, 4 yrs 2 eves wkly €1000pa
Trinity College 2 (8961000) - (8961768) - postgrad dip, 24wks
STOCK MARKET see also Financial services / Banking
UCD Adult Education Centre Belfield (7167123) - intro to the Stock Market; the Stock Market - next level: 10 wks ea
STONE SETTING see Jewellery

STOREKEEPING see also Management/ Supervision
STORES
FAS Training Centre Tallaght Cookstown Indl Est 24 (4045200)
STRESS MANAGEMENT see also Health
Alexander Technique Postural Re-education Frank Kennedy 35 Callary Rd Mt Merrion (2882446) - alexander technique/ health education - also day
Brahma Kumaris WSU Raja Yoga Centres 5 Leeson Pk Ave 6 (6687480) - 3wk free
Dún Laoghaire CFE, 17 Cumberland St Dún Laoghaire (2809676) - 7.30-9.30 10 wks Wed, €95
Forde Clinic 316 Howth Road Raheny 5 (8339902) - mind yoga for stress management (breathing, relaxation, meditation, visualistion - not exercise), Tues, 8-9.30m, 6wks, €80
Irish Yoga Association PO Box 9969 7 (4929213/ 087 2054489) - qualified teachers available all over Ireland/ 4 yr Teacher Training courses
LIFEWORKS Yoga Margaret Forde (8339902) - a yoga class in your workplace? also, mind yoga (relaxation, stress management, no exercises), 6wk courses
Margaret Macken Yoga Stephen's Gr/Adelaide Rd/Clontarf (8332954) - Iyengar Yoga, 6 wk course; also relaxation, stress management and meditation
Old Bawn Community School Tallaght 24 (4526137) - Thurs 7.30-9.30 €90
Shirley McClure (2865997) - & relaxation, workshops and courses for community groups & voluntary organisations, also day
T'ai Chi Energy Centre Milltown Pk Conference Centre Sandford Rd Ranelagh 6 (4961533) - t'ai chi/qi gong - & wkend workshops
The Professional Training and Coaching Consultancy (087 6379765/ 045 865783) - manage stress effectively, 4 wk, Terenure / Lucan / Dundrum
Time Out (4591038) - also wkend
Tony Quinn Centre 66/67 Eccles St 7 (8304211) - relaxation & personal development; also Dún Laoghaire (2809891)
Walmer College & Holistic Centre First Floor, River Hse Raheny Shopping Centre 5 (8329645) - ITEC dip
STUDY & RESEARCH SKILLS
Coláiste Dhúlaigh CFE,Barryscourt Rd Coolock 17 (8481337) - research methodologies, 8 wks Mon 5.10-6.40
NCAD 100 Thomas St, 8 - research for arts practice
Our Lady's Hospice Harold's Cross 6 (4068806 4068810) - research for beginners, 16 Oct 1 day 10-4pm €100 incl lunch
Roebuck Counselling Centre 59 Rathgar Rd 6 (4971929) - assistance with learning at 3rd level for adults, Tues eve ongoing
SUB-AQUA see Scuba
SUPERVISION / LINE MANAGEMENT see also Management
Bray Institute of FE, Novara Ave Bray (2866111 / 2829668) - supervisory, IMI cert, 1st yr Tues €460/ 2nd yr Mon: €380
Coláiste Dhúlaigh CFE, Barryscourt Rd Coolock 17 (8481337) - IMI supervisory management, 1st & 2nd yrs, Mon + Tues, 6.45/7.30
Colaiste Ide Cardiffsbridge Rd Finglas W 8443233 11 (8342333) - sport & recreation

supervisory management, Tue & Thurs 20 wks 7pm ISRM €550

Coolmine Community School Clonsilla 15 (8214583) - NCI dip in first line management, 2 yr course: Mon 7-9.30pm €1150

Crumlin College of FE, Crumlin Rd 12 (4540662) - IMI cert in frontline management: yr 1 management fundamentals, understanding organisations, leadership principals, Tue & Thurs 6.45-9.45; yr 2, business practice, human resources, Mon & Wed 6.45-9.45

DIT Faculty: Business Aungier St 2 (4023000) - IMI cert in supervisory management, 2 pts, €811

DIT Faculty: Tourism & Food Cathal Brugha St 1 (4023000) - bartending supervision, 1 yr 9am-1pm €75 exam fee

Dorset College 64 Lr Dorset St/ 8 Belvedere Pl 1 (8309677) - first line management, ILM level 3, cert

Dún Laoghaire CFE, 17 Cumberland St Dún Laoghaire (2809676) - cert in supervisory management (IMI), 22 wks, 7-10pm, Mon+Wed, €595

Institute of Technology Tallaght ITT Dublin, Tallaght 24 (4042101) Cert in Production & Inventory Management 2 yrs IPICS/ Cert in Supervisory Management 2 yrs IMI

Malahide Community School Malahide (8460949) - first line management, NCI dip, Tue 7.30 24 wks €1150 pa

National College of Ireland Mayor St IFSC 1 (4060500/ 1850 221721) - NCI Diploma in First line Management (Day Release), 1 year, €2,300; NCI Diploma in First line Management (Evening), 2 years, 1 eve, €1,150

Plunket College Swords Rd, Whitehall 9 (8371689) - NCI dip in first line management, 2 yrs €1150 pa (4498591)

SUPPLY CHAIN see Purchasing & Materials

SURFING see also Board Sailing

Surfdock Grand Canal Dockyard Sth Dock Rd Ringsend 4 (6683945) - surf trips/ wkends

SURVEYING

DIT Faculty: Built Environment Bolton St 1 (4023000) - co-ordinate ref systems for spacial data, 9 wks €900 / GIS course, 6 modules, 20 wks €550 / also global nav sat systems 12 wks online course 5 ECTS credits €850

SWEDISH see also Languages

Old Bawn Community School Tallaght 24 (4526137) - conversation for holidays/ business, Thurs 7.30-9.30 €90

Sandford Language Institute Milltown Pk Sandford Rd 6 (2601296) - all levels, 15 wks €285

Taney Parish Centre Taney Rd Dundrum 14 (2985491) - Sat (2814747)

SWIMMING see also Adventure Sports / Water Safety

Clondalkin Sports & Leisure Centre Nangor Rd Clondalkin 22 (4574858) - also day

Clontarf Swimming Club N O'Meara 5 Grange Pk Cl Raheny 5 (086-8116566) - National Aquatic Centre (NAC) Tue 7-9pn Sept-April / Guinness Swimming Pool, Wed 9-10pm Sept to May/ St Vincent's Swimming Pool Sat 5.10-6.15pm Sept - April

Coláiste Dhúlaigh CFE, Barryscourt Rd Coolock 17 (8481337) - Mon, improvers 10am/ beginners 11am: 10 wks each

Corporate Club 24 Elmcastle Green Tallaght 24 (4610935)

National Aquatic Centre Snugborough Rd Blanchardstown 15 (6464300) - all levels; also ladies only; ongoing

Network Club 24 Elmcastle Green Tallaght 24 (4524415)

Portmarnock Sports & Leisure Club Blackwood Lane Carrickhill Portmarnock (8462122)

Public Pools Ballymun Leisure Centre (8623508); Coolock (8477743), Crumlin (4555792); Finglas Leisure Centre, Mellows Pk (8642584); Irishtown Stadium (6697211); Northside Shopping Centre (8477743); Rathmines (4961275); Sean McDermott St (8720752); Townsend St (6729121)

Stewart's Sport Centre Waterstown Ave Palmerstown 20 (6269879) - club & classes, teenage lengths class, Masters Training/ yogalates, step aerobics

Swim Ireland Sport Hq, 13 Joyce Way Park West 12 (6251120) - assistant teacher cert/ teacher (2 parts)/ Aquafit (2 parts)/ adult & child

SYSTEMS ANALYSIS see also Computer Programming

Irish Academy of Computer Training 98 St Stephen's Green 2 (4347662) - website development & HTML 6 wks/ access 8 wks/ visual basic; C: 8 wks ea/ intro to programming; structured prog design & development, 4-8 wks/ C++; visual C++; java; visual J++: each 12 wks/ also day

T'AI CHI see also Meditation / Relaxation / Stress management / Health or Healing

Ballymun Trinity CS, Adult Ed Centre 9 (8420654) - Tue 7.30 10 wks €80

Bray Institute of FE, Novara Ave Bray (2866111 / 2829668) - beginners, Wed / continuation, Mon: each 7-8.30 10 wks €70

Cabinteely Community School Johnstown Rd 18 (2857455) - yang style, Tues, 10 wks, €70

Centre Studios 15 Upr Rathmines Rd 2 (4066812) - 8wks €125

Connolly House Nth Strand (by 5 Lamps) 1 (8557116) - Wed 7pm 10 wks €50

Coolmine Community School Clonsilla 15 (8214583) - 1 & 2: Mon, Tue, 7-8.20, 8.30-9.50: 10 wks €60

DATE Centre CFE, Dundrum 14 (2964322 (9.30am-12pm)) - beginners/ improvers, 10 wks €97 day

Donahies Community School Streamville Rd 13 (8482217) - Wed 7.30pm, 10 wks €70

Dún Laoghaire CFE, 17 Cumberland St Dún Laoghaire (2809676) - Wed, 10 wks, 7pm, €95/ chi-kung, 10 wks Wed 8.30pm €80

Foxrock Institute Kill o' the Grange, Kill Lane Blackrock (4939506) - Tue eve 8 wks €105

Frank Dunphy (6777258 086 8308757) - chuan, beginners/ intermediate, Thurs, eve 8pm, 10 wks €100 Clontarf 3; Mon 8pm, southside Dublin 8 Wed

Greendale Community School Kilbarrack 5 (8322735) - Thurs, 7.30-9.30pm, 10 wks, €95

Hartstown Community School Clonsilla 15 (8209863) - 10 wks, €60

Irish T'ai Chi Ch'uan Assoc St Andrew's Resource Centre 114 Pearse St 2 (6771930) - preparation, level 1-4, 2mths/beginners /short form, long form, sword form and other aspects, 10 wks, various centres

Kylemore College Kylemore Rd 10 (6265901) - Thurs 10 wks 7-9pm

Marino College 14-20 Marino Mart 3 (8332100) - 6pm Wed 1pm 10 wks €60

Newpark Adult Education Centre Newtownpark Ave Blackrock (2884376 / 2883725) - beginners €95 / improvers €95, Tue or Thurs

Old Bawn Community School Tallaght 24 (4526137) - beginners, energy awareness,

Tues/Thurs, 10 wks €90

Palmerstown CS - Pobailscoil Iosolde, Kennelsfort Rd 20 (6260116) - beginners/ intermediate, Mon 7&8.15pm 10 wks €70

Phibsboro Gym 1st Floor, Phibsboro SC 7 (8301849)

Pobalscoil Neasáin Baldoyle 13 (8063092) - Tue eve 3 classes, 10 wks €80

Pobalscoil Rosmini Adult Ed Grace Pk Rd 9 (8371015) - beginners Wed, 1.30-2.50pm; 7-8.20pm €90 each/ chen style, Tue 7 & 8.30pm €90

Rathmines CFE - Senior College, Town Hall 6 (4975334) - Mon, 10 wks, €70

School of T'ai Chi Chuan c/o 12 Winton Ave Rathgar 6 (4905818)

School of Traditional Reiki Ivy House Sth Main St Naas (045 898243 086 3084657) - T'ai chi chi gung

St MacDara's CC, Wellington Lane Templeogue 6W (4566216) - healing, 7pm/ chuan, 8.15, Tue 8 wks €52 ea

St Tiernan's Community School Parkvale Balally 16 (2953224) - beginners 10 wks Mon 7.30 €80

T'ai Chi Energy Centre Milltown Pk Conference Centre Sandford Rd Ranelagh 6 (4961533) - t'ai chi/qi gong - & wkend workshops

Tai Chi Ireland PO Box 8276 6 (087 9795042) - - Old Yang and Wu style Tai Chi, Professional Tuition, 7wk €120/ workshops

Taney Parish Centre Taney Rd Dundrum 14 (2985491) - Fri (2783188), also day

The Sanctuary Stanhope Street 7 (6705419) - with Joan Mccormack, 8 wks €95

Walmer College & Holistic Centre First Floor, River Hse Raheny Shopping C 5 (8329645)

Yang's Martial Arts Assoc Blackrock (2814901) - Yang's Martial Arts Association/ & qi gong - all levels

TABLE-TENNIS

Corporate Club 24 Elmcastle Green Tallaght 24 (4610935)

Irish Table Tennis Assoc Sport HQ 13 Joyce Way Park West 12 (6251135)

Network Club 24 Elmcastle Green Tallaght 24 (4524415)

St Anthony's House St Lawrence Rd Clontarf 3 (8335300) - 7.30-9.30p.m.

TAE KWON DO

Taekwon-Do Centre 10 Exchequer St 2 (6710705)

TANGO see also Dance

Dance Club Rathmines & Rathgar (2893797)

Marino College 14-20 Marino Mart 3 (8332100) - tue 8pm 10 wks €65

TAP DANCING

Bray Institute of FE, Novara Ave Bray (2866111 / 2829668) - Mon 9-10pm, 10 wks, €45

Tapestry Dance Company 309 Errigal Rd Drimnagh 12 (087- 7438923)

TAPESTRY & CREATIVE TEXTILES

Old Bawn Community School Tallaght 24 (4526137) - Thurs 7.30-9.30 €90

TAROT CARDS

Bray Institute of FE, Novara Ave Bray (2866111 / 2829668) - beginners, Mon 7.30-9.30 10 wks €65

Catherine Woods - Prof Tarot Card Reader 12 Church St E East Wall 3 (8552799) - including numerology, meditation: Sat morn 11am-1pm, 14 wks, €30 per class

Harvest Moon Centre 24 Lr Baggot St 2 (6627556) - secrets of, 6 wks €220

Healing House 24 O'Connell Ave Berkeley Rd 7 (8306413) - Tarot reading introductory & refresher, w/end workshop €150

KAIES-Knocklyon Community Centre, 16 (4931213) - Mon 10am 8 wks €90

Lucan Community College Esker Drive (6282077) - Tue 7.30-8.30 10 wks €130

Marino College 14-20 Marino Mart 3 (8332100) - Thurs 6.30pm 10 wks €65

Old Bawn Community School Tallaght 24 (4526137) - Thurs, 7.30-9.30pm, 10 wks €90

TACT St Dominic's School St Dominic's Rd Tallaght 24 (4596757)

Walmer College & Holistic Centre First Floor, River Hse Raheny Shopping C 5 (8329645)

TAXATION see also Accounts / PAYE

Institute of Taxation in Ireland 19 Sandymount Ave 4 (6688222) - associateship of Irish Taxation Inst, eve 3yrs, or distance learning; cert as professional Tax Consultant / tax technician programme (TMITI) 1 yr, wkend

Newpark Adult Education Centre, Newtownpark Ave Blackrock (2884376 / 2883725) - accounts & txation wed 7.30-9.45pm 10 wks 4120

Plunket College Swords Rd, Whitehall 9 (8371689) - IATI cert, p/time day Mon & Wed 11-12.30

TEACHING / TEACHERS COURSES see also Adult Educators / Classroom Assistant / English Teaching / Sailing

Ashfield Computer Training Main St Templeogue 6W (4926708) JEB - Teaching training dip in ICT, morns, eves and accelerated

Betty Ann Norton Theatre School 11 Harcourt St 2 (4751913) - speech & drama dip

Coláiste Dhúlaigh CFE, Barryscourt Rd Coolock 17 (8481337) - JEB dip in IT, Mon 18 wks/ Tue 20 wks/ teaching & eduction principals JEB cert, Mon 6.30-8.30 18wks/ classroom assistant, 12 wks Thurs/ special needs assistant, 25 wks Mon & Tue: NCEF certs

Colaiste Ide Cardiffsbridge Rd Finglas W 8443233 11 (8342333) - IT, Tues & Thurs, 6.30pm, 25 wks, €700, JEB cert

Coolmine Community School Clonsilla 15 (8214583) - special needs assistant (Coll of Prog Ed course), Tue 7-9.45, €550

CTA Computer Training Academy, St James's Tce Malahide (8454070) - train the trainer, day/eve/Sat

Dance Classes & Ballroom of Romance Presentation Primary Sch Terenure 6 (6211514/ 087 2484890) - ballroom dancing teacher's courses, cert/ medal test to syllabus of All Ireland Board of ballroom dancing

Donahies Community School Streamville Rd 13 (8482217) - special needs assistant, College of Prog Ed cert, Mon 7pm 18 wks €850

Dorset College 64 Lr Dorset St/ 8 Belvedere Pl 1 (8309677) - JEB teacher's dip in ICT Skills & MOS, Mon, Wed 6-10pm 20 wks; Sat 11am-3, 20 wks/ CIPD cert in training practice, Tue & Thurs, 24 wks/ TEFL teacher training Tue & Thurs + Sat, 8 wks

Dublin Adult Learning Centre 3 Mountjoy Sq 1 (8787266) - voluntary tutor training in adult literacy, free

Dublin Business School 13/14 Aungier St 2 (4177500) - JEB Teacher's Dip in IT, 2 eves, 6.15-9.30pm, 16 wks

Dublin School of English 10-12 Westmoreland St 2 (6773322) - TEFL part time and full time courses ACELS cert

Dyslexia Association of Ireland 1 Suffolk St 2 (6790276) - course for qualified teachers

Eden Computer Training Rathfarnham 16 & 1 Green St 7 (4953155) - JEB dip, IT

FAS Training Centre Tallaght Cookstown Indl Est 24 (4045200)

Finglas Adult Reading & Writing Scheme Colaiste Eoin Cappagh Rd 11 (8340893) - literacy tutor training, 12 wks Tues 7-9pm

Foxrock Institute Kill o' the Grange, Kill Lane Blackrock (4939506) - for tutors in ladies colour analysis, Wed eve

I.T. Blanchardstown Rd North 15 (8851000) - MA in language teaching (French & German) 2 yr €2900 pa p/time

IPPA - the Early Childhood Org, Unit 4 Broomhill Business Complex, 24 (4630010) - teaching adult learners C&G cert, 1 yr1 day or eve per wk

Irish Computer Society / ICS Skills Crescent Hall, Mount St Crescent 2 (6447820) - certified training professional CPT development prog, training for new trainers, 12 weekly workshops: €2500/ 3 day workshop + projects, training for experienced trainers €1200: both FAS/EI Nat Training Register eligibility

Irish Health Culture Association 66 Eccles St 7 (8304211) - yoga teacher's dip, 11 wkends €3650/ wkend & concentrated courses/ ask for prospectus

Irish Yoga Asociation PO Box 9969 7 (4929213/ 087 2054489) - qualified teachers available all over Ireland/ 4 yr Teacher Training courses

Montessori Education Centre 41-43 Nth Gt George's St 1 (8780071) - Montessori teacher training dip: course (1 nursery) 0-6 yrs, eve 9 mths Mon & Tue 6.30-8.30 €2100; also by distance learning; (2 junior) 6-9 yrs, (3 primary) 9-12 yrs: by distance learning, 10 mths, €1500, dip

Moresoft IT Institute 44 Lr Lesson St 2 (2160902) - JEB dip in ICT for tutors/ trainers Morn, eve, Sats, 12 wk

National College of Ireland Mayor St IFSC 1 (4060500/ 1850 221721) - Certificate in Training Practice (CIPD), 15 days, €2,000

Old Bawn Community School Tallaght 24 (4526137) - thurs 7-9.45 18wks, 2 Sats €850 Froebel & FETAC 5 module (College of Progressive Ed)

Palmerstown CS - Pobailscoil Iosolde, Kennelsfort Rd 20 (6260116) - special needs, cert Mon 7pm 18 wks €825/ diploma Tue 10 wks €500

Portobello School 43 Lr Dominick St 1 (8721277) - montessori FETAC conpetency cert, 1eve per wk, 32 wks

Senior College Dún Laoghaire, CFE Eblana Ave Dún Laoghaire (2800385) - JEB IT skills, €795

Swim Ireland Sport Hq, 13 Joyce Way Park West 12 (6251120) - teacher's swimming courses: adult & child, aquafit, assistant teacher, various dates /also swimirelandawards@btinternet.com

Trinity College 2 (8961000) - (8961989/1290) - in-career programmes for teachers/ IT & learning, MSc, 2 yrs, 24 wks per yr (8962182)

UCD Adult Education Centre Belfield (7167123) - courses on adult education: adults teaching adults; course delivery; philosophy of adult ed; supporting the learner; facilitation skills, group learning; new ideas in; contemporary issues: eachl 6-10 wks

TEAMWORK see also Management / Teachers

Eden Computer Training Rathfarnham 16 & 1 Green St 7 (4953155) - management, motivation, leadership

Maynooth NUI Adult & Community Ed Dept (7084500) - NUI cert, group work theory & practice: Ballymun Axis Arts Centre (8832134)

National College of Ireland Mayor St IFSC 1 (4060500/ 1850 221721) - Certificate in Managing Teams (online), 12 weeks, €915

TECHNOLOGY see also Engineering / Computer / Electronic etc

DIT Faculty: Engineering Bolton St 1 (4023000) - prog logic controllers, 10 wks €350; C&G cert 20 wks €500/ hydraulics 1 yr/ mechanical power transmission 1 yr

Institute of Art, Design & Technology Dún Laoghaire (2414631) - various courses

Institute of Technology Tallaght ITT Dublin, Tallaght 24 (4042101) - MSc in Distributed and Mobile Computing NFQ Level 91 yr/ BSc in Information Technology NFQ Level 7 3 yrs/ BA Technology Management NFQ Level 7 1 yr/ BSc (Hons) Technology Management NFQ Level 8 1 yr (add on)

The Open University Enquiry/Advice Centre Holbrook House, Holles St 2 (6785399)

TELECOMMUNICATIONS see also Electronics / Radio

DIT Faculty: Engineering Bolton St 1 (4023000)

Irish Academy of Computer Training 98 St Stephen's Green 2 (4347662) - networking; 12 wks; MCSA 2003 cert, 24 wks; internet, 12 wks, cert/ also day

TELEVISION PRODUCTION see also Broadcasting

Ballyfermot CFE, Ballyfermot Rd 10 (6269421) - TV/video, Fetac 5 Mon/Wed 7-10pm 22 wks

St Kevin's College, Clogher Rd Crumlin 12 (4536397) - TV & video, 20wks

TENNIS

Corporate Club 24 Elmcastle Green Tallaght 24 (4610935)

Dundrum Family Recreation Centre Meadowbrook 16 (2984654) - tennis coaching

Network Club 24 Elmcastle Green Tallaght 24 (4524415)

Portmarnock Sports & Leisure Club Blackwood Lane Carrickhill Portmarnock (8462122)

Tennis Ireland Dublin City University Glasnevin 9 (8844010) - coaching levels 1 & 2: mini, midi and full court

People's College

EVENING COURSES
October 2006 to March 2007

ART APPRECIATION

COMPUTERS

COUNSELLING

CREATIVE WRITING

CURRENT AFFAIRS/POLITICS

ENGLISH FOR ALL

ENGLISH FOR FOREIGNERS

ENVIRONMENT/BIRDS

FILM STUDIES

GARDENING

GUITAR (Classical)

HISTORY

LITERATURE

MEDITATION & RELAXATION

MUSIC APPRECIATION

PAINTING

PHOTOGRAPHY

PUBLIC SPEAKING

TIN WHISTLE

THEATRICAL WIG &
    HAIRDRESSING (Jan. 2007)

YOGA

LANGUAGE COURSES

FRENCH, ENGLISH, IRISH, ITALIAN, SPANISH, GERMAN

Cost of Courses: €30.00 to €80.00

Prospectus available (mid-August) for collection from:

**People's College, 31 Parnell Square,
Liberty Hall, Dublin 1,**

and

Central Library, Ilac Centre.

or S.A.E. (60c) to

31 Parnell Square, Dublin 1.

ENROLMENTS

Dates: **Monday 11th to Thursday 14th September 2006**
Time: **5.30 p.m. to 8.30 p.m.**
Dates: **Monday 18th to Wednesday 27th September 2006**
Time: **10.00 a.m. to 5.00 p.m. (including lunch-time)**
Venue: **People's College, 31 Parnell Square, Dublin 1.**

Tel: 8735879 Fax: 8735164 E-mail: peopcoll@iol.ie

TEXTILE PAINTING

Jean Strong (2892323) - ongoing/beginners, improvers, 10 wks, €170/also day:- Blackrock & Dundrum

Marino College 14-20 Marino Mart 3 (8332100) - tue 6.30 10 wks €65

TEXTILE PRINTING

NCAD Centre for Continuing Educ 100 Thomas Street 8 (6364214) - c. 22wk

THAI see also Languages

Sandford Language Institute Milltown Pk Sandford Rd 6 (2601296) - all levels, 15 wks €350

THEATRE see also Acting / Drama / Literature / Speech & Drama

Corporate Club 24 Elmcastle Green Tallaght 24 (4610935)

Inchicore CFE, Emmet Rd 8 (4535358) - studies: acting & foundation; dance; set design & construction; stage management; sound & lighting; costume & wardrobe - day courses/ HND in tectnical theatre cert

KLEAR Grange Park View Kilbarrack 5 (8671845) - enjoying theatre, day

Maynooth NUI Adult & Community Ed Dept (7084500) - performance / directing: Kilkenny campus 056 7775910

People's College for Continuing Education & Training 32 Parnell Sq 1 (8735879) - theatrical wig & hairdressing, €60

Saor-Ollscoil na hÉireann 55 Prussia St 7 (8683368) - film & theatre studies

THEOLOGY see also Distance Learning

All Hallows College Gracepark Rd Drumcondra 9 (8373745) - intro to moral theology (Tue); to systematic theology (Wed); ecclesiology (Mon); sacramental theology (Mon): each on Tue 6.50-8.25, 24 wks €390 / theology of truth - justice, peace & ecology: 1, 24 wks Mon 8.30 €390; & 2, 24 wks Tue 6.50 €390. ECTS credits option

Brahma Kumaris WSU Raja Yoga Centres 5 Leeson Pk Ave 6 (6687480) - the theology of yoga, 3 wk free

Milltown Institute Milltown Pk 6 (2776331) - dip/BA (NUI) Theology, eve 2yrs: Tue & Thurs 6.30-9.45 €1800pa or €240 per module/ NUI cert, theology 2 yrs Tue 7.30-10pm; six wkends: €750/ thrology & spirituality, 1 yr day/ also online modular courses

Trinity College 2 (8961000) - traditions of christian thinking; the question of God; religion & science: each 11 wks €150

THIRD WORLD STUDIES See Development Studies

TIMBER TECHNOLOGY

DIT Faculty: Built Environment Bolton St 1 (4023000) - woodcutting machinery, 1 yr €1950

TIME MANAGEMENT

Eden Computer Training Rathfarnham 16 & 1 Green St 7 (4953155)

Kilroy's College Wentworth House Grand Canal Street Lr 2 (6620538 1850-700700) - tutor supported home study: dip course

Training Options Plus 6-8 Wicklow St 2 (6717787) - 1 day, cert

TIN WHISTLE see also Music

Abbey School of Music 9b Lr Abbey St 1 (8747908) - Michael McGrath

Clontarf School of Music 6 Marino Mart 3 (8330936 087 8054963)

Comhaltas Ceoltóirí Éireann 32 Belgrave Sq Monkstown (2800295)

Donahies Community School Streamville Rd 13 (8482217) - Mon 7pm 10 wks €85

Greenhills College Limekiln Ave Walkinstown 12 (4507779/4507863) - Mon/Tue, 10 wks €130

Holy Family Community School Rathcoole (4580766)

Kylemore College Kylemore Rd 10 (6265901) - thurs 10 wks 7-9pm

People's College for Continuing Education & Training 32 Parnell Sq 1 (8735879) - €60

Pobalscoil Rosmini Adult Ed Grace Pk Rd 9 (8371015) - Mon 7-8.20pm €90

Portmarnock Community School Carrickhill Rd (8038056) - beginners/ 7.30/ improvers 8.30 (Ms C McGlynn): Mon 10 wks €80

Scoil Shéamuis Ennis, Naul, Co Dublin (8020898 087 7870138)

Waltons New School of Music 69 Sth Gt George's St 2 (4781884) - also day, see ad page 155

TOASTMASTERS CLUBS see Public Speaking

TOURISM see also Travel Management

Colaiste Ide Cardiffsbridge Rd Finglas W 8443233 11 (8342333) - standard dip/ advanced dip: in Travel & Tourism, Tues & Thurs, 7-10pm, 18 wks, €550 each, IATA/UFTAA

DIT Faculty: Tourism & Food Cathal Brugha St 1 (4023000) - MSc in tourism management, 2yrs p/t, €1900pa

Dorset College 64 Lr Dorset St/ 8 Belvedere Pl 1 (8309677) - cert travel & tourism, Mon & Wed 6.30-9pm, 1 yr

Harcourt Business School HSI 89 Harcourt St 2 (4763975) - cert in travel & tourism

Inchicore CFE, Emmet Rd 8 (4535358)

Pearse College Clogher Rd Crumlin 12 (4536661/4541544) - languages for business & tourism, 1 yr day FETAC cert

Portobello School 43 Lr Dominick St 1 (8721277) - travel & tourism, eve 32 wks ICM dip/ Galileo travel reserv/ British Airways level 1; Virgin Air fares & ticketing: eve 16 wks each

Westmoreland College for Management Studies 11 Westmoreland St 2 (6795324/7266) - ICM cert, dip travel & tourism

TRADE see also Gobalisation / International

Comhlamh 10 Upr Camden St 2 (4783490) - global issues

Export Edge Training Ltd 57 Merrion Square 2 (6619544) - prof dip in global trade & e-business, eve 1 yr, 60% Fás funded

Institute of International Trade of Ireland 28 Merrion Square 2 (6612182) - prof. dip in Global Trade / documentary credit compliance, 1 day/ customs compliance, 2 day/ dangerous goods safety awareness & advisor; various locations

UCD Adult Education Centre Belfield (7167123) - international trade & export, Tue 10 wks

TRADITIONAL MUSIC see also Music/ Irish Traditional

Comhaltas Ceoltóirí Éireann 32 Belgrave Sq Monkstown (2800295) - all traditional instruments / group playing/ singing: venues at: Artane, Balbriggan, Ballymun, Beaumont, Clontarf, Finglas, Kinsealey, Monkstown, Malahide, Navan Rd, Portmarnock, Raheny, Santry

Dún Laoghaire Music Centre 130A Lr George's St Dún Laoghaire (2844178)

Scoil Shéamuis Ennis, Naul, Co Dublin (8020898 087 7870138)

Waltons New School of Music 69 Sth Gt George's St 2 (4781884), see ad page 155

TRAINING COURSES see also Teachers / Comnputer / VTOS etc

- wide range of trainer / tutor courses, day & eve as well as general training & apprenticeship courses available from FAS Training centres (6070500) www.fas.ie

TRANSACTIONAL ANALYSIS

Transactional Analysis in Ireland (4511125) - in everyday situations, mthly wkshop, donation

TRANSLATION / TRANSLATORS COURSES

Alliance Francaise 1 Kildare St 2 (6761632); Alliance-Sud Foxrock Ave 18 (2898760) - contact Alliance for details of translators courses

DIT Online (4024944) - French, German, Spanish: suitable training for Institute of Linguists' Diploma: 27 wks, €600, 5 ECTS credits

WORDS Language Services 44 Northumberland Rd 4 (6610240) - French/German/ Italian/Portugese/Spanish, by correspondence & e-mail

TRANSPORT see also Distance learning

Bray Institute of FE, Novara Ave Bray (2866111 / 2829668) - CPC in road transport, cert, Mon & Wed 7-10pm 20 wks, €450

DIT Faculty: Engineering Bolton St 1 (4023000) - road transport studies, yr 1 €650, yrs 2&3 €950, IRTE cert of professional competency

Institute of International Trade of Ireland 28 Merrion Square 2 (6612182) - dangerous goods safety awareness advisor (road, sea air) 4 days/ customs compliance, 2 day

Tallaght Community School Balrothery 24 (4515566) - transport management, cert, CPC, 30wk, €550 (pay €275 x 2)

TRAVEL MANAGEMENT see also Tourism

Harcourt Business School HSI 89 Harcourt St 2 (4763975) - cert in airline &

cabin crew operations

Inchicore CFE, Emmet Rd 8 (4535358) - travel & tourism management

Pearse College Clogher Rd Crumlin 12 (4536661/4541544) - languages for business & tourism, day/ Galileo cert

Portobello School 43 Lr Dominick St 1 (8721277) - travel & tourism, ICM dip, eve 32 wks

Westmoreland College for Management Studies 11 Westmoreland St 2 (6795324/7266) - ICM cert, dip travel & tourism

TROMBONE

Bray Music Centre Florence Rd Bray (2866768)

Newpark Music Centre Newtownpark Ave Blackrock (2883740) - also day

TRUMPET

Bray Music Centre Florence Rd Bray (2866768)

Newpark Music Centre Newtownpark Ave Blackrock (2883740) - also day

TURKISH

Sandford Language Institute Milltown Pk Sandford Rd 6 (2601296) - all levels, 15 wks €285

Trinity College 2 (8961000) (8961560) intro to Turkish language & culture/ post-beginners/ intermediate: each 24 wks €365

TYE-DYE see Batik

TYPESETTING & PHOTOSETTING see Desk Top Publishing / Printing

TYPING see also Keyboard / Teachers / Word Processing

Cabinteely Community School Johnstown Rd 18 (2857455) - & keyboard skills, 10wk, €95

CTA Computer Training Academy, St James's Tce Malahide (8454070) - 15 hrs intro / speed development: day/eve/Sat

Donahies Community School Streamville Rd 13 (8482217) - touch typing & speed, Wed 7.30 10 wks €110

Dublin Public Libraries Admin Hq, 138-144 Pearse St 2 (6744800) - self-learning €free

Newpark Adult Education Centre Newtownpark Ave Blackrock (2884376 / 2883725) - 10wks, €120, Tue 7.30-9.30

Pitman Training Centre 6-8 Wicklow St 2 (6768008) - data entry: keyboard, speed, audio, 8 to 30 hrs cert; day eve sats

Tallaght Community School Balrothery 24 (4515566) - & keyboard skills, beginners & improvers, 7.30-9.30 10wk, €80

UILLEANN PIPES see also Music / Traditional Music

Comhaltas Ceoltóirí Éireann 32 Belgrave Sq Monkstown (2800295)

Na Piobairi Uilleann 15 Henrietta St 1 (8730093) tues, 7.30-10pm, beginners, intermediate, advanced

Scoil Shéamuis Ennis, Naul, Co Dublin (8020898 087 7870138)

Waltons New School of Music 69 Sth Gt George's St 2 (4781884) - also day, see ad page 155

UPHOLSTERY

College of Further Education Main St Dundrum 14 (2951376)

Malahide Community School Malahide (8460949) - beginners, Tue 10 wks €80

Newpark Adult Education Centre Newtownpark Ave Blackrock (2884376 / 2883725) - beg/advanced, 10wks, €130, Tue-Thurs 7.30-9.45

URDU (Language of Pakistan)

Sandford Language Institute Milltown Pk Sandford Rd 6 (2601296) - all levels, 15 wks €285

VEGETARIAN COOKERY

Bray Institute of FE, Novara Ave Bray (2866111 / 2829668) - European, Wed 7.30-9.30 10 wks €90

Vegetarian Society of Ireland PO Box 3010 Dublin 4

VIDEO PRODUCTION see also Film

Ballyfermot CFE, Ballyfermot Rd 10 (6269421) - camcorder edit, 15 wks Mon 7-10pm

Crumlin College of FE, Crumlin Rd 12 (4540662) - digital camcorder home movie making (with own camcorder) 10 wks Wed 8.15-9.45

Digital Film School contact Julianne: (086 8206144) - beginners, recreational film-making

Dún Laoghaire CFE, 17 Cumberland St Dún Laoghaire (2809676) - video editing, Wed 7-10pm, 10 wks €260

New Media Technology College, 13 Harcourt St 2 (4780905) - digital video production & online broadcasting

St Kevin's College, Clogher Rd Crumlin 12 (4536397) - tv & video, 20wks

VIETNAMESE

Sandford Language Institute Milltown Pk Sandford Rd 6 (2601296) - all levels, 15 wks €350

VIOLA

Dún Laoghaire Music Centre 130A Lr George's St Dún Laoghaire (2844178)

Waltons New School of Music 69 Sth Gt George's St 2 (4781884) - also day, see ad page 155

VIOLIN see also Music

Abbey School of Music 9b Lr Abbey St 1 (8747908) - Mary Fahy

Bray Music Centre Florence Rd Bray (2866768)

Clontarf School of Music 6 Marino Mart 3 (8330936 087 8054963) - classical, 18wk - day only

Dún Laoghaire Music Centre 130A Lr George's St Dún Laoghaire (2844178)

Leinster School of Music Griffith College Campus South Circular Rd 8 (4150467)

Melody School of Music 178E Whitehall Rd W Perrystown 12 (4650150) - all day W/S & Sat; w/ends, Sat-Sun, 12 wks

Newpark Music Centre Newtownpark Ave Blackrock (2883740) - also day

Waltons New School of Music 69 Sth Gt George's St 2 (4781884) - also day, see ad page 155

VISUAL ARTS / EDUCATION see also Art Appreciation

Portmarnock Community School Carrickhill Rd (8038056) - visual awareness (Mr D Higgins), Mon 7.30-9.20, 10 wks €100

Portobello School 43 Lr Dominick St 1 (8721277) - visual display, dip: eve 32 wks

VISUALISATION

Healing House 24 O'Connell Ave Berkeley Rd 7 (8306413) - support group - healing & visualisation, Mon 8-10pm €10/ 1 day workshop march 07 €55

VOICE PRODUCTION see also Music / Singing

Betty Ann Norton Theatre School 11 Harcourt St 2 (4751913)

Clontarf School of Music 6 Marino Mart 3 (8330936 087 8054963) - voice development, day & eve, 17 wks

Dún Laoghaire Music Centre 130A Lr George's St Dún Laoghaire (2844178)

Hollywood Academy Dublin 13-14 Sackville Pl 1 (8786909) - from 4-8pm: 11 mths €75 per mth, cert

Kylemore College Kylemore Rd 10 (6265901) - voice training, Wed 10 wks 7-9pm

Leinster School of Music Griffith College Campus South Circular Rd 8 (4150467)

MD Communications 38 Spireview Lane off Rathgar Rd 6 (4975866)

Parnell School of Music & Performing Arts 13-14 Sackville Pl 1 (8786909) - vocal training, from 4-8pm 1 yr €75 per mth, cert

Rachel Dempsey Global Harmonies Smithfield 7 (086 3097232) - free the voice/ vocal jamming: 8 wks each various venues €100

Waltons New School of Music 69 Sth Gt George's St 2 (4781884) - also day, see ad page 155

VOLLEYBALL / MINI VOLLEYBALL

Corporate Club 24 Elmcastle Green Tallaght 24 (4610935)

Network Club 24 Elmcastle Green Tallaght 24 (4524415)

Portmarnock Community School Carrickhill Rd (8038056) - 16 wks 5-7pm

VOLUNTARY WORK / VOLUNTEERING MANAGEMENT see also Community Development / Mental Health

Comhlamh 10 Upr Camden St 2 (4783490) - options and issues in global development/ lobby skills

Dublin Simon Community Margaret Dent Volunteer Coordinator 1 (6749200) - training for Simon volunteers

Junior Chamber Ireland - email pro@jci-ireland.org for info

National Adult Literacy Agency 76 Lr Gardiner St 1 (8554332) - info on becoming a voluntary literacy tutor

National College of Ireland Mayor St IFSC 1 (4060500/ 1850 221721) - NCI Certificate in Managing Organisations in the Voluntary Sector, 60 hours, €840

Sli Eile Volunteers 20 Upr Gardiner Street 1 (8880606) - opportunities for 18-35 yr olds to work as volunteers in educational projects in North Inter City. Training on 'Working for Justice' and Christian basis for 'social justice work' also provided

Volunteering Ireland Coleraine House Coleraine St 7 (8722622) - volunteering management courses: volunteer support & supervision 7 Sept/ volunteering & working with migrant communities 21 Sept/ developing volunteer policy 5 Oct/ relationship between volunteers & paid staff 17 Oct/ building effective volunteer teams 9 Nov/ motivation volunteer 23 Nov: 10am-4pm €100/€125

VTOS COURSES

Crumlin College of FE, Crumlin Rd 12 (4540662) - IT with CISCO/ network technician/ software sys/ web design/ advertising & graphics/ selling, sales management/ security/ accounting technician admission level/ office admin/ reception/ tourism & travel/ marketing/ hotel & catering/ sports therapy/ exercise/ beauty therapy/ hairdressing & cosmetic/ make-up for fashion/ merchandising/ fashion management

Pearse College Clogher Rd Crumlin 12 (4536661/4541544) - leaving cert/university foundation/ PLC studies - day/ for 8 wk taster courses - contact 4544013

WALKING see also Adventure Sports / Hiking / Mountaineering

Corporate Club & Network Club 24 Elmcastle Green Tallaght 24 (4524415)

WALTZING

Dance Club Rathmines & Rathgar (2893797)

WARDEN SERVICE

Civil Defence Esplanade Wolftone Qy 7 (6772699) - various centres

WATER COLOURS see also Art / Painting

Ashfield College Main St Templeogue 6W (4900866) - 7.30-9.30, 8 wks

Ballsbridge CFE, Shelbourne Rd 4 (6684806) - intro, Mon 6pm/ Thur 6pm & 7.45: 10 wks, €80 ea

Brian Byrnes Art Studio 3 Upr Baggot St 4 (6671520 / 6711599) - 8wk, €150, also day

Cabinteely Community School Johnstown Rd 18 (2857455) - beginners/improvers, 10wk, €95 each

Coláiste Eanna, Kilkieran Rd Cabra 7 (8389577) - 10wks, Tue 7-9pm

College of Further Education Main St Dundrum 14 (2951376) - beginners, Thurs 7-9pm 8 wks €104

Crescent Studios 15 Ballyroan Cres Rathfarnham 16 (4947507) - watercolours & basic drawing beginners, Mon; private tuition

DATE Centre CFE, Dundrum 14 (2964322 (9.30am-12pm)) - beginners, Mon 9.30am/ & drawing, Tue 9.30 & 11.10am, 10 wks each €97

Donahies Community School Streamville Rd 13 (8482217) - 7.30 Mon, 10 wks, €85

Greendale Community School Kilbarrack 5 (8322735) - Thurs 7.30pm 10 wks, €95/ also Wed 10.30 am

Hartstown Community School Clonsilla 15 (8209863) - 10wks, €85

Holy Family Community School Rathcoole (4580766)

Jean Strong (2892323) - ongoing, beginners-improvers, 10wks, €170/also day:- Blackrock & Dundrum

Kilternan Adult Education Group Ballybetagh Rd Kilternan 18 (2952050) - Mon 11.45/ beginners Thur 11.30/ Fri 9.30 & 12: all 10 wks €130

Kylemore College Kylemore Rd 10 (6265901) - beginners, Wed 7-9pm 10 wks

Malahide Community School (8460949) - Tue, Thurs, 10 wks, beginners/ improvers €90

Meridian Art Group c/o St Paul's College Raheny 5 (8310688)

NCAD Centre for Continuing Educ 100 Thomas Street 8 (6364214) - techniques of, c.22wk

Newpark Adult Education Centre, Newtownpark Ave Blackrock (2884376 / 2883725) - Mon/ Thurs, 10 wks

Newpark Adult Education Centre Newtownpark Ave Blackrock (2884376 / 2883725) - 10wks, €120, Mon/ Thurs 7.30-9.45

Palmerstown CS - Pobailscoil Iosolde, Kennelsfort Rd 20 (6260116) - level 1&2, Mon 6.45/8.15, 10 wks €80 ea

Pobalscoil Rosmini Adult Ed Grace Pk Rd 9 (8371015) - beginners & improvers, Mon or Tue 8.30-9.50 €95 each

St Tiernan's Community School Parkvale Balally 16 (2953224) - Wed 7.30 10 wks, €95

WATER POLO

Irish Water Polo Association N O'Meara, Leinster Branch, 5 Grange Pk Close Raheny 5 (086 8116566)

WATER SAFETY

Clondalkin Sports & Leisure Centre Nangor Rd Clondalkin 22 (4574858)

Colaiste Ide Cardiffsbridge Rd Finglas W 8443233 11 (8342333) - pool lifeguard, Thurs 7pm, Fri 8pm 8 wks RLSS €450

Sea & Shore Safety Services Ltd. Happy Valley Glenamuck Rd 18 (2955991) - personal survival techniques, 1 day €165/ safety & social responsibility, 1 day €100/ elementary fire fighting; crowd management; crisis management:each, half-day €100/ fast rescue boat, €2000/ CPSC 5 day €5100 or €510 pp: all STWC'95 approved

WEB DESIGN see also Computers / Graphic

Adelaide Computers 14 Pembroke Lane Ballsbridge 4 (2696213) - all levels/ frontpage/ publisher

Ballsbridge CFE,, Shelbourne Rd 4 (6684806) - intro to, Tue 6.15-9.15, 10 wks €250

Ballymun Trinity CS, Adult Ed Centre 9 (8420654) - Mon 7.30-9.30 10 wks €130

Bray Institute of FE, Novara Ave Bray (2866111 / 2829668) - level 2 C&G cert, web design, Mon 7.30 22 wks, €350

BCT Institute, 30 Fitzwilliam St 2 (6616838 /891) Web site design (dreamweaver fireworks flash), Wed, 6.45-9pm 11 wks/ CIW e-commerce designer, Wed 6.45-9pm 15wks; CIW site development foundations, Tue 6.45-9pm 10wks; CIW site designer, Wed 6.45-9pm 15 wks/ internet technical professional, i-net+, Fri 6.45-9pm 10 wks

CITAS 54 Middle Abbey St 1 (8782212) - html, dreamweaver, 6 wks Tue 6-9pm, €600

Coláiste Dhúlaigh CFE,Barryscourt Rd Coolock 17 (8481337) - Tue 7.30-9.30pm 10 wks

Crumlin College of FE, Crumlin Rd 12 (4540662) - management of, f/time day

CTA Computer Training Academy, St James's Tce Malahide (8454070) - day/ eve/ Sat

Dublin Business School 13/14 Aungier St 2 (4177500) - Dip in Web Design/Advanced Dip in Web Development, 1 eve 6.15-9.30pm, 10 wks

Dún Laoghaire CFE, 17 Cumberland St Dún Laoghaire (2809676) - Tue, 20 wks, 7-9pm, €300

Eden Computer Training Rathfarnham 16 & 1 Green St 7 (4953155)

FAS Training Centre Baldoyle 13 (8167400) - 10 wks; Ballyfermot 10 (6055900); Cabra Bannow Rd 7 (8821400) - 10 wks; Finglas Jamestown Rd 11 (8140200) - 10 wks; Jervis St 1 (8044600) - intro to, 6-9pm 10 wks; Wyattville Rd, DL (2043600) - intro, 10 wks

Irish Academy of Computer Training 98 St Stephen's Green 2 (4347662) - IACT webmaster course in web design, 12 wks dip

Moresoft IT Institute 44 Lr Lesson St 2 (2160902) - flash mx & dreamweaver: intro & advanced: each 6-9pm 5 wks

New Media Technology College, 13 Harcourt St 2 (4780905) - web authoring 1 html; 2 dreamweaver; 3 java, CGI scripts, style sheets/ digital imaging, adobe photoshop/ animation - flash, director/ also p/time day/ web programming active server pages/ also, corporate training options

Palmerstown CS - Pobailscoil Iosolde, Kennelsfort Rd 20 (6260116) - Thurs 8.30pm 10 wks €80

Pitman Training Centre 6-8 Wicklow St 2 (6768008) - 12-18 hrs, cert/ business skills dip & web design, full/pt-time; day eve sats

Pobalscoil Rosmini Adult Ed Grace Pk Rd 9 (8371015) - beginners, Wed 7-9pm €200

Rathmines CFE - Senior College, Town Hall 6 (4975334) - Tue, 7.30pm 10 wks €115

Ringsend Technical Institute Cambridge Rd 4 (6684498) - introduction to, 10 wks €105

School of Computer Technology 21 Rosmeen Gdns Dún Laoghaire (2844045) - C&G cert 36 hrs €750/ also day

Senior College Dún Laoghaire, CFE Eblana Ave Dún Laoghaire (2800385) - cert in web authoring, FETAC 25 wks, €310/ computer imaging FETAC €310

WEBSITE DEVELOPMENT

Connolly House Nth Strand (by 5 Lamps) 1 (8557116) - build your own, Wed 6.30 10 wks €105

Crumlin College of FE, Crumlin Rd 12 (4540662) - build your first website, Tues 6.45 10 wks

Dorset College 64 Lr Dorset St/ 8 Belvedere Pl 1 (8309677) - certified internet webmaster - CIW v5: foundations/ site designer/ e-commerce: Tue & Thurs 6.30-9pm 8 wks each

FAS Net College (2043732 ecollegeinfo@fas.ie) - online courses

WEIGHT LIFTING / TRAINING

Motions Health & Fitness Training (087 2808866) - Fitness Instructor training diploma course (ITEC), part-time, 9 hours per week. Venue Citywest Hotel & Leisure Centre, Naas Rd

Tony Quinn Centre 66/67 Eccles St 7 (8304211)

WELDING see also Art Metal Work

DIT Faculty: Engineering Bolton St 1 (4023000) -welding: MMA & oxy-acetylene; gas shielded arc; MMA advanced plate & pipe; pipe fabrication; inspection & testing NDT; welding repair & maintenance: each course 20 wks, cert, 1 eve weekly, €500

FAS Training Centre Ballyfermot 10 (6055900)

FAS Training Centre Tallaght Cookstown Indl Est 24 (4045200)

WELFARE SERVICE

Civil Defence Esplanade Wolftone Qy 7 (6772699) - various centres

The Open University Centre Holbrook House, Holles St 2 (6785399) - & health studies

WILDLIFE see also Conservation / Natural History / Ornithology / Zoo

WIND-SURFING see also Board Sailing

Corporate Club 24 Elmcastle Green Tallaght 24 (4610935)

Fingall Sailing School Malahide (8451979)

Irish Sailing Assoc 3 Park Rd Dún Laoghaire (2800239) - all levels, all yr, all ages, apply for provider list

Network Club 24 Elmcastle Green Tallaght 24 (4524415)

Surfdock Grand Canal Dockyard Sth Dock Rd Ringsend 4 (6683945) - beginners/ also wkend/ corporate groups

WINE APPRECIATION / MAKING see also Cookery

Ashfield College Main St Templeogue 6W (4900866) - tasting & appreciation / gourmet cookery & wine selection, 8 wks each

Cabinteely Community School Johnstown Rd 18 (2857455) - Tues, 8 wks, €135

Coolmine Community School Clonsilla 15 (8214583) - 6 wks, Mon €120

Dún Laoghaire CFE, 17 Cumberland St Dún Laoghaire (2809676) - Wed 10 wks 7.30-9.30 €170

Hartstown Community School Clonsilla 15 (8209863) - appreciation, 6wks, €95

KAIES-Knocklyon Community Centre, 16 (4931213) - Tues 8pm 6 wks €135

Malahide Community School Malahide (8460949) - tasting, 6 wks, Tues €95

Marino College 14-20 Marino Mart 3 (8332100) - Thurs 10wks, €160 (incls wine), Thurs

Newpark Adult Education Centre Newtownpark Ave Blackrock (2884376 / 2883725) - appreciation - beginners, €180, Mon/Tue 7.45-9.45

Old Bawn Community School Tallaght 24 (4526137) - Thurs 10 wks €140

St Tiernan's Community School Parkvale Balally 16 (2953224) - beginners, Wed 7.30 6 wk Wine Dev Board course: €210

Wine Development Board of Ireland 14 Whitefriars, Peter's Row Aungier St 2 (4757580) -wine appreciation WSET: intermediate cert/ advanced dip

WOMEN'S STUDIES / ISSUES

Ballyfermot CFE, Ballyfermot Rd 10 (6269421) - - NUI (UCC) dip, 100 hrs x 2 yrs, Mon 7-10pm

Maynooth NUI Adult & Community Ed Dept (7084500) - Liberties College 8 (4542100); St Kilian's Bray (2864646)

Trinity College 2 (8961000) - (8968589) identifying gender: intro. lectures, 9 wks €60

WOMEN, COURSES / ACTIVITIES FOR

KLEAR Grange Park View Kilbarrack 5 (8671845) - various, day only

League of Health (Irl) 17 Dundela Pk Sandycove (2807775) - individual centres listed under KEEP FIT

WOODCARVING / CRAFT

Bray Institute of FE, Novara Ave Bray (2866111 / 2829668) - carving, Mon 7.30 10 wks, €85

Newpark Adult Education Centre Newtownpark Ave Blackrock (2884376 / 2883725) - 10wks, €130, Mon 7.30-9.45/ wood turning, Wed 10 wks €150, 7.30-9.45

Pobalscoil Neasáin Baldoyle 13 (8063092) - wood turning, tue 7.30-9.30, 10 wks

WOODWIND see also Music

Dún Laoghaire Music Centre 130A Lr George's St Dún Laoghaire (2844178)

Waltons New School of Music 69 Sth Gt George's St 2 (4781884) - also day, see ad page 155

WOODWORK

Ballymun Trinity CS,s Adult Ed Centre 9 (8420654) - woodturning, level 1 Mon €140 / level 2 Tue: each 7.30-10pm €140: 10 wks

Bray Institute of FE, Novara Ave Bray (2866111 / 2829668) - woodturning, Wed 7.30 10 wks, €85

DIT Faculty: Built Environment Bolton St 1 (4023000) - wood turning, Mon 7-10pm, 10 wks €300

Dún Laoghaire CFE, 17 Cumberland St Dún Laoghaire (2809676) - Mon 7-9.30pm 10 wks €130

Greenhills College Limekiln Ave Walkinstown 12 (4507779/4507863) - woodturning, 10 wks, €228

Hartstown Community School Clonsilla 15 (8209863) - woodturning, 10wks, €90

Holy Family Community School Rathcoole (4580766)

Kylemore College Kylemore Rd 10 (6265901) - DIY Thurs 12 wks 9.30-12.30/ furniture making FETAC 2 Thurs 1.30-4.40

Malahide Community School Malahide (8460949) - for beginners, Thurs 7.30pm 10 wks €95

Newpark Adult Education Centre Newtownpark Ave Blackrock (2884376 / 2883725) - beginners,10wks, €130, Tue, Wed, Thurs 7.30-9.45

Plunket College Swords Rd, Whitehall 9 (8371689) - beginners Tue 7.30 10 wks €112

Pobalscoil Rosmini Adult Ed Grace Pk Rd 9 (8371015) - basic skills, tue 7pm & 8.30 €95 each

Ringsend Technical Institute Cambridge Rd 4 (6684498) - beginners, Mon €90/ intermediate Tue €140: 10 wks each

Saint Tiernan's Community School Parkvale Balally 16 (2953224) - woodturning, 10 wks: Mon €80/ Wed, Thurs (8 per class) 10 wks, €150

WORD PROCESSING see also Computer / Keyboard / Secretarial / Typing

College of Further Education Main St Dundrum 14 (2951376) - Tue & Thurs 7-9pm 8 wks €140

Coolmine Community School Clonsilla 15 (8214583) - word & email, Mon 20 wks €200/ Tue, €100, 10wks, 7.30-9.30

Crumlin College of FE, Crumlin Rd 12 (4540662) - ecdl / ms office, Mon, Tue, Wed

CTA Computer Training Academy, St James's Tce Malahide (8454070) - ms word, basic/ intermediate/ advanced/ ecdl/ mos: day/ eve/ Sat

Dún Laoghaire CFE, 17 Cumberland St Dún Laoghaire (2809676) - Mon 20 wks 8-10pm €300

Eden Computer Training Rathfarnham 16 & 1 Green St 7 (4953155)

FAS Training Centre Loughlinstown Wyattville Rd, DL (2043600) - MOS word core 10 wks

Grange Community College Grange Abbey Rd Donaghmede 13 (8471422) - ms word, 10wks

Greenhills College Limekiln Ave Walkinstown 12 (4507779/4507863) - desk top publishing and wp, Tue, 20 wks €292 FETAC cert

Kilroy's College Wentworth House Grand Canal Street Lr 2 (6620538 1850-700700) - tutor supported home study: computer basics, ECDL, keyboard & typing

Pitman Training Centre 6-8 Wicklow St 2 (6768008) - ms word, day eve sats, cert

St Kevin's College, Clogher Rd Crumlin 12 (4536397) - word for windows level 2, NCVA, 20wks

WRESTLING

Irish Amateur Wrestling Assoc Michael McAuley, 9 (8315522/ 087-2627452) Hercules amateur wrestling & weightlifting club 9 Lurgan st 7: general club: daily/ 9.30am -9pm training Tuesday &Thurs 6.30 7.30 juniors seniors 7.30 pm 9pm,

pitman°
training

The Experts in Computer & Office Skills Training

6 wicklow street dublin 2 ● 6768008 ● pitmand@iol.ie ●

Sunday 11am 1pm / UCD "Gladiators" Belfield 4: 8-10pm Mon, 5-7.30 Fri/ "No Fear" BJJ & Wrestling club Greenmount Av 6 open 6 days wkly/ "The Eagles" wrestling club Coolmine Centre Blanchardstown/ "Spartan Club" Firhouse scout den Tallaght/ for children: "Vulcan" Larkin College, Champions Av 1 Wed-Fri 11am/ St. Mary's College Rathmines 10am 12.am / "Wolverines Club" St. Mary's College Rathmines Sundays 11am -1pm open classes.

WRITING (CREATIVE) see also Creative Writing / Songwriting

Ashfield College Main St Templeogue 6W (4900866) - 7.30-9.30, 8 wks

Balymun Comprehensive School Adult Ed Centre 9 (8420654) - workshops, Mon 7-8.30 10 wks €100

BookConsulT 68 Mountjoy Square 1 - creative writing / poetry workshops / editorial reports & assessments / getting published / writing

Bray Institute of FE, Novara Ave Bray (2866111 / 2829668) - screen writing, Mon 7.30 10 wks €85

Cabinteely Community School Johnstown Rd 18 (2857455) - 10wk, €95

Coolmine Community School Clonsilla 15 (8214583) - Mon, 10wk, €80/ workshop Sat 7 Oct 10am-1 €25

DATE Centre CFE, Dundrum 14 (2964322 (9.30am-12pm)) - writers groups: Tue: beginners 9.30am/ improvers 11.10/ Fri: poetry fiction drama, 9.30&11.10am: each10 wks, day €97

Dún Laoghaire CFE, 17 Cumberland St Dún Laoghaire (2809676) - Tue 7.30-9.30, 10wks €110

Dún Laoghaire-Rathdown Co Council Public Library Service - Dalkey Library Writer's Group (2855277) & Deansgrange Library Writers' Workshop (2850860): meet Thurs 6-7.30, fortnightly, free, new members always welcome

Finglas Adult Reading & Writing Scheme Colaiste Eoin Cappagh Rd 11 (8340893) - for improving basic reading writing skills, 10 wks Mon 11-12.30

Firhouse Community College Firhouse Rd 24 (4525807) - Mon 7.30-9.30pm 8 wks €104

Foxrock Institute Kill o' the Grange, Kill Lane Blackrock (4939506) - 8 wks, €105

Gaiety School of Acting Sycamore St Temple Bar 2 (6799277) - 10 wk course: dramatic writing

Greenhills College Limekiln Ave Walkinstown 12 (4507779/4507863) - beginners/improvers, writers workshop, 10 wks, €130

Irish Writers' Centre 19 Parnell Sq 1 (8721302) - beginners / intermediate / advanced: each 12 wks Tue / Wed / Thurs: 6.30-8.30pm/ wkend courses also

Kilroy's College Wentworth House Grand Canal Street Lr 2 (6620538 1850-700700) - tutor supported home study: for adults & children, dip courses

Kilternan Adult Education Group Ballybetagh Rd Kilternan 18 (2952050) - Wed 10am-1, 10 wks €130

KLEAR Grange Park View Kilbarrack 5 (8671845) - beginners, day

Marino College 14-20 Marino Mart 3 (8332100) - Tues, 7.30 10 wks €90

Newpark Adult Education Centre Newtownpark Ave Blackrock (2884376 / 2883725) - memoir writing/ writers' workshop, beginners/improvers: 10wks, €120: Mon-Tue, Thurs 7.30-9.45

People's College for Continuing Education & Training 32 Parnell Sq 1 (8735879) - €60

Rathmines CFE - Senior College, Town Hall 6 (4975334) - workshop, Wed 7-9pm 10 wks €90

St Peter's College Collins Ave 5 (8337686) - beginners, Tue: 7-8.30, 10 wks €65

Tallaght Community School Balrothery 24 (4515566) - 8wk, 7.30-9.30 €70

UCD Adult Education Centre Belfield (7167123) - 10 week courses: the creative edge; discovering and channelling creativity; editing techniques; enjoy writing; literature history and romance; unblocking the block - creative writing for beginners; write that novel; writers workshop in children's fiction; development workshop in children's fiction; writing fiction the short story & beyond, also, module 2; writing for radio/ the business of writing, 1 Sat spring / writing for the screen, Sat 2 day

WRITING SKILLS

Irish Academy of Public Relations (2780802) - courses at UCD, Belfield: cert in pr and pr writing, 12 wks 1 ev, €730; cert in journalism and print, 12 wks 1 ev, €730; practical journalistic writing skills, 1 yr, by email or corresp, €390/€440

Kilroy's College Wentworth House Grand Canal Street Lr 2 (6620538 1850-700700) - tutor supported home study: freelance journalism, creative, dip

Our Lady's Hospice Harold's Cross 6 (4068806 4068810) - academic writing skills, 25 August 10-4pm €100 incl lunch

Pobalscoil Rosmini Adult Ed Grace Pk Rd 9 (8371015) - practical course, letters/ essays/ etc, Wed 7-8.20 €90

WORDS Language Services 44 Northumberland Rd 4 (6610240) - general writing skills / business writing / technical writing skills: all online courses

WRITING, BASIC and READING see also Basic Education / Dyslexia / English Literacy

National Adult Literacy Agency 76 Lr Gardiner St 1 (8554332) - national referral service for adults/literary resource room available/ family literacy/ English as a second language

Ringsend Technical Institute Cambridge Rd 4 (6684498)

WWW see Computer Programming, Internet & Email, Web Design

YACHTMASTER'S CERTIFICATE / OFFSHORE / OCEAN

Glenans Irish Sailing Club 5 Lr Mount St 2 (6611481)

Irish Sailing Assoc 3 Park Rd Dún Laoghaire (2800239) - apply for list of providers

Sea-Craft 3 Newcourt Ave Bray (2863362) - eve, Yachtmaster's coastal/ offshore/ ocean: ISA RYA certs

YOGA

Alan Pelly Mercy College Coolock 5 (8476440 / 087 2749011) - Tues 8pm 8 wks €90; also at St Brigid's Resource Cntr, Killester, Wed 8pm

Balbriggan Community College Pine Ridge Chapel St (8412388/9) - Mon/ Tue 7.30-9pm 8 wks €78 each

Ballsbridge CFE, Shelbourne Rd 4 (6684806) - Mon & Thur, 6pm & 7.45, each 10 wks €80

Ballymun Trinity CS,s Adult Ed Centre 9 (8420654) - Mon 6.30 & 8pm 10wk, €90

BASE Ballyboden Adult Social Education Whitechurch Library Taylor's Lane 16 (4935953) - 10 wks

Brahma Kumaris WSU Raja Yoga Centres 5 Leeson Pk Ave 6 (6687480) - raja, 7 wk free

Bray Institute of FE, Novara Ave Bray (2866111 / 2829668) - beginners, Mon, Wed/continuation, Tue: 7 or 8.30 10wks, €85 each

Cabinteely Community School Johnstown Rd 18 (2857455) - beginners/continuing 10wk, 1.5 hrs, €70 each

Centre Studios 15 Upr Rathmines Rd 2 (4066812) - Ashtanga; Hatha; yoga-pilates fusion; each 8wks €125; also day / teen yoga 8 wks day €80 / pre-natal 8wks €125

Classical Hatha Yoga 5 Leeson Pk Ave 6 (6687480) - Hatha yoga, posture & breathing, 6 wks €90 - also day

Coláiste Dhúlaigh CFE, Barryscourt Rd Coolock 17 (8481337) - beginners & continuation: Mon 7.30-9, Tues 6.30 &8pm, 10 wks/ also day Wed 1-2.30pm, 10 wks, mixed ability

Coláiste Eanna, Kilkieran Rd Cabra 7 (8389577) - beginners, Thurs, 7.30 & 9pm, 10wk

College of Further Education Main St Dundrum 14 (2951376) - beginners/ continuation: Tue & Thurs 7-9pm 8 wks €104

Coolmine Community School Clonsilla 15 (8214583) - Tue 1 & 2: / Mon, Wed: each 7.30, 10 wks €70

Crumlin College of FE, Crumlin Rd 12 (4540662) - beginners/continuation, 10 wks Mon, Tue, Wed 6.45/8.15

Dance Theatre of Ireland Bloomfields Centre, Lr George St Dún Laoghaire (2803455) - Hatha Yoga, Fri, 6.30 & 8; also 8-9.30 Fri 2 classes, 10 wks €80

DATE Centre CFE, Dundrum 14 (2964322 (9.30am-12pm)) - beginners/improvers/ mixed ability: each 10 wks, €97 day

Donahies Community School Streamville Rd 13 (8482217) - beginners/ advanced, Tues, Wed, 7 & 8.30, 10 wks, €70

Dublin Buddhist Centre 42 Lr leeson St (Basement) 2 (6615934) - 5wks, €64

Dún Laoghaire CFE, 17 Cumberland St Dún Laoghaire (2809676) - Mon 7.30 & Tues 7pm/ mixed ability Tues 8.30-10: ea 10 wks, €95 each

Dundrum Family Recreation Centre Meadowbrook 16 (2984654)

Firhouse Community College Firhouse Rd 24 (4525807) - Mon, Tue 7.30-9pm 8 wks €78

Foxrock Institute Kill o' the Grange, Kill Lane Blackrock (4939506) - healing and Yoga, 8 wks, €105

Grange Community College Grange Abbey Rd Donaghmede 13 (8471422) - for relaxation, beginners 8 wks

Greendale Community School Kilbarrack 5 (8322735) - basic Tue 7pm / beginners Thurs 7pm/ continuation 8.30pm: 10wks €90 each

Greenhills College Limekiln Ave Walkinstown 12 (4507779/4507863) - 10 wks, €130

Harmony Yoga Ireland 233 St James Rd Walkinstown 12 (087 8263778) - pregnancy yoga 4 day, yoga for babies 3 day

Hartstown Community School Clonsilla 15 (8209863) - 10wks, €60

Harvest Moon Centre 24 Lr Baggot St 2 (6627556) - 6 wks €120

Healthy Way Ralph Square Leixlip Co Kildare (6244288) - mixed ability, Mon, Tue, Wd, Thurs: various times, 10 wks €120/ advanced Tue, 6.30 10 wks €120

Holistic Healing Centre 38 Dame St 2 (6710813)

Holy Family Community School Rathcoole (4580766)

Inchicore CFE, Emmet Rd 8 (4535358)

Irish Health Culture Association 66 Eccles St 7 (8304211) - yoga teacher's dip, 11 wkends €3650/ wkend, & concentrated courses/ ask for prospectus

Irish Health Culture Association Yoga Teachers 66 Eccles St 7 (8500493/ 8304211) - see display listing: MIHCA yoga teachers

Irish Yoga Asociation PO Box 9969 7 (4929213/ 087 2054489) - qualified teachers available all over Ireland/ 4 yr Teacher Training courses

Jackie Skelly's Fitness 42 Clarendon St, 2; Park West, Nangor Rd, 12 & Applewood Village, Swords, & Ashbourne (6770040) - gym membership incl classes

Jean McDonald IYA (2722317) - venues: Fitzpatrick's Castle Killiney, Wed / St Anne's Resource Centre: multiple sclerosis class, Fri morns / Kriya yoga, Navara Centre Bray (by appt)

Kilternan Adult Education Group Ballybetagh Rd Kilternan 18 (2952050) - Mon, Tue: 10 wks, day/eve €97

KLEAR Grange Park View Kilbarrack 5 (8671845) - beginners, intermediate, 20 wks/
yoga for the golden years - day only

Kylemore College Kylemore Rd 10 (6265901) - Tue 6.45 & 8pm each 10 wks

LIFEWORKS Yoga Margaret Forde (8339902) - a yoga class in your workplace?
also, mind yoga (relaxation, stress management, no exercises), 6wk courses

Lucan Community College Esker Drive (6282077) - hata, beginners/ improvers:
7.15/8.30 10 wks €82 ea

Malahide Community School Malahide (8460949) - beginners, 10 wks Tues & Thurs,
7.30 & 8.30, €80 ea

Margaret Forde Yoga (8339902) - venues: Raheny, St Paul's College, Sybil Hill, 6
wks Mon & Wed, 7.30/ Baggot St 2: 12.30pm & 5.30pm/ also pregnancy & birth
yoga classes

Margaret Macken Yoga Stephen's Gr/Adelaide Rd/Clontarf (8332954) - Iyengar
Yoga, 6 wk course; also relaxation, stress management and meditation

Marino College 14-20 Marino Mart 3 (8332100) - hata: Tues beginners/ Thurs: 10wks
€45/€65

Melt, Temple Bar Natural Healing Centre 2 Temple Ln 2 (6798786) - Ashtangat yoga,
Thurs+ Fri 6 wks €105; Iyengar Mon Tue+ Wed, 8 wks €89/€105

Newpark Adult Education Centre Newtownpark Ave Blackrock (2884376 / 2883725)
- Iyenger for beginners, improvers,10wks, €95, Mon to Thurs, 6.45 or 8.30

IRISH HEALTH CULTURE ASSOCIATION YOGA TEACHERS

Regular classes mainly for 1¼ to 1½ hrs/6-8 weeks. Phone individual teachers.

Dublin 1 & 7: Tony Quinn Centre Eccles Street 7 8304211; *DUBLIN 2;* Valerie Ward – pregnancy yoga 087 2852293; *DUBLIN 3/5:* Margaret Forde **Clontarf/Raheny** 8339902; Joan Gleeson **Clontarf** 8331917; Thérése McCormack **Donnycarney/Clontarf** 8333890; Helena Podesta **Malahide/Artane** 8312326; Alan Pelly **Killester/Dollynount** 8476440; Denise Vanhoutte **Raheny/Killester** 085 7162789; *DUBLIN 6* Susan Kelly **Churchtown & Dublin 6** 086 8801683; Lorraine Brady **Rathmines** 8348705; Yvonne Sherry **Terenure** 086 838 3347; *DUBLIN 9/11:* Lorraine Brady **Glasnevin** 8348705; John Daly **Whitehall** 8307885; Marianne Dunn **Northside** – for children/teens 085 7329654; *DUBLIN 13:* Cathy Barron Sutton/Bayside 8324682; *DUBLIN 14:* Maebh Thornton **Churchtown** 086 8383347; Susan Kelly **Churchtown** 086 8801683; Yvonne Sherry **Churchtown** 086 8383347; *DUBLIN 15:* Harriett O'Doherty **Blanchardstown/Castleknock** 8389415; *DUBLIN 16:* Stephanie Clayton **Knocklyon/ Rathfarnham/ Tallaght** 087 2051947; Teresa Duggan **Rathfarnham/Ballinteer** 4941212; Madeline Page **Firhouse/ Tallaght /Knocklyon/ Templogue** 4938005; *NORTH CO DUBLIN:* Niamh Daly **Skerries** 8494362; Louise Fagan **Skerries/Rush/Dunboyne/ Clonee** 8494513; Carmel Farnan **Rush** 843 9891; Collete Ferguson **Fingal area** 849 1941; *SOUTH CO DUBLIN/WICKLOW:* Maria Gavin Stillorgan VEC 280 6404; Genny & Tim Rice **Dunlaoghaire/Deansgrange/Stillorgan** 235 2015; Katherine Scheip **Shankhill/Bray** 086 3775108; Deirdre Souchere **Stillorgan** 087 253 6801; *WEST CO. DUBLIN/KILDARE/MEATH:* Sylvia Braun **Slane/Navan** 046 9053146; Margaret Browne 045 867139 & Deborah Browne 087 8156 055 **Blessington/Naas/Newbridge;** Mary Cromwell **Navan**. 046 9071097; Linda Elliott **Lucan** – pre/post natal 6105410; Janet Fitzsimons **Ashbourne** 8357393; Alison Flynn Citywest Business Campus 087 6302694; Linda Keen **Ashbourne** 8354441; Annmarie Kennedy **Kells** 086 8911647; Pamela McDermott **Lucan** 086 4053882; De Lourde Scallan **Celbridge/Naas/Rathcool** 086 838 7781; Yvonne Sherry **Lucan** 086 8383347; The Yoga Sanctuary **Lucan/Leixlip/Celbridge** 085 7487611

Obus School of Healing Therapies, 53 Beech Grove Lucan (6282121) - morns & eves, 10 wks €100

Old Bawn Community School Tallaght 24 (4526137) - 7,30-9.30, Tues 10wks €90 / yoga pregnancy, Tues 6-7.30 10 wks €68/ Yoga for men, Thurs 7-9pm €90

Palmerstown CS - Pobailscoil Iosolde, Kennelsfort Rd 20 (6260116) - levels 1&2, Tues & Thurs, 7 & 8.15: 10 wks €60 ea

People's College for Continuing Education & Training 32 Parnell Sq 1 (8735879) - €80

Phibsboro Gym 1st Floor, Phibsboro SC 7 (8301849) - Fri 6.30-7.30, 8 wks

Physio Extra 37 Upr Grand Canal St 4 (087 7818300 6685048) - yoga with pilates

Plunket College Swords Rd, Whitehall 9 (8371689) - beginners/ continuation, Tues, 10 wks, €67 ea

Pobalscoil Neasáin Baldoyle 13 (8063092) - Tue 7.30-9pm, 10 wks

Pobalscoil Rosmini Adult Ed Grace Pk Rd 9 (8371015) - Wed 7-8.20/ beginners Mon, Tue: 7pm Wed 8.30pm/ continuation, Mon, Tue, Wed 8.30pm: each €90

Portmarnock Community School Carrickhill Rd (8038056) - beginners, Mon 8 wks 8-9.15 €100

Rathmines CFE - Senior College, Town Hall 6 (4975334) - beginners Tue 6pm/ improvers, continuation: Tue + Wed: 7-9pm, 10 wks €70

Ringsend Technical Institute Cambridge Rd 4 (6684498) - hatha: beginners/improvers, Mon/Tue 10wks, €70; spring term 15 wks Mon €105

Saint Finian's Community College Swords (8402623) - 8 wks

Saint Tiernan's Community School Parkvale Balally 16 (2953224) - beginners with Mella, Mon, 7.30-9pm, 10 wks, €80/ advanced with Mella (087 9771116) Wed

St Anthony's House St Lawrence Rd Clontarf 3 (8335300)

St Kevin's College, Clogher Rd Crumlin 12 (4536397) - 10wks

St MacDara's CC, Wellington Lane Templeogue 6W (4566216) - beginners, Mon/Tue: 7.30-8.30pm, 8 wks, €78 each

St Peter's College Collins Ave 5 (8337686) - Mon & Tue, 10wk, 7.30 & 8.30, €60 ea

Stillorgan Senior College Old Road Stillorgan (2880704) - Mon 7.30 8 wks €78

TACT St Dominic's School St Dominic's Rd Tallaght 24 (4596757)

Tallaght Community School Balrothery 24 (4515566) - beginners 7-8.15/ improvers 8.20-9.30, 10wk, €70 each

Taney Centre Taney Rd Dundrum 14 (2985491) - Tue, Thurs: 2982880; Tue: 6767551; Mon, Wed, Thurs: 2962608/ also day

TARGET St Kevin's School Newbrook Rd, Donaghmede 13 (8671967) - 10 wks, day only, beginners, improvers

The Sanctuary Stanhope Street 7 (6705419) - beginners / intermediate: satyanda & hatha, each 10 wks €120

Tony Quinn Centre 66/67 Eccles St 7 (8304211) - 6 wk courses, lunchtime courses; also local area venues

Valerie Ward, Yoga Teacher city centre & southside (087 2852293) - 6wks, €65 / pregnant yoga classes

Walmer College & Holistic Centre First Floor, River Hse Raheny Shopping C 5 (8329645)

Yoga Dublin Dartmouth Pl Ranelagh 6 (4982284) - all types daily, also pilates & massage; day & eve. See website

Yoga Therapy Ireland 20 Auburn Drive Killiney (2352120) - accredited teacher training dip / post-grad course/ tutor training / yoga workshops & seminars/ classes countrywide. Qualified insured teachers

YOUTH COURSES / INFORMATION CENTRES

Catholic Youth Care 20-23 Arran Qy 7 (8725055) - centres at: Bray (2828324); Swords (8405100); Clondalkin (4594666); Dún Laoghaire (2806147); E Wicklow (0402-39646); Finglas (8341436); Lucan/Nth Kildare (6280465); Ronanstown (4570363)

Maynooth NUI Adult & Community Ed Dept (7084500) - NUI cert Youth Studies: Liberties College 8 (4542100)

Youth Info Centres - info on education, training, employment, careers, rights & entitlements, travel, sport & leisure - Main St, Blanchardstown (8212077) Dundrum (4938284); Monastery Rd, Clondalkin (4594666) Bell Tower, Dún Laoghaire (2809363); Main Rd, Tallaght

ZOO

Dublin Zoo Education Dept Phoenix Pk 8 (4748932) - conservation & wildlife

ZOOLOGY see also Natural History

Kylemore College Kylemore Rd 10 (6265901) - Mon 10 wks 7-9pm

A Directory of Email & Website addresses
relating to courses at most of the Centres included

1000 FACES: International School of – www.geocities.com/college 1000 faces

ACCA – students@ie.accaglobal.com – www.ireland.accaglobal.com

ACCORD – marriagepreparation@dublin.accord.ie – www.accord.ie

Acupuncture Foundation Training School – acufound@eircom.net – www.acupuncturefoundation.com

Adelaide Computers – question@ireland.com – www.etrainingireland.com

Aikido Federation of Ireland – Irelandaikikai@eircom.net – www.aikido.ie

Aisling Ireland – aisirl@iol.ie – aisling-ireland.com

Alan Pelly – discoveryoga@eircom.net – www.discover-yoga.com

Alexander Technique – frankkennedy@eircom.net – www.alexandertech-dublin.com

Alix Gardner Catering – dublincookery@yahoo.com – www.dublincookery.com

All Hallows College – jcleary@allhallows.ie – www.allhallows.ie

Alliance Francaise – info@alliance-francaise.ie – www.alliance-francaise.ie

An Oige – mailbox@anoige.ie – www.irelandyha.org

Ann Faherty – annfaherty@esatclear.ie

Ashfield College – info@ashfield-college.com – www.ashfield-college.com

Ashfield Computer Training – info@ashfieldcomputertraining.ie – www.ashfieldcomputertraining.ie

Asian Institute – info@theasianinstitute.com – www.theasianinstitute.com

Aspen's College – neelaminfo@aspensireland.com – www.aspensireland.com

Astroleg – mail4@astroleg.dk – www.astroleg.net

Astronomy Ireland – info@astronomy.ie – www.astronomy.ie

Athletics Association – admin@athleticsireland.ie – www.athleticsireland.ie

Ballinteer Community School – ballcom@eircom.net – www.ballinteercs.ie

Ballsbridge CFE – info@ballsbridge.cdvec.ie – www.ballsbridgecollege.com

Ballyfermot CFE – night school@bcfe.cdvec.ie – www.bfe.ie

Ballymun Men's Centre – info@ballymunmenscentre.com

Ballymun Trinity Comprehensive School – compaded@eircom.net

Basketball Ireland – info@basketballireland.ie – www.basketballireland.ie

Bel Canto Singing – reception@thesingingschool.com – www.belcantohouse.com

Belly Dance Ireland – valdance@eircom.net – www.BellydanceIreland.com

Clondalkin Ad Ed: Berni Grainger – berni_grainger@yahoo.co.uk

Betty Ann Norton Theatre School – bettyannnorton@eircom.net – www.bettyann-nortontheatreschool.com

Bill Brady School of Guitar – bbguitar@eircom.net

Birdwatch Ireland – info@birdwatchireland.org – www.birdwatchireland.ie

Blue Sky Meditation Centre – info@bluesky.ie – www.bluesky.ie

Bluefeather School of Languages – info@bluefeather.ie – www.bluefeather.ie

BookConsulT – cprojectsltd@eircom.net

Brahma Kumaris Yoga – dublin@ie.bkwsu.org – www.bkwsu.org

Bray Institute of FE – nightschool@bife.ie – www.bife.ie

Bray Music Centre – braymusiccentre@iolfree.ie

Bray Sailing Club – training@braysailingclub.ie – www.braysailingclub.ie

Brennanstown Riding School – info@brennanstownrs.ie

Broadmeadows Equestrian Centre – brianduffshowjumping@eircom.net – www.irelandequestrian.com

Bronwyn Conroy Beauty School – info@bronwynconroy.com – www.bronwynconroy.com

Brooks Academy – terry@pipers.ie

Buddhist Centre – info@buddhism.ie – www.buddhism.ie

Business Computer Training Institute – info@bct.ie – www.bct.ie

Cairde Rince Ceili na hEireann – www.ceilidancing.com

Calliaghstown Riding Centre – info@calliaghstownridingcentre.com – www.calliaghstownridingcentre.com

Carl Alfred – carltalf@hotmail.com

Catholic Youth Care – info@cyc.ie – www.cyc.ie

Central Library – cicelib@iol.ie – www.dublincity.ie/living-in-the-city/ libs

Centre for Professional Development – marycurran@coachcentre.com – www.coachcentre.com

Centre Studios – info@centrestudios.com – www.centrestudios.com

Ceramic Forms – michelle@ceramicforms.com – www.ceramicforms.com

Childminding Ireland – training@childminding.ie – www.childminding.ie

Children's Books Ireland – info@childrensbooksireland.com – www.childrensbooksireland.com

Christine Courtney – info@aromatherapytraining.com – www.aromatherapytraining.com

CITAS College – courses@citas.ie – www.citas.ie

Civil Defence – carol.butler@dublincity.ie – www.dublincivildefence.com

Clanwilliam Institute – training@clanwilliam.ie – www.clanwilliam.ie

Classical Hatha Yoga – bknick@eircom.net

Cle, Irish Book Publishers Assoc – info@publishingireland.com – www.publishingireland.com

Clondalkin Sports & Leisure – scdls@eircom.net – www.clondalkin.co.cslc

Clontarf School of Music – paulcsmusic@eircom.net

Clontarf Swimming & Water Polo – nickolas_omeara@entemp.ie

Coiscéim Dance Theatre – info@coisceim.com – www.coisceim.com

Colaiste Dhúlaigh CFE – fept.dhulaigh@gmail.com – www.aecd.co.nr

Colaiste Eanna – info@colaiste-eanna.com – www.colaiste-eanna.com

Colaiste Eoin – info@eoin.cdvec.ie – www.colaisteeoin.ie

Colaiste Ide – general.enquiries@ide.cdvec.ie – www.colaisteide.ie

CFE Dundrum – info@cfedundrum.com – www.cfedrundrum.com

College of Progressive Education – info@progressivecollege.com – www.progressivecollege.com

Colliers School of Motoring – colliersdrivingschool@eircom.net – www.colliersdrivingschool.ie

Comhaltas Ceoltóirí Éireann – enquiries@comhaltas.com – www.comhaltas.com

Comhlámh – info@comhlamh.org – www.comhlam.org

Communications & Management Inst – info@cmi-ireland.com – www.cmi-ireland.com

Conradh na Gaeilge – eolas@cnag.ie – ww.cnag.ie

Consumers Association – cai@consumerassociation.ie – www.consumerassociation.ie

Contract Bridge Assoc of Ireland – irebridg@iol.ie

Coogan Bergin College– info@cooganbergin.com – www.cooganbergin.com

Coolmine CS– adulted@coolmine.ie – www.coolminecs.ie/adulted

Corballis Public Golf Course – corballis@golfdublin.com – www.golfdublin.com

Cormac Cuffe – cormac.cuffe@Gmail.com – www.irishjewellerycourses.com

Corporate Club – info@corporateclub.ie – www.corporateclub.ie

Crossroads Set Dancers – jgryan@eircom.net

Crumlin CFE – adulted@ccfe.cdvec.ie – www.crumlincollege.ie

CTA Computer Training – info@ctac.ie – www.ctac.ie

Cumann Camogaiochta– info@camogie.ie – www.camogie.ie

Dance Theatre– info@dancetheatreireland.com – www.dancetheatreireland.com

Danzon – hilary@danzon.ie – www.danzon.ie

DATE Centre – adte04@eircom.net – www.southadulted.ie

Digital Film School – info@digitalfilmschool.ie – www.digitalfilmschool.ie

DIT admissions office – admissions@dit.ie – www.dit.ie

Dominick Reilly PGA – dominicreilly@iol.ie

Donahies Community School – donahcs@eircom.net

Dorset College – info@dorset-college.ie – www.dorset-college.ie

Driving Instructor Register – info@dir.ie – www.dir.ie

Dublin Adult Learning Centre – info@dalc.ie – www.dalc.ie

Dublin Airport Singers – tonymadden@eircom.net – www.dublinairportsingers.new

Dublin Buddhist Centre – info@dublinbuddhistcentre.org – www.dublinbuddhistcentre.org

Dublin Business School – admissions@dbs.edu – www.dbs.edu

Dublin Camera Club – info@dublincameraclub.ie – www.dublincameraclub.ie

Dublin City Morris Dancers – alancorsini@eircom.net

Dublin City Public Libraries – dublinpubliclibraries@dublincity.ie – www.iol.ie/dublincitylibrary/

Dublin Folk Dance – interdance@eircom.net – dublinfolkdancegroup.com

Dublin Gliding Club – www.dublinglidingclub.ie

Dublin Institute of Design – info@dublindesign.ie – www.dublindesign.ie

Dublin Naturalists Field Club – dnfc@eircom.net – www.dnfc.net www.butterflyireland.com

Dublin School of Dance – annecc@inybco.com – www.inybco.com

Dublin School of English – admin@dse.ie – www.dse.ie

Dublin School of Guitar – alangrundy@eircom.net

Dublin School of Horticulture – info@dfh.ie – www.dfh.ie

Dublin Shotokan Karate – www.dublinski.com

Dublin Simon Community – mdent@dubsimon.ie – www.dublinsimon.ie

Dublin Zoo – education@dublinzoo.ie – www.dublinzoo.ie

Dun Laoghaire CFE – info@dlcfe.ie – www.dlcfe.ie

Dun Laoghaire-Rathdown Co Council – www.dlrcoco.ie/library

Dunsink Observatory – cwoods@dunsink.dias.ie – www.dunsink.dias.ie

Dyslexia Association – info@dyslexia.ie – www.dyslexia.ie

East Coast Shooting Club – ww.eastcoastshootingclub.net

Eden Computer Training – info@eden.ie

Edwin Williamson Singing – reception@thesingingschool.com – www.belcantohouse.com

EireCopter Helicopters – info@eirecopter.ie – www.eirecopter.ie

electronic Business School – info@ebsi.ie – www.ebsi.ie

Elmgreen Golf Centre – elmgreen@golfdublin.com – www.golfdublin.com

ENFO - Information on the Environment – info@enfo.ie – www.enfo.ie

English Language Institute – info@englishlanguage.com – www.englishlanguage.com

Enriching Careers – www.enrichingcarreers.com

Esperanto Assoc of Ireland – www.esperanto.ie

ETC Consult – etcc@iol.ie, info@etcconsult.com – www.etcconsult.com

Export Edge Business College – training@export-edge.com – www.export-edge.com

FACTS Training – facts@indigo.ie

FAS eCollege – ecollegeinfo@fas.ie – www.fas.ie

FAS Training Centres– www.fas.ie

FAS Training Centre Loughlinstown – loughevening@fas.ie – www.fas.ie

FAS Training Centre Tallaght – tallaghtnight@fas.ie – www.fas.ie

FETAC – information@fetac.ie – www.fetac.ie

Film Institute of Ireland – info@irishfilm.ie – www.irishfilm.ie

Fingal Co Libraries – libraries@fingalcoco.ie – www.fingalcoco.ie/LivingInFingal/Libraries

Fingal Sailing School – info@fingalsailingschool.com – www.fingalsailingschool.com

Finglas Read & Write – cora.rafter@eoin.cdvec.ie

Firhouse Community College – firhousecollege@eircom.net

Fitzwilliam Institute Ltd – fitzinst@iol.ie – www.fitzwilliam-institute.ie

Football Assoc of Ireland – www.fai.ie

Forde Clinic – yogalife@eircom.net

Foxrock Institute – info@foxrockinstitute.ie – www.foxrockinstitute.ie

Froebel College of Education – chairman@nurture.ie – www.nurture.ie

Gael Linn – www.gael-linn.ie

Gaelchultúr Ltd – eolas@gaelchultur.com – www.gaelchultur.com

Gaiety School of Acting – info@gaietyschool.com – www.gaietyschool.com

Gallery Art Centre – galleryartcentre@yahoo.com – www.galleryartcentre.com

Gallery of Photography – gallery@irish-photography.com – www.irish-photography.com

Galligan Beauty Group – info@galligangroup.com – www.galligangroup.com

Geraldine Brand – info@geraldinebrand.com – www.geraldinebrand.com

Glenans Irish Sailing Club – info@gisc.ie – www.gisc.ie

Goethe-Institut – german@dublin.goethe.org – www.goethe.de/dublin

Grafton Academy– info@graftonacademy.com – www.graftonacademy.com

Grange Community College – grangeadmin@eircom.net – www.grangecc.ie

Greendale Community School – sshiels@greendalecs.com – www.iol.ie/~gcs

Greenhills College – info@greehillscollege.ie – www.greenhills-college.com

Griffith College Dublin – admissions@gcd.ie – www.gcd.ie

Hanly Centre – info@thehanlycentre.com – www.thehanlycentre.com

Harcourt Business School – hsidublin@eircom.net – www.hsi.ie/dublin

Harmony Yoga Ireland – harmonyyogaireland@utvinternet.ie – www.harmonyyogaireland.utvinternet.ie

Hartstown Community School – adult_ed@eircom.net – www.hartstown-cep.com

Harvest Moon Centre – peter@harvestmoon.ie – www.uou2.com

Hazel Byrne – hazelbyrne@usa.net

Healing House – info@healinghouse.ie – www.healinghouse.ie

Health Promotion Unit – www.doh.ie

Hegarty Health Systems – yogametrics@eircom.net – www.yogametrics.com

Hi-Tech Training – hitech@indigo.ie – hitechtraining.ie

Holistic Healing Centre – info@hhc.ie – www.hhc.ie

Holistic Sourcing Centre – info@holisticsourcingcentre.com – www.holisticsourcingcentre.com

Hollywood Academy Dublin –
  info@thehollywoodacademydublin.com – www.thehollywoodacademydublin.com

Holy Family Community School – hfcs@iol.ie

I.T. Blanchardstown – student.helpline@itb.ie – www.itb.ie

IICH Education – iich@eircom.net – www.therapyireland.org

Inchicore CFE – enquiries@inchicore.cdvec.ie – www.inchicorcollege.ie

Institute of Accounting Technicians in Ireland – info@iati.ie – www.iati.ie

Institute of Art, Design & Technology – info@iadt.ie – www.iadt.ie

Institute of Certified Public Accountants (CPA) Ireland – sdowling@cpaireland.ie – www.cpaireland.ie

Institute of Clinical Hypnotherapy & Psychotherapy – hypnosis@iol.ie – www.hypnosiseire.com

Institute of Creative Counselling & Psychotherapy – iccp@eircom.net – www.iccp.ie

Institute of Education – info@ioe.ie – www.ioe.ie

Institute of International Trade of Ireland – iiti@irishexporters.ie – www.iiti.ie

Institute of Professional Auctioneers & Valuers – info@ipav.ie – www.ipav.ie

Institute of Public Administration – educ@ipa.ie – www.ipa.ie

Institute of Taxation in Ireland – students@taxireland.ie – www.taxireland.ie

Institute of Technology Tallaght – parttimeinfo@ittdublin.ie – www.ittdublin.ie

Instituto Cervantes – cendub@cervantes.es – www.dublin.cervantes.es

International Foundation for Adult Education – ifae@postmaster.co.uk

International Study Centre – isc@indigo.ie – www.iscdublin.com

IPPA - the Early Childhood Organisation – info@ippa.ie – www.ippa.ie

Irish Academy of Computer Training (IACT) – info@iact.ie – www.iact.ie

Irish Academy of Public Relations – info@irishacademy.com – www.irishacademy.com

Irish Academy of Training – info@academy.ie – www.academy.ie

Irish Aikido Association – aikidoireland@iol.ie – www.aikidoireland.ie

Irish Amateur Boxing Assoc – iaba@eircom.net – www.iabc.ie

Irish Amateur Wrestling Assoc – mcauley@indigo.ie – www.irishwrestling.com

Irish Association of Holistic Medicine – ihcaoffice@eircom.net – www.holistic-psychotherapy.org

Irish Astronomical Society – ias1937@hotmail.com – www.irishastroasoc.org

Irish Auctioneers & Valuers Institute (IAVI) – education@iavi.ie – www.realestate.ie

Irish Canoe Union – office@irishcanoeunion.com – www.irishcanoeunion.com

Irish Chinese Cultural Society – irishchineseculturalsociety@hotmail.com – www.ucd.ie/iccs

Irish College of English – info@iceireland.com – www.iceireland.com

Irish College of Traditional Chinese Medicine – ictcm@enablis.co.uk – www.chinesemedicine.ie

Irish Computer Society / ICS Skills – info@ics.ie – www.ics-skills.ie

Irish Deaf Society (Linkup) – brian@irishdeafsociety.ie – www.irishdeafsociety.ie

Irish Federation of Sea Anglers – ifsa@gofree.indigo.ie – www.ifsa.ie

Irish Georgian Society – info@igs.ie – www.igs.ie

Irish Health Culture Association – ihcaoffice@eircom.net – www.healthculture.net

Irish Hockey Association – info@hockey.ie – www.hockey.ie

Irish Institute for Integrated Psychotherapy – iiipnolan@eircom.net

Irish Management Institute – regoffice@imi.ie – www.imi.ie

Irish Martial Arts Commission – brd@iol.ie – www.martialarts.ie

Irish National Sailing School – ssailing@inss.ie – www.inss.ie

Irish Payroll Association (IPASS) – ask@ipass.ie – www.ipass.ie

Irish Peatland Conservation Council – bogs@ipcc.ie – www.ipcc.ie

Irish Red Cross Society/ Crois Dhearg na ∏ireann – amaceoin@redcross.ie – www.redcross.ie

Irish Rugby Football Union – info@irishrugby.ie – www.irishrugby.ie

Irish Sailing Assoc – training@sailing.ie – www.sailing.ie

Irish School of Ecumenics (TCD) – www.tcd.ie/ise

Irish School of Homoeopathy – info@homoeopathy.ie – www.homoeopathy.ie

Irish School of Shamanism – dermot@celticshaman.com

Irish School of Shiatsu – shiatsu@eircom.net – www.shiatsu.ie

Irish Squash – irishsquash@eircom.net – www.irishsquash.com

Irish T'ai Chi Ch'uan Assoc – info@irishtaichi.com – www.irishtaichi.com

Irish Table Tennis Assoc Ltd – itta@eircom.net – www.irishtabletennis.com

Irish Underwater Council – info@scubaireland.com – www.irishunderwatercouncil.ie

Irish Water Polo Assoc – nickolas_omeara@entemp.ie

Irish Writers' Centre – info@writerscentre.ie – www.writerscentre.ie

Irish Yoga Association – info@iya.ie – www.iya.ie

Italian Alternative – info@myitalt.com – www.myitalt.com

Jackie Skelly's Fitness Club – info@jackieskellyfitness.com – www.jackieskellyfitness.com

James Joyce Cultural Centre – info@jamesjoyce.ie – www.jamesjoyce.ie

Jean McDonald IYA – www.jeanmcdonald.ie

John Murphy Guitar Studio – johnmurphy04@eircom.net – www.guitarlessonsd16.com

John Ward – johnwardmusic@yahoo.co.uk

Junior Chamber Ireland – pro@jci-ireland.org – www.jci-ireland.org

Just Dance – danceireland@hotmail.com

Karen Ward – kward@iol.ie – www.karenwardholistictherapist.com

Keytrainer Ireland – train@key.ie – www.key.ie

Killester CFE – nightcourses@kcfe.cdvec.ie – www.killestercollege.ie

Kilroy's College – homestudy@kilroyscollege.ie – www.kilroyscollege.ie

Kilternan Adult Education Centre – info@codubvec.ie

Kimmage Development Studies Centre – info@dsckim.ie – www.dsckim.ie

Kinesiology Institute – kinesiologyinstitute@eircom.net

KLEAR – kleared@eircom.net – www.kleared.ie

KMI Institute of Theology & Cultures – adminkmi@eircom.net

Kylemore College – info@kylemore.cdvec.ie

Langtrain International – info@langtrain.ie

Language Centre – language.centre@nuim.ie – www.nuim.ie/language

League of Health (Irl) – mcdaidm@gofree.indigo.ie – www.leagueofhealth.com

Leinster School of Music – leinster.school@gcd.ie – www.gcd.ie

Liberties College – maryrose.o'connor@liberties.cdvec.ie – www.libertiescollege.cdvec.ie

LIFEWORKS Yoga – yogalife@eircom.net

Litton Lane Training – info@littontraining.com – www.littontraining.com

Lucan Community College – admin@lucancc.ie – www.lucancc.ie

Malahide Community School – adulted@malahidecs.ie

Margaret Forde Yoga – yogalife@eircom.net

Marino College – adulteducation@marino.cdvec.ie – www.marino.college.com

Marketing Institute – education@mii.ie – www.mii.ie

Maynooth NUI Adult Ed Centre – adcomed@nuim.ie

McKeon Murray Business Training Services – info@mckeonmurray.ie – www.mckeonmurray.ie

Melody School of Music – tumi@gofree.indigo.ie

Melt, Temple Bar Natural Healing Centre – info@meltonline.com – www.meltonline.com

Merriman School of Singing and Music – reception@thesingingschool.com – www.belcantohouse.com

Metropolitan College of Music – eokeeffe@indigo.ie

Milltown Institute – info@milltown-institute.ie – www.milltown-institute.ie

Montessori Education Centre – info@montessori-ed-ctr.com – www.montessori-ed-ctr.com

Moresoft IT Institute – training@moresoft.ie – www.moresoft.ie

Motions Health & Fitness Training – motions@iol.ie – www.motions.ie

Motorcycling Ireland – office@motorcycling-ireland.com – www.motorcycling-ireland.com

Na Piobairi Uilleann – info@pipers.ie – www.pipers.ie

National Adult Literacy Agency – literacy@nala.ie – www.nala.ie www.literacytools.ie

National Aquatic Centre – info@nac.ie – www.nac.ie

National College of Communications – info@theopencollege.com – www.theopencollege.com

National College of Complementary Medical Ed – info@ntc.ie – www.ntc.ie

National College of Ireland – info@ncirl.ie – www.liveandlearn.ie

National Flight Centre Flight School – info@nfc.ie – www.nfc.ie

National Gallery of Ireland – info@ngi.ie – www.nationalgallery.ie

National Library of Ireland – info@nli.ie – www.nli.ie

National Training Authority – info@nta.ie – www.nta.ie

National Training Centre – info@ntc.ie – www.ntc.ie

Natural Health Training Centre – aikido01@eircom.net – www.aikido.ie

NCAD Centre for Continuing Educ – cead@ncad.ie – www.ncad.ie

Network Club – info@networkclub.ie – www.networkclub.ie

New Media Technology College – info@hypermedia7.com – www.hypermedia7.com

Newpark Adult Education Centre – newparkedu@eircom.net – www.newparkadulted.ie

Newpark Music Centre – www.newparkmusic@eircom.net

Newpark Sports Centre – info@ymaa.ie – www.ymaa.ie

NIFAST Liberty Risk Services – info@nifast.ie – www.nifast.ie

Nth Dublin Radio Club – famads7@iol.ie – www.iol.ie/~fammads/ei0ndr.htm

Nurture Institute – chairman@nurture.ie – www.nurture.ie

OBUS School of Healing – OBUS@eircom.net – www.aromatherapytraining.com

Old Bawn Community School – obcsaded@indigo.ie – www.indigo.ie~obcsaded

Open Golf Centre – opengolf@iol.ie

Open University – ireland@open.ac.uk – www.open.ac.uk

Order of Malta – info@orderofmalta.ie – www.orderofmalta.ie

Oscail – oscail@dcu.ie – www.oscail.ie

Our Lady's Hospice – education@olh.ie

Palmerstown Community School – info@adulted.ie – www.adulted.ie

Park House International – www.parkhouse.ie

Parnell School of Music – info@thehollywoodacademydublin.com – www.thehollywoodacademydublin.com

Peannairí, Irish Scribes – www.calligraphy.ie

Pearse College – information@pearse.cdvec.ie – www.pearsecollege.ie

People's College Debating Soc – peopcoll@iol.ie

People's College – peopcoll@iol.ie – www.peoplescollege.ie

Phoenix TEFL Centre – info@phoenixtefl.com – www.phoenixtefl.com

Physio-Extra – physioextra@eircom.net – www.e-physio.ie

Pilates Institute (NTC) – info@ntc.ie

Pitman Training Centre – pitmand@iol.ie – www.pitman-training.ie

Plunket College – info@plunket.cdvec.ie – www.plunketcollege.ie

Pobalscoil Neasáin – modaded@hotmail.com - www.psn.ie

Pobalscoil Rosmini – adulted@pobalscoilrosmini.ie – www.pobalscoilrosmini.ie

Portmarnock Community School – office@portcs.iol.ie

Portmarnock Sports & Leisure Club – pslc@eircom.net – www.pscl.ie

Portmarnock Sub-Aqua Club – colinmurray@esatclear.ie – www.psac.net

Portobello School – info@portobelloschool.ie

Positive Success Group – evening@PositiveSuccessGroup.com

Public Relations Institute of Ireland – info@prii.ie – www.prii.ie

Public Service Aikido Club – psac@aikidoinireland.org – www.psac.aikidoinireland.org

Pulse Recording College – pulserecording@pulserecording.com – www.pulserecording.com

Quantum Communications – kenmccy04@yahoo.co.uk

Rachel Dempsey – racheldempsey@hotmail.com

Rakassah Belly Dance School – azirah99@yahoo.co.uk

Rathmines College of FE – info@rsc.cdvec.ie

Retirement Planning Council of Ireland – information@rpc.ie – www.rpc.ie

Rigpa Tibetan Buddhist Meditation Centre – dublin@rigpa.ie – www.rigpa.ie

Ringsend Technical Institute – info@ringtec.cdvec.ie – www.ringtec.ie

Roebuck Counselling Centre – roebuckcounsellingcentre@eircom.net – www.roebuck-counselling.com

Sales Institute of Ireland, The – info@salesinstitute.ie – www.salesinstitute.ie

Sam Young – samy@iolfree.ie

Sandford Language Institute – info@sandfordlanguages.ie – www.sandfordlanguages.ie

Saor-Ollscoil na hEireann

School of Business & Humanities – info@iadt.ie – www.iadt.ie

School of Computer Tech – info@sct-ireland.com – www.sct-ireland.com

School of Philosophy & Economic Science – spes@eircom.net – www.practicalphilosophy.ie

Sea & Shore Safety Services Ltd – seaandshore@eircom.net – www.seaandshoresafety.com

Sea-Craft – www.seacraft.ie

Seamus Ennis Cultural Centre – seamusenniscentre@eircom.net

Seamus Lynch – seamuslynchacu@eircom.net – www.iol.ie/~Seamus Lynch

Shiatsu Ireland – enquiries@shiatsuireland.com – www.shiatsuireland.com

Shirley McClure – mcclures@gofree.indigo.ie

Ski Club of Ireland – sci@skiclub.ie – www.skiclub.ie

Sli Eile Volunteers – volunteering@sli-eile.com – www.sli-eile.com

Society of Change Ringers – www.cccdub.ie

Sound Training Centre – soundtrainingcentre@gmail.com – www.soundtraining.com

South Dublin Adult Learning Centre – sdalc@eircom.net

South Dublin Libraries – www.southdublinlibraries.ie

Spawell Golf Centre – d-lavelle@oceanfree.net

Speed Reading Centre – www.speedreading.ie

SPI – spionline@eircom.net

St John Ambulance Brigade – educationsec@sjab.ie – www.sjab.ie

St Kevin's College – info@stkevins.cdvec.ie – www.stkevinscollege.ie

St MacDara's Community College – stmacdaras@eircom.net

St Vincent's Shotkan Karate Club – gearoid.quinn@eircom.net – www.karateireland.com/stvincents

Stewart's Sport Centre – www.stewartshospital.com

Suaimhneas Reflexology – carol@suaimhneas.com – www.suaimhneas.com

Success Partners – info@successpartners.ie – www.successpartners.ie

Surfdock – courses@surfdock.ie – www.surfdock.ie

Swim Ireland – admin@swimireland.ie – www.swimireland.ie

T'ai Chi Ireland – taichi@indigo.ie – www.taichiireland.com

TACT – tact@oceanfree.net

Taekwon-Do Centre – info@inta.ie – www.inta.ie

Tag N Rye Dog Services – tagnrye@eircom.net – www.tagnrye.com

Tallaght Community School – tallaghtcs@eircom.net – www.tallaghtcs.com

Tallaght Photographic Society – j.byrne@ntlworld.ie – www.tallaghtphotographicsociety.com

Taney Parish Centre – parishoftaney@eircom.net – www.taneyparish.ie

Tapestry Dance Company – info@tapestry.ie – www.tapestry.ie

Tara Buddhist Centre – taracentredublin@eircom.net – www.meditateinireland.com

TARGET – info@targeteducation.net – www.targeteducation.net

TEFL Training Institute – dublang@iol.ie – www.tefl.ie

Templeogue Castle Bridge Club – frafar@eircom.net – www.templeoguebridgecentre.com

Tennis Ireland – info@tennisireland.ie – www.tennisireland.ie

The Garden School – ciaran@dfh.ie – www.dfh.ie

The Professional Training and Coaching – g.kingston@esatclear.ie

The Sanctuary – enquiries@sanctuary.ie – www.sanctuary.ie

Thornton Pk Equestrian Centre – info@thorntonpark.ie – www.thorntonpark.ie

Toastmasters International Clubs – www.toastmasters.org.uk

Tony Quinn Centre – www.healthculture.net

Training Options Plus – top1@iol.ie – www.trainingoptions.ie

Transactional Analysis – elizabeth.cleary@gmail.com – www.homepage.eircom.net/~liztai37

Trinity College – www.tcd.ie

Trisailing Ltd – info@trisailing.ie – www.trisailing.ie

U-Learn Language Centre – ulearn@eircom.net – www.u-learn.ie

UCD Adult Ed Centre – adult.education@ucd.ie – www.ucd.ie/adulted

Vegetarian Society of Ireland – vegsoc@ireland.com

Veronica – spiritdancer84@iol.ie

Volunteering Ireland – nancy@volunteeringireland – www.volunteeringireland.com

Walmer College & Holistic Centre – info@walmer.ie – www.walmer.ie

Waltons New School of Music – info@newschool.ie – www.newschool.ie

Westmoreland College for Management & Business –

admissions@westmorelandcollege.ie – www.westmorelandcollege.ie

Whitehall CFE – general.enquiries@whsc.cdvec.ie – www.whitehallcollege.com

Wine Development Board of Ireland – info@wineboard.com

WORDS Language Services – info@wls.ie – www.wls.ie

Yellow Brick Road – stacey@yellowbrickroad.ie – www.yellowbrickroad.ie

Yoga Dublin Studios – info@yogadublin.com – www.yogadublin.com

Yoga Therapy Ireland – yti@eircom.net – www.yogatherapyireland.com